THE ENGLISH REFORMATION REVISED

THE
ENGLISH REFORMATION
REVISED

EDITED BY
CHRISTOPHER HAIGH
Christ Church, Oxford

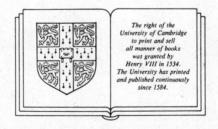

The right of the
University of Cambridge
to print and sell
all manner of books
was granted by
Henry VIII in 1534.
The University has printed
and published continuously
since 1584.

CAMBRIDGE UNIVERSITY PRESS
Cambridge
London   New York   New Rochelle
Melbourne   Sydney

Published by the Press Syndicate of the University of Cambridge
The Pitt Building, Trumpington Street, Cambridge CB2 1RP
32 East 57th Street, New York NY 10022, USA
10 Stamford Road, Oakleigh, Melbourne 3166, Australia

First published 1987

Printed in Great Britain by the University Press, Cambridge

British Library cataloguing in publication data
The English Reformation revised.
1. Reformation – England
I. Haigh, Christopher
274.2′06   BR375

Library of Congress cataloguing in publication data
The English Reformation revised.
Includes index.
1. Reformation – England. 2. England – Church history – 16th century.
I. Haigh, Christopher.

BR375.E54 1987   274.2′06   86–24484

ISBN 0-521-33337-7   hard covers
ISBN 0-521-33631-7   paperback

CONTENTS

v

ILLUSTRATIONS

GRAPHS

TABLES

ACKNOWLEDGEMENTS

Cambridge University Press and the editor wish to thank publishers, editors and authors for permission to reprint the following:

Chapter 1 from *Historical Journal*, XXV (1982)
Chapter 2 from R. O'Day and F. Heal, eds., *Continuity and Change: Personnel and Administration of the Church in England, 1500–1642* (Leicester University Press, 1976)
Chapter 3 from *History*, LXVIII (1983)
Chapter 4 from *Bulletin of the Institute of Historical Research*, XL (1977)
Chapter 5 from F. Heal and R. O'Day, eds., *Church and Society in England, Henry VIII to James I* (Macmillan, 1977)
Chapter 7 from *Journal of Ecclesiastical History*, XXV (1974)
Chapter 8 from *History*, LX (1975)
Chapter 9 from *Past and Present*, XCIII (1981)

Chapter 6 is printed for the first time, with thanks to the author.

PREFACE

This collection of essays outlines an alternative history of the Reformation in England. It has been assembled in response to complaints from teachers and students that there is, at present, no 'revisionist' textbook to set alongside classic studies such as A. G. Dickens's *The English Reformation* (1964) and T. M. Parker's *The English Reformation to 1558* (1950). Although it is hoped that the volume will remain useful thereafter, it is in some respects a holding operation until proposed new books on the Reformation are finally written! The essays have therefore been selected in an attempt to piece together a more or less coherent interpretation – which is why the editor's own work is over-represented. The contributors do not necessarily agree in all respects, and their chapters illustrate different aspects of recent research, from the detailed analysis of diocesan courts to the broad survey of popular attitudes. But, taken together, the essays show how a new version of Reformation history can be constructed. The volume is an incomplete history, of course, though the new 'Introduction' and 'Conclusion' try to plug some of the gaps: it is thin on politics and on Protestants, but other Reformation studies have given such subjects at least their due. All of the main essays except for Chapter 6 have been published before in journals or collections: the editor is grateful to authors and publishers for their permission to reprint, and especially to Ronald Hutton for allowing his essay to be published here for the first time.   C. A. H.

ABBREVIATIONS

A.P.C.	*Acts of the Privy Council of England*
B.I.H.R	*Bulletin of the Institute of Historical Research*
B.I.Y.	Borthwick Institute of Historical Research, York
B.L.	British Library
C.Q.R.	*Church Quarterly Review*
C.R.O.	West Sussex Record Office, Chichester
C.R.S.	*Catholic Record Society*
E.H.R.	*English Historical Review*
G.L.R.O.	Greater London Record Office
H.J.	*Historical Journal*
J.E.H.	*Journal of Ecclesiastical History*
L.A.O.	Lincoln Archives Office
L.J.R.O.	Lichfield Joint Record Office
L.P.	*Letters and Papers, Foreign and Domestic, of the Reign of Henry VIII*
L.P.L.	Lambeth Palace Library
P. & P.	*Past and Present*
P.R.O.	Public Record Office
R.O.	Record Office
S.P.	State Papers
T.B.G.A.S.	*Transactions of the Bristol and Gloucestershire Archaeological Society*
T.R.H.S.	*Transactions of the Royal Historical Society*
V.C.H.	*Victoria County History*

INTRODUCTION

The excitement of history lies in its uncertainty. Except for the vital matter of accuracy in detail, there are no solved problems or authoritative conclusions in historical study. There is always more to be done – more documents to discover, more refined methods to apply, more issues to be considered, more thought to be given. So no history book, no matter how eminent the author or balanced the argument, can provide a definitive version of the past. It is not a defect of any particular work that it will be overtaken by later research, it is a characteristic of the historical discipline. Students should not be surprised that a well-established textbook is eventually challenged – rather they should be impressed that it has carried conviction for so long. For twenty years, Professor A. G. Dickens's *The English Reformation* stood in unrivalled mastery of its field, and it remained the best single-volume survey of the subject. It has been the standard text for teachers and students, and its pervasive influence could be detected in History examination scripts at all levels. But two decades of further research, much of it by historians inspired by the example of Dickens himself, have undermined old answers and raised new questions. Some recent writers would wish only to adjust the detail and emphases of 1964, but others suggest the need for a more fundamental revision of perspective.

One of the reasons for the popularity of the Dickens version of the Reformation is that it built upon a well-established tradition in English historical consciousness. *The English Reformation* is a highly sophisticated exposition of a story first told by John Foxe in 1563. Professor Dickens had set himself 'three special objectives' in writing his book: to describe the deep-seated causes of the dramatic changes of 1529–59; to emphasise the role of Protestant ideology, rather than of political or constitutional pressures, in producing those changes; and to show the impact of religious revolution upon ordinary people.[1] But these were exactly the themes of Foxe's *Acts and Monuments*. Foxe, too, had investigated the pre-history of the Reformation, and had contrasted the superstition and tyranny of the medieval

[1] A. G. Dickens, *The English Reformation* (London, 1964), p.v.

Catholic Church with the honest piety of discontented proto-Protestants. Foxe, too, had stressed the growing power of Protestantism, which was furthered by politicians and preachers as a state religion and a popular creed. And Foxe, too, had examined the ideas and experiences of those ordinary Christians who escaped from priestly control. Of course, Foxe had written Protestant propaganda, designed to carry forward the Reformation by discrediting Catholics and extolling the 'true humble martyrs and servants of God';[2] Dickens wrote sensitive and highly professional history, designed to communicate the fruits of thirty years of research. But their standpoints and their sources were more than a little similar: both traced the rise of reforming Protestantism at the expense of deficient Catholicism, and both used the trials of heretics as evidence for the spread of Protestant beliefs.

The perspective and the method of the Foxe–Dickens approach have been undermined by the impact of 'revisionism'. Now all historical argument is subject to revision, and in a loose sense all historians are 'revisionists', since they seek to improve upon earlier accounts of the past. But a number of recent attempts to revise the history of early modern England have had common features, and they have been classified as examples of 'revision*ism*'. The revisionist attack was first mounted against prevailing interpretations of the origins of the English Civil War. The existence of long-term constitutional or social discontents was disputed, the significance of parliamentary puritanism as a progressive ideological movement was doubted, the continuing power and prestige of the monarchy was stressed, and political conflict was explained as the outcome of factional competition for office and influence. This specific application has been extended into a more general revisionist critique of 'whig–Protestant' versions of English history, which sought to chart the triumph of progressive forces. For the history of England from the mid-fifteenth century to the mid-seventeenth had been seen in terms of a number of 'rises' – the rise of new monarchy, the rise of Protestantism, the rise of the gentry, the rise of puritanism, and the rise of parliament, movements culminating in the cataclysm of civil war. But revisionist historians have questioned the power of such modernising forces, and suggested that the 'rises' may not have risen very far; conservatism and continuity may be much more in evidence than radicalism and revolution.[3]

When applied to the Reformation, the revisionist strategy can produce a re-casting of history very similar to that achieved in the early-Stuart period. The existence of long-term religious discontents can be disputed, the significance of Protestantism as a progressive ideological movement can be doubted, the continuing popularity and

[2] J. Foxe, *Actes and Monuments*, ed. G. Townsend (London, 1843–9), IV, pp. 587–8.

[3] For a general statement of revisionism *avant la lettre*, see G. R. Elton, 'A High Road to Civil War?', in his *Studies in Tudor and Stuart Politics and Government* (Cambridge, 1974, 1983), II, pp. 164–9, and for a careful application of revisionist techniques to the pre-Civil War period see C. Russell, *Parliaments and English Politics, 1621–1629* (Oxford, 1979).

prestige of the Catholic Church can be stressed, and the political Reformation can be explained as the outcome of factional competition for office and influence. In fact, the revising of the English Reformation is only in small part a consequence of the deliberate use of revisionist approaches. It is much more the result of the exploitation of neglected evidence and the execution of regional studies. But revisionist attitudes and recent researches have combined to challenge the 'Foxe version' of Reformation history endorsed by Professor Dickens.

The historian who seeks long-term causes for the English Reformation can easily find them, as Dickens did in the first five chapters of his book. Because the Reformation happened, it is tempting to assume that it was necessary, that it was a justifiable protest against appalling defects in the late-medieval Church. But the search for flaws is a dangerous undertaking, and their contemporary significance can be exaggerated. There are many examples of religious beliefs and practices in the pre-Reformation Church which seem like far-fetched superstitions to the modern mind, but Keith Thomas and John Bossy have shown how conventional religion could provide both magical protection against the risks of rural life, and mechanisms of social conciliation and eternal salvation.[4] One man's superstition is another's spirituality: what mattered was that the simple rituals of village religion were functional – they apparently worked! Much the same is true of the structures of the Church: what would be flaws in the twentieth century were functions in the sixteenth. The pre-Reformation leaders of the Church may seem like careerist bureaucrats and its courts like oppressive inquisitions, but many of the bishops showed real concern for the supervision of their clergy and the maintenance of pastoral care, while their courts provided fairly cheap and convenient resolutions for local disputes.[5] In Chapter 2, Stephen Lander shows that in the diocese of Chichester the bishop revitalised administration, tightened clerical discipline, and tried to ensure that laymen fulfilled their religious duties. But the Reformation attack upon ecclesiastical jurisdiction weakened the authority of the courts, and prevented a continuation of the programme of improvement: Reformation blocked reform.

Generations of historians tracing the origins of the Reformation have cited examples of negligence and immorality among the clergy. There were scandals, it is true – but they were very rare. The inmates of a few of the religious houses could live in opulent idleness, but most monasteries were workaday communities offering charity, education, employment, and prayers for departed souls.[6] Some parish priests

4 K. Thomas, *Religion and the Decline of Magic* (London, 1971), pp. 27–188; J. Bossy, *Christianity in the West, 1400–1700* (Oxford, 1985), pp. 1–75.
5 S. Thompson, 'The Pastoral Work of the English and Welsh Bishops, 1500–1558' (University of Oxford D. Phil. thesis, 1984), *passim*; R. Houlbrooke, *Church Courts and the People during the English Reformation, 1520–1570* (Oxford, 1979), pp. 10–11, 42, 50–1, 95–6, 114–15, 263, 271–2.
6 D. Knowles, *The Religious Orders in England* (Cambridge, 1948–59), III, pp. 3–137, 241–303; C. Haigh, *Reformation and Resistance in Tudor Lancashire* (Cambridge, 1975), pp. 118–26.

were neglectful, but many more were thoughtful ministers to the needs of their people. It would be difficult to explain the high levels of lay benefactions to the Church and of lay recruitment to the priesthood if the clergy had really been as slothful and self-seeking as Protestant historians have suggested.[7] We should not isolate the evidence of deficiencies in the Church, and ignore the evidence of efficiency. On balance, the Church was a lively and relevant social institution, and the Reformation was not the product of a long-term decay of medieval religion. Indeed, as we shall see, Catholic piety was expanding rather than contracting in the years before the Reformation. Henry VIII did not challenge a moribund Church and a declining religion: he attacked institutions and forms of piety which were growing and vigorous.

The fact that there *was* a Reformation does not mean that it was wanted: it does not imply that there was a deep-seated popular demand for religious change. But Professor Dickens found in Lollardy and anticlericalism indications of widespread alienation from institutional Catholicism. It is difficult to assess the contribution of the Lollard heretics. Dickens thought that they formed a constituency from which Protestant preachers could recruit support, and it has been suggested that the sacramentarian views of Lollards influenced the theology of the reformers.[8] Both arguments have some force, but the numerical significance of the Lollards is far from clear. The evidence for Lollard activity is mainly drawn from the records of heresy trials, much of it collected by John Foxe. However such evidence raises two major problems. Firstly, suspects were interrogated by canon lawyers and theologians, whose questions and reports may have created a coherent heretical position out of the scepticism and misunderstandings of ordinary people.[9] Secondly, the apparent incidence of heresy varied with the intensity of official investigations: a 'rise of Lollardy' may show simply a sharpening of persecution.[10] So, in both its content and its distribution, Lollardy was a problem created by the authorities, and it formed a mirror image of their own fears. Lollardy was not quite a figment of episcopal imaginations, but it was a highly amorphous phenomenon.

Heresy appears to have been geographically and socially restricted in the early sixteenth century. There were certainly heretical groups in the main towns, especially London, Bristol, Coventry and Norwich, and in the clothworking villages of Buckinghamshire, Essex and Kent, but elsewhere there were no more than occasional

[7] See below, pp. 70–2. The best examinations of the pre-Reformation parish clergy are M. Bowker, *The Secular Clergy in the Diocese of Lincoln, 1495–1520* (Cambridge, 1968) and P. Heath, *The English Parish Clergy on the Eve of the Reformation* (London, 1969).

[8] Dickens, *English Reformation*, pp. 33–7; J. F. Davis, *Heresy and Reformation in the South East of England, 1520–1559* (Royal Historical Society Studies in History, London, 1983), pp. 41–65.

[9] A. Hudson, 'The Examination of Lollards', *B.I.H.R.*, XLVI (1973), pp. 145–59; J. A. F. Thomson, *The Later Lollards, 1414–1520* (Oxford, 1965), pp. 226–30.

[10] The chronology of heresy prosecutions is charted in Thomson, *Later Lollards*, pp. 237–38.

aberrant individuals. There were certainly heretics among the lesser merchants of
London, but usually Lollards were drawn from weavers and other artisans.[11] It may
be objected that the detected Lollards were just the tip of a more significant iceberg,
but the popular hostility towards heresy[12] suggests that the detection rate would
be high and the submerged section of the iceberg small. Perhaps Lollardy was
expanding on the eve of the Reformation – or perhaps that is an illusion created by
the determination of some bishops to root out heresy and purify their dioceses. At
least in the diocese of Lincoln, it seems that the Lollard problem was brought under
control; by the 1540s Bishop Longland had almost destroyed Buckinghamshire
Lollardy, which had seemed such a threat twenty years earlier.[13] So it is far from
clear what we should make of the Lollards. Because the Protestant Reformation
ultimately succeeded, there is a danger that historians will exaggerate these
proto-Protestants into a powerful movement. The Lollards do show that there were
dissidents from the late-medieval Church, and that some of them were organised
into an underground sect. But they seem also to show that heresy was rare, and that
heretics were much disliked by their orthodox neighbours. If the Lollards are our
evidence of a demand for Reformation, then the demand was limited – and in some
places it was declining.

Modern scholars have generally admitted that the Lollards were a small minority,
and it would be hard to argue otherwise in the face of the overwhelming proofs
of the Catholic orthodoxy of the majority. But many historians have assumed that
the Catholic majority became hostile to the Church, through a combination of the
deficiencies of the clergy and the aspirations of the laity. The concept of
anticlericalism plays a crucial role in recent accounts of the English Reformation,
for it helps to explain how a largely Catholic country had a largely peaceful
Reformation. The English may have loved the mass, but they hated the priests and
were eager to see them humbled.[14] But the Reformation was not the product of
a long-term clash between laity and clergy. It is argued in Chapter 3 that relations
between priests and parishioners were usually harmonious, and the laity complained
astonishingly infrequently against their priests. There were local tensions, certainly,
but they were individual rather than institutionalised, occasional rather than endemic.
In a frantic search for the causes of Reformation, we must not wrench isolated cases
of discord from their local contexts, and pile them together to show a growing chorus

---

[11] Dickens, *English Reformation*, p. 30. Groups of Midlands heretics are carefully described in
    J. Fines, 'Heresy Trials in the Diocese of Coventry and Lichfield, 1511–1512', *J.E.H.*, XIV
    (1963), pp. 160–74.

[12] Thomson, *Later Lollards*, pp. 7–8, 143–6, 152–3; Haigh, *Reformation and Resistance*, pp. 78, 84–6.

[13] M. Bowker, *The Henrician Reformation: the Diocese of Lincoln under John Longland, 1521–1547*
    (Cambridge, 1981), pp. 178–83.

[14] This case is argued by Dickens, *English Reformation*, pp. 90–102, and G. R. Elton, *Reform and
    Reformation: England 1509–1558* (London, 1977), pp. 8–11, 51–8, 118–19.

of dissatisfaction: we must not construct a false polarisation between Church and people. There was no general hostility towards the clerical estate, and such criticism as there was came from specific interest groups, especially lawyers, London merchants, and the political enemies of Cardinal Wolsey. The English people had not turned against their Church, and there was no widespread yearning for reform. The long-term causes of the Reformation – the corruption of the Church and the hostility of the laity – appear to have been historical illusions.

So the first phase of the revisionist strategy, the denial of underlying causes of the Reformation, can be executed with some success. The second phase, the reduction of the role of Protestantism as a progressive ideological movement, is a little more difficult. For the rehabilitation of Protestant allegiance as a powerful contributor to the Reformation process was the main aim of Professor Dickens's work, and he has argued his case with style and determination. He has sought to show the growth of Protestant commitment among ecclesiastical and political leaders, the processes of evangelisation which took the new religion to the nation at large, and, above all, the enthusiastic response of ordinary people to the liberating theology of the reformers. He has, in short, challenged any distinction between the official, state Reformation and the popular, spiritual Reformation, and demonstrated their interaction in a dynamic process of religious revolution. In Chapter 1, the argument that the spread of Protestantism was rapid and popular is set out, and some of its assumptions refuted. In sixteenth-century conditions, Protestantism was not, and could not be, an attractive religion at the grass-roots level. Although *some* illiterate workers were converted to the new faith, its stress upon Bible-reading and its insistence upon justification by faith and predestination limited its popular appeal. It was not until the middle of the reign of Elizabeth I that the universities produced a generation of committed Protestant ministers who could take the evangelical faith to the parishes, and even then great difficulties were encountered.[15] The growth of Protestantism was not fast, and it was not easy.

England had a Protestant Reformation, but it was not made by a powerful Protestant movement. The Reformation was not an inexorable process, carried forward by an irresistible ideological force; it was a succession of contingent events which, in total, tended towards Protestant victory. The term 'Reformation' embraces a number of distinct changes in religious organisation, practice and belief – a reduction of clerical authority, an abolition of papal supremacy, a suppression of monasteries and chantries, an introduction of a vernacular Bible, a replacement of the mass by Protestant services, and a re-definition of the Church's theology. These stages in the English Reformation sequence stretched across more than thirty years,

---

[15] For the impact of Protestantism on Elizabethan England, see P. Collinson, 'The Elizabethan Church and the New Religion', in C. Haigh, ed., *The Reign of Elizabeth I* (Basingstoke, 1984), esp. pp. 176–94.

and each step was taken, not because it formed the next item on a preconceived Reformation agenda, but because it suited the immediate interests of princes and politicians. England had an ersatz Reformation, an anaemic substitute for the real thing. In Germany, the Netherlands, Scotland and Switzerland, even in France, where it failed, the Reformation came with passion and violence; in England it came with restraint, in orderly obedience to royal instruction. Elsewhere, Catholic altars and images were destroyed by mob action; in England, as we shall see in Chapter 6, they were taken down by hired masons and carpenters, on the orders of the Crown. So there was no cataclysmic Reformation, to be explained by mass enthusiasm or a revolutionary party. Instead, there was a piecemeal Reformation, to be explained by the chances of day-to-day politics.

Professor Dickens has argued that a version of Reformation history which fails to recognise the power of Protestantism makes the Elizabethan Settlement inexplicable.[16] His protest illustrates the difference between 'whiggish' and 'revisionist' strategies of explanation. A whig approach to the legislation of 1559 will seek the progressive force which caused it or made it possible, and the fact of the legislation becomes evidence for the strength of that force. A revisionist approach will examine the political circumstances of 1559, and assess the interests and calculations of the participants. Elizabeth's advisers and supporters were themselves Protestants, the men who had helped make the Edwardian Reformation and who had turned to the reversionary interest in the reign of Mary. They, and the daughter of Anne Boleyn, would prefer a Protestant Church if they could get one – and the circumstances of 1558–9 gave them their chance. With the Catholic episcopate depleted by deaths and England at war with both the pope and the francophile Catholic claimant to the throne, the anti-Protestants were temporarily weakened and Elizabeth's party had its way.[17] Thereafter, the settlement of 1559 survived not because it endorsed the aspirations of the Protestants but because the queen moderated its terms and restrained its enforcement; it succeeded not because it was popular but because Elizabeth made it less unpopular. So only the balance of politics in 1559 made the Elizabethan Settlement a largely Protestant one, and only the balance of advantage afterwards made the decision of 1559 a lasting 'settlement'.

Of course, our assessment of the strength of Protestantism should not be determined by an analysis of Elizabeth's Settlement, and our reading of 1559 should not be decided by a preference for revisionist rather than whiggish explanations. What matters is the evidence for the distribution of Protestant allegiance. In Chapter 5,

[16] A. G. Dickens, review of J. J. Scarisbrick, *The Reformation and the English People* (Oxford, 1984), in *J.E.H.*, XXXVI (1985), pp. 125–6.

[17] This interpretation of the making of the Elizabethan Settlement has been developed by N. L. Jones, *Faith by Statute: Parliament and the Settlement of Religion, 1559* (Royal Historical Society Studies in History, London, 1982), and W. S. Hudson, *The Cambridge Connection and the Elizabethan Settlement of 1559* (Durham, North Carolina, 1980).

David Palliser examines a number of indicators of the extent of Protestant support, and the picture he reveals is a complex one. From his investigation of heresy prosecutions, wills, clerical marriage, religious rebellions, and Marian exiles and martyrs, only two things seem clear: that there was considerable regional and local variation in the incidence of Protestant loyalties, and that even the areas of most obvious Protestant advance saw vigorous Catholic resistance. The Reformation was not a Protestant walkover, it was a hard-fought and long drawn-out contest.[18] The new religion had not claimed the devotion of the people of England by 1559; probably everywhere it was a minority faith, and in many places it was a tiny sect. Except in London, the widespread preaching of reformed religion first took place in the reign of Elizabeth, not in that of her brother or her father. The establishment of Protestantism as a mass religion was thus a consequence, not a cause, of the political Reformation. The Reformation brought Protestantism, not Protestantism the Reformation.

The role of Protestantism as a progressive ideological force in the English Reformation can, therefore, be reduced (though it cannot be eliminated), and the second phase of a revisionist strategy more or less completed. The revisionist version is said to leave Protestantism out of the Reformation, but the Foxe–Dickens version had almost left out the Catholics – except as bemused victims of the historical process. So the third phase of the revisionist programme is a stress upon the continuing popularity of Catholicism, and much recent research has supported this assertion. In Chapter 6, Ronald Hutton's examination of almost 200 sets of churchwardens' accounts shows that Catholic devotion retained its vitality at the parish level until the very moment of the official Reformation's impact. An important study of the south-west of England has demonstrated that the veneration of images and the endowment of prayers continued unabated until the mid-1530s,[19] and Professor J. J. Scarisbrick has revealed the vigour of religious guilds and confraternities.[20] With a rising level of recruitment to the priesthood, a buoyant market for religious books, and more and more altars and images crammed into the churches,[21] Catholic piety was flourishing in the years immediately before the Reformation. Although it is true that some aspects of traditional devotion collapsed

---

[18] This was true even in London: see S. Brigden, 'The Early Reformation in London, 1520–1547: the Conflict in the Parishes' (University of Cambridge Ph. D. thesis, 1979), and her forthcoming book *London and the Reformation*.

[19] R. Whiting, 'Abominable Idols: Images and Image-breaking under Henry VIII', *J.E.H.*, XXXIII (1982), pp. 31–9; '"For the Health of my Soul": Prayers for the Dead in the Tudor South-West', *Southern History*, V (1983), pp. 66–72. See also A. Kreider, *English Chantries: the Road to Dissolution* (Cambridge, Mass., 1979), pp. 86–92.

[20] Scarisbrick, *Reformation and the English People*, pp. 19–39.

[21] See below, pp. 70–1 and 115–16.

when proscribed by the state,[22] Ronald Hutton's chapter shows that Catholic piety flourished once again in Mary's reign. Altars, images, crucifixes and candlesticks were restored to the churches with alacrity, and the extent of local investment in service equipment suggests religious enthusiasm rather than reluctant conformism.

The rehabilitation of Marian Catholicism is one of the most striking developments in the revision of the Reformation. In Chapter 7, Rex Pogson shows that the Marian Church inherited a huge problem of alienated revenues, dilapidated churches, impoverished clergy and weakened authority, but that Cardinal Pole formulated far-sighted plans for reform. Gina Alexander indicates in Chapter 8 that Mary's bishop of London was not merely 'bloody Bonner', persecutor of Protestants, but a careful diocesan who sought to rebuild Catholic commitment in an impressively systematic fashion. Other bishops and Catholic writers promoted a purified version of traditional religion, more solidly based on the Bible and the sacraments and less dependent on ingrained habits and popular superstitions.[23] It seems that Catholicism recovered well in Mary's reign, and prospects for the future seemed good. In parish churches at least, the damage done by the Reformation was repaired, and clerical recruitment boomed again for the first time since the 1520s. In despair, Protestant writers in exile called for rebellion, to overturn Mary's regime before the reconstruction of Catholicism became irreversible.[24] But, as modern English historians have usually supposed, God was on the side of the Protestants: he intervened before the followers of Ponet, Knox and Goodman could act, and Mary and Pole died within hours of each other. The Marian Church did not become the foundation for a continuing Catholic England – but it did become the foundation for a continuing Catholic community. Chapter 9 shows that conservative religious allegiance remained widespread, and suggests that clergy who had served in Mary's Church organised a separated Catholic denomination in the reign of Elizabeth. English Catholicism was not destroyed by the Reformation: it fought back, reorganised itself, and survived.

So there was no deep-seated hostility to the late-medieval Church, Protestantism remained weak until the late sixteenth century, and Catholicism remained vibrant

---

[22] Whiting, 'Abominable Idols', pp. 39–46; '"For the Health of my Soul"', pp. 79–85. For attempts to resist or evade official proscriptions, see Scarisbrick, *Reformation and the English People*, pp. 61–121.

[23] J. Loach, 'The Marian Establishment and the Printing Press', *E.H.R.*, c (1986), pp. 138–41; A. Bartholomew, 'Lay Piety in the Reign of Mary Tudor' (University of Manchester M.A. thesis, 1979), esp. pp. 1–42. See, for example, the stress on the need for real contrition, not merely external penance, in E. Bonner, *A profitable and necessarye doctryne* (London, 1555), 'The exposition of the Sacrament of Penaunce', and T. Watson, *Holsome and Catholyke doctryne* (London, 1558), fos. cv–cxxxv.

[24] D. M. Loades, *The Reign of Mary Tudor* (London, 1979), pp. 338–55 (though Professor Loades's emphasis is rather different); Haigh, *Reformation and Resistance*, pp. 195–208.

and popular. Why then was there a Reformation? John Morrill was once accused
of having explained why no civil war broke out in 1642;[25] other revisionists are
said to have explained why there was no Reformation! But there was a Reformation —
of sorts — and an explanation has to be offered if the revisionist position is to carry
any conviction. It is, however, necessary to recognise what it is we must explain — not
a dramatic Protestant revolution, but a series of specific chances and decisions which,
in the end, added up to Reformation. So we may attempt the fourth phase of the
revisionist strategy, and account for the political Reformation by factional
competition for office and influence. A number of recent historians have discussed
Tudor politics in factional terms, but the significance of factional conflict for our
understanding of the Reformation is clearest in the work of David Starkey and Dale
Hoak. Starkey has suggested that the political Reformation in the reign of Henry
VIII was 'the work of a Court faction'. He has shown how the rise of Ann Boleyn,
tool of the opponents of Cardinal Wolsey, split Court and Council into competing
factional alliances, and made religious principle a polarising issue in politics.[26]

The ecclesiastical implications of Henry's divorce project made religion a matter
for political calculation, and ambitious men espoused causes as their calculations of
interest dictated. The religious future of England was then in some measure
dependent upon who was in favour with the king. Henry's determination to have
his divorce from Katherine of Aragon, the financial and foreign policy consequences
of the break from Rome, and the political and administrative skills of Thomas
Cromwell gave reformist factions the advantage in the 1530s — though in the crisis
of 1536 the conservatives were able to destroy Anne Boleyn and her allies. The
dominance of the evangelicals was broken in the coups of 1539–40, when Henry's
distaste for radical religion and for Anne of Cleves allowed conservatives to reverse
religious policy and overthrow Cromwell. The 1540s saw a struggle between a
conservative-controlled Privy Council and an evangelical Privy Chamber, which in
Henry's last year became a desperate battle for control of the future. In the spring
and summer of 1546 the conservative leaders tried to break the influence of reformers
about the king, and the Howard family asserted its claim to a regency in the next
reign. But some adroit manoeuvring in favourable circumstances enabled the
evangelicals to discredit the Howards and Bishop Gardiner of Winchester, and they
consolidated their control of the dying king. If Henry had died in the summer of
1546, he would have left conservatives to dominate his young successor; but he died
in January 1547, and by then a reformist alliance was directing affairs.

Dale Hoak has shown how the Duke of Somerset established himself as Protector

[25] J. Morrill, *The Revolt of the Provinces* (London, 1980 ed.), p. x.
[26] D. Starkey, *The Reign of Henry VIII: Personalities and Politics* (London, 1985), esp. pp. 9, 15–16,
29–30.

in 1547, and remodelled the Privy Council to weaken the conservative opposition. Somerset pursued an ecclesiastical policy of moderate Protestant reform, but the trouble this provoked in 1549 allowed a conservative grouping to topple him from power. The Earl of Warwick had participated in the alliance against Somerset, but he calculated that his own role would be minimal in a conservative regime. So he threw in his lot with the reformers, allied with Somerset, ensured his own domination of the Council and followed an unambiguously Protestant policy.[27] In 1553 Warwick, now Duke of Northumberland, played the Protestant card once again. He attempted to exclude the Catholic Mary from the throne, partly on grounds of her religion, and to raise Protestant support for the claims of Jane Grey. But his stratagem was blocked, by a popular rebellion in East Anglia and by the decisive action of Catholic gentry in proclaiming Mary queen in several counties.[28] The Reformation had been carried forward by hard-headed politicians: their own religious principles, their assessments of self-interest, and the evolving patterns of domestic and international advantages had favoured the pieces of the piecemeal Reformation. And, as we have seen, the same was to be true in 1558–9, after Mary's death had cut short the Catholic restoration: the Elizabethan Settlement, too, was made by a Court faction seeking to maintain itself in power.

So it is possible to offer an explanation of the Reformation which does not presuppose a powerful Protestant movement or the collapse of Catholicism. The momentum of day-to-day politics may have provided the moving force for religious change, and a narrative of Court intrigue may serve as our explanatory tool. But this fourth phase of the revisionist strategy is perhaps the least likely to command assent. Historians may prove reluctant to cast Henry VIII as the puppet rather than the puppeteer of politics, and a recent interpretation of the events of 1539–40 has stressed the leading role of the king himself.[29] There is certainly strong resistance to the proposition that the Protestant Reformation can be explained by the machinations of a tiny power elite.[30] For if the Reformation was made by a self-interested political clique, against the wishes of the nation, how did it come to be

[27] D. E. Hoak, *The King's Council in the Reign of Edward VI* (Cambridge, 1976), pp. 231–68; 'Rehabilitating the Duke of Northumberland: Politics and Political Control, 1549–53', in J. Loach and R. Tittler, eds., *The Mid-Tudor Polity, c. 1540–1560* (Basingstoke, 1980), pp. 35–40.

[28] D. MacCulloch, 'The *Vita Mariae Angliae Reginae* of Robert Wingfield of Brantham', *Camden Miscellany*, XXVIII (1984), pp. 188–91. Outside East Anglia, it was usually the conservatives who took the lead in proclaiming Mary Queen: see *The Chronicle of Queen Jane*, ed. J. G. Nichols (Camden Society, 1850), p. 12.

[29] G. Redworth, 'A Study in the Formulation of Policy: The Genesis and Evolution of the Act of Six Articles', *J.E.H.*, XXXVII (1986), pp. 42–67; 'The Political and Diplomatic Career of Stephen Gardiner' (University of Oxford D. Phil. thesis, 1985), pp. 35–64.

[30] See, for example, K. Thomas in *Times Literary Supplement* (1982), p. 479, and A. G. Dickens in *J.E.H.*, XXXVI (1985), pp. 125–6.

accepted? Why was such an unpopular Reformation such a peaceful Reformation?
This seems to be a crucial difficulty for any revisionist approach to the Reformation,
but there are several escape-routes available.

Robert Whiting has shown that, in the diocese of Exeter, the erection of images
and the endowment of prayers ceased when such devotions were attacked by royal
policy. In Chapter 6, Ronald Hutton demonstrates that churchwardens rapidly
complied with official orders to suppress Catholic worship. Their explanations for
the almost instant obedience of the parishes are much the same – not local approval
of Protestant policies, but local recognition of the power and prestige of the
monarchy.[31] There is certainly much in this view – especially after Cromwell had
sharpened the treason laws and made dissent from royal policy a risky business. By
instructing justices to watch priests, priests to watch justices, and everyone to watch
the commons, Cromwell instituted, if not a reign of terror, at least a reign of
nervousness.[32] The parishioners of Ashlower in Gloucestershire turned their vicar
over to the authorities just in case – 'forasmuch as your poor orators and subjects
be men not knowing whether the act thus done by the said vicar in manner as afore
is expressed be treason or no, and fearing that if it so should be that they in not
uttering of it should not do their duties according as your true subjects ought,
therefore your said orators and subjects have in discharge of their duties opened and
declared the act of the said vicar'. When open criticism could lead to a treason charge,
sullen silence was safest: as a London priest said in 1536, 'I will pray for [the pope]
as the chief head of Christ's Church, and so I will advise all men to do secretly.
But we may say nothing openly, for the knaves hath our heads under their girdle.'[33]

But we must be careful not to exaggerate the extent of local obedience, for evasion
was common. The royal Injunctions of September 1538 ordered that images which
had been the objects of particular devotion should be pulled down, and that the
practice of burning candles before images should cease. The churchwardens' accounts
show that the use of candles stopped almost immediately, since to continue with
them risked an order for the destruction of images as superstitious. But the accounts
also show that hardly any images were taken down, and parishes had made the
concession on candles to ensure that their images were safe.[34] Where, as in Kent,
an officious commissary tried to enforce the removal of images, trouble ensued.
At Milton and Sholden, images which had been pulled down by the commissary's
order were replaced by local people when he had moved on, and at Elmstead the

[31] Whiting, 'Abominable Images', pp. 46–7; see below, pp. 137–8.
[32] G. R. Elton, *Policy and Police: the Enforcement of the Reformation in the Age of Thomas Cromwell*
(Cambridge, 1972), pp. 217–62, 327–82.
[33] P.R.O., Star Chamber 2/21/120; S. P. 1/102, fos. 73–4 (*L. P.*, x, 346). I am grateful to Professor
Elton for these references.
[34] H. Gee and W. J. Hardy, eds., *Documents Illustrative of English Church History* (London, 1896),
pp. 277–8; see below, p. 117.

parishioners petitioned the archbishop for the restoration of the image of St James, since lights had *not* been burned before it. At Aldington and Lydd priests still encouraged their people to venerate images, and at Eastwell and North Mongeham devotion to images continued.[35] But usually there was compromise: the grosser superstitions were dropped, but parishes kept their images and proudly cleaned and painted them as before.

On images, Henry VIII got half of his way: on Bibles in churches he got even less. No doubt part of the resistance to the 1538 instruction that each parish should buy a Bible for use in the church came from the cost of the purchase, but the general association of English Bibles with heresy was also responsible. In Kent, after the Bible order was published, one man warned his fellows not to read the Bible until doomsday, and a priest at Wincanton denounced 'these new-fangled fellows which read the new books, for they be heretics and knaves and pharisees'. James Fredewell, a Kent priest, raged that 'he had liefer that all the New Testaments in England were burned than he would buy any or look upon any'.[36] So it is not surprising that parishes were slow to get their Bibles. In the spring of 1539, four-fifths of the churches in three Lincoln deaneries still had no Bible, and the vicar-general was doing nothing to enforce purchase. By the end of 1540, hardly any parishes outside London and the cathedral cities had their Bibles, though churchwardens had had more than two years to get them. In May 1541, an angry royal proclamation complained that 'his royal Majesty is informed that divers and many towns and parishes within this his realm have negligently omitted their duties in the accomplishment thereof, whereof his Highness marvelleth not a little'; parishes were given six months to comply, on pain of a fine of £2. Thereafter there was grudging and gradual obedience, and by the end of 1545 most wardens had made their purchases – though some country parishes complied only in 1547, when visited by Edward VI's commissioners.[37] It had taken a decade for the order to be fully enforced: slow Reformation indeed!

Sometimes apparent conformity to the Reformation process masks common prudence or self-interested manipulation. When benefactions to images and for prayers began to dwindle after 1536, it was not because Catholic beliefs were weakening but because the suppression of monasteries showed ecclesiastical endowments were at risk. When corporations or families reclaimed lands or animals given to churches by predecessors, they were forestalling official confiscation, not signalling the advance of Protestantism.[38] Professor J. J. Scarisbrick has noted that men could

---

[35] *L.P.*, XVIII (2), 546, pp. 296, 297, 299, 301, 303, 317.

[36] Elton, *Policy and Police*, p. 25.

[37] Bowker, *Henrician Reformation*, p. 170; *L. P.*, *XIV* (2), 214; P. L. Hughes and J. F. Larkin, eds., *Tudor Royal Proclamations* (New Haven, 1964), I, p. 296; see below, pp. 116, 118.

[38] Whiting, '"For the Health of my Soul"', pp. 74–8; A. G. Dickens, *Lollards and Protestants in the Diocese of York, 1509–1558* (Oxford, 1959), pp. 205–9.

oppose the dissolutions while cheerfully profiting from them; the English gentry may have been Catholics, but they were certainly not fools.[39] Margaret Bowker shows in Chapter 4 that the Henrician Reformation brought improvements in the career prospects of the clergy, and suggests that this made conformity more rewarding: priests acquiesced in changes they might otherwise have resisted. The English Reformation was accepted, not because it was popular but because in some respects it was convenient.

That lay Catholics bought Church lands and that clerical Catholics held on to their benefices has been supposed to suggest a lack of real commitment to their religion, but cautious compliance could sometimes be the wisest policy. Bishop Fisher of Rochester held out for the papal primacy, and went to the block for his beliefs – but he was soon replaced at Rochester by the Protestant John Hilsey, who then carried forward the Reformation in the diocese. In Lincoln, however, John Longland kept his see, and was able to delay the impact of Protestantism on his diocese until after his death in 1547: perhaps it was Longland, not Fisher, who served the Catholic cause well.[40] Of course, the conservative conformists did not necessarily keep their places in selfless devotion to their faith: their motives were mixed. Students of the Reformation tend to assume that religious issues had priority, and that participants in the Reformation ought always to have put religion first. But the men and women of Reformation England were, Catholic or Protestant, generally confused ordinary mortals, not saints and martyrs. The conservative bishops, with the exception of Fisher, conformed to the Henrician Reformation. They sought to block the king's constitutional and religious changes, but, on issue after issue, they finally obeyed. They did so because they accepted the rights of king and parliament in the regulation of religion, and because the unity of the realm was more important to them than the unity of Christendom.[41] The fact that they shared the king's view that statutes took priority over canon law, and that they wished to maintain the stability of the kingdom, does not make them weak Catholics, or demonstrate a fatal defect at the heart of conservative allegiance. It shows only that they were Tudor bishops, with secular as well as ecclesiastical responsibilities, and duties to the king as well as to the Church.

So the prestige of the monarchy predisposed conservatives towards conformity, and for those with inadequate predisposition there was Cromwellian intimidation. Some orders were evaded or their implementation delayed, so their offensiveness

[39] Scarisbrick, *Reformation and the English People*, pp. 68–74. See also D. M. Palliser, *Tudor York* (Oxford, 1979), p. 237.
[40] P. Clark, *English Provincial Society from the Reformation to the Revolution: Religion, Politics and Society in Kent, 1500–1640* (Hassocks, 1977), p. 36; Bowker, *Henrician Reformation*, pp. 176, 181.
[41] J.-P. Moreau, *Rome ou L'Angleterre? Les Réactions Politiques des Catholiques Anglais au Moment du Schisme (1529–1553)* (Paris, 1984), pp. 27–176.

was blunted. Some measures which were objectionable in theory were acceptable in practice: monasteries were good things, but a share in the spoils made their loss more bearable. Catholic leaders were reluctant to disrupt the social order by encouraging disobedience, or to risk foreign invasion while the country was divided. There were many good reasons for the compliance of the conservatives – but were they good enough? This was, after all, the Protestant Reformation, and surely the Catholics ought to have rejected it? But it was, until late in the day, far from obvious that it *was* the Protestant Reformation. At first it was simply the king's divorce, and a petty squabble with the pope. 'Remember how often in times past these ways hath been attempted, and what end the authors thereof hath come unto', Dr John London told his reformist nephew in 1534. 'Remember this world will not continue long. For although the king hath now conceived a little malice against the bishop of Rome because he would not agree to this marriage, yet I trust that the blessed king will wear harness on his own back to fight against such heretics as thou art!'[42]

There was no need to resist the insignificant and the temporary, for God would soon put matters right. In 1536 a London priest told a man in confession, 'Be you of good comfort, and be steadfast in your faith and be not wavering, and God shall reward us the more. For these things will not last long, I warrant you; you shall see the world change shortly.'[43] A Sussex priest said of the English Bible in 1538, 'Lightly it came, and lightly it will be gone again', and in Kent in 1543 a parishioner told his priest and churchwardens that 'such ways should continue but a while, and that they should see shortly'.[44] So common sense suggested patient conformity, for even kings were mortal men: 'If it fortune the king to die, you shall see this world turned up-so down or clear changed', said a priest at St Albans in 1535.[45] Because the Reformation came piecemeal, the significance of the pieces was not recognised, and this was the key to its success. The conservative people of England would find a wholesale Reformation distasteful – indeed, they gagged in 1536 when they were asked to swallow, in rapid succession, the suppression of monasteries, reformist Injunctions, and the abrogation of saints' days. But the meal was more manageable when fed in tiny morsels, and the English ate their Reformation as a recalcitrant child is fed its supper, little by little, in well-timed spoonsful – 'one for Cardinal Wolsey, one for Queen Katherine, one for the pope, one for the monks, one for pilgrimages...' – until the plate had been emptied and Reformation had happened.

Even Catholic bishops did not realise what was happening around them until it was too late. 'Oh, that I had holden still with my brother Fisher, and not left him

---

[42] Elton, *Policy and Police*, p. 353.
[43] P.R.O., S.P. 1/102, fos 73–4 (*L.P.*, x, 346).
[44] *L.P.*, XIII (1), 1199(2); XVIII (2), 546, p. 299. It was reported of Suffolk in 1538 that 'they say all things shall be as it hath been, and than all shall be nought again' (*L.P.*, XIII (2), 1179).
[45] Elton, *Policy and Police*, p. 27.

when time was', wailed Bishop Stokesley of London on his deathbed in 1539.[46] If
the conservatives had known that Henry's break with Rome was not going to be
just a tactical manoeuvre to get the king his divorce, then perhaps others would have
stood with Fisher in 1535 – but they did not know, and they could not know. For
to accuse them of lack of foresight is to adopt the false perspective of inevitable
Reformation. They did not recognise that the break would be final, because it was
not necessarily going to be final: Thomas Cromwell wanted it to be final, and Henry
VIII was willing for it to be final, but only the chances of politics would make it
final. For the Reformation almost didn't happen. In 1536 Anne Boleyn was
overthrown, Henry married a conservative pawn, and Cromwell was at risk. In
1539–40 Protestant beliefs were outlawed, Cromwell was destroyed, and Henry
married another tool of the conservatives. In 1543 Archbishop Cranmer was under
threat, in 1546 Queen Catherine Parr. Six months before Henry's death, the
reformers were close to final defeat, and conservatives almost ensured their
ascendancy in the next reign. In 1549 the Duke of Somerset was brought down, and
there was talk of a Marian regency. In Mary's own reign, the mass, papal authority
and the heresy laws were restored with astonishingly little difficulty, and only the
queen's death gave Reformation another chance.

By 1559, of course, it was clear that a Protestant Reformation was happening.
When the Catholic bishops were then asked to accept a total Reformation, they voted
against the enacting bills in parliament and refused to obey the statutes which were
passed. But, even then, it was far from certain that the political see-saw had come
to rest and that Reformation was irreversible. Just before Mary's death, a Lancashire
justice had admitted 'that this new learning shall come again, but for how
long? – even for three or four months and no longer'. In 1560 the bishop of Lichfield
complained of parishes which 'hath not only yet their altars standing, but also their
images reserved and conveyed away, contrary to the Queen's Majesty's injunctions,
hoping and looking for a new day'.[47] The bishop of Carlisle reported in 1562 that
his people were expecting a reversal of religion and preparing for it, and in 1565 there
were rumours in Lancashire that altars and crucifixes were to be restored.[48] These
expectations were unfulfilled, but their existence is important. History is, after all,
made by people who usually don't know what *is* happening and certainly don't know
what *will* happen. They could not recognise a composite Reformation–event, they
could see only the little events which might, in sum, add up to a Reformation. The
political activists of Tudor England did not elect for or against 'the Reformation'

[46] P. Hughes, ed., *St. John Fisher: the Earliest English Life* (London, 1935), p. 160.
[47] Foxe, *Actes*, VIII, p. 563; M. R. O'Day, 'Thomas Bentham: a Case Study in the Problems of
the Early Elizabethan Episcopate', *J.E.H.*, XXIII (1972), p. 145.
[48] H. N. Birt, *The Elizabethan Religious Settlement* (London, 1907), p. 311; Haigh *Reformation and
Resistance*, p. 220.

in a single do-or-die decision, they made a number of lesser choices – for or against Wolsey in 1529, for or against canon law in 1532, for or against the Aragon marriage in 1533, for or against papal power in 1534, for or against higher clerical taxes in 1535, and so on. The overall revisionist strategy, by dissolving the Reformation into its constituent elements, makes acquiescence explicable. At any one time, there was not much Reformation to accept, and England accepted its Reformation because it didn't quite see what it was doing. The piecemeal Reformation was a peaceful Reformation.

I

THE RECENT HISTORIOGRAPHY OF THE
ENGLISH REFORMATION

CHRISTOPHER HAIGH

The English Reformation was not a specific event which may be given a precise date; it was a long and complex process. 'The Reformation' is a colligatory concept, a historians' label which relates several lesser changes into an overall movement: it embraces a break from the Roman obedience; an assertion of secular control over the Church; a suppression of Catholic institutions such as monasteries and chantries; a prohibition of Catholic worship; and a protestantisation of services, clergy and laity. Though the political decision to introduce each phase of change and the legislative alteration of statutes and canons may be dated easily enough, it is much harder to ascribe responsibility and motive for such measures. Moreover, as the interest of historians has in recent years moved on from such political issues towards the administrative enforcement of new rules and popular acceptance of new ideas, so the identification and explanation of change have become even more difficult: the pace is likely to have varied from area to area, and the criteria by which progress should be measured are far from clear. It is therefore not surprising that there has been much dispute over the causes and chronology of developments in religion, and recent interpretations of the Reformation in England can, with some simplification, be grouped in relation to two matrices. One matrix relates to the motive force behind the progress of Protestantism: at one extreme, it could be suggested that Protestant advance was entirely the result of official coercion, while at the other it could be said that the new religion spread horizontally by conversions among the people. The second matrix relates to the pace of religious change: on the one hand, it could be suggested that Protestantism made real progress at an early date and had become a powerful force by the death of Edward VI, while on the other it could be said that little had been achieved in the first half of the century and the main task of protestantising the people had to be undertaken in the reign of Elizabeth. These two matrices provide us with four main clusters of interpretations.

First, there are those historians, usually political historians and biographers, who have seen the English Reformation as taking place rapidly as a result of imposition from above. The *doyen* of this school is, without doubt, G. R. Elton, who has presented the Reformation as one aspect of the great reform programme which was initiated and carried far by Thomas Cromwell in the 1530s. The political Reformation saw the 'nationalisation' of the Church, and a religious Reformation sought to purge the parishes of superstition. These changes were enforced from the centre by deliberate governmental action: the people were persuaded to accept new policies by a carefully orchestrated campaign of preaching and printed propaganda, encouragement to conform was provided by a sharpening of the treason laws, and local dignitaries were instructed to report deviants to Cromwell for investigation. The reformist thrust was, according to Professor Elton, carried very much further under Edward VI, with the imposition of a Protestant liturgy, the destruction of Catholic church furniture, and a preaching campaign to carry the Gospel into the villages: 'The fact is that by 1553 England was almost certainly nearer to being a Protestant country than to anything else.'[1] This picture of a 'rapid Reformation from above' has received powerful support from Peter Clark's study of Kent: it is clear that Cromwell paid close attention to this strategically important county and built up, by the exercise of patronage, a reformist group among the governing gentry and in the urban oligarchies. Within the Church in Kent, Archbishop Cranmer and the preachers he brought in were crucial to the progress of Protestantism, and reformers took control of the administrative machine. Clark claims that changes in the formulae of wills and the political complexion of town governments show that, under pressure from the archbishop, there was a Protestant breakthrough in the mid-1540s: indeed, by this point the 'Reformation from above' had been so successful that 'Reformation from below' may have taken over, and Clark has suggested that a swing to Protestantism in the Home Counties forced Henry VIII 'to commit himself to the Protestant cause' in 1546-7.[2]

Elton and Clark are in a well-established tradition of English Reformation historiography, and a picture of officially inspired and imposed reform is presented by several of the older and briefer textbooks. They have, however, added to earlier descriptions of statutes and injunctions studies of the enforcement machinery in action and of the changing political structure of a well-governed area. But one may have doubts on the wider applicability of such an interpretation of the Reformation. Elton has shown how Cromwell's reform programme came to be accepted at the political centre, and how Cromwell attempted to impose his policies on the localities: he has not, however, shown that reform was, to any significant degree, accepted in the provinces, and a growing number of local studies suggest that there was little

---

[1] G. R. Elton, *Reform and Reformation: England 1509–1558* (London, 1977), especially pp. 157–200, 273–95, 353–71, with the passage quoted at p. 371; *Policy and Police: the Enforcement of the Reformation in the Age of Thomas Cromwell* (Cambridge, 1972).

[2] P. Clark, *English Provincial Society from the Reformation to the Revolution: Religion, Politics and Society in Kent, 1500–1640* (Hassocks, 1977), pp. 34–68.

progress. 'Reformation from above' depended for its effectiveness upon the co-operation of the justices of the peace and diocesan administrators, who seem to have been unsatisfactory proponents of reform. Even in the early part of the reign of Elizabeth there remained a strong conservative element on the commissions of the peace, and to avoid crippling county government the commissions could be remodelled only slowly,[3] while the social influence of bishops was weakened by expropriation and lesser diocesan officials were a distinctly conservative group.[4] It is true that in Peter Clark's Kent both secular justices and ecclesiastical administrators co-operated with the reforming regime, but the county was a far from typical area: Kent was close to London, so the gentry were embroiled in the web of Court politics; it was a maritime county, so the Continental Protestant influence was strong; and at its head was an activist reforming archbishop who patronised Protestants and harassed conservatives. Elsewhere, in circumstances less favourable to the Reformation, local government proved a block rather than a spur to religious change.[5]

The most influential of the historians who have detected a 'rapid Reformation from below' in early Tudor England is A. G. Dickens, though his general view has been supported by, for example, Claire Cross.[6] Professor Dickens has stressed the religious rather than the political roots of the English Reformation, and has sought to demonstrate that links between an expanding late Lollardy and early Protestantism led to swift Protestant advance at the popular level. The seedbed of Protestantism had been prepared by Bible-reading Lollard conventicles and by itinerant Lollard evangelists, and the interaction between native Lollardy and new Protestantism was symbolised by the exchange of Wycliffite texts for Tyndale New Testaments arranged by Robert Barnes.[7] The higher clergy of the Catholic Church were too involved in politics and the lower clergy were too poor and uneducated to meet

---

[3] W. R. Trimble, *The Catholic Laity in Elizabethan England* (Cambridge, Mass., 1964), pp. 25–6, 52–3; R. B. Manning, 'Catholics and Local Office Holding in Elizabethan Sussex', *B.I.H.R.*, XXXV (1962), pp. 47–61; J. H. Gleason, *The Justices of the Peace in England, 1558–1640* (Oxford, 1969), pp. 68–72; C. Haigh, *Reformation and Resistance in Tudor Lancashire* (Cambridge, 1975), pp. 213, 284–6; D. MacCulloch, 'Catholic and Puritan in Elizabethan Suffolk', *Archiv für Reformationsgeschichte*, LXXII (1981), pp. 232–5.

[4] F. Heal, *Of Prelates and Princes: a Study of the Economic and Social Position of the Tudor Episcopate* (Cambridge, 1980), pp. 101–327; R. Houlbrooke, *Church Courts and the People during the English Reformation, 1520–1570* (Oxford, 1979), pp. 24–5; Haigh, *Reformation and Resistance*, pp. 210, 212; F. D. Price, 'An Elizabethan Church Official: Thomas Powell, Chancellor of the Gloucester Diocese', *C.Q.R.*, CXXVIII (1939), pp. 94–112.

[5] Elton, *Policy and Police*, pp. 85–9; Haigh, *Reformation and Resistance*, pp. 102–7, 140–2, 213, 284–90; R. B. Manning, *Religion and Society in Elizabethan Sussex* (Leicester, 1969), pp. 61–125; Chapter 5 below, pp. 109–10.

[6] A. G. Dickens, *The English Reformation* (London, 1964); 'Heresy and the Origins of English Protestantism', in J. S. Bromley and E. H. Kossman, eds., *Britain and the Netherlands* (London, 1964), II, pp. 47–66; C. Cross, *Church and People, 1450–1660* (London, 1976).

[7] Dickens, *English Reformation*, p. 34; M. Aston, 'Lollardy and the Reformation: Survival or Revival', *History*, XLIX (1964), pp. 161–3.

the rising lay demand for a more personal involvement in religion or to combat the dynamic force of a Bible-based evangelical Protestantism: Reformation was easy and it was fast. Although legislative changes created a climate in which reform could triumph, the Dickens Reformation is one of conversion rather than coercion, with Protestantism spreading in the localities by the unco-ordinated efforts of radical clergy, itinerant clothworkers and Bible-reading anticlerical gentry. This analysis is, in part, based upon Dickens's own pioneering study of the progress of religious change at the popular level in Yorkshire, and his general conclusions have gained support from other local studies of areas where Lollardy had made progress and where early Protestant clergy were active: it seems that there was a 'rapid Reformation from below' in Essex, Bristol and the textile villages of Gloucestershire.[8] It could, however, be argued that, in concentrating their attentions upon the atypical heretics whose cases reached the pages of Foxe, Strype, episcopal registers and court act books, historians of this school are in danger of losing perspective on the pace of religious change. Of course there were Protestant heretics in the 1520s, and there were more in the 1530s, but they formed a very small minority whose real significance has been exaggerated because their own rejection of Catholicism was, much later and for accidental political reasons, to triumph nationally.

Acceptance of an overall interpretation of the English Reformation which presents it as rapid and essentially popular depends upon two assumptions which are being increasingly questioned by recent scholarship. First, we must assume that the institutions, personnel and beliefs of the English Catholic Church did not command the respect and commitment of the people, who were therefore open to the influence of new and heterodox ideas. But as Reformation historians have moved from the study of the Church through the printed propaganda of its anticlerical critics to the study of the Church through the records of its work, a picture of a moribund, dispirited and repressive institution which failed to meet the needs of its people becomes more and more difficult to sustain. We now know that the parish clergy were *not* negligent, immoral and inadequately educated clerics embroiled in regular conflicts with their parishioners over tithe and mortuaries: if their standards of spirituality and academic achievement would not satisfy the late-twentieth-century mind, they seem to have satisfied Tudor villagers, who complained remarkably infrequently about their priests.[9] Though the early Tudor bishops have been

---

[8] A. G. Dickens, *Lollards and Protestants in the Diocese of York, 1509–1558* (Oxford, 1959); J. E. Oxley, *The Reformation in Essex to the Death of Mary* (Manchester, 1965); K. G. Powell, *The Marian Martyrs and Reformation in Bristol* (Bristol, 1972); 'The Beginnings of Protestantism in Gloucestershire', *T.B.G.A.S.*, xc (1971), pp. 145–8.

[9] M. Bowker, *The Secular Clergy in the Diocese of Lincoln, 1495–1520* (Cambridge, 1968); P. Heath, *The English Parish Clergy on the Eve of the Reformation* (London, 1969); Houlbrooke, *Church Courts and the People*, pp. 177–9.

dismissed as lordly prelates rather than spiritual pastors, we know now that in the dioceses of Chichester, Ely, Lincoln, Norwich and Winchester, and probably elsewhere, colleagues of Thomas Wolsey were attempting to overhaul diocesan administration, improve clerical standards and exert pastoral discipline over the laity.[10] Our assessment of the ecclesiastical courts and response to them is no longer based upon the 1532 'Commons Supplication against the Ordinaries', an *ex parte* political statement which tells us little about real conditions: we now know that the courts were, by sixteenth-century standards, honest, speedy and cheap, that their discipline was accepted with little criticism, and that they met important social needs in the resolution of disputes and the regulation of relationships.[11] Those 'faults' of the late medieval Church which have been presented as symptoms of decline or causes of lay criticism are now shown to have been very much less significant than had been supposed, and it therefore seems unlikely that there was any serious alienation of the laity from the institutional Church. Indices such as will-benefactions to the Church and the demand for religious books show a stable or even increasing lay involvement in the conventional piety sanctioned by authority,[12] and the 'anti-clericalism' seen by many historians as the springboard for religious change may not have been a widespread phenomenon. Much of the evidence cited for anticlericalism comes from literary sources (primarily the work of Protestant propagandists and not necessarily reflective of any wider opinion), or from the grievances of particular groups with their own specific interests (such as London merchants in conflict with Wolsey), or from assumptions that there must have been a revulsion against the Church's flaws – flaws we now know were not usually serious. London, which was jealous of its civic rights and where it was difficult to operate an effective parochial system, presented special problems, but there is surprisingly little solid evidence of conflict between clergy and laity elsewhere: the diocese of Lichfield, with over 600 parishes, produced only ten tithe suits in 1525 and four in 1530, while in the 252 parishes of Canterbury diocese there were only four cases in 1531. Tithe appears to

[10] *Ibid.*, pp. 10–11; Chapter 2 below, pp. 37–46, 52–4; F. Heal, 'The Parish Clergy and the Reformation in the Diocese of Ely', *Proceedings of the Cambridge Antiquarian Society*, LXVI (1975), pp. 147–50; Bowker, *Secular Clergy*, pp. 18–20, 33, 36, 90.

[11] M. Bowker, 'The "Commons Supplication against the Ordinaries" in the Light of some Archidiaconal *Acta*', *T.R.H.S.*, 5th series, XXI (1971), pp. 61–77; *The Henrician Reformation: the Diocese of Lincoln under John Longland, 1521–1547* (Cambridge, 1981), pp. 51–7; Houlbrooke, *Church Courts and the People*, pp. 42, 50–1, 95–6, 114–15, 263, 271–2.

[12] Bowker, *Henrician Reformation*, pp. 48, 93, 147–8, 176–9; A. Kreider, *English Chantries: the Road to Dissolution* (Cambridge, Mass., 1979), pp. 89–92; W. K. Jordan, *The Charities of Rural England, 1480–1660* (London, 1961), pp. 438–40; H. S. Bennett, *English Books and Readers, 1475–1557* (London, 1952), pp. 57–8, 65–70, 74–5; J. Rhodes, 'Private Devotion in England on the Eve of the Reformation' (University of Durham Ph.D. thesis, 1974), I, pp. 6–7, 181; 194; II, pp. 98–9.

have become a seriously divisive problem in the parishes only from the 1540s and
it is difficult to see, in the early Tudor period, the breach in lay–clerical relations
necessary to a 'rapid Reformation from below'.[13]

The second assumption which underpins an interpretation of the English
Reformation as swift and popular relates to the attractiveness and the presentation
of evangelical Protestantism. A 'rapid Reformation from below' means that the new
religion soon seized the imaginations of artisans and peasants, but that this happened
on any widespread scale seems improbable. Protestantism was above all the religion
of the Word, the printed word and the preached word, and it stressed salvation
through a God-given faith supported by a reading of the Scriptures and an attendance
at sermons. It was therefore a religion which had a much stronger appeal in the towns
than in the countryside. We know that in the late sixteenth century tradesmen were
five times more likely to be literate than husbandmen, and that regular and popular
preaching was a feature of the towns rather than the rural parishes.[14] This means
that country people were less likely than townsmen to be introduced to the new
religious ideas, and that such ideas were less attractive to them: a number of local
studies have shown that Protestantism could spread quite easily among the merchants
and artisans of English towns,[15] but the Reformation shift from a ritualistic to a
bibliocentric presentation of religion was a disaster in the countryside. Richard
Greenham preached six sermons a week to his parishioners at Dry Drayton in
Cambridgeshire, but after twenty years of effort he left for London in 1591, partly
because of 'the intractableness and unteachableness of that people amongst whom
he had taken such exceeding great pains'. An experienced Lancashire evangelist
recorded sadly in 1614:

> It doth not a little grieve the ministers of the Gospel to take great pains in teaching
> the truth, and that in good manner, and yet see most of their hearers to receive little
> or no profit at all, but still remain, after many years' teaching, as ignorant, as popish
> and profane as they were at the first. Yet let them not be dismayed, it was Christ's
> own case; the fault is in the hearers, not in the teachers.[16]

[13] S. Brigden, 'The Early Reformation in London, 1520–1547: the Conflict in the Parishes'
(University of Cambridge Ph.D. thesis, 1979), pp. 23–86; Heath, *English Parish clergy*, p. 152;
Houlbrooke, *Church Courts and the People*, pp. 146–7, 273–4; Bowker, *Henrician Reformation*,
pp. 135–6; *Secular Clergy*, pp. 3, 110–11, 114, 152; Haigh, *Reformation and Resistance*, pp. 14,
56–62.

[14] D. Cressy, *Literacy and the Social Order: Reading and Writing in Tudor and Stuart England*
(Cambridge, 1980), pp. 146, 152; P. Seaver, *The Puritan Lectureships* (Stanford, 1970), pp. 77–117,
121, 297–300.

[15] Chapter 5 below, pp. 105–7; W. J. Sheils, 'Religion in Provincial Towns: Innovation and
Tradition', in Heal and O'Day, eds., *Church and Society*, pp. 156–76.

[16] S. Clarke, *A General Martyrology* (London, 1677 edn.), pp. 12–15; W. Harrison, *The Difference
of Hearers* (London, 1625 edn.), Sig. A3. On the ineffectiveness of evangelism in some areas,
see my 'Puritan Evangelism in the Reign of Elizabeth I', *E.H.R.*, XCII (1977), pp. 30–58, and
the chorus of complaints from Elizabethan preachers too numerous to note here.

If Protestant proselytising in the countryside often encountered hostility or sullen resentment, the reasons are not difficult to find. An earlier generation of English Protestant historians too often assumed that the new Gospel taught by Luther was so obviously *true* that sensible Englishmen would abandon without hesitation the superstitions of their forefathers. But more recent scholars have adopted a functionalist approach to popular religion, and have recognised that the magical and communal rituals of the late-medieval Church met important parish needs. Rituals which were related to the harvest year and which offered protection from the hazards of agricultural life, and ceremonies which reconciled disputes in villages built upon willing co-operation, were not readily relinquished: it has, indeed, been suggested that when the enforcement of the Elizabethan settlement drove magic from the churches, the people sought from charms and 'cunning men' the protection from evil which had formerly been provided by the Church.[17] The Reformation abolished the symbolic rituals which had been at the centre of rural religion, and attempted to impose a brand of personalised religion more suited to the needs of the gentry and the literate townsmen: as a result, some members of the rural poor found the official Church had little to offer them. Late in the reign of Elizabeth the Kentish preacher Josias Nichols examined 400 communicants in one parish and found that only ten per cent understood basic Christian doctrine and only one per cent expected to be saved through faith rather than works. In the 1640s John Shaw found the people of Furness 'exceedingly ignorant and blind as to religion', and he met an old man who, when told he would be saved through Christ, said 'I think I heard of that man you spake of once in a play at Kendal called Corpus Christi play, where there was a man on a tree and blood ran down'.[18]

It has been argued here, then, that a picture of a 'rapid Reformation', whether it is thought to have been imposed from above or to have spread among the people, cannot properly be derived from rural England as a whole. Though religious change proceeded more rapidly in some areas than elsewhere, this was usually as the result of special circumstances. Kent had trading contacts with Protestant centres abroad, and Bible translations and propaganda were smuggled in through Dover to be distributed among the Lollard groups of the clothing towns, while it is clear that the role of Archbishop Cranmer was crucial in the growth of Protestant opinion.[19] In Bristol and Gloucestershire the position appears to have been similar: there were already Lollards in the weaving villages, some of the county gentry were influenced by Tyndale through family contacts, members of the Bristol merchant oligarchy

[17] K. Thomas, *Religion and the Decline of Magic* (London, 1971), pp. 27–188, 252–332; J. Bossy, 'Blood and Baptism: Kinship, Community and Christianity in Western Europe from the Fourteenth to the Seventeenth Centuries', in *Studies in Church History*, x (1973), pp. 129–43.

[18] J. Nichols, *The Plea of the Innocent* (n.p., 1602), pp. 212–13; *Yorkshire Diaries and Autobiographies* (Surtees Society, LXV, 1877), p. 137. See also Clark, *English Provincial Society*, pp. 155–7.

[19] *Ibid.*, pp. 36, 40, 47, 60, 74.

supported Latimer's evangelical preaching, and when he became bishop he organised a preaching campaign. Under Edward VI, Bishop Hooper was not only an active proselytiser, but he also exercised, through visitation and his consistory court, unusually careful pastoral supervision of the diocese of Gloucester. But despite the vigour of these efforts, the destruction of Catholic allegiance in Gloucestershire proved much easier than the creation of positive Protestantism, and though the county was later to become one of the most distinctively Protestant of the western counties it had not moved far in that direction by 1558.[20] In Kent and the Bristol area the twin influences of a port and episcopal pressure seem to have been significant, but in Hampshire the protestantising influence of the port of Southampton was apparently neutralised by the long rule of a conservative bishop, and in the reign of Elizabeth Catholicism remained surprisingly strong in this Channel county. In Sussex, a little further east, continental influences established Protestant groups in the ports of Rye and Winchelsea under Henry VIII, but the conservative Bishop Sherburne and his officials at Chichester prevented radical inroads in the west of the county.[21] Even the diocese of London may help to show the need for both Protestant trade links and activist Protestant bishops if there was to be a 'rapid Reformation'. In the 1530s and 1540s Bishops Stokesley and Bonner tried hard to limit Protestant penetration, and there was a good deal of conservative resistance from clergy and laity in the City to the spread of the new religion. It may be significant that the main early Protestant centres in the diocese, outside the City itself, were in the north-east of Essex, close to the port of Harwich, while Elizabethan Catholic recusancy was to be concentrated closest to London itself, where episcopal influence had been strongest.[22] Of course, the forces which dictated the pace of religious change in a region were more numerous and complex than those discussed here, but it seems clear that Kent and Gloucestershire were far from typical counties, and the conjunction of pressures from a Protestant port and a Protestant bishop was an unusual one.

A third group of historians has presented a Reformation which was imposed from above by authority, but which had only a slow impact upon the localities. Penry Williams has suggested that the early Reformation infected the statute book more

---

[20] K. G. Powell, 'The Social Background to the Reformation in Gloucestershire', *T.B.G.A.S.*, XCII (1973), pp. 96–120; F. D. Price, 'Gloucester Diocese under Bishop Hooper', *T.B.G.A.S.*, LX (1939), pp. 51–151.

[21] Houlbrooke, *Church Courts and the People*, pp. 227, 237–8; J. E. Paul, 'The Hampshire recusants in the reign of Elizabeth I' (University of Southampton Ph.D. thesis, 1958), pp. 128–30, 391; S. J. Lander, 'The Diocese of Chichester, 1508–1558' (University of Cambridge Ph.D. thesis, 1974), *passim*; Manning, *Religion and Society in Elizabethan Sussex*, pp. 37–8.

[22] Brigden, 'Early Reformation in London', pp. 127–34, 141–5, 227–61; Oxley, *Reformation in Essex*, pp. 210–37; M. O'Dwyer, 'Catholic Recusants in Essex, c. 1580 to c. 1600' (University of London M.A. thesis, 1960), pp. 27–40.

effectively than the parishes, and that popular Catholicism was broken only by official preaching, printing and prosecution in the reign of Elizabeth. A. L. Rowse has seen the Reformation in Cornwall as a struggle for power between two parties, the winner gaining an opportunity to dictate the religion of the 'mentally passive people'. There was a good deal of hostility in the 1530s and under Edward VI towards attempts to impose religious change upon the Cornish, though the repression which followed the Western Rebellion of 1549 may have weakened popular resistance. But major Protestant advance came only as a result of a political coup in the late 1570s: a coalition of aggressive, reformist coastal gentry with privateering interests broke the power of the conservative inland gentry, and thereafter there was no effective bar to the imposition of religious reform.[23] In Sussex the popular Reformation had barely begun by 1558 and Protestantism made real headway only from the 1570s, when the bishop brought in radical preachers from Cambridge and enforcement of the Elizabethan settlement was improved by the remodelling of the commission of the peace.[24] In northern counties, too, the early Reformation was ineffective, and there was substantial religious change in the reign of Elizabeth only as a result of the redistribution of political power. The new religion had made minimal progress among the ruling order of Durham and Northumberland by 1564, but the crippling of the Percy and Neville interests after the Revolt of the Earls proved to be a turning point: in Durham the bishop became the main dispenser of patronage and focus of political aspirations, so that authority passed into the hands of supporters of the Reformation. In Lancashire, too, Protestantism had little impact until after a political reconstruction: in 1568 the Ecclesiastical Commission was purged, in 1572 the conservative third Earl of Derby was succeeded by a son more open to the influence of the Court, in 1579 the clearly Protestant Bishop Chadderton arrived at Chester and in 1587 the commission of the peace was remodelled. Thereafter the anti-Catholic laws were enforced in the well-governed parts of the county, and there radical preachers could work unmolested.[25]

A group of scholars who embrace a 'slow Reformation from below' might be sought among the most sophisticated of the recent historians of puritanism, who are presenting what had been seen as a post-Reformation radical deviation as the mainstream of Protestant advance. Patrick Collinson has treated Elizabethan puritanism as the evangelical phase of the English Reformation, following the first

[23] P. Williams, *The Tudor Regime* (Oxford, 1979), pp. 253–92; A. L. Rowse, *Tudor Cornwall* (London, 1941), pp. 184, 253–4, 257–8, 263–89, 320, 345–65.
[24] R. B. Manning, 'The Spread of the Popular Reformation in England', in C. S. Meyer, ed., *Sixteenth Century Essays and Studies* (St Louis, Ohio, 1970), pp. 36–8; *Religion and Society in Elizabethan Sussex*, pp. 63–4, 154, 256–60.
[25] 'Letters from the Bishops to the Privy Council, 1564', ed. M. Bateson, in *Camden Miscellany*, IX (1895), pp. 65–7; M. E. James, *Family, Lineage and Civil Society* (Oxford, 1974), pp. 51, 67–70, 78–9, 147; Haigh, *Reformation and Resistance*, pp. 209–46; 295–315.

political phase, in which the new religion was carried to the parishes by the preachers, who created a godly community of committed Protestants. In Cambridgeshire, Margaret Spufford found that though there was little opposition to the offical changes of the early Reformation and a few villages may have had handfuls of Protestants in the 1540s, in most parishes Protestantism had an impact only from the 1560s and not until the 1590s is there substantial evidence of Protestant enthusiasm. Similarly, Bill Sheils had found that, except for a very few parishes, there is little sign of shifts in religious allegiance in Northamptonshire and Rutland before the reign of Elizabeth, and that Protestant loyalties developed significantly among the laity only from the late 1560s, when the influence of new Protestant ministers was felt.[26] But interpretations of the English Reformation as a slow and tortuous process, whether it proceeds by official coercion or popular conversion, are, not surprisingly, as flawed as works of the 'rapid Reformation' school. If 'rapid Reformation' historians too easily assumed that an absence of serious recorded opposition to, let us say, the Edwardian reforms suggest acquiescence and even approval, then 'slow Reformation' writers are too willing to conclude that an absence of serious recorded heresy under Mary shows that the early Reformation had failed.[27] Again, if those who think change was swift exaggerate the importance of Henrician heresy cases, those who argue that Protestantism gained ground only slowly may exaggerate the significance of Elizabethan recusancy returns.[28] If the case for a 'rapid Reformation' is usually substantiated from areas where social and political conditions were favourable to change, the argument for a 'slow Reformation' tends to be supported with evidence from counties with poor communications and less effective government. Reformation historians have, in the main, concentrated their attentions upon the counties near to London, such as Essex and Kent, where both the official and popular Reformations are most likely to have been effective, and upon the outlying areas, Cornwall, Lancashire and York, where change was necessarily slower: it has been possible to argue that both groups represent special cases.

The publication of the second stage of Margaret Bowker's painstaking study of the diocese of Lincoln is therefore of great significance, for Lincoln cannot be dismissed as untypical. The diocese sprawled across nine counties of midland England

[26] P. Collinson, *The Elizabethan Puritan Movement* (London, 1967), especially pp. 14–15; 'Towards a Broader Understanding of the Early Dissenting Tradition', in C. R. Cole and M. E. Moody, eds., *The Dissenting Tradition: Essays for Leland H. Carlson* (Athens, Ohio, 1975), pp. 10–13; M. Spufford, *Contrasting Communities* (Cambridge, 1974), pp. 239–65, 320–44; W. J. Sheils, *The Puritans in the Diocese of Peterborough, 1558–1610* (Northamptonshire Record Society, xxx, 1979), pp. 14–24.
[27] For example Elton, *Reform and Reformation*, pp. 367–71; Haigh, *Reformation and Resistance*, pp. 183–5, 190.
[28] For example Dickens, *Lollards and Protestants*, pp. 240–6; Haigh, *Reformation and Resistance*, pp. 269–78.

and had within it a representative sample of geographical locations. If the early Reformation could be effective, it surely ought to have been in Lincoln: it was a well-administered diocese which included one university and came close to the other; it embraced, in the Chilterns, an area of strong Lollard influence; and there were, in Leicester, Northampton and Stamford, important towns. But if Lincoln clergy conformed to the Henrician changes it was only because there were powerful career inducements; the bishop combated Protestantism, and Buckinghamshire Lollardy was contained; and there is little evidence of shifts in belief among the laity until the late 1540s. Lincoln emerges as a classic case of 'slow Reformation', and Mrs Bowker concludes that when Bishop Longland died in 1547 'he left a diocese with priests and laity as conservative as he was'.[29] In the county of Lincolnshire the Edwardian Reformation seems to have been entirely destructive in its impact, and though the Marian visitations discovered isolated critics of Catholic doctrine and practice there was no substantial sympathy for the new religion. The Protestant breakthrough came only in the reign of Elizabeth, through the evangelistic efforts of a new generation of university-trained ministers.[30] The case of Lincoln is likely to shift the consensus of historical generalisation towards a recognition that the early phases of the Reformation were indecisive, and that major Protestant advance took place mainly in the Elizabethan period. It was only in the latter part of the sixteenth century, when a Protestant regime remodelled commissions of the peace and diocesan administrations to give power to supporters of reform, when the redistribution of clerical patronage weakened conservative interests and when the universities produced a supply of committed preachers of the new religion, that Protestantism had a real and widespread impact.

Such an interpretation is far from universal among historians of the English Reformation, and on a crude head-count it may not even be the majority opinion, but it seems to be the natural conclusion of trends in recent historiography. Much of the achievement of the last twenty years of English Reformation scholarship has been built upon the insights and example of A. G. Dickens and G. R. Elton. Professor Dickens led students of the Reformation from the pages of Foxe, Bale and Fish to the folios of visitation act books and sheafs of consistory cause papers. In these under-used sources was recorded not the Reformation of the politicians and preachers but the Reformation of the people, and it has proved possible to trace the impact of the official Reformation upon the parishes and the growth of reformed opinion. Perhaps Dickens did not follow through the implications of his own archival

---

[29] Bowker, *Henrician Reformation*, especially pp. 181–5.

[30] R. B. Walker, 'Reformation and Reaction in the County of Lincoln, 1547–58', *Lincolnshire Archaeological and Architectural Society*, IX (1961), pp. 50, 58–9; 'The Growth of Puritanism in the County of Lincoln in the Reign of Queen Elizabeth I', *Journal of Religious History*, 1 (1961), pp. 148–9, 150.

revolution, for in rightly attacking the myth of the thorough backwardness of the Tudor North he tried to show that even unpromising areas could be made to fit into the chronology and categories of established 'rapid Reformation' historiography.[31] Those who have followed Professor Dickens into the record offices of English counties and dioceses have more often challenged the Protestant orthodoxy and stressed the diversity of local responses to the Reformation pressure. If Dickens led a breakthrough in the provinces, G. R. Elton led one at the centre, taking historians from the pages of the statute book to the state papers and administrative records, from the enactments of parliament to the processes of policy formation and enforcement. Scholars are now constructing an account of the political struggles within Court, administration and parliament which produced the erratic official Reformation, and a historiography which stressed theologians and preachers is being replaced by a Reformation of factions, parties and coups.[32] But perhaps of even greater significance for Reformation historians was Professor Elton's stress on the problems of enforcement, a stress which resulted from his examination of the reports of disaffection in the counties as the Henrician changes were imposed. Elton thus became the first serious non-Catholic or non-Anglo-Catholic historian to present the English Reformation as a major struggle.[33] It is true that Elton's admiration for the achievements of Thomas Cromwell has led him to exaggerate the progress the Reformation had made by the time of that minister's fall, and to minimise the importance of the resistance which was to occur thereafter,[34] but others have carried his themes of coercion and conflict into the later stages of the Reformation.

Some of the historians who have followed through the insights of Dickens and Elton have now abandoned the conventional interpretation of the English Reformation, an interpretation which came to appear archetypally 'whiggish' in the sense exposed by Herbert Butterfield. The task of the historian is the explanation of events: he tries to show why things turned out as they did. Since the eventual outcome of the Reformation was a more or less Protestant England, too often 'the history of the English Reformation' has been written as 'the origins of English Protestantism': we have been given a history of the progressives and the victors in which those men, ideas and issues seen as leading towards the final Reformation result are linked together in a one-sided account of change. The Reformation in England thus appears, in the pages of 'whig' historians, as an inexorable process, a necessary sequence unfolding easily to a predetermined conclusion: the medieval Church was

---

[31] Dickens, *Lollards and Protestants*, pp. 1–7 and *passim*.
[32] Professor Elton has summarised much of this work in *Reform and Reformation*, pp. 250–310, 328–52, 376–81.
[33] Elton, *Policy and Police*, pp. 1–170.
[34] *Ibid.*, pp. 393–6; *Reform and Reformation*, pp. 198, 294–5. See the remarks by C. S. L. Davies in *E.H.R.*, XCIII (1978), pp. 873–5.

in decline, the laity was anticlerical, Lutheran ideas were readily accepted, a centralising state espoused reform, superstition was attacked and, after a brief Marian fiasco, a finally Protestant England was recognized in the legislation of 1559, the date at which many Reformation textbooks stop. But the Reformation in England was not an inevitable development, it was the contingent product of a series of conflicts and crises and of the interaction of social, geographical and political influences which varied from region to region.

So far, only one general account of the period has accepted the possibility of another outcome and presented the Reformation as a long and hard-fought contest.[35] But many more specific studies have supported a view of the Reformation as a struggle, a struggle to achieve political victory at the centre and a struggle to secure enforcement in the localities. It is clear from the work of, for example, Guy, Starkey, Ives, Elton, L. B. Smith, Slavin and Hoak[36] that the main period of the early Reformation, from 1527 to 1553, was one of swirling factional conflict at Court, in which religious policy was both a weapon and a prize. At a number of points, in 1529, 1532, 1536, 1538, 1539, 1540, 1543, 1546–7, 1549–50 and 1553, events could have developed in dramatically different ways if the balance of power had shifted only slightly. It may be that the settlement of 1559 was the result of a preconceived plan by Elizabeth and her advisers rather than, as Neale thought, of pressure from Protestants in parliament, but the outcome was decisively influenced by the challenge of conservatives in the House of Lords and the government had to fight hard for even its qualified victory.[37] Thereafter, there were still times when a political decision to revert to Catholicism was not entirely beyond the bounds of possibility.[38] In the counties, too, the Reformation was a struggle between the reformers and both deliberate Catholic resistance and the strong force of inertia – there were, in the middle of the reign of Elizabeth, still places like Ripon in Yorkshire and Weaverham in Cheshire where religious change had had hardly any effect.[39] At the local level

[35] C. S. L. Davies, *Peace, Print and Protestantism, 1450–1558* (London, 1977). See also J. J. Scarisbrick, *The Reformation and the English People* (Oxford, 1984).

[36] J. A. Guy, *The Public Career of Sir Thomas More* (Brighton, 1980); D. Starkey, *The Reign of Henry VIII: Personalities and Politics* (London, 1985); E. W. Ives, 'Faction at the Court of Henry VIII: the Fall of Anne Boleyn', *History*, XLVII (1972), pp. 169–88; G. R. Elton, 'Thomas Cromwell's Decline and Fall', in his *Studies in Tudor and Stuart Politics and Government* (Cambridge, 1974), I, pp. 189–230; 'Tudor Government: The Points of Contact. III. The Court', in *Studies* (Cambridge, 1983), III, pp. 38–57; L. B. Smith, 'Henry VIII and the Protestant Triumph', *American Historical Review*, LXXI (1966), pp. 1237–64; A. J. Slavin, 'The Fall of Lord Chancellor Wriothesley' *Albion*, VII (1975), pp. 265–86; D. E. Hoak, *The King's Council in the Reign of Edward VI* (Cambridge, 1976).

[37] N. L. Jones, *Faith by Statute: Parliament and the Settlement of Religion* (London, 1982).

[38] W. MacCaffrey, *The Shaping of the Elizabethan Regime* (London, 1969), pp. 77–8, 108, 211–12, 276.

[39] Chapter 9 below, pp. 180n, 183; K. R. Wark, *Elizabethan Recusancy in Cheshire* (Chetham Society, 1971), p. 16.

the Reformation was not a walkover for the Protestants, it was a real contest: at
Bristol, Gloucester, Oxford and Rye in the 1530s, at Canterbury and London in the
1540s, at Poole, Bodmin and Exeter in the reign of Edward VI and at Hereford and
York in the 1560s there was powerful opposition to the Reformation in the towns.[40]
The 1570s in Cornwall and Norfolk and the 1580s in Suffolk and Lancashire saw
fierce battles for supremacy between conservative and reformist gentry, and only
the political victories of the latter allowed an easier growth of Protestantism.[41] Sullen
hostility towards novelty was apparently widespread in the countryside, and it took
the Elizabethan episcopate some fifteen years to impose reasonable observance of the
Prayer Book upon clergy and parishioners;[42] there was more militant opposition
to aspects of the official Reformation from nine counties in 1536, at least six counties
in 1549 and two counties in 1569. Such resistance was not the despairing reflex
response of a defeated cause, and its influence on the development of the Reformation
at the centre and in the localities suggests that there was nothing inevitable about
the final Protestant victory. The plans and achievements of the reign of Mary show,
too, that there was no inevitability in the final Catholic failure. Rex Pogson's work
on Cardinal Pole and studies of specific dioceses indicate a far-sighted approach to
the needs of English Catholicism,[43] and some officials were attempting to present
the old religion in forms more palatable to the articulate laity.[44] Marian visitations,
even of Bonner's London, demonstrated that the bishops faced not an intractable
problem of crushing entrenched heresy but a rather more solvable difficulty in
re-indoctrinating a partially indifferent people.[45] It has, indeed, been argued that until
as late as the mid-1570s conservative priests were quite successful in sustaining
Catholic allegiance at the popular level, and that collapse came only when the Marian
generation was replaced by missionary priests with new priorities.[46]

[40] Elton, *Policy and Police*, pp. 85–90, 93–100, 112–23; Clark, *English Provincial Society*, pp. 63–4,
84; Brigden, 'Early Reformation in London', pp. 235–61, 322–7; *Narratives of the Days of the
Reformation*, ed. J. G. Nichols (Camden Society, 1859), pp. 71–84; Rowse, *Tudor Cornwall*, pp.
262, 264, 276; J. Cornwall, *Revolt of the Peasantry, 1549* (London, 1977), pp. 57–8, 100–1,
110–11; 'Letters from the Bishops', ed. Bateson, pp. 14–15, 19–23; J. C. H. Aveling, *Catholic
Recusancy in the City of York*, (C.R.S., 1970), pp. 25, 26, 27–8, 31–2, 33–4, 39.

[41] Rowse, *Tudor Cornwall*, pp. 345–65; A. Hassell Smith, *County and Court: Government and Politics
in Norfolk, 1558–1603* (Oxford, 1974), pp. 181, 201–3, 211–28; MacCulloch, 'Catholic and
Puritan in Elizabethan Suffolk', pp. 236–47; Haigh, *Reformation and Resistance*, pp. 285–90,
313–15.   [42] Chapter 9 below, pp. 178–84.

[43] Chapter 7 below; R. H. Pogson, 'Reginald Pole and the Priorities of Government in Mary
Tudor's Church', *H.J.*, XVIII (1975), pp. 3–20; Haigh, *Reformation and Resistance*, pp. 195–207;
Heal, *Of Prelates and Princes*, pp. 156–61; Chapter 8 below, pp. 170–2.

[44] A. Bartholomew, 'Lay Piety in the Reign of Mary Tudor' (University of Manchester M.A.
thesis, 1979), especially pp. 1–42; Chapter 8 below, pp. 170–1.

[45] *Ibid.*, pp. 168–9; Houlbrooke, *Church Courts and the People*, p. 238; Walker, 'Reformation and
Reaction in the County of Lincoln', pp. 58–9.

[46] C. Haigh, 'From Monopoly to Minority: Catholicism in Early Modern England', *T.R.H.S.*,
5th series, XXXI (1981), pp. 129–47.

These are some of the strands from which an 'anti-whig' interpretation of an overall 'slow Reformation' might be constructed, but the production of a revised synthesis will be difficult. The great advantage of a view of the English Reformation which stressed its speed and its one-sidedness was that it made the subject manageable; the narrative method lends itself easily to a 'whig' interpretation of events, as progressives implement their policies step by step. But the writing of studies which do justice to the Catholics as well as the Protestants, to the ignorant as well as the theologians, which demonstrate the interplay of factions and forces at the centre and in the localities, and which trace the shifts in popular opinion in different parts of the country, will be a much more arduous task. History, however, must not be made to fit the convenience of the historian, still less the demands of the publisher; we must show the past in all its variety and irreducible complexity, no matter how far art has to be sacrificed to accuracy.

2

CHURCH COURTS AND THE REFORMATION IN THE DIOCESE OF CHICHESTER, 1500–58

STEPHEN LANDER

It was largely through visitations and the regular sessions of his courts that a bishop sought to maintain the standards of the clergy and the religious life of his diocese, and to settle disputes over ecclesiastical matters. The state had also assigned to the Church the right of proving wills and of administering the goods of those who died intestate. Consequently, the spiritual welfare of a diocese depended to a large extent upon the efficiency and authority of its church courts, especially those of the bishop. It has long been known that these courts were left constitutionally untouched by the Reformation, and it has even been suggested that they actually had their jurisdiction strengthened by the legislation of the time of Henry VIII. It is the argument of this article, however, albeit on the basis of the evidence for one diocese, that the courts were undergoing reform in the last decades before the break with Rome, but that officially-inspired attacks upon them during the 1530s undermined their authority permanently.

In the diocese of Chichester, as in nearly every other diocese, the multiplicity and complexity of jurisdictions had come during the later Middle Ages to present a limitation upon the bishop's authority. In the city of Chichester, for example, archbishop, bishop and dean exercised ecclesiastical as well as temporal jurisdiction, while across the bishop's park, the diocesan of Exeter had jurisdiction over the royal college at Bosham.[1] It is hardly surprising that most bishops of Chichester, like other diocesans whose authority in their cathedral cities was limited, chose normally to reside at one of their episcopal manors outside the city.[2]

At the end of the fifteenth century there were as many as nine different ecclesiastical courts at work in the county of Sussex, which, apart from peculiar

---

[1] *The Acta of the Bishops of Chichester, 1075–1207*, ed. H. Mayr-Harting (Canterbury and York Society, LVI, 1962), pp. 55–6, 198; J. H. Denton, *English Royal Free Chapels* (Manchester, 1970), pp. 44–6, 113–14.

[2] *The Episcopal Register of Robert Rede, Bishop of Chichester, 1397–1415*, ed. C. Deedes, I (Sussex Record Society, VIII, 1908), p. xxiv; *Extracts from the Episcopal Register of Richard Praty, Bishop of Chichester, 1438–45*, ed. C. Deedes (Sussex Record Society, IV, 1905), p. 89; C.R.O., Ep. I/1/4–5.

jurisdictions, was at that date very nearly coterminous with the diocese of Chichester. Of the diocesan courts, the most important was the consistory court of the bishop. This court, which usually sat in the cathedral, dealt with the whole range of ecclesiastical jurisdiction.[3] Theoretically it acted for the whole diocese, but the majority of its cases were from the archdeaconry of Chichester. Like the consistory courts at Ely, it had developed a wider scope than consistory courts in a number of larger dioceses which only dealt with instance cases.[4] Probably because the office of commissary at Chichester was of comparatively late development, its bishops do not seem to have been regularly active in the correction of offenders, and the business arising from its small number of parishes was usually light.[5]

In the two archdeaconries of Chichester and Lewes, the bishop's commissaries and the two archdeacons shared jurisdictional rights, and both commissaries made regular trips away from the city, usually to the ruridecanal churches, to hold courts.[6] Commissaries had probably first been appointed at Chichester as elsewhere, to contest the monopoly of first instance jurisdiction claimed by archdeacons, and their activities had made a settlement of archidiaconal and episcopal rights essential.[7] It is not clear whether the agreement that had been reached at Chichester before the end of the fifteenth century had come about as the result of a dispute, like those between the archdeacons of Ely and Lincoln and their bishops, but it strongly favoured the bishop.[8] Archdeacons were unable to act in any case which involved the goods of those who died intestate, they could not deprive priests of their benefices, and they were unable to decide matrimonial, incest or heresy cases, or those arising on any of the bishop's thirteen Sussex manors.[9] In those cases that were not specifically reserved to the bishop, however, the archdeacons and commissaries exercised concurrent jurisdiction, with the result that confusion and competition were likely. The fact that the settlement reached between the archdeacon of Chichester and the bishop was still thought worthy of note as late as 1481, moreover, probably shows

---

[3] C.R.O., Ep. I/1/1, fo. 5; Ep. I/10/1, fos. 1–49.

[4] M. E. Aston, *Thomas Arundel* (Oxford, 1967), pp. 41, 53–68; R. W. Dunning, 'Wells Consistory Court in the Fifteenth Century', *Proceedings of the Somerset Archaeological and Natural History Society*, CVI (1962), pp. 48, 50, 56–8; R. A. Marchant, *The Church under the Law* (Cambridge, 1969), p. 60; C. Morris, 'A Consistory Court in the Middle Ages', *J.E.H.*, XIV (1963), 150–9; also probably true of Lichfield: L.J.R.O., B/C/1/1–2.

[5] C.R.O., Ep. I/1/1, fos. 10, 12: sequestrators rather than commissaries were still acting in the late fourteenth century; C.R.O., Ep. I/1/1–6.

[6] C.R.O., Ep. I/10/1–2, 6–7; Ep. II/9/1.

[7] C. Morris, 'The Commissary of the Bishop in the Diocese of Lincoln', *J.E.H.*, X (1959), pp. 50–63; R. M. Haines, *The Administration of the Diocese of Worcester in the First Half of the Fourteenth Century* (London, 1965), p. 116.

[8] Morris, 'Commissary of the Bishop', pp. 60–1; Aston, *Thomas Arundel*, pp. 53–68; cf. Haines, *Administration of Worcester*, pp. 40–4, 52–3.

[9] C.R.O., Ep. I/1/4, fo. 17; Ep. VI/4/1, fos. 5–72.

that there was still rivalry between the two at that date. In curtailing archidiaconal rights which represented a limitation upon his own, therefore, Robert Sherburne, the last pre-Reformation bishop of Chichester, was to have a profound effect upon the spiritual administration of his diocese.

The peculiar jurisdictions within the see also presented limitations to episcopal authority, and were often particularly badly administered. In the city of Chichester, the dean exercised ordinary jurisdiction over the Close, all the parishes of the city, except All Saints in the Pallent, and over the parishes of Fishbourne and Rumboldswyke in the suburbs. This peculiar was only subject to episcopal control during triennial visitation and during a vacancy of the deanery, the usual administration of its parishes being exercised by the dean or his official in a peculiar court. It is known that such a court, dealing with all types of cases from the city, was active during the last twenty-five years of the fifteenth century. In the archdeaconry of Chichester, archiepiscopal manors formed the peculiar of Pagham and Tarring, and in the archdeaconry of Lewes, the exempt deanery of South Malling. Exercise of ordinary jurisdiction over these two deaneries belonged to their dean or his commissary and was subject to the archbishop of Canterbury as diocesan during a vacancy and not to the bishops of Chichester.[10]

Finally, of monastic exemptions from episcopal jurisdiction, that claimed by Battle Abbey seems to have been a source of extended conflict with the see, not least because it gave the priest who served the parish of Battle, called the dean, jurisdiction over his parish. He had the right, which was retained until the nineteenth century, to decide all cases, except for matrimonial disputes which were reserved to the bishop, who otherwise could only correct offenders from the parish of Battle if the dean failed to do so.[11]

The limitations placed upon the bishop's authority by this variety of jurisdictions are clear. To bring a persistent offender to justice, which was never an easy task with the poor roads over the South Downs cutting off the city of Chichester and the consistory court from most of the diocese, was rendered harder still, since the culprit could remove himself from the bishop's jurisdiction to escape the attentions of the apparitors. If he lived in the Selsey peninsula, for example, he was within easy reach of the diocese of Winchester, of the dean of Chichester's peculiar, and of the exempt deanery at Pagham. Rivalry between courts, moreover, could be dangerous to the spiritual welfare of the parishes, since where there was competition for business,

[10] C.R.O., Ep. III/4/1; F. W. Steer and Isabel M. Kirby, *Diocese of Chichester: A Catalogue of the Records of the Bishop, Archdeacons and Former Exempt Jurisdictions* (Chichester, 1966), pp. xxii–xxiii; C.R.O., Ep. IV/2/1–2; Ep. V/3/1.

[11] *Register of Rede*, II, pp. 439–42; *The Chartulary of the High Church of Chichester*, ed. W. D. Peckham (Sussex Record Society, XLVI, 1946), nos. 274, 905; C.R.O., Ep. VI/1/3, fo. 82; Ep. VI/1/4, fos. 199–200.

judges and proctors tended to treat instance cases far more seriously than disciplinary cases, because the former brought in far higher fees. The official of the archdeacon of Canterbury, for example, only began to ferret out offenders when instance business declined sharply after 1500.[12] In the diocese of Chichester during the first years of the century the dean's peculiar court, the archdeaconry of Chichester commissary court, and the consistory court all spent a disproportionate amount of time in dealing with instance cases. Between September 1506 and September 1507, in fact, the last two courts tried nearly four times as many instance as office cases, and this was at a time when the former invariably took at least three months to complete, and the latter seldom more than two or three weeks.[13] What this meant in practice is only too clear. Clerical incontinence appears to have been quite a serious problem at this date with some fifteen per cent of parishes in the archdeaconry troubled by it, but the courts spent little time in dealing with offenders, did not press charges against some, and treated the majority of those who were convicted with great leniency. In one notorious case the judge actually respited the penance of an incumbent who had confessed fornication with one of his parishioners. Only when there were aggravating circumstances were offending priests removed from the churches they had profaned by their conduct.[14]

It is not known how active the archdeacons' courts were at the turn of the century in this diocese but in some areas such courts were particularly inefficient at correcting offenders. This may have been because archdeacons were even more likely to be absent from supervising their courts than a bishop was from his, and their officials were often of a lower calibre. The official of the archdeacon of Chester, for example, whose principal held a prebend at Lichfield and usually resided there, seems to have been particularly ineffective, and was regarded with contempt in his archdeaconry. Since most archdeacons of Chichester and Lewes were also absentees, the situation may well have been little better in Sussex. However it would be dangerous to argue too much from this evidence, as in other areas archdeacons' courts may have been inactive where the bishop's consistory was active and *vice versa*.

It seems likely, therefore, that any attempts at reform in the diocese of Chichester at a parochial level which were to be carried out through visitations and the regular sessions of the courts would have been seriously handicapped had Sherburne not gone some way towards eliminating the diversity of jurisdictions in his diocese, and coming to terms with those that remained. His reforms were chiefly concerned with the jurisdictional rights of the two archdeacons. No proceedings have survived for either of their courts, but a few references show that the archdeacon of Chichester

[12] B. L. Woodcock, *Mediaeval Ecclesiastical Courts in the Diocese of Canterbury* (London, 1952), p. 79.

[13] C.R.O., Ep. III/4/1, fos. 97–119; Ep. I/10/1.

[14] C.R.O., Ep. I/10/1, fos. 19, 21, 36–7, 40–2, 44–5, 63, 75, 78, 80, 90, 96–7, 102, 113.

or his official, at least, was still active judicially during the vacancy following the translation of Bishop Fitzjames to London in June 1506.[15] Moreover, a comparison of episcopal income from probate fees in 1506–8 with the very much larger sums received during the 1520s, when it is known that virtually all probate was granted by episcopal officers, leads to the inescapable conclusion that both archdeacons had ordinary rights as late as 1508.[16] Sherburne was not slow in realizing that the concurrent jurisdiction of archdeacon and commissary no longer fulfilled a useful purpose, and, on the collation of his former receiver-general, William Norbery, to the archdeaconry of Chichester in April 1512, he appointed him commissary for that archdeaconry, thus in effect amalgamating the two jurisdictions. A similar process was in operation at this time in a number of other dioceses, such as Lincoln, where, perhaps significantly, Sherburne had been an archdeacon.[17]

This partial reorganization of the courts in the archdeaconry of Chichester continued in force until October 1518 when Sherburne brought a number of new men into the diocese to reform and revitalise his spiritual administration. Pre-eminent amongst these new officers were John Worthial, William Fleshmonger and John Stilman, who were to be at the centre of the bishop's administration at Chichester throughout the remainder of Sherburne's episcopate and beyond. Worthial, a B.Cn.L. in 1508, was principal of New Inn Hall at Oxford from 1510 to 1520, and proceeded to his doctorate in 1525. He appears to have started his career as an ecclesiastical lawyer in the Lincoln courts, being a proctor in the audience court of Bishop Atwater in 1517. It may have been on the recommendation of Atwater, whom Sherburne much repected, or because of his standing at Oxford that the bishop chose to bring him to Chichester, but he eventually monopolised the posts of commissary-general, official principal and chancellor, and proved a trustworthy and industrious servant who reaped his reward in livings from a grateful bishop. Surviving letters show just how important he was thought by contemporaries to be in the diocesan administration.[18]

William Fleshmonger, who became dean of Chichester in 1518 and was Sherburne's chancellor and official principal until the mid-1520s, was also from the diocese of Lincoln. A doctor of civil and canon law by 1514 and a member of Doctors' Commons by 1522, he was, like Sherburne, a Wykehamist, and it is

[15] C.R.O., Ep. I/1, fo. 57; Ep. I/10/1, fos. 44, 46–7, 67.

[16] L.P.L., Register Warham 2, fo. 50; C.R.O., Ep. VI/4/1, fos. 8–9, 20–1.

[17] B.L., Egerton MS. 2383(2); C.R.O., Ep. I/1/5, fo. 24; STC I/1, fo. 1; cf. Morris, 'Commissary of the Bishop', pp. 62–3.

[18] *An Episcopal Court Book for the Diocese of Lincoln, 1514–20*, ed. Margaret Bowker (Lincoln Record Society, LXI, 1967), p. 52; A. B. Emden, *A Biographical Register of the University of Oxford, 1501–40* (Oxford, 1974), p. 638; *Statutes and Constitutions of the Cathedral Church of Chichester*, ed. F. G. Bennett, et al. (Chichester, 1904), p. 60; C.R.O., Ep. I/1/5, fos, 29, 31–2; Ep. I/1/4, fos. 66–8, 70, 73; Cap. I/14/4a, fos. 11–19.

probable that he came to the bishop's notice through New College where he had been a fellow. That Sherburne was eager to have him as dean may be indicated by the fact that the previous incumbent, Thomas Larke, resigned on the large pension of £42 to make way for him. Sherburne's hopes were justified, for the fruitful co-operation that followed between them stands out in comparison with the troubled history of relations between the Chichester chapter and see, and Fleshmonger provided added authority to Worthial's pronouncements in the consistory court during the latter's first years as an ecclesiastical judge.[19]

John Stilman, a public notary, was from the diocese of Bath and Wells, a married man with a family like others of his profession. He was active as both episcopal and capitular registrar by August 1518, and, until his death or retirement in 1543, was a crucial figure in the administration of the cathedral and diocese. With the judge of an ecclesiastical court, the registrar was the most important official both in the regular sessions of the courts and at visitation. He was responsible for issuing citations, for taking depositions, recording visitation presentments and collecting evidence, for keeping a note of the proceedings of the courts and for registering wills, for compiling and preserving the records of the bishop's administration, and for ensuring that the judge's instructions and orders were obeyed.[20] Stilman's industry is much in evidence in the records that survive. He made fresh copies of both of Sherburne's registers, in which he included records of four episcopal visitations, a complete list of subsidy exemptions, and a large collection of vicarage ordinations and similar documents. He sat in the commissary court for the archdeaconry of Chichester as well as the consistory court for over twenty years, took part in all the episcopal and probably all the Chichester archidiaconal visitations in this period as well, and in an elegant book hand transcribed copies of espiscopal statutes.[21] After his death, the diocese had to wait until the 1570s before it had another registrar who approached his experience and industry, and whose work was of the same quality.

The arrival of Worthial, Fleshmonger and Stilman, and of a number of less important officials such as the proctors Richard Gybon, William Bolton, William Frende, Laurence Woodcock and William Draper, and the appointment of larger

[19] Emden, op. cit., II, 700–1; Statutes and Constitutions, pp. 54–80; P.R.O., E. 135/8/34; C.R.O., Ep. I/1/5, fos. 43–5; M. E. C. Walcott, The Early Statutes of the Cathedral Church of Chichester (London, 1877), p. 79; W. R. W. Stephens, Memorials of the South Saxon See and Cathedral Church of Chichester (London, 1876), p. 127; Register of Rede, I, p. 24; R. B. Manning, Religion and Society in Elizabethan Sussex (Leicester, 1969), pp. 72–6; C.R.O., Ep. I/1/3, fos. 5–12; E-p. I/10/2, fos. 22, 41, 47, 69; Ep. I/10/3, fos. 6, 27; Ep. I/10/4, fo. 7.

[20] C.R.O., Cap. I/14/5, fos. 5–12; The Acts of the Dean and Chapter of the Cathedral Church of Chichester, 1472–1544, ed. W. D. Peckham (Sussex Record Society, LII, 1952), p. xxiv; Woodcock, Medieval Ecclesiastical Courts, pp. 38–50.

[21] C.R.O., Ep. I/1/5, fos. 3–142; Ep. I/1/4, fos. 46–111; Ep. I/10/2–7; Ep. I/18/2–3; Cap. I/14/1–3, 5; C. E. Welch, 'Bishop Sherburne of Chichester and His Donations', Notes and Queries (1954), pp. 191–3.

numbers of apparitors, shows that Sherburne made a thorough reorganization of his spiritual administration at this time.[22] These men provided him with the tools to carry out a more far-reaching reform of the courts than had previously been possible. No compositions or commissions survive to bear witness to the changes that took place, although it is reasonably clear what happened. Both archdeacons were induced to surrender all of their jurisdictional rights, except those exercised summarily at visitation, in return for a proportion of the fees accruing to the episcopal courts.[23] The ground had been well prepared for such a change in the archdeaconry of Chichester with Norbery as commissary and archdeacon, and it seems probable that a similar arrangement had been made under Mr Oliver Pole, the archdeacon of Lewes, who was for a time the bishop's chancellor.[24] It is not known what proportion of fees was reserved to the archdeacons, although it seems from the evidence about probate fees that they struck a good bargain, sometimes receiving as much as half of the sums collected.[25]

Although the most important union of jurisdictions begun at this time, this was not the only one. Probably from as early as Fleshmonger's election as dean in 1518, although certainly from 1520, jurisdiction over the dean's peculiar was exercised through the consistory court.[26] This was not the result of a formal composition, but of fortuitous appointments, for Sherburne appears to have appointed Worthial to preside in the consistory court at the time, as Fleshmonger was using him to act as his official.[27] Deans had before, like Fleshmonger, acted as episcopal officers, but it had not led to a union of their respective jurisdictions.[28] That it did in this case is a clear indication of the trust between Fleshmonger and Sherburne, a trust that was advantageous to both. It brought the bishop control over the city which was the centre of his diocese, and increased the power and prestige of his consistory court on the one hand, while on the other it brought greater authority to bear upon offenders in the peculiar than the dean alone could muster. That it was a success is evident from the fact that it survived, for a time, both Sherburne's resignation in 1536 and Fleshmonger's death in 1541.[29]

This period saw one further jurisdictional development, although it was one that could be paralleled in other dioceses. It became the practice of the dean of Pagham and Tarring to appoint a proctor of the consistory court at Chichester to sit in his

[22] C.R.O., Ep. I/10/2–3.
[23] C.R.O., Ep. I/18/10, fos. 1–12: 1560, Archdeacon of Chichester visited in person, but thereafter appointed the bishop's official to act for him – see STC III/4, 34, 41, 46, 50.
[24] C.R.O., Cap. I/14/4a, fo. 24; Ep. I/1/5, fo. 28.
[25] C.R.O., Ep. VI/4/1, fos. 8–9, 14–15, 27–8, 73–4.
[26] C.R.O., Ep. I/10/2.
[27] C.R.O., STC I/2, fo. 38; Ep. I/10/5, fo. 79: separate appointment as dean's official.
[28] C.R.O., Cap. I/1/2, 87; Ep. I/1/3, fo. 76; Ep. III/4/1.
[29] See below, p. 51.

peculiar court in the church of All Saints, Chichester.[30] This appears to have happened for the first time, perhaps significantly, while Thomas Milling was dean. Like Sherburne and a number of the proctors whom he appointed as commissaries, he had been at New College, and it is probable that he was known to Sherburne before he was collated to the deanery in August 1513. Such an arrangement had advantages for both of them. The dean could in this way attract to his court a better-trained and more experienced canon lawyer than might otherwise have been possible, for the evidence shows that when a proctor was not acting, Milling had to depend on such humble figures as Simon Oxley, the vicar of Tarring, or the notoriously immoral Alexander Shawe, vicar of Pagham. On the other hand, the bishop was able through his officers to bring influence to bear upon the peculiar jurisdiction. This was especially true when, for a time, Worthial himself acted as commissary for Milling.[31]

These jurisdictional changes and reforms were accompanied by a remarkable improvement in the efficiency and effectiveness of the episcopal courts, in the archdeaconry of Chichester at least. The consistory court which had sat on only 19 court days in 1507, sat on 36 in 1520, and 45 in 1524, and, until the number of sessions declined again during Sherburne's last years at Chichester, this increase was accompanied by a growth in business before the courts.[32] The authorities were able to speed their dispatch of probate and instance business, and, most importantly for the spiritual life of the diocese, to deal in greater numbers with those, whether cleric or lay, who offended against the Church's teachings. The evidence shows that it was in this last field that Sherburne's reforms had the most significant results, and also where the efficiency of his courts stands in sharpest contrast with the situation under the Reformation bishops who were his successors at Chichester.

Between September 1506 and September 1507, the consistory and archdeaconry of Chichester commissary courts had dealt with 220 instance cases, but only 65 office cases, while in the year 1520, soon after the jurisdictional changes, they dealt with a very similar number of instances cases, 227, but with as many as 195 office cases.[33] This remarkable increase in activity, which was maintained during the 1520s, was, in part, caused by the union of jurisdictions which brought cases formerly heard by the archdeacon to the episcopal courts, but it was also undoubtedly the result of new and extensive attacks on abuses that were made by Bishop Sherburne and his officers through the courts.[34] They were active in many fields, but most noticeably

---

[30] C.R.O., Ep. I/10/2–5; STA I/1A, fos. 12, 24, 54, 76, 100; Ep. IV/2/1–2.
[31] L.P.L., Register Warham 2, fo. 349; Emden, *Biographical Register*, II, 1333; C.R.O., STA I/1A, fos. 49, 98–9, 100–3; *L.P.*, XIII(1), 1273.
[32] C.R.O., Ep. I/10/1, fos. 14–33; Ep. I/10/2, fos. 2–128; Ep. I/10/3, fos. 2–35; no pre-1550 court books survive for the archdeaconry of Lewes.
[33] C.R.O., Ep. I/10/1, fos. 1–29, 52–98; Ep. I/10/2, fos. 2–131.
[34] C.R.O., Ep. I/10/3, 3a, 4.

in attempts to improve the repair of church fabric and the performance of the clergy in the parishes. During 1507, the authorities in the archdeaconry of Chichester had only brought six cases against those responsible for disrepair of church fabric, but in 1520, Sherburne's officers brought seventy-one such cases, and this was at a time when the problem of dilapidations was less serious than previously, if the evidence of visitation *comperta* is to be believed.[35] Moreover, during 1520 the authorities were apparently successful at getting repairs carried out, and fragmentary evidence shows that they continued to lavish attention on the problem until the early years of the Reformation Parliament.[36] They were also busy correcting beneficed clergy who were absent from their livings without licence. In February 1521, a diocesan official was sent to London to report on the behaviour of a Chichester priest who was thought to be disporting himself there, and he reported to Worthial that the priest was 'fussing and croaking in London', and only 'serveth his benefice by a canon'. By the time his parish was visited in September of that year, he had been forced to reside.[37] Others who were absent without leave were treated severely. John Williamson, the vicar of Binsted, was threatened with deprivation if he did not appear at his benefice within five days, the vicars of Houghton and Amberley were threatened in their absence with large fines, and the eight incumbents who were found to be absent without licence at the episcopal visitation of 1521 had the fruits of their livings sequestered. A similar severity, which had not been shown hitherto, was accorded to incontinent priests, even though clerical incontinence was also less of a problem than previously.[38]

These were not the only fields in which the courts were used extensively and successfully under Sherburne. They were also used, to an extent hitherto unknown, to coerce inefficient monastic heads, for example; and in a concerted effort to resist attempts by parishioners to withhold from their parish church or priest what they owed them in tithes, offerings, or church dues.[39] Furthermore, it was in the regular sessions of the courts that judicial enquiries were undertaken into the endowments of unserved chantries and of inadequately endowed parish benefices, as a prelude to action being taken to re-use the former and improve the latter – a feature of Sherburne's episcopate.[40]

[35] C.R.O., Ep. I/10/1, fos. 33, 65, 69, 83, 102; Ep. I/10/2, fos. 5, 20, 64, 71–2, 93, 107–8, 117, 125; Ep. III/4/1, fos. 82–3; Ep. I/18/2, fos. 6–8.
[36] Most faults discovered in 1520 had been repaired by summer 1521; see B. L., Add. MS. 34317, fo. 63; C.R.O., Ep I/10/4, fos. 5, 12, 15.
[37] C.R.O., Cap I/14/4a, fo. 14; Ep. I/18/2, fo. 25.
[38] C.R.O., Ep. I/10/3a, fo. 10; Ep. I/18/2, fos. 17, 20, 24, 29–32, 34; Ep. I/1/5; for incontinent priests see e.g. B.L., Add. MS. 34317, fo. 52.
[39] Examples: C.R.O., Ep. I/10/2, fo. 26; Ep. I/10/3, fos. 31–2, 35–6, 38, 40; Ep. I/10/2, fos. 27–8, 31, 37. The vast majority of cases brought by incumbents to recover dues were won in the 1520s; this was not true at other times.
[40] C.R.O., Ep. I/1/5, fos. 52–84, 88–9, 135–6; Ep. I/10/2, fos. 32, 32a, 105; Ep. I/10/3, fo. 8; Ep. I/10/3a, fos. 7, 9.

The courts could not have been used to such an extent had they not been able to deal with cases very rapidly, so it is not surprising to find that office cases against both laymen and clerics were being dealt with more quickly, and offenders were being made to appear before the courts more easily, during the 1520s than previously, as the table below makes clear. This was not, however, because unjustified charges,

The duration of office cases in the courts of the archdeaconry of Chichester[41]

	Number of office cases before courts	Number of appearances sought by courts in these cases	Average number of appearances needed to deal with one case
Nov. 1506–Nov. 1507	(77) 43	95	2.2
Jan. 1520–Jan. 1521	(78) 195	279	1.4

which had subsequently to be dropped, were being brought against laymen, as was later alleged of church courts, for the evidence seems to show that a majority of defendants were guilty.[42] The difficulty of making an assessment of guilt or innocence from the surviving records is well illustrated by the case of Thomas Moreland, the vicar of Bosham, who in 1536 was alleged to have confessed fornication with Agnes Pers. When proceedings began in the consistory court, he claimed that the woman was honest and that he had made no confession and it was subsequently established that one of his parishioners had made up the whole story.[43] Moreover there is stray evidence from elsewhere that the process of compurgation was unreliable and open to severe abuse.[44] It does still seem possible to make a reasonably accurate assessment of the guilt or innocence of those laymen who were cited to answer charges *ex officio*, however, by analysing the number of cases dropped after a preliminary hearing. The table on page 44 gives the results of such an analysis.

The ease with which the authorities were able to secure the appearance of those cited during the 1520s meant that they were also able to provide a less costly and time-consuming service for plaintiffs in instance cases, and a quicker dispatch of the probate of wills. In instance cases it was very common for plaintiffs to give up their suit because of the costs involved before an agreement or a definitive sentence had been reached, so it speaks well of the courts over which Worthial presided that definitive sentences were far more common in the 1520s than at other times. Between September 1506 and December 1507 only one case was concluded in this

[41] C.R.O., Ep. I/10/1, fos. 8–32, 60–103; Ep. I/10/2.
[42] See p. 44.   [43] C.R.O., Ep. I/10/5, fos. 99–100, 104.
[44] For example C. Hill, *Society and Puritanism* (London, 1964), p. 310.

way, but between January and July 1520, six definitive sentences were promulgated, and a number of others are to be found among proceedings that survive for 1524–6.[45] Sherburne's courts were able to provide a service for plaintiffs in which the conclusion of suits, where no interim agreement had been reached, was financially feasible. This did not mean, however, that his officers pushed cases to this expensive

The results of office cases against laymen during the 1520s[46]

Probable results	Consistory court Jan. 1520 to Jan. 1521	Commissary court Jan. 1520 to Jan. 1521	Consistory court Jan. 1524 to Jan. 1525
Confessed	14	8	7
Guilty (injunctions issued or failed in purgation)	16	24	11
Probably guilty (not admitted to purgation or often absent from court)	11	8	10
Total	41	40	28
Innocent (succeeded at purgation or dismissed)	5	11	8
Probably innocent (no action taken against defendant)	9	4	2
Total	14	15	10
Result uncertain	24	27	5
Total number of cases	79	82	43

conclusion, for they often used arbitrators to try to settle disputes away from the courts. During 1520, for example, it is known that Worthial introduced arbitrators to settle fifteen cases.[47] The speed with which instance cases passed through the courts, however, and their outcome, depended as much upon the parties involved as upon the authorities. When executors came to the courts with wills to prove, on the other hand, official efficiency was of the greatest importance, and the speed with which wills were dispatched during Sherburne's episcopate was remarkable, for the majority of them were proved within eight weeks of being written, and over eighty per cent

[45] C.R.O., Ep. I/10/1, fo. 27; Ep. I/10/2, fos. 7, 22, 38, 41, 47, 69; Ep. I/10/3, fos. 6, 27; Ep. I/10/4, fos. 7, 26.
[46] C.R.O., Ep. I/10/2, 3.
[47] C.R.O., Ep. I/10/2, fos. 3, 8, 23, 34–5, 39, 60, 65, 70, 74, 95, 116, 126, 133.

were proved within twelve weeks.[48] Obviously Dr Kitching's warning against
confusing speed with efficiency and justice must be heeded here, although the
circumstances were probably somewhat different in diocesan probate. Moreover, the
complicated processes involved in dealing with the goods of deceased bankrupts
were carried out reasonably quickly at this time also, and the courts were proving
wills very cheaply.[49] The preamble to the 1529 Probate Act accused ordinaries of
taking as much as £2 or £3 for the probate of a will, and the new scale introduced
by the Act provided for fees of 6d. for goods valued under £5 rising to 5s. for those
valued over £40. At Chichester, however, except for those who were granted
probate *in forma pauperis*, the standard fee was 10d.[50]

The church courts at Chichester were clearly particularly busy and efficient in the
years that followed Bishop Sherburne's jurisdictional reforms. This seems to have
been because he retained a personal interest in them, and made efforts to protect
and expand their activities. Sherburne was himself a respected and experienced
ecclesiastical judge and monastic visitor, and, like some other bishops who showed
a lively concern for the maintenance of their episcopal rights, was active on a number
of occasions in defending the jurisdiction of his courts from the depredations of
outsiders. In 1516, he had availed himself of the occasion of the dispute over probate
jurisdiction in the southern province to win from the archbishop of Canterbury a
number of minor concessions over the extent of the Prerogative jurisdiction as it
affected his diocese, for example.[51] In 1520-1, he successfully defended his recent
reorganisation of the courts from an attempt by a former archdeacon of Lewes to
recover the archdeaconry and the jurisdictional rights that had previously gone with
it.[52]

Probably more important than either of these successes, however, was the
agreement made with Wolsey during the 1520s which kept his legatine court, one
of 'the most aggressive and powerful tribunals in the history of the English Church',
from interfering with the work of the Chichester courts. The details of the settlement
do not survive, although Sherburne was accused in 1530 of allotting half the value
of his casualties to Wolsey for the right to retain his jurisdiction unchecked, and a
damaged draft of a dean and chapter document seems to indicate that in 1527
Sherburne was paying over to him as much as £20 a year. The evidence so far
adduced of actual payments of such a sum, however, seems highly unreliable. It is

---

48 For example C.R.O., Ep. I/1/5, fos. 109–14.
49 For example C.R.O., Ep. I/10/2, fos. 43–4, 98–100.
50 21 Henry VIII, c. 5; *The Lay Subsidy Rolls for the County of Sussex, 1524–5*, ed. J. C. K. Cornwall
    (Sussex Record Society, LVI, 1956), pp. 13–28.
51 C.R.O., Ep. VI/1/4, fos. 6–7; M. Kelly, 'Canterbury Jurisdiction and Influence During the
    Episcopate of William Warham, 1503–32' (University of Cambridge Ph.D. thesis, 1963), pp.
    55–93.
52 C.R.O., Cap. I/14/4a, fos. 14, 24; B.L., Add. MS. 34317, fos. 19, 24.

clear that Sherburne was prepared to pay for independence, an independence moreover which appears to have been maintained, for the meagre surviving evidence reveals that Wolsey's legatine court took cases from many dioceses, but not from Chichester.[53]

Sherburne's interest in his courts was not limited to jurisdictional matters. Although Worthial usually presided, the bishop retained and exercised the right to hear important cases himself. The evidence of his own judicial activity is almost certainly incomplete, but he clearly dealt with a wide range of cases. He sat to decide the augmentation of two vicarages in 1513–14, for example, to grant pensions from livings, to hear a difficult matrimonial dispute between members of local gentry families in 1533, and to try a notorious heretic in 1534.[54] Moreover, he clearly exercised a close control over the everyday work of the courts. Their activities, especially with regard to clerical residence and church finance, reflect the bishop's own preoccupations, and he appears to have intervened in cases that interested him. He was involved in the expulsion from the diocese of the curate of Cowfold, for example, showed interest in the proceedings over the bankrupt Robert Toprat's estates, and on occasions initiated charges against offenders.[55] A letter that survives from Sherburne's registry gives a good indication of his close control over quite minor matters. A local landowner, one of whose servants had been before the courts, wrote: 'Whereupon and at my special desire your said commissary respited the penance *which was only by your commandment*, and therefore I heartily thank your good lordship and glad I shall be to redress my servant in all things that your lordship shall think necessary.'[56]

Sherburne was clearly fortunate in finding able and industrious officers, but it appears to have been his jurisdictional reforms and protection of the courts, and his continuing interest in their activities, that were ultimately responsible for their effectiveness. Unfortunately for the future history of the diocese, however, his jurisdictional reforms and judicial activity were not developed or continued by his successors, and the church courts at Chichester were never again as effective as they had been during the 1520s.

This decline in effectiveness was largely the result of influences from outside the diocese which began to be felt during Sherburne's episcopate – though Bishop Richard Sampson's later neglect of his see for work in London was also important – for the evidence shows that national events after 1530 had a direct and dismal effect

[53] Kelly, *op. cit.*, pp. 178–89; J. J. Scarisbrick, 'The Conservative Episcopate in England 1529–35' (University of Cambridge Ph.D. thesis, 1956), pp. 117–21; J. J. Scarisbrick, 'The Pardon of the Clergy', *H.J.*, XII (1956), pp. 25–7; B.L., Add. MS. 34317, fo. 33.

[54] C.R.O., Ep. I/1/5, fos. 43–51, 136; Ep. I/1/4, fos. 75–9; Ep. I/10/5, fos. 9, 80–90.

[55] B.L., Add. MS. 34317, fos. 28, 49; C.R.O., Ep. I/10/2, fos. 26, 43–4, 98–100; Cap. I/14/4a, fo. 10.

[56] C.R.O., Ep. I/10/3, fo. 21; Cap. I/14/4a, fo. 2.

upon the exercise of spiritual jurisdiction at Chichester. There is little doubt that the church courts were unpopular with some of the laity in the years preceding the 1529 Parliament, perhaps because of their very efficiency, but the violence of anticlerical feeling in the Commons in 1529, and the extent of the attacks upon ecclesiastical jurisdiction made in Parliament in the next five years, were unprecedented.[57] The scope and purpose of these attacks have been the subject of much debate, but their actual effect upon the courts in the localities has not. They cannot be judged in isolation, however, since this period also saw a number of potentially more serious threats to the exercise of ecclesiastical jurisdiction by the bishops. Plans for far-reaching reform of the courts were clearly circulating during the Reformation Parliament, for example, and a draft bill, possibly connected with the agitation of 1532, proposed the prohibition of all *ex officio* actions except in heresy cases. This could have destroyed at a stroke the ability of the bishops to maintain ecclesiastical discipline in their dioceses or carry out reforms through their courts. Other plans went further, and Richard Pollard, one of Cromwell's servants, even proposed the abolition of the separate spiritual jurisdiction altogether. The courts had their defenders, however, and in the event nothing came of these plans. The threat of change, however, especially to the important office jurisdiction, and the knowledge that reform of the canon law was being discussed during this period, clearly hung over the courts. At Chichester this undoubtedly contributed to a dramatic decline in their activity.[58]

Cranmer's metropolitical visitation of 1534–5, which was undertaken with royal support, was the first of the southern province for over a century, and represented a direct challenge to episcopal authority. Mr Richard Gwent, one of the visitors, came to the diocese of Chichester in the summer of 1535. He visited Chichester cathedral in July, and at the start of August wrote to Cromwell to report what he had found. While the visitation lasted, Sherburne's jurisdiction was inhibited, and no episcopal court sat between 10 April and 24 July 1535. For this bishop, who had kept Wolsey's commissaries from interfering in his diocese, this must have been a severe blow, even though it was an indignity to which other bishops were also subjected. It must have been the more so for Sherburne since its purpose was to enforce the royal supremacy to which he was opposed.[59] Potentially more serious threats to episcopal power and prestige followed, for the inhibition for the famous

---

[57] M. Bowker, 'Some Archdeacons' Court Books and the "Commons Supplication against the Ordinaries" of 1532', in D. A. Bullough and R. L. Storey (eds), *The Study of Mediaeval Records: Essays in Honour of Kathleen Major* (Oxford, 1971), pp. 282–316.

[58] See S. E. Lehmberg, *The Reformation Parliament 1528–36* (Cambridge, 1970), pp. 81–104, 127–8; G. R. Elton, *Reform and Renewal* (Cambridge, 1973), pp. 130–5; for decline in courts' activity see below, p. 49. Probably the reform was being discussed in the summer and autumn of 1535: F. D. Logan, 'The Henrician Canons', *B.I.H.R.*, XLVII (1974), 99–103.

[59] P.R.O., S.P. 1/93, fos. 67, 71; S.P. 1/79, fo. 165a; S.P. 1/83, p. 243; S.P. 1/84, p. 119.

royal visitation was issued in September 1535, Layton, one of the visitors, was in Sussex during September and October, and Cromwell's vicegerential court was at work by the middle of October if not before.[60]

In the event, however, although the royal visitors did come to Sussex, and the vicegerential court was active in London until 1540, the threat posed by the inhibition and the court, in the diocese of Chichester at least, proved more theoretical than actual. Sessions of the consistory court continued uninterrupted throughout the period, and only one Chichester case appears among all the surviving records of the vicegerential court, and that involved a will which would probably normally have come before the Prerogative Court of Canterbury rather than a diocesan court.[61]

The threat of change and the damage caused by these events was real enough, however, and their effect upon Sherburne and upon the ecclesiastical officers of his diocese was profound. The office jurisdiction which they had used so effectively during the 1520s was under attack in Parliament and seemed on the point of abolition. Their right to settle tithe, perjury and defamation cases was contested, and the cherished independence of their courts had been destroyed by the archiepiscopal and royal visitors who had descended upon the diocese. It is not surprising that they took fright and drastically reduced the much abused *ex officio* activity of their courts. Nor is it surprising that potential plaintiffs were far less willing than before to use the Chichester courts to settle their disputes.[62] Moreover, they now had less opportunity to do so, because the authorities also reduced the number of court sessions, in the case of the consistory court from 45 in 1524 to 24 in 1534 and 23 in 1536.[63] As a result, there was a very sharp decline in office and instance business during Sherburne's last years at Chichester, and only the probate business of courts remained unaffected, as the table opposite shows.

The table also shows that the business of the courts only recovered slowly and that even in the 1550s office and instance business had not returned to pre-Reformation levels. There were reasons within the diocese for this. The preamble to the 1536 Tithe Act stated that many people 'have attempted in late time past to disobey condemn and despite the process, lawes and decrees of the Ecclesiastical courts of this realm, in more temerous and large manner than before this time hath been seen',[64] and it is clear that under Sherburne's successors the courts had greater and greater difficulty in ensuring the appearance of those cited, and in getting their orders obeyed. This was particularly unfortunate, for it meant that office proceedings were often ineffectual, that potential plaintiffs were deterred from starting proceedings, and that the courts declined in authority and effectiveness. In the 1520s few office cases had

---

[60] L.P., IX, nos. 444, 509; B.L. Add. MS. 48022, fo. 83; P.R.O., S.P. 1/97, p. 93.
[61] C.R.O., Ep. I/10/5, fos. 60, 62–3, 66–70, 72–3, 75; P.R.O., PROB 11/26, fo. 77.
[62] Lehmberg, Reformation Parliament, pp. 119, 128.
[63] C.R.O., Ep. I/10/3, fos. 2–35; Ep. I/10/5, fos. 25–48, 84, 69–79, 91–105.
[64] 27 Henry VIII, c. 20.

Cases before the courts of the archdeaconry of Chichester[65]

	Jan. 1520 to Jan. 1521	July 1533 to July 1534	Feb. 1537 to Feb. 1538	Oct. 1556 to Oct. 1557
Office cases				
Consistory court	90	27	31	Not separate
Commissary court	105	58	47	Not separate
Both courts	195	85	78	122
Instance cases				
Consistory court	136	31	30	Not separate
Commissary court	91	53	43	Not separate
Both courts	227	84	73	73
Probate cases				
Consistory court	50	16	20	Not separate
Commissary court	71	85	80	Not separate
Both courts	121	101	100	287
All cases				
Consistory court	276	74	81	Not separate
Commissary court	267	196	170	Not separate
Both courts	543	270	251	482

required more than one session to complete, but by the 1550s many took two or three sessions, and some dragged on and on.[66] The case of Robert Fowler of Albourne, who was cited to all the consistory court sessions between December 1556 and June 1557, was one that did, and other cases before the courts of both archdeaconries during the 1550s show that his was by no means exceptional.

The main reason for the courts' difficulties was the growing disrespect that was shown to spiritual sanctions, a legacy of the denigration heaped on the courts during the 1530s and a reflection of the unsettled times. In the 1520s, the Church's censures, as used in this diocese, had had a telling force. People actually fled the diocese to escape a suspension, and this lesser penalty was usually perfectly adequate to enforce obedience. The large numbers of those suspended in office proceedings who sought an absolution before the next session of the court shows how serious this lesser penalty was considered before 1530, and the fact that the threat of excommunication or merely of being judged contumacious without censure often had the desired effect, indicates how strong the authorities' position then was.[67] After Sherburne's death,

[65] C.R.O., Ep. I/10/2; Ep. I/10/5, fos. 12–37, 84, 108–41; Ep. I/10/6, fos. 1–34; Ep. I/10/7, fos. 1–27; Ep. I/10/10, fos. 5–48.
[66] C.R.O., Ep. I/10/10, fos. 5–47: between October 1556 and October 1557, 317 appearances sought to deal with 122 office cases.
[67] C.R.O., Ep. I/10/2, fos. 12, 34, 47, 60–1, 81, 89, 103; Ep. I/10/3, fos. 22, 25, 38; Ep. I/10/6, fo. 24.

however, the situation changed very noticeably, although it did not reach dire
proportions in Sussex until Catholic recusants challenged the Elizabethan
settlement.[68] The following table, by showing the marked rise in the use of
excommunication and decline in that of suspension at Chichester over the early
Reformation, gives a clear indication of the debasement of both penalties, and seems
to show that the change had occurred by 1537:

The use of ecclesiastical censures in office cases by the courts of the archdeaconry
of Chichester[69]

Date	Total office cases	Excommunications	Suspensions
Jan. 1520–Jan. 1521	105	1	41
July 1533–July 1534	85	1	21
Feb. 1537–Feb. 1538	78	10	16
Oct. 1556–Oct. 1557	122	13	20

There were also more specifically local reasons why the courts at Chichester did
not recover from the shocks of the 1530s. Richard Sampson left his spiritual officers
virtually unassisted, and, without episcopal guidance, Worthial proved a less
industrious servant. He had been nearly thirty when he first came to the diocese, so
that by 1540 he was over fifty, and by then had clearly lost some of his early energy.
He was also more heavily involved elsewhere than he had been in the 1520s. He
became a residentiary of the cathedral in 1530, and by Fleshmonger's death in 1541
he became the senior, and acted as president of the chapter. From then until his death
in 1554, chapter business took up more and more of his time. It is not, therefore,
surprising that he left the city of Chichester for the peripatetic sessions of the
commissary court considerably less often during the 1540s than he had during the
1520s.[70] This meant that judicial activity for the archdeaconry became more
concentrated on the consistory court at Chichester, an unfortunate process which was
to be taken considerably further by Worthial's successor as commissary and official
principal, Richard Brisley.[71]

This was not all, however, for after 1543 Worthial was having to preside as judge
without the help of a long-standing and able assistant, for it was in that year that

[68] Manning, *Religion and Society*, pp. 27–31.
[69] C.R.O., Ep. I/10/2; Ep. I/10/5, fos. 12–37, 108–41; Ep. I/10/6, fos. 1–34; Ep. I/10/7, fos. 1–27; Ep. I/10/10, fos. 5–48.
[70] *Sussex Chantry Records*, ed. J. E. Ray (Sussex Record Society, XXXVI, 1931) pp. 50, 59; *Acts of the Dean and Chapter*, no. 449; C.R.O., Ep. I/1/6, fos. 65–8, 89–96; Cap. I/23/2, fos. 52–99; Cap. I/4/8/1.
[71] C.R.O., STC I/8, fo. 104; STC III/A, fo. 1.

John Stilman died. It is not surprising that he now showed less vigour in hunting out and dealing with offenders, or that the attacks on abuses made under Sherburne were not resumed.[72]

Structural changes to the courts after Worthial's death in 1554, however, were far more detrimental to the effectiveness of episcopal jurisdiction. In the very month in which Worthial made his will, a dean's peculiar court began to act again apart from the consistory court.[73] Consequently, the parishes of the cathedral city of the bishops of Chichester were once again outside episcopal control, except during triennial visitation, and it seems probable that the difficulties experienced by Bishop Curteys in the city in the 1570s were one result. Moreover, the dean's court provided far less efficient justice for the city than had the consistory court. It met so infrequently, was so taken up with the administrative acts involved in instituting and inducting priests to benefices, and in proving wills, that there was little inclination or opportunity to correct offenders or to try ecclesiastical disputes.[74]

Steps even more detrimental to the courts were taken by Worthial's successor as judge, Richard Brisley. He was often dilatory in proceeding with offenders, and dealt with cases outside the proper court sessions in his own house. On one such occasion, moreover, a penance was commuted to a money payment at the request of the defendant. He also received irregular fees. Thomas Hide and Alice Davie, who had consented to marry after being prosecuted for fornication, for example, were required to pay the judge 4s., and, for a will proved in London, Brisley personally received 3s. 4d. These few references do not show corruption as serious as that later found in the diocese of Gloucester, but there had evidently been a decline in standards since the 1520s.[75] Consequently, it is not surprising to find that although the authorities attacked heresy and witchcraft during Mary's reign, they made none of the efforts of Sherburne's officers to root out the more widespread problems of clerical non-residence and poverty, and of dilapidated churches.[76]

More serious for the future work of the courts was Brisley's amalgamation of the commissary court for the archdeaconry of Chichester and the consistory court. Throughout Worthial's dominance at Chichester these two courts had functioned separately, even though the judge, registrar and proctors were usually the same in both, and regular, although latterly declining, numbers of circuits were undertaken into the deaneries each year. Brisley, however, was so involved in heresy trials that

[72] As the visitation returns show: C.R.O., Ep. I/18/4–8.
[73] C.R.O., Ep. III/4/2, fo. 2; STC I/8, fos. 109–10.
[74] C.R.O., Ep. III/4/2, fos. 3–12.
[75] C.R.O., Ep. I/10/10, fos. 29, 31, 34–5, 41, 45, 47–9; cf. F. D. Price, 'An Elizabethan Church Official: Thomas Powell, Chancellor of the Gloucester Diocese', C.Q.R., cxxviii (1939), pp. 94–112; F. D. Price, 'The Abuses of Excommunication and the Decline of Ecclesiastical Discipline under Queen Elizabeth', E.H.R., lvii (1942), pp. 106–15.
[76] C.R.O., I/1/6; Ep. I/18/8–9; B.L., Harleian MS. 421, fos. 105–10; 425, fos. 102–5.

he made no effort to distinguish between his activities as commissary and official principal, and between March 1556 and November 1557 made only four trips into the deaneries.[77] This meant that judicial activity for the archdeaconry away from Chichester became very infrequent, and in the 1560s it became more infrequent still, being limited to summary hearings at visitation.[78] This had two most unfortunate results. First, it became more inconvenient for potential plaintiffs, for those with wills to prove, and for those cited to the courts to answer charges or at the instance of a third party. When there had been regular sessions in each rural deanery, no parish was more than a day's travel from the hearings of an ecclesiastical court, but now that the vast majority of cases were dealt with at Chichester, the cost and inconvenience involved must have increased considerably. This was especially so since the city, where the consistory court sat, was particularly badly placed as a judicial centre for the archdeaconry, let alone the diocese.

Second, and perhaps of even greater importance for the office jurisdiction of the courts, the removal of court sessions from the localities placed the burden of detecting faults more squarely upon episcopal and archidiaconal visitations, and therefore on the shoulders of the already harassed churchwardens, whose reliability had always been in question. This was one reason why the Elizabethan authorities had such difficulty in detecting and stamping out recusancy in the diocese in the 1570s and 1580s, and why Bishop Curteys recommended the establishment of a branch of the Ecclesiastical Commission in Sussex.[79]

It was in this context, therefore, equally unfortunate that the commissary court in the archdeaconry of Lewes was also becoming settled, in this case in one of the parish churches in Lewes. Courts were still being held regularly in outlying areas by Mr Robert Taylor, the commissary of Lewes, as late as 1557, but after his deprivation in 1559, this occurred only at visitation. By the early 1560s, in fact, the ecclesiastical courts in both archdeaconries of this diocese had taken on the form they were to retain until the nineteenth century.[80] It was a form, moreover, the inadequacy of which was to be ruthlessly exposed by the resistance of papists and puritans.

It could reasonably be argued that the picture here presented of the Chichester courts at the Reformation, one of reform and efficiency during the 1520s, but of decline thereafter, owed more to specifically local circumstances, such as the presence of an active resident bishop during the 1520s and early 1530s, or the failings of Worthial and Brisley in the 1540s and 1550s, than to national events, and that,

---

[77] C.R.O., Ep. I/10/2, fos. 6–8; STC III/A, fos. 1–4; Ep. I/10/10, fos. 1–49.

[78] C.R.O., STC III/A; Ep. I/18/11.

[79] Manning, *Religion and Society*, pp. 29–30, 43, 131–3, 149.

[80] See *ibid.*, p. 22; C.R.O., Ep. II/9/1, fos. 113–24; Ep. I/18/9, fo. 47; Ep. I/1/7, fo. 18; Ep. I/18/11, fos. 22–37, 54–66.

consequently, the diocese was something of a special case. There are enough parallels between the changes at Chichester and developments in other dioceses, however, to cast doubt upon such a conclusion. Bishop Fox of Winchester noted with approval the efficiency of his chancellor during the 1520s, and boasted to Wolsey in 1527 that there was 'as little openly known sin or enormous crimes, both in persons spiritual and temporal' in his diocese, 'as is within any diocese of this realm'.[81] Historians have noted an upsurge of business in the 1520s, similar to that at Chichester, in the Lichfield and Canterbury courts, and the latter were also using excommunications with care at this date.[82] Moreover, episcopal courts were clearly not the only ones that were flourishing. At Chester, where the archdeacon's authority was virtually episcopal, for example, the official made an unsuccessful attempt to broaden the activity of his court in the early 1520s by holding some sessions elsewhere than in Chester, and the efficiency of some archdeaconry courts in the Lincoln diocese at this date has received special mention.[83] Furthermore, it is clear that Sherburne was by no means the only bishop in the last decades before the break with Rome who was interested in his diocesan courts. Bishop Atwater of Lincoln presided in person over something like regular sessions of an audience court, Bishop Stokesley is known to have tried London cases in person, and many of Sherburne's contemporaries on the bench were active visitors.[84] Also, it seems inconceivable that bishops West of Ely, Nykke of Norwich, Booth of Hereford and Fox of Winchester, like Sherburne, should have gone to the trouble and expense of resisting the interference of Wolsey's commissaries had they attached no importance to the work of their diocesan courts and considered them as little more than a source of revenue and prestige, and the same may, to some extent, be said of the resistance shown by bishops Longland, Gardiner, Stokesley, Reppes and Veysey to Cranmer's metropolitical visitation.[85] To these bishops on the very eve of the Reformation, ecclesiastical courts were still an

[81] *The Letters of Richard Fox, 1486–1527*, ed. P. S. Allen and Helen M. Allen (Oxford, 1929), pp. 146–51.

[82] Woodcock, *Medieval Ecclesiastical Courts*, pp. 84, 100; *V.C.H. Staffs.*, III (1970), p. 37; see p. 49 above.

[83] P. Heath, 'Mediaeval Archdeaconry and Tudor Bishopric of Chester', *J.E.H.*, XX (1969), pp. 243–52; Cheshire R.O., EDC 1/3, fos. 18–27: I am grateful to Dr C. A. Haigh for drawing my attention to this phenomenon; Bowker, 'Some Archdeacons' Court Books', pp. 286–316.

[84] *Episcopal Court Book*, ed. Bowker, *passim*; C. A. McLaren, 'An Early Sixteenth Century Act Book of the Diocese of London', *Journal of the Society of Antiquaries*, III (7) (1968), pp. 337–8; *Bishop Geoffrey Blythe's Visitations, c. 1515–25*, ed. P. Heath (Staffordshire Record Society, 1973), pp. lviii–lix, xi–xiv; D. Knowles, *The Religious Orders in England*, III (Cambridge, 1959), pp. 70–3; *Visitations of the Diocese of Norwich, 1492–1532*, ed. A. Jessop (Camden Society, 1888) pp. 65–319.

[85] A. F. Pollard, *Wolsey* (London, 1929), pp. 193–202; Scarisbrick, 'The Conservative Episcopate', pp. 114–21; *Letters of Fox*, pp. 150–1; Kelly, 'Canterbury Jurisdiction', p. 178; J. Ridley, *Thomas Cranmer* (1962), pp. 79–81.

essential and effective part of diocesan organization. Their reform might be discussed in Convocation, as it was in 1532, but they must be defended from interference from above or resentment from below.

There were also later parallels with the situation at Chichester. The most notorious example of corrupt and inefficient courts is probably that provided by the Gloucester evidence for the early years of Elizabeth's reign, and, although the Gloucester experience was probably extreme and untypical, there were certainly other inefficient courts in the decades after 1540. For example, those of another Henrician diocese, that of Chester, in the 1540s and 1550s, were presided over first by a man who was a frequent litigant in his own court, and then by another who fathered, by three different women, one bastard under Henry VIII, five legitimate children under Edward VI and another bastard under Mary.[86] Their court could hardly have commanded respect. At Lichfield in the 1560s, moreover, Bishop Bentham had considerable difficulty in enforcing the 1559 Injunctions and in making any headway against Catholic recusants, and the same could be said of almost every diocese.[87] Church courts in general revived during the latter part of Elizabeth's reign as litigation increased, but even then the continuing use of ecclesiastical commissions indicates contemporary recognition of the inability of the old episcopal courts to deal with those, whether Catholic or puritan, who repudiated the jurisdiction of the Church. Moreover, even if recusants are excluded from calculations, the same pattern emerges, as at Chichester, of failure to enforce obedience to court procedures and of numerous excommunications. This was true of the comparatively well-administered diocese of London, for example, of archdeaconries in the dioceses of York, Norwich and Chester, and of certain deaneries in the archdeaconry of Taunton.[88]

The Chichester courts may present an especially clear picture of reorganisation and reform in the 1520s and of decline in business and efficiency over the early Reformation, but it was a picture, especially with regard to the 'rapidly growing contempt of the laity' for the Church's 'strictures and fulminations', that is apparently applicable in varying measure to other dioceses.

It is clear that in Chichester as elsewhere the decade or so before the Henrician Reformation witnessed the efforts of an energetic bishop to breathe fresh life into the diocesan administration. Sherburne sought to bring the control of his diocese

---

[86] C. Haigh, 'A Mid Tudor Ecclesiastical Official', *Transactions of the Historic Society of Lancashire and Cheshire*, CXXII (1970), pp. 6, 17–18.

[87] *V.C.H. Staffs.*, III, pp. 47–9.

[88] R. Peters, 'The Administration of the Archdeaconry of St Albans, 1580–1625', *J.E.H.*, XIII (1962), pp. 61–75; H. G. Owen, 'The Episcopal Visitation: Its Limits and Limitations in Elizabethan London', *J.E.H.*, XI (1960), pp. 179–85; Marchant, *Church under the Law*, pp. 204–35.

into his own hands, defying the attempts of rival jurisdictions. Meeting with success, he then tried to turn the attention of the courts away from their preoccupation with instances cases and towards the business of discipline. There is every sign that this bishop made the consistory effective where correction cases were concerned and the work of the court in all its aspects was rendered more efficient (although whether more just we have no means of knowing). It has been possible to demonstrate that the years 1530 to 1557 saw a weakening of the consistory's effectiveness and authority – presumably as a result of the shocks administered to the system by the Reformation and its unsettled aftermath.

3

ANTICLERICALISM AND THE
ENGLISH REFORMATION

CHRISTOPHER HAIGH

Thinking is a difficult business, and most of us prefer to do as little of it as possible. To avoid the anguish and responsibility of independent thought, we explain the past with historical clichés, we play with labels rather than grapple with the complexities of detail. We rely upon 'the decay of medieval religion', 'the growth of an articulate laity', 'the rise of Lollardy' and 'the dynamic impact of Protestantism' for an exposition of the origins of the English Reformation. But such categories are only the convenience-foods of historical study, which give us our past pre-packaged and frozen, in ready-mixed meals needing only to be warmed in the moderate oven of a mediocre essay or lecture: with such fast-foods to hand, the over-worked cook need not formulate his own recipe or cope with his own ingredients. These concepts are sometimes no more than convenient fictions, which survive not because the evidence justifies them but because they are the necessary foundations for a conventional interpretation.

'Anticlericalism' is just such a fiction, and owes its popularity to utility not veracity: G. G. Coulton argued seventy years ago that the clergy *must* have been unpopular or the Reformation would be inexplicable.[1] The need to explain the Protestant outcome of the English Reformation imposes a perspective which finds in 'anticlericalism' both a cause of religious change and a reason for its acceptance. The concept provides a crucial explanatory tool, which links together the statutes of 1489, 1497 and 1512 on benefit of clergy, the Hunne and Standish affairs of 1512–15, hostility to Cardinal Wolsey, the so-called 'anticlerical legislation' of 1529 and the Commons' Supplication of 1532, to demonstrate a rising tide of lay discontent which led naturally to support for the break with Rome, the suppression of the monasteries, and an attack on the superstitions which had buttressed clerical power. A whiggish teleology which traces the inexorable progress of protest and reform does not notice that agitation about spiritual jurisdiction died down after 1515, and that the Parliament of 1523, despite its struggle with Wolsey over taxation,

[1] G. G. Coulton, *Ten Medieval Studies* (Cambridge, 1930 edition), pp. 137–8.

had nothing to say about the Church. Much is made of the 'anticlerical' drama of the first session of the Reformation Parliament but, except for the official manoeuvres which led to the Pardon of the Clergy, we hear less of the second session, when statutes were passed to deal with aliens, apprentices, beggars, gypsies, poisoning, the wool trade and the draining of Plumstead Marsh: the Church received minimal attention. A House of Commons which, according to the chonicler Edward Hall, had spent November and December 1529 venting its accumulated fury against Churchmen, was apparently satisfied by three petty acts, and in 1531 members sat about getting irritated because the Council gave them nothing to do.[2] As the compelling force we need if we are to explain a cataclysmic Reformation, 'anticlericalism' is distressingly unconvincing, sustained as it is by selective citation and an embarrassingly narrow range of examples.[3] But, fortunately, explanation of the Reformation does not pose quite the challenge it did in Coulton's day, since what once seemed a swift and momentous revolution now often appears as a long drawn-out struggle which owed more to the contingencies of politics than to ideology or social movements.[4] In these hard, revisionist times, 'anticlericalism' runs the risk of redundancy.

Despite the prominent place it occupies in Reformation textbooks, the concept of 'anticlericalism' has been given surprisingly little analysis and the phenomenon it seeks to describe has not often been studied. Although it is often recognised that there were different branches of 'anticlericalism' (the ideology of erastian reformers, the theology of the priesthood of all believers, the gut reaction of neglected parishioners), such distinctions are usually glossed over and hostility to the clergy is explained as a unitary force, as the opposition of a self-conscious laity to a distinctive clerical caste. But the evidence for sharp divisions and critical reactions between clergy and laity is not strong, and is usually little more than speculative. Much of the argument for substantial 'anticlericalism' is of the 'must have been' variety: men 'must have been' hostile to a corrupt, worldly, wealthy and inefficient Church, so we are offered examples of the explanatory '-isms' of the Reformation: absenteeism, pluralism, nepotism, legalism. Such a view is based on modern rather than Tudor attitudes towards the Church and its function, and it has been severely dented by recent scholarship, which has questioned whether the alleged abuses were really widespread and whether they really caused discontent. On the issues of clerical education, morality and pastoral care, it has been demonstrated in a number of regional studies that deficiencies were exaggerated by earlier historians and that

---

[2] S. E. Lehmberg, *The Reformation Parliament, 1529–1536* (Cambridge, 1970), pp. 81–9, 118–26, 130; G. R. Elton, *Reform and Reformation* (London, 1977), pp. 141, 144–5.

[3] The Hunne case is usually cited as the example of friction over mortuaries, and the issue of tithe is illustrated by the troubles of Henry Gold as rector of Hayes.

[4] See Chapter 1 above.

clerical standards apparently satisfied parishioners. In visitations of over a thousand
parishes in the diocese of Lincoln between 1514 and 1521, officials found only
twenty-five reports of priestly misconduct with women; in 1527–8, only eleven cases
were found in 230 parishes of the archdeaconry of Winchester; and in 1538 eight
priests were charged from 200 Norwich parishes. The thousand Lincoln parishes
yielded few complaints of clerical negligence: there were seventeen accusations that
services were irregular, twelve that services were not performed properly, seven that
priests did not preach or visit the sick, and in five parishes the priest was too old
or infirm for his duties.[5] It is true that we know only of reported offences and others
may have been concealed, but it would be strange if an allegedly anticlerical laity
had not charged the idle and the incontinent: we must assume that either most
parish priests obeyed the rules or, if they did not, their people did not object strongly
enough to complain. Indeed, if visitation presentments of clergy are used as an index
of lay attitudes rather than clerical conduct, it seems that the volume of criticism
rose sharply under Elizabeth and this may reflect a new *post*-Reformation
antagonism.[6] Perhaps 'anticlericalism' was a result rather than a cause of the
Reformation.

There were individual cases of greed and misconduct among parish priests, and
at higher levels there were scandalous examples of ostentation and easy living. But
when for every Cardinal Wolsey and every Prior More of Worcester there were
hundreds of poorly-paid and hard-working curates,[7] it is not clear that specific defects
would discredit the clergy as a whole. We cannot presume a clear distinction and
likely friction between priests and laymen, for the lower clergy and poorer laity had
much in common and both were oppressed by their social superiors:[8] each priest
was a son, a brother, an uncle – sometimes a father! – a member of the village
community, usually working in or near his native parish, and not an alien intruder.[9]
At Westminster there may have been a drawing up of ranks in times of crisis, and

[5] M. Bowker, *The Secular Clergy in the Diocese of Lincoln, 1495–1520* (Cambridge, 1968), pp. 3,
114, 116; R. A. Houlbrooke, *Church Courts and the People during the English Reformation* (Oxford,
1979), pp. 178–9. See also C. Haigh, *Reformation and Resistance in Tudor Lancashire*
(Cambridge, 1975), pp. 27–30, 50–1; P. Heath, *English Parish Clergy on the Eve of the Reformation*
(London, 1969), pp. 104–19.

[6] See, for example, Houlbrooke, *Church Courts*, pp. 200, 204; Haigh, *Reformation and Resistance*,
pp. 240–6; R. A. Marchant, *The Church under the Law* (Cambridge, 1969), p. 219; P. Tyler,
'The Church Courts at York and Witchcraft Prosecutions, 1567–1640', *Northern History*, IV
(1969), pp. 94–5.

[7] For the incomes of curates in the 1520s see M. L. Zell, 'Economic Problems of the Parochial
Clergy in the Sixteenth Century' in R. O'Day and F. Heal, eds., *Princes and Paupers in the English
Church* (Leicester, 1981), p. 26.

[8] See, for example, the resistance by both clergy and laymen in Kent to the Amicable Grant
in 1525 (P. Clark, *English Provincial Society from the Reformation to the Revolution* (Hassocks,
1977), p. 21), and the refusal by London curates, backed by laymen, to pay their share of the
praemunire fine in 1531 (E. Hall, *Henry VIII*, 2 vols (London, 1904), II, pp. 200–1).

[9] Haigh, *Reformation and Resistance*, pp. 40–1.

in 1515 the clerk of the parliaments closed his account of the session with regret for the conflict 'inter Clericum et Secularem Potestatem, super Libertatibus Ecclesiasticis', but social and political divisions were much more complex than a simple cleavage between clergy and laity. Bishops and abbots shared property interests and a common social life with the country nobles and gentry who were their stewards, bailiffs, lessees and neighbours,[10] though relations between the prelates and the lawyers and merchants were, as we shall see, more strained. One need not be a Marxist historian to suspect that the crucial social cleavage in early Tudor England was horizontal, between the propertied and the propertyless, rather than vertical, between laymen and priests, no matter how often we are told that there 'must have been' lay resentment of ecclesiastical abuse and privilege.

If this speculative, indirect evidence for 'anticlericalism' is weak, the direct evidence presented to demonstrate lay antagonism is no stronger. The jaunty poems of John Skelton, Jerome Barlow's scurrilous *Burial of the Mass*, the *Supplication for the Beggars* by Simon Fish, and William Tyndale's *Practice of Prelates*, slashing attacks on the morals, power and wealth of the clergy, are cited as examples of broader hostility, but these writers were partisan propagandists advancing a cause. Barlow, Fish and Tyndale were energetic Lutheran activists, and Fish's tract was distributed in the streets of London as the Reformation Parliament was opened: not without reason, Fisher, Gardiner and More thought attacks on the clergy were part of a Lutheran conspiracy to discredit the Church and weaken its resistance to heresy.[11] Skelton's 'anticlerical poems', 'Speak, Parrot', 'Colin Clout' and 'Why Come Ye Not To Court?', were directed against Wolsey rather than the clergy, and they were written in 1521–2 as part of the attack mounted by his patrons, the Howards, and other Court nobles on the dominant position of the Cardinal.[12] Such diatribes as these are not independent evidence of wider attitudes, and they would only have been influential if their charges rang true. But while no charge against Wolsey was too gross to be possible, Wolsey was not the Church, and the priests most men knew were chaste and ill-paid pastors. Barlow and Fish may only be cited as examples if it can be shown that their views were widespread, but this cannot be done. Contemporary comments on lay attitudes which seem to show 'anticlericalism' come from foreign observers such as Polydore Vergil, who had a personal grievance against Wolsey and had a sharp eye for attacks upon him, or the Imperial ambassador Eustace Chapuys, whose concern for Katherine of Aragon's position made him

[10] F. Heal, *Of Prelates and Princes: a study of the economic and social position of the Tudor episcopate* (Cambridge, 1980), pp. 35–8, 76–8.

[11] J. Foxe, *Actes and Monuments*, 8 vols (London, 1837–41), IV, p. 659; Lehmberg, *Reformation Parliament*, pp. 87, 146; T. More, *The Apology* (Yale Edition of the Complete Works of St Thomas More, IX, New Haven, 1979), p. 64. Cf. S. W. Haas, 'Simon Fish, William Tyndale and Sir Thomas More's Lutheran Conspiracy', *J.E.H.*, XXIII (1972), pp. 125–36.

[12] H. L. R. Edwards, *Skelton* (London, 1949), pp. 182–225; J. J. Scarisbrick, *Henry VIII* (London, 1971 edition), pp. 164–8.

hyper-sensitive to any challenge to the pope or Church courts.[13] The main chronicle source which seems to show 'anticlericalism' in London and among members of Parliament is also the work of a prejudiced observer: Edward Hall was a London lawyer and parliamentary ally of Thomas Cromwell, and a main theme of the Tudor section of his narrative is how Henry VIII and his people threw off clerical oppression.[14] Such literary evidence as this, or the opinion of Christopher St German in *A Treatise Concerning the Division Between the Spiritualty and Temporalty*, cannot be discounted, but it is significant only if offered with supporting material from less committed sources.

The inconclusive literary evidence finds some corroboration in legislative action, especially the 'anticlerical statutes' of 1529, but again it may be doubted if the acts reflected widely-held attitudes or genuine grievances. The complaints of 1529 were brought forward by specific interest groups, especially the Mercers' Company, which, like other Londoners, had been involved in long tussles with Wolsey over war taxation, trading privileges and the 1528 disruption of the cloth trade which resulted from the Cardinal's foreign policy.[15] The Mercers' five articles (only one of which concerned the Church) were presented to a House of Commons in which, as Lehmberg has shown, lawyers and merchants were well represented, and these and other complaints were worked into bills by a committee of lawyers:[16] lawyers and merchants had particular reasons for criticising the Church and, especially, Wolsey. When Parliament met, the issue of the moment was not reform of the Church, or even the king's marriage, but the future of the Cardinal of York: the three ecclesiastical issues on which the Commons chose to proceed, mortuaries, pluralism and probate, arose from Wolsey's own career and may have been part of a campaign to secure his permanent exclusion from power. The Mortuaries Act was perhaps designed to remind members of the Hunne affair and Wolsey's part in defusing the crisis of 1515 and preserving the privileges of the Church. The Pluralities Act was an obvious reference to the excesses of the Cardinal himself, and there is some evidence that his pluralist chaplains were unpopular in London.[17] If probate was a problem, it was a problem of Wolsey's own creation, since he had tried to arrogate probate jurisdiction to himself as legate: indeed, the Probate Act was helped

[13] E. J. Davis, 'The Authorities for the Case of Richard Hunne', *E.H.R.*, xxx (1915), p. 481; *The Anglica Historia of Polydore Vergil*, ed. D. Hay (Camden Society, 1950), pp. x, 229–35, 257–61; 325; *Calendar of State Papers, Spanish*, IV (i), p. 367.
[14] S. T. Bindoff, ed., *The House of Commons, 1509–1558*, 3 vols (London, 1982), II, pp. 279–82; Hall, *Henry VIII*, esp. II, p. 167.
[15] H. Miller, 'London and Parliament in the Reign of Henry VIII', *B.I.H.R.*, xxxv (1962), pp. 143–5; S. E. Brigden, 'The Early Reformation in London, 1520–1547' (University of Cambridge Ph.D. thesis, 1979), pp. 26–9.
[16] Lehmberg, *Reformation Parliament*, pp. 19–28, 81–3.
[17] Brigden, 'Early Reformation in London', pp. 28 and n, 69 and n.

through the Commons by a speech from Sir Henry Guildford, comptroller of the king's household and a long-standing enemy of Wolsey, who made improbable allegations about fees charged by the Cardinal.[18]

It seems unlikely that the three statutes of 1529 were honest attempts to tackle real difficulties. The Mortuaries Act imposed a scale of cash payments based on the value of the goods of the deceased, but it is difficult to assess the difference this made since local practice varied so much: some parishes had already abandoned the custom of giving an animal or an item of clothing in favour of a scale of charges. Though mortuaries were presumably as unpopular as unavoidable taxes always are, two things seem clear. The first is that, though the cost to an individual estate might be anything up to £1 or more, few mortuaries were actually taken and in practice the poor seem to have been exempt. The second is that, though some were vigorous, mortuary disputes were rare: the Hunne case was *not* an example of widespread resistance. In the archdeaconry of Chester there were only eight mortuary suits in the twenty-eight years before the statute (though there were thirteen in 1530 while the implications of the act were worked out), and in the diocese of Norwich there were only six cases between 1519 and 1529.[19] The Pluralities Act is even more problematical, since it was so hedged about with provisos that any priest influential enough to secure two benefices would surely qualify to hold them. While a fifth or a quarter of parishes had pluralist incumbents, it seems that adequate curates almost always substituted for non-residents and neglect only rarely resulted. The statute did nothing to improve pastoral care or benefit parishioners, since it could not make a pluralist reside in all his benefices: the only beneficiaries were a few priests who became incumbents when they might have remained curates.[20] Once again, if pluralism and neglect caused discontent, it was presumably after the Reformation rather than before, since pluralism increased only as the supply of priests fell and by the reign of Elizabeth there were too few clergy to provide services in all churches.[21]

[18] A. F. Pollard, *Wolsey* (London, 1965 edition), pp. 192–8; Hall, *Henry VIII*, II, p. 166. It is unlikely that even Wolsey really demanded a thousand marks for probate of a will worth £4,485 (G. W. Bernard, 'The Rise of Sir William Compton, early Tudor courtier', *E.H.R.*, XCVI (1981), p. 772), since this was fifteen times the usual rate, and impossible that he could have done so without provoking some recorded resistance.
[19] Heath, *English Parish Clergy*, pp. 153–6, 167; Haigh, *Reformation and Resistance*, pp. 57–8; Houlbrooke, *Church Courts*, p. 125. The Canterbury consistory heard only one mortuary case a year, and though there is some suggestion that trouble was more common in the archdeaconry of Leicester the evidence there is scrappy and inconclusive. B. L. Woodcock, *Medieval Ecclesiastical Courts in the Diocese of Canterbury* (London, 1952), p. 86; M. Bowker, *The Henrician Reformation: the diocese of Lincoln under John Longland* (Cambridge, 1981), p. 53.
[20] Bowker, *Secular Clergy*, pp. 90–1, 104–5; Bowker, *Henrician Reformation*, p. 43; Heath, *English Parish Clergy*, pp. 56–69.
[21] J. I. Daeley, 'Pluralism in the diocese of Canterbury during the administration of Matthew Parker', *J.E.H.*, XVIII (1967), pp. 42–3; R. B. Manning, *Religion and Society in Elizabethan Sussex* (Leicester, 1969), pp. 55–9; Haigh, *Reformation and Resistance*, pp. 239, 241.

The Probate Act may also have benefited few, for though the new scale of fees exempted the poor and reduced the payments of the rich, it threw a heavier burden on middling groups. It is not easy to gauge the impact of the act, since the practice of diocesan courts had varied and the evidence is sometimes scrappy. But in the archdeaconry of Norwich in the 1520s the poor had already been released from probate fees, and forty per cent of wills were proved free, except for a shilling to the scribe for registration. In the dioceses of Canterbury and Lincoln, probate fees were still levied in accordance with a scale introduced by Archbishop Stratford in 1341 and now eroded by inflation, though in two Lincoln archdeaconries there is evidence of profiteering in scribal fees; in Chichester diocese, probate fees were considerably lower than the Stratford scale. If probate ever was a genuine grievance, it was probably confined to prosperous townsmen: the issue was raised in 1529 by the London Mercers, and, since fees were charged on the value of moveable goods and not land, the system discriminated against merchants and favoured landowners.[22]

Thus the three statutes of 1529 were not the product of popular clamour or widespread discontent: the issues seem to have been raised by specific interest groups, and the objective may have been an attack on Wolsey and his allies rather than the clergy in general. Though the draft bills were perhaps more explosive, the acts which were passed were the dampest of squibs, dramatic only in comparison with the claims made by their proponents and minor changes in comparison with ecclesiastical practice. The statutes were certainly not an anticlericals' charter, and in the next six years there were only 210 prosecutions in the Exchequer Court for clerical breaches of the statutes: these charges were mainly brought by informers and troublemakers, and only fourteen of them were pressed to a conclusion, while 'anticlerical' Londoners charged only seven of their priests in the 1530s.[23] One is tempted to propose that the significance attached to the 1529 statutes is entirely unwarranted, and probably results from the selective report of the session given by Edward Hall. It is surely misleading to label as 'The Anticlerical Commons' a body which in 1529 passed twenty-six bills, only three of them on ecclesiastical issues and the rest mainly on criminal law, land tenure and trade.[24] The legislative evidence of the first session of the Reformation Parliament does not demonstrate the existence of general 'anticlericalism'.

The third session, however, returned to ecclesiastical problems, and the 'Commons Supplication against the Ordinaries', a broad attack on Church courts, was presented

---

[22] Bowker, *Henrician Reformation*, pp. 51–3; Houlbrooke, *Church Courts*, pp. 95, 114–15; Woodcock, *Medieval Ecclesiastical Courts*, p. 73; Chapter 2 above, p. 45.

[23] J. J. Scarisbrick, 'The Conservative Episcopate in England, 1529–1535' (University of Cambridge Ph.D. thesis, 1955), pp. 88–94; Brigden, 'Early Reformation in London', p. 32.

[24] Lehmberg, *Reformation Parliament*, pp. 97–9. Professor Lehmberg subtitles his chapter on the 1529 session 'The Anti-Clerical Commons'.

to the king. The 'Supplication' poses three difficulties for historians: its authorship and intention; the accuracy of its charges; and the representativeness of the opposition it declares. Each of these raises complex and technical problems, which cannot be discussed in detail here, but a few general comments and some supporting evidence may be offered. The origin of the 'Supplication' is a controversial matter, though the involvement of Thomas Cromwell in the early drafts of 1529 and the final version of 1532 seems clear. It was suggested by the late J. P. Cooper that the 'Supplication' was put into its final form in response to 'anticlerical' agitation in the Commons from early in the 1532 session, while G. R. Elton thought that the document was introduced to the House by Thomas Cromwell to raise a new wave of protest and carry through a preconceived attack on Church courts.[25] The balance of evidence and probability seems to lie with Professor Elton, and J. A. Guy has stressed the role of Cromwell even more vigorously, arguing that the presentation of the 'Supplication' was an independent initiative by Cromwell, an audacious attempt to use the Commons to press the king towards a more radical ecclesiastical policy.[26] Whether Cromwell would have dared to undertake such a dangerous manoeuvre is doubtful, but it may be that he had little choice.

In the 1532 session the competence of Cromwell as a manager of Crown business in the Commons was in question: he had failed to secure passage of bills on uses and a subsidy, and the bill designed to further the king's annulment by challenging papal annates was likely to be blocked – Henry and his minister had to make unprecedented efforts to get the Annates Bill through. It may not be a coincidence that the 'Supplication' was presented to the king on the day before the House of Lords finally gave the bill its third reading, with almost all the lay peers voting in favour, or that the Commons was asked to discuss the bill after having been reminded of clerical greed and oppression by discussion of Church courts. Even so, the Annates Bill was forced through the Commons only with great difficulty, after Henry VIII had ordered that those who opposed him should, quite literally, stand up and be counted.[27] The bill was opposed in the Lords by the bishops and abbots, and perhaps in the Commons it was the merchants who took the lead, as they would in 1533 against the Appeals Bill for fear of economic retaliation by Charles V.[28] If there was, in 1532, a tacit alliance between the prelates and some members of the Commons then the 'Supplication' focused cleverly on just those issues which would divide them: the speed and cost of litigation in Church courts; the relationship between secular and ecclesiastical jurisdictions (which was of obvious interest to lawyers and

[25] J. P. Cooper, 'The Supplication against the Ordinaries Reconsidered', *E.H.R.*, LXXII (1957), pp. 616–41; G. R. Elton, *Studies in Tudor and Stuart Politics and Government*, 2 vols (Cambridge, 1974), II, pp. 107–36; Elton, *Reform and Reformation*, pp. 150–5.

[26] J. A. Guy, *The Public Career of Sir Thomas More* (Brighton, 1980), pp. 186–92.

[27] Lehmberg, *Reformation Parliament*, pp. 132–8; Elton, *Reform and Reformation*, pp. 149–50.

[28] Lehmberg, *Reformation Parliament*, pp. 137–8, 174–5.

sometimes caused friction in cathedral cities[29]); and the Church's treatment of independent-minded laymen – and, for good measure, the document added extraneous issues to drum up any further support which was available.[30] The 'Supplication' may thus have been a desperate tactical ploy by Cromwell, designed to turn the Commons against the bishops, and thus save both the Annates Bill and a promising political career. Certainly, the 'Supplication' was of no more than temporary significance, for the Commons showed no interest in pressing their complaints after presenting them to the king (even asking for Parliament to be dissolved), and, though the theoretical implications of the concessions the bishops finally had to make were enormous, their practical consequences were minimal.

Though the 'Supplication', to be effective, must have appealed to the ambitions and interests of some, we now know that the specific charges it made were largely untrue. The burden of the case against the Church courts was that they were dilatory, inefficient, expensive and operated to maximise profits for officials rather than provide justice for litigants, but evidence from the dioceses of Chichester, Lincoln, Norwich and Winchester suggests that the case cannot be substantiated.[31] Probate was granted speedily, and if litigation was unhurried it was certainly handled faster and more effectively than in common law courts, while court fees were in reality much lower than was claimed. That a large majority of those prosecuted admitted charges against them suggests that accusations were not made for the sake of fees, and in cases between parties judges aimed to secure early agreement rather than press matters on to an expensive conclusion. The bishops were clearly baffled by the complaints made against the courts, and while they admitted there might be individual faults they insisted that the system was generally fair.[32] It has, however, been argued that the real grievance which moved the Commons was fear of heresy prosecutions and the inability of laymen to provide a convincing defence: 1531–2 saw a spate of burnings for heresy, of educated clergy and Londoners rather than ignorant Lollards, and it was certainly thought that the Church was attempting to stifle criticism by repression.[33] But there remains the general issue of principle raised

[29] See, for example, Clark, *English Provincial Society*, pp. 28, 39, for Canterbury, where there was trouble in 1531.

[30] As well as the legal issues, the 'Supplication' complained about the cost of institutions to benefices and about nepotism by the bishops (issues which presumably bothered only the lower clergy); that there were too many holidays in harvest time; and that clergy were employed in estate administration. See the text of the 'Supplication' in C. H. Williams ed., *English Historical Documents, 1485–1558* (London, 1971), pp. 732–6.

[31] Chapter 2 above, pp. 44–5; M. Bowker, 'The Commons Supplication against the Ordinaries in the light of some Archidiaconal *acta*', *T.R.H.S.*, 5th series, XXI (1971), pp. 62–74; Houlbrooke, *Church Courts*, pp. 42, 95–6; 112, 114–16, 263.

[32] Bowker, 'Commons Supplication', pp. 76–7; H. Gee and W. J. Hardy, *Documents Illustrative of English Church History* (London, 1896), pp. 154–76.

[33] Bowker, 'Commons Supplication', pp. 75–6; Guy, *Public Career of Sir Thomas More*, pp. 164–74; Lehmberg, *Reformation Parliament*, pp. 83, 84.

by the 'Supplication' – the range of the jurisdiction of the Church's canons and courts – and while historians have tended to question the real significance of this matter it was probably a major reason why the 'Supplication' found support in the Commons.

There was one obvious group which stood to gain from an attack on the jurisdiction of the Church, and that was the common lawyers: they had for some time been trying to claim classes of litigation from the Church for themselves, and the scope of the 'spiritualty' was a lively issue among them.[34] For reasons which are still far from clear, there had been a marked decline in the business of the Westminster courts of King's Bench and Common Pleas since the early fifteenth century, and although there had been temporary recoveries the volume of litigation had sunk to crisis level by the 1520s. There was thus a serious imbalance between the supply of common lawyers and the demand for their services, and in the 1520s this may partly have been because of competition from Chancery and from Star Chamber and the 'under courts' of the Council.[35] Though it is still not certain that the decline of common law litigation resulted from a transference of business to other courts, it is not surprising if the lawyers thought it was; indeed, in the 1460s and after, the consistory court of Canterbury was certainly dealing with a mass of litigation on debt and breach of contract (under the rubric of 'breach of faith') which would earlier have gone to Common Pleas. From the reign of Henry VII, common lawyers attempted to reclaim business which they regarded as properly their own: a series of prohibitions and especially *praemunire* writs challenged the Church's power to hear contract cases, and from 1492 this class of business dwindled rapidly at Canterbury.[36] *Praemunire* cases in King's Bench tested the Church's jurisdiction in other spheres, and from 1508 King's Bench began to hear defamation cases in which the slander related to a secular offence, while Chancery and the Council courts were also subjected to common law attacks.[37] Thus the common lawyers who were, as we have seen, an important group in the Commons and who staffed the committee which had produced the drafts from which the 'Supplication' was constructed, had narrow professional reasons for pressing on the political front the campaign against the Church they were already waging in the courts and in print. The 'Supplication' may have been a lawyers' tactic, with other issues added to the central problem of jurisdiction to seek wider support; more probably it was a Cromwellian measure, brought forward with confidence that the selfish interests of the lawyers would lead them to back it.

[34] *The Reports of Sir John Spelman*, ed. J. H. Baker, 2 vols (Selden Society, 1977), II, pp. 65–8.
[35] M. Blatcher, *The Court of King's Bench, 1450–1550* (London, 1978), pp. 15–28; E. W. Ives, 'The Common Lawyers in Pre-Reformation England', *T.R.H.S.*, 5th series, XVIII (1968), pp. 165–7; J. A. Guy, *The Cardinal's Court* (Hassocks, 1977), pp. 41–3, 51–78.
[36] Woodcock, *Medieval Ecclesiastical Courts*, pp. 89–92; Houlbrooke, *Church Courts*, pp. 8–9; *Reports*, ed. Baker, II, pp. 48, 53, 65–8.
[37] *Ibid.*, pp. 237–43, 73, 77–9.

The 'Supplication' certainly advanced the professional interests of lawyers and its charges against Church courts were largely unjust, but the protest may nevertheless exemplify a wider hostility towards Church courts; it may still reflect 'anti-clericalism'. Assessment of public attitudes towards ecclesiastical courts is not easy, for most extended treatments of the issue come from the partial pens of common lawyers and erastian reformers and more pungent comments are usually from aggrieved victims of the Church's justice. One may easily find examples of verbal abuse of courts and their officials, and such characteristically anal humour need not be reproduced here. What we should make of such vituperation is less clear, since it has always been the habit of losing teams to blame referees. One can hardly treat such acrimony statistically, but it does seem to have been rare (or rarely reported) before the Reformation,[38] and this may be linked to other evidence of obedience to – if not necessarily respect for – Church courts. In comparison with secular courts and the position in Church courts later, a remarkably high proportion of those cited to appear before ecclesiastical tribunals did so. In Canterbury diocese in the late fifteenth century, three-quarters of defendants in instance suits appeared, and almost as many appeared to answer office prosecutions in the early sixteenth century. The higher courts of the diocese of Lincoln secured a high level of co-operation from defendants: in the first thirty years of the sixteenth century only one man refused to appear before the court of audience, tearing up his citation, and almost all those accused admitted the charges against them. The lower courts, however, in Lincoln and elsewhere, found it more difficult to enforce attendance, and only about a third of defendants admitted charges in the courts of archdeacons. But even in the lesser courts the level of resistance did not cause major problems, and the courts could transact their business with reasonable efficiency.[39]

But, from the 1530s, as preaching of reformed religion and official limitation on the coercive power of the Church weakened respect for its institutions and its sanctions, the courts found it more difficult to enforce appearance and obedience. From the mid-1530s the consistory at Chichester had to use the sterner sanction of excommunication rather than merely suspension to bring the recalcitrant to order, and the same change of policy took place at Norwich fifteen years later. In the diocese of Chester in the reign of Mary, more than eighty per cent of those presented at visitation were still appearing at correction courts, but by the 1590s this had collapsed to about thirty per cent at both diocesan and metropolitan visitations: a national average for the rate of appearances seems to be about forty per cent by the early seventeenth century. At the Gloucester consistory in the middle of Elizabeth's reign,

[38] Bowker, *Henrician Reformation*, pp. 54–5.

[39] Woodcock, *Medieval Ecclesiastical Courts*, p. 100; Bowker, *Henrician Reformation*, pp. 54–6; Haigh, *Reformation and Resistance*, pp. 14–17.

two-thirds of defendants failed to appear before the court and had to be excommunicated, and in the 1580s the Chester consistory was excommunicating an average of 112 people a year from roughly twice as many cases.[40] Although it cannot be demonstrated systematically, it may be that this rising level of contumacy was accompanied by an increasing volume of abuse of courts, judges and apparitors, though this may be an illusion of the evidence as nervous officials tried harder to stifle criticism.[41] While one could hardly argue that obedience to the pre-Reformation courts demonstrated affection and later disobedience showed new 'anticlericalism', it does seem that the Reformation changed the attitude of those summoned from grudging respect to widespread contempt.

We have so far discussed the view of Church courts taken by two groups who felt themselves victims of ecclesiastical jurisdiction, the common lawyers and defendants. But the opinion of those who instituted court proceedings was presumably different, since they chose to use the courts for their own purposes. The volume of instance litigation before the Church courts declined from the 1490s, with the common lawyers' use of prohibitions and *praemunire* to capture contract business from the Church and with the development of new forms of action which made the common law more attractive to businessmen. Though there seems to have been a recovery in the period of Wolsey's dominance, the attack on ecclesiastical jurisdiction made in the *praemunire* charge of 1531 and the 'Supplication' of 1532 led to a collapse of court business in the 1530s: the Chichester and Norwich consistories had in 1534 only half the litigation they had dealt with a decade earlier. But when the official campaign against Church jurisdiction went no further, business began to return, and from the 1530s to the 1590s the volume of litigation boomed. It is true that part of the increase is to be explained by the expansion of tithe business, in which the plaintiffs were often clergy, but laymen too initiated larger numbers of cases and at Chester, Norwich, Winchester and York defamation and testamentary business together increased from a quarter to a half of the total.[42] Thus, except for the loss of one whole class of litigation (which, indeed, the Church had only gained from the common law courts in the fifteenth century) and a temporary uncertainty which resulted from official policy, ecclesiastical courts retained their appeal as dispute-resolving agencies – and they did so because they were accessible, efficient

---

[40] Chapter 2 above, p. 50; Houlbrooke, *Church Courts*, p. 49; Haigh, *Reformation and Resistance*, pp. 232, 235; Marchant, *Church under the Law*, pp. 204–9; F. D. Price, 'The Abuse of Excommunication and the Decline of Ecclesiastical Discipline under Queen Elizabeth', *E.H.R.*, LVII (1942), pp. 109–11.

[41] Houlbrooke, *Church Courts*, p. 49; Haigh, *Reformation and Resistance*, p. 16.

[42] *Reports*, ed. Baker, II, pp. 48, 53, 65–7; Woodstock, *Medieval Ecclesiatical Courts*, p. 84; Chapter 2 above, p. 49; Houlbrooke, *Church Courts*, pp. 37–8, 273–4, Haigh, *Reformation and Resistance*, p. 227 and n; Marchant, *Church under the Law*, pp. 16–20, 61–2.

and relatively cheap. Whatever defendants may have thought, the courts seem to have been popular among plaintiffs and the instance side of their work was well supported.

It is therefore impossible to define a general 'layman's view' of the ecclesiastical courts, since attitudes varied according to the interests of individuals. The poor, whose sexual irregularities made them the most numerous victims of the disciplinary powers of the Church, might abuse the churchwardens who presented them, the apparitors who called them to correction and the judges who imposed penance. But the respectable parishioners, who wished to ensure there would be no bastard children to be supported by the parish, determinedly presented suspected fornicators, and if they had a complaint it was not that the discipline of the Church was oppressive but that it was sometimes ineffective.[43] There is little evidence in the work of the courts that lay hostility might have been provoked, and court records give minimal support for any presumption of wide spread 'anticlericalism'. But, once again, if the courts ever did contribute to lay antagonism towards the Church it was probably after the Reformation rather than before. From the 1580s onwards, concern for a 'reformation of manners' increased the prosecution of sexual offenders and presumably expanded the number of resentful victims.[44] In this respect, too, 'anticlericalism' was an Elizabethan consequence of the Reformation and not a Henrician cause.

The act books and cause papers of consistory courts do, however, enable us to investigate an issue which is assumed to have been a potent cause of friction between priests and people and a major reason for 'anticlericalism' – tithe. If the case of Richard Hunne was not typical of lay attitudes towards mortuaries, then the troubles of Henry Gold at Hayes in Middlesex do not exemplify common views of tithe: these were isolated clashes, not examples of endemic conflict. There *were* local struggles over the payment of tithe, and in a few cases they dragged on for years and caused obvious bitterness, but we must keep such disputes in perspective. Tithe litigation was almost always about interpretation of local custom rather than the principle of tithing, and it was, at least before the mid-sixteenth century, rare.[45] We do not know how many parish quarrels there were over tithe, only how often rectors and vicars (and also lay lessees) sued tithe-resisters – but, since it was claimed by lawyers that the clergy were too ready to sue for tithe when a polite request or a compromise might have worked,[46] 'anticlericals' might regard suits as a high

---

[43] Houlbrooke, *Church Courts*, pp. 75–9, 86–7.
[44] K. Wrightson and D. Levine, *Poverty and Piety in an English Village: Terling, 1525–1700* (New York, 1979), pp. 119, 126–7; K. Wrightson, *English Society, 1580–1680* (London, 1982), pp. 209–12.
[45] The disagreements which produced tithe litigation are discussed in Houlbrooke, *Church Courts*, pp. 122–36. See also Haigh, *Reformation and Resistance*, pp. 25–6, 58–62.
[46] Cf. the complaint about unnecessary mortuary suits in the 'Supplication', in Williams, ed., *English Historical Documents*, p. 735.

proportion of quarrels! In the late-medieval diocese of Canterbury, with about 250 parishes, there were fourteen tithe suits in 1482 and four in 1531; Norwich diocese produced only ten cases from 1148 parishes in 1524; Winchester had three cases from 339 parishes in 1529; and the 650 parishes of the diocese of Lichfield yielded ten cases in 1525 and four in 1530.[47] There were particular difficulties in London, with the intractable problem of personal tithes, and there were disputes between the clergy and the City over tithing terms in 1519, 1528 and 1533–4. But even in the litigious metropolis, only one-third of parishes produced tithe suits between 1521 and 1546, and Londoners had some conscience over tithe – seventy per cent of testators left money in their wills for 'forgotten tithes'.[48] One may hardly suppose that tithe-paying was popular, and certainly there is evidence that the payment of tithe to non-resident pluralists was resented, but in general tithe does not seem to have been a divisive issue before the Reformation. It became so, it seems, only from the 1540s, as inflation reduced the real value of commuted cash payments and incumbents sought to overthrow *modi*: parishioners resisted, and the annual number of tithe causes before the courts doubled between the 1540s and the 1560s in Norwich and Winchester, with similar increases elsewhere.[49] If tithe caused 'anticlericalism', it can hardly have done so before the middle of the sixteenth century.

Thus the three classes of evidence which historians have used to try to demonstrate 'anticlericalism' – literary, legislative and litigatory – are weak foundations for such a significant edifice. They show only that some individuals and interests had grievances against Wolsey, that certain small groups in society (such as Lutherans and lawyers) had their own reasons for attacking the Church, that those who lost their suits sometimes complained about the courts, and that there was friction in a few parishes between priest and people. The evidence yields cases of special pleading or of localised tension, not examples of a general clash between laity and clergy. Court material shows conflict, and in the nature of things that is what the sources record – but the conflict is isolated, occasional and individual. We may find individual clerics who by negligence or quarrelsomeness fell out with some of their parishioners; we find problems in the interpretation of tithing or mortuary customs. But we do not find enough cases and sufficient evidence of bitterness to justify a general concept of 'anticlericalism' in the early sixteenth century. There is not very much evidence, beyond that drawn from common lawyers, that men thought in terms of distinct

[47] Woodcock, *Medieval Ecclesiastical Courts*, p. 86; Houlbrooke, *Church Courts*, pp. 273, 274; Heath, *English Parish Clergy*, p. 152.
[48] Brigden, 'Early Reformation in London', pp. 44–60. Bequests for 'forgotten tithes' were also common among townsmen in York diocese, and may have been a response to the neglect of personal tithes: D. M. Gransby, 'Tithe Disputes in the Diocese of York, 1540–1639' (University of York M.Phil. thesis, 1966), pp. 45–6.
[49] Houlbrooke, *Church Courts*, pp. 146–50, 273, 274; Bowker, *Henrician Reformation*, pp. 135–6; Haigh, *Reformation and Resistance*, pp. 58–61, 152; Marchant, *Church under the Law*, p. 62.

categories of laity and clergy, and that priests were identified as a homogeneous caste which could be uniformly condemned. There was, in the 1510s and 1520s as there had ever been, complaint about inadequate parish clergy and parasitic monks, but criticism came as strongly from Colet, Fisher and Longland as from any 'anticlerical' laymen. When both bishops and educated laymen pressed for improvement in clerical education and in pastoral care, and by more careful examination of ordination candidates[50] and bequests for stipendiaries and preachers set about achieving improvement, it seems absurd to divide the reform movement and label one part of it 'anticlerical'. We should also not exaggerate the volume and significance of the moralists' protest, since when we examine visitation returns which show the frequency of lay complaint we find a quiescence which is, given the alleged prevalence of 'anticlericalism', surprising.

But if we approach the question of lay–clerical relations from a different perspective, determined to understand the nature of late medieval religion and community life rather than to explain the Reformation, the infrequent presentment of priests is not at all strange. The parish priest was, after all, the dispenser of saving sacraments, the pastor and reconciler, and one of the leaders of the village. In any form of collective action, whether tenants negotiating with a landlord, local riots over enclosure or a full-scale rebellion, clergy were in the forefront, not only because they were literate and could frame articles of complaint, but also because their presence gave legitimacy to protest and their people naturally turned to them for guidance. In the Pilgrimage of Grace, rebels from Howdenshire and the Vale of York marched in parish contingents, each group led by its priest carrying the church cross, while the Cumbrian rebels nominated four Chaplains of Poverty.[51] Though not all priests were worthy of it, the clerical state had enormous prestige. Clergy were, after all, laymen who had elected to become priests, and the high level of recruitment to the secular clergy does not suggest that laymen were contemptuous of priesthood. The financial attractiveness of priestly life in the early sixteenth century was low and falling, since the majority of ordinands would spend their careers as ill-paid assistants because there were too many recruits for the places available,[52] so the evidence of ordinations is all the more impressive. Recruitment rates varied enormously between areas, and southern England (especially London) produced proportionately fewer ordinands than the Midlands and North, but these discrepancies had existed for at least 150 years. Recruitment of secular clergy was in decline in the late fourteenth and early fifteenth centuries, but this was later reversed and

---

[50] Bowker, *Henrician Reformation*, pp. 39–40.
[51] M. Bateson, ed., 'The Manner of the Taking of Robert Aske', *E.H.R.*, v, (1890), p. 334; *L.P.*, XI, 729; XII (1), 687.
[52] Zell, 'Economic problems of the parochial clergy', pp. 19–30.

there were peaks in ordinations in the 1510s and 1520s. Although the population in the 1520s was about the same as it had been a century earlier, in several dioceses the level of recruitment was significantly higher. In the diocese of Lichfield, roughly twice as many priests were ordained in each year between 1504 and 1529 as had been ordained on average between 1364 and 1384, and in some years there were three times as many; average annual ordinations at York in the 1520s were about fifty per cent higher than they had been in the late fourteenth century or the mid fifteenth.[53]

The registers of Lichfield and Lincoln, dioceses which between them covered the bulk of midland England, suggest that ordinations reached their highest levels in the 1510s, the decade of Hunne and Standish. Recruitment fell back somewhat in the 1520s, but only relatively, and it remained vigorous; perhaps heavy clerical taxation for Wolsey's wars was responsible, or career prospects may have declined still further after the boom recruitment of the 1510s. But the attacks upon the clergy which began in 1529 had an immediate impact on ordinations, which collapsed in Hereford, Lichfield, London and York in 1530 (though the fall did not come until 1536 in Lincoln).[54] It seems likely that the agitation against Churchmen did begin to change public attitudes, and in consequence fewer candidates for the priesthood presented themselves. If ordinations provide some index of the prestige of the clergy, the Reformation was accompanied but not preceded by a decline in their reputation. It is difficult to believe that if laymen *had* been 'anticlerical' before 1529 they would have entered the priesthood in anything like the numbers they did, or that they would have provided financial support for such large numbers of priests. We now know that perhaps as many as half of the serving parish clergy were not beneficed incumbents but curates, chaplains and stipendiaries, and there was an unknown additional number of private chaplains and mass-priests living off trentals or short-term endowments. Some of the unbeneficed were paid as deputies by absentee incumbents or as assistants, and others received the profits from endowments, but many were supported by the voluntary offerings of the laity. In south Lancashire in 1541, seventy priests were paid by local gentlemen, twenty-six from parish offerings and six by groups of laymen (as against thirty-three paid by incumbents), and in Winchester diocese seventy-five were paid by gentlemen, nineteen by parishioners and nine by fraternities (though almost 200 were paid by incumbents

---

[53] R. L. Storey, 'Recruitment of English Clergy in the Period of the Conciliar Movement', *Annuarium Historiae Conciliorum*, VII (1977), pp. 290–312; L.J.R.O., B/A/1/14(i) (Reg. Blythe); B.I.Y., R/I/27 (Reg. Wolsey). I am grateful to Dr W. J. Sheils for help with the York figures.

[54] L.A.O., Bishops' Registers 25 and 26 (Reg. Atwater and Reg. Longland); *Register of Charles Bothe*, ed. A. T. Bannister (Canterbury and York Society, 1921); Guildhall R.O., MS. 9531/10 (Reg. Tunstall), fos. 152–63; Chapter 4 below, pp. 78–9. I am grateful to Mrs M. Bowker and to Dr S. E. Brigden for help with Lincoln and London figures.

or from tithe leases).[55] Other clergy had an uncertain living from bequests for masses, and, while it would not be fair to adduce benefactions to religious purposes as direct evidence of attitudes towards priests, it can at least be said that if there was hostility to clergy it did not inhibit giving: bequests to the Church, like recruitment, peaked in the 1510s and fell rapidly only in the 1530s and after.[56]

In sum, therefore, those numerical indicators which ought in some way to be related to approval of the clergy – recruitment and benefactions – increased before the Reformation and fell during it; those indicators which show conflict, such as mortuary and tithe litigation, were at a low level before the Reformation and rose thereafter. Personal abuse of clergy seems not to have been common before the Reformation, and rarely led to defamation suits, but this changed from the 1530s: no Lancashire priests sued laymen for slander in the 1520s, but three did so in the 1530s (all after 1536) and ten brought cases in the 1540s, while by the reign of Elizabeth verbal abuse of ministers was commonplace.[57] There were cases of conflict and cases of co-operation, but in the years before religious change was thrust upon an unwilling people the co-operation was very much more evident than the conflict. From the point of view of the parishes, the Reformation was an external, autonomous event, which they had in no sense chosen, caused or contributed towards, for even where there was some friction between clergy and people it contributed little to religious change. There had been tension between ecclesiastical bodies and civic authorities in Canterbury and York before the Reformation, but both cities were important conservative centres as late as the 1560s and Protestant advance was resisted by civic leaders.[58] The Lancashire parishes of Chipping and Ribchester were riven by long and apparently bitter tithe disputes in the 1540s, with churchwardens pawning church plate to sustain cases against the absentee incumbent of both rectories, but by the end of Elizabeth's reign they were notable areas of Catholic recusancy.[59] There was no necessary incompatibility between criticism of priests and a strong commitment to orthodox Catholicism, as the commonplace book of John Collins, a London mercer, demonstrates. Collins was a member of the company which had campaigned most vigorously against Wolsey in 1529, and his book contains a large number of poems critical of prelates in general and Wolsey in particular, who were blamed for 'the ruin of a realm'. But Collins headed each page 'Jhus', copied out stories of Catholic devotion and miracles, and reproduced pious prayers for souls in purgatory: when he made his will in 1538 it was orthodox

[55] Haigh, *Reformation and Resistance*, p. 65; *Register of Stephen Gardiner*, ed. H. Chitty (Canterbury and York Society, 1930), pp. 174–85.

[56] W. G. Bittle and R. T. Lane, 'Inflation and Philanthropy in England: a Re-assessment of W. K. Jordan's Data', *Economic History Review*, 2nd series, XXXIX (1976), p. 209.

[57] Haigh, *Reformation and Resistance*, pp. 56, 221, 242; Tyler, 'Church Courts at York', pp. 94–5.

[58] Clark, *English Provincial Society*, pp. 26, 28, 98, 140–1, 154; D. M. Palliser, *Tudor York* (Oxford, 1979), pp. 55, 88–90, 244–8.

[59] Haigh, *Reformation and Resistance*, pp. 60–1, 253, 284, 316–17, 318.

in tone and he provided for masses for his soul.[60] If his views are to be labelled 'anticlerical', then it was the 'anticlericalism' of Catholic reform, not that of Protestantism or secularist lay rebellion, and it is difficult to see how such opinions can have contributed to the Reformation.

If we seek the origins of the Reformation, we shall find them not in any general 'anticlericalism' but in the aspirations of particular interest groups: the common lawyers who coveted ecclesiastical litigation and the Court politicians who aimed to make or salvage careers by taking advantage of the king's concern for the succession. Nor need we hope to find in 'anticlericalism' an explanation for easy acceptance of religious change, since we now know that enforcing the Reformation was a much more difficult task than was once thought.[61] We need not assume, on the basis of a collection of individual conflicts and an impressionistic survey of propagandist criticism, that there was any widespread hostility towards priests. If the spiritual aspirations of some laymen were increasing, these were met in the flood of pious books for laymen published in the 1520s: a convincing 'discontented anticlerical' should hardly be sought among readers of the works of Richard Whitford.[62] The mechanical observances of the rural poor would not have satisfied London merchants such as John Collins, but it is a common error to regard Church and clergy as monolithic structures: a range of specialised religious products was on offer to each sector of the market, from intense spirituality under the direction of Carthusians and Brigittines to simple services from Sir John Lack-Latin. The English Church had trouble with its laity not before the Reformation, when the product range was wide, but from the middle of the reign of Elizabeth, when the variety of provision contracted and a more homogeneous sales-force marketed only one brand at a fixed, high price. The single orthodoxy of late-Tudor England, a religion of spartan services and long, moralising sermons, provoked the popular anticlericalism which even mortuaries had not caused – Richard Hunne notwithstanding. The minister who stressed Bible-reading to a largely illiterate congregation, who denigrated the cycle of fast and feast linked to the harvest year, who replaced active ritual with tedious sermons to pew-bound parishioners, and who refused to supply protective magic for this world and the next, was naturally less popular than his priestly predecessor. Hence, as Keith Thomas has noted, the rise of the cunning men and wizards, whose prevalence is a demonstration of the shortcomings, from the parishioners' point of view, of the reformed clergy.[63]

If it was clericalism which begat anticlericalism, we shall find the latter in the

[60] B.L., Harleian MS. 2252, discussed in Brigden, 'Early Reformation in London', pp. 35–7.
[61] G. R. Elton, Policy and Police (Cambridge, 1972), esp. pp. 1–170; Chapter 1 above, p. 27.
[62] J. Rhodes, 'Private Devotion in England on the Eve of the Reformation' (University of Durham Ph.D. thesis, 1974), pp. 155, 176–95, 309–10, 385.
[63] K. Thomas, Religion and the Decline of Magic (London, 1973 edition), pp. 27–89, 209–332, 762–5.

Elizabethan Church: the post-Reformation ministry, with its university education and professional cohesion, was much more clericalist than the pre-Reformation priesthood.[64] The numerical decline of the unbeneficed created a more uniformly prosperous ministry, while a tithe-supported clergy was less dependent upon the laity, despite the illusion created by town lectureships. Educated clerics served where college patronage took them, not in their native parishes, while clerical inter-marriage and synods and exercises may have created a horizontal nexus of clerical contacts at the expense of parochial relationships. The minister may have come to seem an outsider rather than a member of the community, who intruded only to complain about alehouses and present fornicators at visitation. It was complained of two Rochdale men in 1585 that

> both of these speak evil and contemptuous words against Mr Midgeley, a godly and approved learned preacher and our vicar, and said that the old religion which he belied was better than that used in these unquiet times, and that he was a Yorkshire plague, and moreover said that he had travailed to bring in Mr Greves and other strange prattling preachers of no good report, who clog with their tongues and only for much wages.

The two malcontents were innkeepers, who led a party among the parishioners opposed to Midgeley's long sermons, compulsory catechism classes and enforcement of Sunday observance.[65] Of course, selective quotation of those who condemned clerical marriage, regulation of conduct, sermons and tithe-gathering will prove post-Reformation anticlericalism no more effectively than it tried to prove pre-Reformation anticlericalism. But the post-Reformation context of criticism was significantly different, and made individual clashes more dangerous. When the ministers preached justification by faith, predestination and the priesthood of all believers, they cut away the theology which had bolstered the position of even unworthy predecessors. The pressure of inflation had made tithe conflict much more common and lay–clerical relations more likely to be soured. The Church was a more obviously repressive institution, with ecclesiastical commissions to hound even the gentry and ever-lengthier presentments of sexual and sabbath offenders. These were the circumstances which prompted lay hostility towards ministers and turned laymen to sullen indifference towards established religion or to separatism.[66] 'Anti-clericalism', in short, was not a cause of the Reformation; it was a result.

[64] R. O'Day, *The English Clergy: the Emergence and Consolidation of a Profession* (Leicester, 1979), pp. 1–23, 126–43.

[65] *Ibid.*, pp. 159–206; C. Haigh, 'Puritan Evangelism in the Reign of Elizabeth I', *E.H.R.*, XCII (1977), pp. 49, 57.

[66] O'Day, *English Clergy*, pp. 205–21; Clark, *English Provincial Society*, pp. 156–9, 177–8, 182–3; C. Haigh, 'The Church of England, the Catholics and the People', in C. Haigh, ed., *The Reign of Elizabeth I* (Basingstoke, 1984).

4

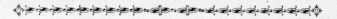

THE HENRICIAN REFORMATION
AND THE PARISH CLERGY

MARGARET BOWKER

'The scanty band of martyrs' to the Catholic cause[1] during the reign of Henry VIII
poses a question for the historian of the Henrician Reformation which is still far from
receiving a wholly satisfactory answer. Whatever the causes of the Pilgrimage of
Grace, however varied the particular regional grievances which fuelled it, it cannot
be regarded solely in terms of religious protest, and it was geographically confined.[2]
The vicar of Podington in Bedfordshire might tell his parishioners in November
1536, 'Take ye heed what ye do, for the Lincolnshire men are up, and they come
for a common wealth and a good intent, and their opinion is good, and yours is
nought', but he did not raise his congregation, and his very words suggest they were
not in sympathy with him even though they did not report him immediately.[3] For
the most part, the people of England appeared to acquiesce in the religious changes
of the 1530s: whether they were won over by the government's policy of propaganda
or whether their silence was a grudging acceptance of the inevitable we do not
know.[4] But it was no small matter to change the basis of authority within the church,
to translate that authority into an active and inquisitorial royal supremacy,[5] and to
accompany these changes with the dissolution of the monasteries[6] and the taxation

---

[1] D. Knowles, *The Religious Orders in England* (3 vols, Cambridge, 1948–59), III, p. 369.

[2] For recent contributions to the controversies surrounding the Lincolnshire Rising and the
Pilgrimage of Grace, see C. S. L. Davies, 'The Pilgrimage of Grace reconsidered', *P.&P.*, XLI
(1968), pp. 54–76; M. E. James, 'Obedience and dissent in Henrician England: the Lincolnshire
Rebellion 1536', *P.&P.*, XLVIII (1970), 3–78; M. Bowker, 'Lincolnshire 1536: Heresy,
Schism or Religious Discontent?', *Studies in Church History*, XI, ed. D. Baker (Cambridge,
1972), pp. 195–212.

[3] G. R. Elton, *Policy and Police: the Enforcement of the Reformation in the Age of Thomas Cromwell*
(Cambridge, 1972), p. 350. There is a misprint here: Postington should be Podington, to which
John Henmarshe was admitted in 1521, L.A.O., Register 27 [Longland], fo. 255.

[4] Elton, *Policy and Police*, p. 395.

[5] See Elton, *Policy and Police*, esp. pp. 217–62; see also M. Bowker, 'The Supremacy and the
Episcopate: The Struggle for Control, 1534–40', *H.J.*, XVIII (1975), pp. 227–43.

[6] Knowles, *The Religious Orders*, III, pp. 206 *seq.*

of the clergy on an unprecedented scale.[7] Doctrinal pronouncements which were
frequently ambiguous might have meant little to those who knew nothing of the
finer points of Catholic and Lutheran theology, but even the simplest villager could
not fail to notice a change when saints' days were abolished, bibles purchased, and
shrines and places of pilgrimage and devotion were removed.[8] Nor could an
administrator like Thomas Cromwell change the religion or the covetous desires of
men's hearts with the speed with which he altered ecclesiastical powers and privileges
on the statute book. His campaign of propaganda and his insistence on the importance
of preaching in advancing the supremacy suggests that he appreciated the difficulty
of the task he had undertaken.[9] What did the parish priest make of these changes?
Was he influenced by propaganda alone or were there other factors besides that of
fear which secured silence in the face of change? Obviously those who were not
of the stuff of martyrs but who were out of sympathy with the new order would
do well not even to speak of their disquiet; unguarded words, like those of James
Mallet, who held many benefices and was treasurer of Lincoln cathedral and resident
within the close for the greater part of the 1530s[10] and was alleged to have said,
'Woo worth them that began the devorce between the Kyng and Quene Kateryne,
for syns we had never good world', could result in a fate similar to his: he was
hanged, drawn and quartered in the middle of Chelmsford in 1542.[11] Not all who
voiced their dislike of the new order suffered so badly, but it behoved men to talk
guardedly and to keep their thoughts to themselves.[12] Yet if we cannot make
windows into men's souls, nor recapture the heart-searching and confusion which
must have featured in every parish of England, we can discover some of the purely

[7] J. J. Scarisbrick, 'Clerical Taxation in England, 1485 to 1547', *J.E.H.*, XI (1960), pp. 41–54.

[8] For the most important royal injunctions see *Visitation Articles and Injunctions of the Period of
the Reformation, 1536–58*, ed. W. H. Frere and W. M. Kennedy (Alcuin Club Collections, XV,
1910), and *Documents Illustrative of English Church History*, ed. H. Gee and W. J. Hardy
(London, 1896, repr. 1972), pp. 269 *seq.* The text of the Injunctions of 1536 given by Frere
and Kennedy includes the order for a Bible in English (*Visitation Articles*, p. 9). Gee and Hardy
did not include it and Professor Elton has also discarded it (*Policy and Police*, p. 247 n 3), but
too hastily. The diocesan injunctions of 1537 for Worcester and Lichfield and Coventry include
the order, and it is highly improbable that a diocesan would proceed in this controversial
matter without the backing of a royal injunction (*Visitation Articles*, pp. 19–25). For the
limitation of holy days see *Concilia Magnae Britanniae et Hiberniae*, ed. D. Wilkins (4 vols, 1737),
III, p. 803; for a fuller text see L.A.O., Register 26, fos. 274v *seq.* For the Ten Articles see
Formularies of Faith put forth by Authority during the reign of Henry VIII, ed. C. Lloyd (Oxford,
1825), pp. xiii–xxxii, 1–19.

[9] Elton, *Policy and Police*, pp. 171 *seq.*

[10] J. Le Neve, *Fasti Ecclesiae Anglicanae 1300–1541*, I, *Lincoln Diocese*, comp. H. P. F. King
(London, 1962), p. 21.

[11] A. B. Emden, *A Biographical Register of the University of Oxford, A.D. 1501 to 1540* (Oxford,
1974), p. 374.

[12] Professor Elton has examined the discrepancy between denunciation and execution in *Policy
and Police*, pp. 393 *seq.*

practical effects of the legislation of the 1530s on the careers of the parochial clergy, and, with them, some material reasons which may have kept the band of martyrs scanty. This is not to argue that the reasons for conformity were purely material; it is simply to suggest that movements of the spirit can rarely be captured or measured, whereas some of the incentives for remaining silent in these years, notably those connected with the prospects for promotion, are capable of measurement and may have weighed heavily in individual cases.

Some important indications of the way in which, on a purely materialistic plane, the expectations of the clergy were changed by the legislation passed between 1529 and 1540 appear from the voluminous registers of John Longland, Bishop of Lincoln from 1521 until 1547, and in the scrappy visitation and court books and the fuller *liber cleri* which survive for his episcopate. The material is stark, repetitive and sometimes defective, but for most of the period ordination lists survive, and the records of institutions to benefices are very nearly complete. For half of the archdeaconries of the diocese we also have an indication of non-residence in these years. Obviously, until the comparable material in other dioceses receives similar attention, it will not be possible to assess the extent to which the diocese of Lincoln indicates a national pattern. But even if the diocese of Lincoln were to prove exceptional, its very size demands that it be given serious study. It accounted for 21.5 per cent of all the parishes in England.[13]

But the diocese of Lincoln is remarkable in the Henrician period for more than just its size. It had been singularly fortunate in its bishops, and while they were no innovators, it certainly seems as though they were reformers in the sense of paying careful attention to the demands of the canon law, particularly over such matters as residence and the pastoral care of churches.[14] John Longland was prominent in this respect, and his preaching and his attention to visiting won from William Warham a warm commendation:

> And of truthe I thynke veryly if all bysshoppes hadde doon ther duetyes as ye have in settyng forthe christes doctryne And repressing of vice by preching and otherwise, the dignytye of the church hadd nott bene soo cold and almost extencte in mennes hertes, and iniquyte hadde nott hadd so grette boldness and strenche (*sic*) as itt hath nowe increasing day by day by the grete scismatyke and heretyque Luther whose malice I beseche almighty god shortely to emende or represse att his pleasur.[15]

Almighty God did not at once answer Warham's entreaties, and Longland continued to combat Lutheranism with every power at his disposal.[16] His zeal in

[13] Figures based on P. Hughes, *The Reformation in England* (3 vols, London, 1950–4), I, pp. 33–4.
[14] For the activities of these bishops see M. Bowker, *The Secular Clergy in the Diocese of Lincoln, 1495–1520* (Cambridge, 1968).   [15] L.A.O., Register 26, fo. 206r–v.
[16] For a discussion of Longland's attitude to heresy see A. G. Chester, 'Robert Barnes and the Burning of the Books', *Huntington Library Quarterly*, XIV (1950–1), pp. 211–21; for his co-operation with Bishop Tunstal see C. Sturge, *Cuthbert Tunstal* (London, 1938), pp. 139–41.

this respect, and his desire to root out heresy in all forms may have resulted in the diocese of Lincoln being more orthodox than other dioceses. Longland's 'feryent zeale for reformation to be made as well of heritycall doctrynes, as of mysbehavioyrs in Maners',[17] which also elicited comment from Warham, may well justify our placing him with his predecessor William Atwater and his colleague Robert Sherburne of Chichester as a Catholic reformer.[18] If reform had not only begun but had been pursued for at least twenty years before the break with Rome, then the problem confronting Cromwell was not merely to effect a Protestant Reformation, with, in the case of the monasteries, strong economic overtones, but it was also to meet the critique of his policy resulting from a previous Catholic Reformation. It is therefore possible that the clergy of the Lincoln diocese may be exceptional but not unique in one particular: Cromwell's activities were not their first experience of 'Reformation' and they may, therefore, have been more aware and more intransigent than their counterparts in less favoured dioceses. If this is so their eventual acquiescence in the changes of the Henrician period is all the more remarkable.

Ironically it was facilitated by the reluctance of the laity to offer themselves for ordination. The number of men seeking ordination to the priesthood in any one year before 1531 (when the record is missing) varied considerably. In 1523 over 100 were ordained, but the number never dropped below fifty-five (see Graph I).[19] The numbers may suggest that ordination was an indiscriminate affair, but this does not appear to have been the case: a careful record survives which suggests that canonical requirements of the examination of ordinands were punctiliously observed. We even know, for some dates, who examined which candidate: on 11 March 1525 ordinands were examined by the suffragan bishop, who was in fact to conduct the service, as well as by the notorious Dr London,[20] and cryptic initials indicate the large number of bishop's commissaries who examined between 1532 and 1535.[21] A sharp decline in the number of men offering themselves for ordination occurred in 1536, and thereafter there were never more than thirty men offering themselves for ordination, and frequently the number was well below that. A similar trend is discernible in the diocese of Durham: between 1536 and 1544 no one was ordained, and thereafter only half a dozen a year were forthcoming and sometimes still fewer. In the diocese of Exeter between 1539 and 1544 only thirty men were ordained in total, and

[17] L.A.O., Register 26, fo. 206.
[18] For Sherburne's activities as a reforming diocesan see S. J. Lander, 'The diocese of Chichester, 1508–58: episcopal reform under Robert Sherburne and its aftermath' (University of Cambridge Ph.D. thesis, 1974).
[19] The ordination lists from which these figures are drawn are in L.A.O., Register 26, fos. 1v–66v.
[20] L.A.O., Register 26, fos. 17–18.   [21] Ibid., fos. 30v seq.

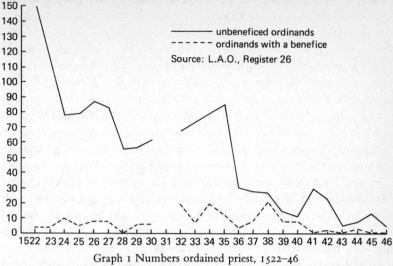

Graph 1 Numbers ordained priest, 1522–46
(the 1531 list is incomplete)

thereafter there were no ordinations until 1551, and there appear to have been no ordinations at York between 1547 and 1551.[22]

In the case of the diocese of Lincoln, the fall in numbers cannot be attributed to the absence of religious in the ordination lists resulting from the dissolution of the monasteries. The registrar kept a separate record of the ordination of religious, and those records cease in 1539 with the ordination in Lincoln cathedral of Edward Eddenham alias Seele, canon of Thornton.[23] A partial explanation for the continuous fall in numbers from their pre-1536 level is suggested by the change in the size of the diocese. In September 1541 a separate diocese of Peterborough was formed, and that removed from the jurisdiction of Lincoln the counties of Northampton and Rutland; in 1542 Oxfordshire was lost to the new see of Oxford.[24] Obviously students at Oxford seeking ordination would now present themselves to the new bishop, and fellows of colleges who are listed as already having a benefice would do the same: the fall in the number of beneficed priests, apparent after 1541, is clearly attributable to the creation of a new diocese. But this explanation does not explain the fall in the numbers of *non-beneficed* priests before 1540, before in fact there were alternative dioceses for would-be priests born in Oxfordshire, Rutland and

[22] Hughes, *Reformation in England*, III, p. 53 n. 1; D. H. Pill, 'The Administration of the Diocese of Exeter under Bishop Veysey', *Transactions of the Devonshire Association*, XCVIII (1966), pp. 269–71.

[23] L.A.O., Register 26, fo. 59v.   [24] Knowles, *The Religious Orders*, III, p. 391.

Northamptonshire, nor does it explain it in other dioceses. It is tempting to attribute this drop solely to the cessation of monastic titles which accompanied the dissolution. How could an ordinand satisfy the canonical requirement that he should have a livelihood guaranteed either by his own patrimony, or by a curacy which was assumed to be guaranteed by a monastic title? In fact all the evidence before 1536 suggests that the title had become a legal fiction,[25] and it was one which, by statute, the recipients of monastic lands might take over as it stood.[26] By 1540, for example, John Howarde of Normanby was made subdeacon to the title of John Sayntpole, and priests were ordained who had titles of royal pensions (which suggests they were ex-religious), of laymen who had received monastic lands and were guaranteeing them a patrimony, as well as titles derived from the dissolved religious houses now in the hands of the court of augmentations.[27] The centre of power had changed, and the laity and the king controlled titles in varying proportions according to the chronology of the sale of individual parcels of monastic land. It is possible that both were more scrupulous and careful in their grant of titles; it is also likely that the search for a title by a would-be ordinand was initially more difficult, not least because all the recipients of monastic lands were not locally based. But however real these difficulties may have been, the fact that any men were ordained at all suggests that the problems besetting the ordinand were not insuperable provided convictions or ambitions were strong. Similarly it is highly improbable that the lay recipients of monastic lands agreed to an unofficial self-denying ordinance by which they did not (with a few exceptions) exercise their right to provide titles and thereby deprived themselves of a source of patronage: effectively such a policy would have limited their choice of incumbents to those who were already in orders on titles supplied by others. Additional factors were clearly at work to deplete ordination lists on such a scale, and it is highly possible that the dissolution of the monasteries which disorientated titles also affected the convictions and ambitions which took men into the priesthood at all.

The fine balance between the difficulty of acquiring a title, conviction and self-interest in any one ordinand's case would be hard to ascertain. For, by 1536, there were some sound material reasons for avoiding the priesthood at least in the immediate future. We know that before 1536 there had been considerable competition for benefices. In 1521, the registrar saw fit to add to the formal particulars of the admission of a candidate to a benefice, the details of when it became vacant. Oliver Osgodby was admitted to the parish of Beelsby, which was in the patronage of the provost and chapter of Southwell, only two hours after the resignation of the last incumbent.[28] Beelsby was not a particularly wealthy living – it was valued

[25] Bowker, *Secular Clergy*, pp. 61–4.
[26] *Statutes of the Realm*, III, pp. 575–8, 27 Hen. VIII, c. 28.
[27] L.A.O., Register 26, fos. 60–61v.   [28] L.A.O., Register 27, fo. 21v.

in 1524 at £8[29] – but Oliver was clearly in a hurry: usually there was a delay of between ten days and two months – a delay necessitated in many cases by the formalities surrounding presentation. But if Oliver made it across the line, there were many who did not. In 1523, 109 men were ordained priests. We do not know what became of fifty-two of them. Some would have died and others probably experienced fates in other parts of the country comparable to those which awaited priests who stayed within the diocese and who are relatively easy to trace. Eighteen of those fifty-two were not born in the diocese and came to it on letters dimissory: some of them were probably at Oxford and none seems to have received either a benefice or a curacy within the diocese. Of the remaining fifty-seven, only twenty-one (nineteen per cent of the total ordained in 1523, or thirty-six per cent of those so ordained whose careers are known to us) received a benefice. The remaining thirty-six were still curates as late as 1543. For the ambitious who lacked the powerful patron to translate their dreams into reality, the path even to so modest an objective as a single benefice was a long one: nearly half of those successful in obtaining a benefice at all took between eleven and twenty years to do so.[30] To men in this position, the influx of the religious on to the benefice market would have been as terrifying as the arrival of a refugee column to a famine-stricken village. The dissolution of the monasteries would have made anyone with an eye for opportunity think very carefully about ordination. The pressure for benefices, always great, would be infinitely greater, and the abuses of patronage even more likely.[31]

The speed with which potential ordinands reacted to the new situation created by the dissolution is surprising, and the awareness of the clergy in the Lincolnshire rising of the perilous nature of their employment suggests that the dissolution was unwelcome on that ground alone. Fears were expressed that the religious would get the benefices, and that existing incumbents would be removed by failing to pass examinations in novel articles of faith.[32] In the event these fears were unjustified, since the fall-off in numbers for ordination was so great that it created opportunities

[29] A Subsidy collected in the Diocese of Lincoln in 1526, ed. H. E. Salter (Oxford Historical Society, LXIII, 1909), p. 21.

[30] These figures have been reached by using the ordination lists of 1523, L.A.O., Register 26, fos. 6v seq., and comparing them with the register of institutions, L.A.O., Register 27, passim, and the extant visitation material and Liber Cleri, L.A.O., Vj. II, Vj. 12, Vij 1; Cj. 3, Cj. 4; and A Subsidy, passim. Records of those holding curacies are not satisfactory for Leicestershire and Northamptonshire, but some idea of personnel can be obtained from H. I. Longden, Northamptonshire and Rutland Clergy from 1500 (16 vols, Northampton, 1938–52) and A. P. Moore, 'Proceedings of the Ecclesiastical Courts in the Archdeaconry of Leicester, 1516–35', Associated Architectural Society Reports and Papers, XXVIII (1905–6), pp. 117–220. 593–662. For additional material on institutions after 1540 see C. W. Foster, 'Institutions to Benefices in the Diocese of Lincoln 1540–70', ibid., XXIV (1897–8), pp. 1–32, 467–525.

[31] The competition for benefices was not confined to 1520–36; see Bowker, Secular Clergy, pp. 70 seq.   [32] Bowker, 'Lincolnshire 1536', pp. 202–5.

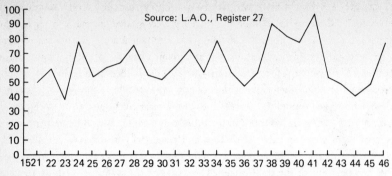

Graph 2 Number of benefices vacant through death of previous incumbent

both for those who already had benefices and for those who were waiting to get them, at just the moment when their prospects seemed so intolerable that it was worth risking rebellion to improve them. That things became easier for the clergy was due partly to chance and partly to the extraordinary effects produced by legislation.

In real terms, opportunities were created for the newly-ordained, or for those serving chantries or curacies, only by the death of an incumbent. His resignation which might leave one benefice vacant might also mean that he was moving to another, so that in absolute terms no new opportunity had been created. The average number of vacancies occurring in livings by the death of the previous incumbent before 1536 was sixty-one per annum and between 1536 and 1546 it was sixty-six (see Graph 2). In the same two periods, the average annual rate of ordination was eighty-two and sixteen respectively. If we leave aside for the moment the problems created by pluralism, it is clear that before 1536 more men were ordained than could possibly get a benefice: necessarily/and usefully the unsuccessful were employed as curates, stipendiaries and chantry priests. But after 1536 there were more vacancies than there were newly ordained priests. On average the difference between the number of new recruits to the priesthood and the number departing from it through death was fifty. Over a ten-year period, therefore, some 500 vacancies would naturally occur through death which were not to be filled through ordination in the Lincoln diocese. The deficit had to be met from the existing pool of clergy who held curacies or chantries, from the religious or from the friars. Alternatively the situation might provide a heaven-sent opportunity for the pluralist to gather an ever-increasing number of benefices to the benefit of his own pocket. In that event the actual cure of the souls in the parishes, where there was a non-resident and pluralist incumbent, would be delegated in its turn either to the ex-religious or to the waning number of seculars whose numbers were not being increased at the actual rate. What seems to have happened?

It is tempting to assume that the vacancies were filled up completely by the ex-religious. Difficult though it is to prove conclusively, this hypothesis seems unlikely. It is very hard to identify all ex-religious, though it is relatively easy to identify some of them. If a monk sought a dispensation to hold a benefice as well as being released from his vows, or if he sought a dispensation less comprehensive in its effect, the chances are that his name will be among the many in the faculty office registers so well calendared by Dr Chambers.[33] But as Dr Chambers meticulously points out, there are gaps in the registers, and some names which other evidence suggests should be included in the lists of ex-religious who were granted 'capacities', as they were called, are not there.[34] If a religious chose a pension rather than a capacity his name may be among the pension lists for the diocese, edited by Dr Hodgett.[35] But those lists are of a comparatively late date, and it is not clear how far the absence of the name in them should be taken as indicative of the death of the pensioner. Michael Bonne, for instance, was a stipendiary priest of All Saints, Huntingdon, who held a dispensation to hold a benefice,[36] but he was also said in 1543 to be in receipt of a pension as a former canon of Huntingdon.[37] He is not listed as receiving a pension in a book of the court of augmentations in 1551.[38] Was he dead? Had he received a living from the king and lost his pension? Had he sold it?[39] Or are the lists very inadequate? In addition there were large numbers of friars and some religious who received no pension and no capacity and so are included in no list.[40] How many were in this category of 'missing ex-religious' we do not know. Yet even when all these limitations to our knowledge are admitted, it seems highly unlikely that the religious filled a large number of the benefices which became vacant after 1536. Only in 1540, when the number of vacancies in benefices, however caused, dropped to ninety-six, did the ex-religious push their known share of institutions to eighteen (see Graph 3). That figure is slight if we remember that, in 1540, seventy-seven of the vacancies occurred as a result of death and only eleven men were newly ordained priests.[41] Even if the figure of ex-religious should be twice that

---

[33] *Faculty Office Registers, 1534–49*, ed. D. S. Chambers (Oxford, 1966), p. xliv.

[34] *Ibid.*, p. xlv.

[35] *The State of the Ex-Religious and Former Chantry Priests in the Diocese of Lincoln, 1547–74*, ed. G. A. J. Hodgett (Lincoln Record Society, LIII, 1959).

[36] *Faculty Office Registers*, p. 151.   [37] L.A.O., Vj.11, fo. 7.

[38] *The State of the Ex-Religious*, p. 26.

[39] For a discussion of these questions see *The State of the Ex-Religious*, pp. xv–xvii.

[40] G. A. J. Hodgett, 'The Unpensioned Ex-Religious in Tudor England', *J.E.H.*, XIII (1962), pp. 195–202. For a discussion of this article see *Faculty Office Registers*, pp. xlii *seq.*

[41] See Graphs 1 and 2.

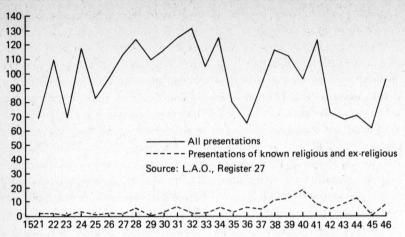

Graph 3 Presentations to benefices and presentations of religious and ex-religious

of known ex-religious, there were still more vacancies than there were ex-religious and newly ordained to fill them. Obviously with the passing of each year, the queue of secular priests waiting for benefices would have thinned, and the chances for seculars and religious alike would improve provided the ordination numbers kept as low as twenty. So we find that as time went on the religious succeeded to a number of benefices. In 1554, for example, fifty-four of the pensioned ex-religious were known to be holding benefices in the diocese, of whom only sixteen had obtained a benefice before 1547.[42] Loyalty and patience got their reward. But it would be a mistake to think that the religious did better than those who had been ordained as secular priests before 1536, or than those who were so ordained after that date. At no time did they receive more than one-seventh of the livings vacant in the diocese in a year. Others were needed to fill the remaining vacancies, and it is instructive to see who exactly did profit from the easing of the pressure on benefices.

The decision to present one man rather than another to a bishop for institution to a benefice rested with the patron. The dissolution of the monasteries changed the distribution of patronage in the Church of England and in so doing determined the fate of ex-religious and seculars who were waiting in the benefice market. Before 1536, 24.5 per cent of all presentations to rectories in the archdeaconries of Buckingham, Lincoln, Stow, Bedford, Leicester and Huntingdon (which were to form the new diocese of Lincoln) was by the religious orders. Additionally in the

---

[42] *The State of the Ex-Religious*, pp. xvi, 77 *seq.* Dr Hodgett's own figures from these lists are different from mine as they are differently compiled. He has counted together both ex-religious and chantry priests and has also counted curacies: hence his conclusion that 'over 52 per cent of the pensioners…had received ecclesiastical preferment' by 1554.

same area, and over the same period, they possessed the patronage of 282 vicarages which brought their share of presentations to just over 40.5 per cent. Individual families in the comparable period possessed nearly 35.5 per cent of the patronage of livings, but no one individual had at his disposal anything like the number of livings possessed by the large religious houses: the knights of St John of Jerusalem had the patronage of thirty-three churches before 1536, and many other houses had over twenty. In contrast the layman with the most patronage at his disposal was Edward Watson who was registrar to the bishop until his death in 1530. Between 1521 and his death he had disposed of eleven livings. The king had the patronage of 4.9 per cent of the total exercised in the diocese and the bishops of Lincoln and other bishops or clergymen held 12.4 per cent. Corporations, mainly Oxford and Cambridge colleges, held the remaining 6.4 per cent. Power in terms of patronage was, therefore, well distributed, but collectively the religious orders possessed more than anyone else.

The dissolution of the monasteries changed this situation. The king emerged after 1536 with 21.5 per cent of the patronage of the diocese, individual lay families with 55 per cent, churchmen with 9.4 per cent, corporations with five per cent and the monasteries, which were in the course of dissolution, with 8.8 per cent destined to go to the king and powerful laymen. In practical terms this meant that the king, in areas which were to form the new diocese of Lincoln, held the patronage of seventy-four vicarages where he had possessed only three before the dissolution, and his share of the patronage of rectories more than doubled. Laymen who had, before the dissolution, presented to forty-five vicarages, were able to present to 138 after it. Charles Brandon, Duke of Suffolk, and his wife had fifteen livings to dispose of after the dissolution compared with only four before it.[43] The king and the laity took the patronage which the religious formerly possessed, and those needing a benefice must press their claims either at court or at the seat of the layman they thought most sympathetic to those claims. This seemed to create the situation most feared by the Lincolnshire rebels of 1536: the concentration of power in London rather than in the locality, to the advantage of the courtier but to the disadvantage of his country cousins. In fact it did not quite happen that way.

Potentially the claims of those who were already at court or serving a powerful layman as a chaplain could outstrip those of a provincial curate. Courtier priests had access to an even greater wealth of patronage than had been available to them hitherto: benefices could be theirs for the asking. But a severe limitation curbed their greed and had the effect of spreading opportunity more widely and offsetting the dangers inherent in the distribution of patronage which followed the dissolution. The limitation was statute. In 1529 and again in 1536, parliament attempted to tackle

[43] These figures are based on L.A.O., Register 27, and in each case a +0.3% rounding figure is needed.

the inter-related questions of non-residence and pluralism. Who might and who might not receive more than one benefice? Were there limits to the number of benefices which even the most favoured should be allowed to accumulate? The intention of the 1529 statute was clear: pluralism was to be limited. One benefice with cure was accepted, as it had been by the canonists, as the norm, but it was recognised that the poverty of certain benefices made a combination of small livings desirable. The statute, therefore, required seculars not to hold more than one benefice over £8 in value. A priest who already held more than one might keep up to four, but for the future no one, however favoured, was to have more than three. Licenses were available to allow members of the king's council to have three benefices, and chaplains to dignitaries, doctors of divinity and episcopal chaplains were to be allowed only two. The obligation of residence was restated but scholars and pilgrims as well as those who were allowed two or three benefices by virtue of their other duties were permitted not to reside. In 1536 a loophole in the residence requirements was filled: to qualify as a scholar, a student must be actually engaged in studying and attending lectures.[44] At a time, therefore, when the dissolution of the monasteries had concentrated a great deal more patronage at court, and the pressure for benefices from the newly-ordained was declining, the courtier had a severe limit put on his activities. Moreover he would need to do some very careful arithmetic before approaching a patron for a benefice. If he were allowed only two benefices he needed to make sure that they were the most lucrative ones. These were not likely to be available together, and the moment would come when he had to resign a poorer benefice to get a wealthier one. But at the moment when this would seem his best course in absolute financial terms, a further statute, first fruits and tenths, stood to deter him. The first year's income of each newly acquired benefice was payable to the Crown after 1534, and no exceptions were made either for the privileged king's servants or for the poor: even those with a benefice worth a meagre eight marks had to pay, though they were not liable until after three years.[45] Not only would a courtier priest need to decide whether the benefices which he had were more or less lucrative than those becoming available, but even supposing a very lucrative rectory came on to the market he would have to consider whether it was worth the sacrifice of one year's first fruits. It is small wonder that in this situation in which ambition had to be measured in terms of cash, and the cure of souls considered almost as a long-term investment for this world quite apart from the next, the bishop of Lincoln singled out simony as the greatest sin of the age. Longland was preaching before the king at Greenwich, on Good Friday 1538, and as he was under some suspicion as a result of the Pilgrimage of Grace, he spoke his mind on the subject of the Bishop of Rome. But he reserved his Ciceronian rhetoric for denouncing the greatest sin of them all:

[44] *Statutes of the Realm*, III, pp. 293–6, 21 Hen. VIII, c. 13; *ibid.*, pp. 668–9, 28 Hen. VIII, c. 13.
[45] *Ibid.*, pp. 493–9, 26 Hen. VIII, c. 3.

That which almoost destroyethe the churche of Chryst...Simony, Simony, Choppynge and chaungynge, byinge and sellynge of benefices and of spirytuall gyftes and promocyons. And noo better marchandyse is now a dayes, then to procure vousons of patrons for benefyces, for prebendes, for other spirituall lyveloode: whether it be by sute, requeste, by letters, by money, bargayne or otherwayes, yee whether it be to bye them or to sell them.[46]

Archbishop Lee of York gave a similar picture in 1540 of priests spying on incumbents of good benefices to see whether they were dying: they 'hearken and gape every day when he will die' in the hope of receiving the living the moment a vacancy occurs.[47] This was not in itself new, as the two-hour vacancy at Beelsby in 1521 showed, but it had been given a new urgency and a new twist by the combination of the statutes limiting pluralism and the later statute imposing first fruits and tenths. The days of quick resignations and hasty exchanges of livings were over.

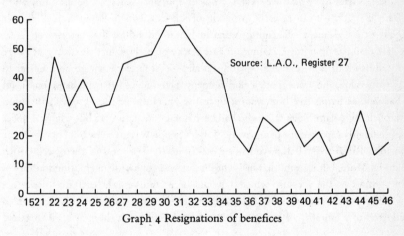

Graph 4 Resignations of benefices

Resignations declined after 1534 (see Graph 4) and presumably this reflects the thought and calculation necessary before a transfer was made from one benefice to another. For those who were fortunate enough to have acquired four benefices before 1529 or who had prebends without cures (which were exempt from the statute) there was no problem. For John Fyley, formerly a monk of Revesby, who had a full capacity to receive a benefice and had been released from his vows, things were harder.[48] He received the rectory of Flixborough from the king in 1538: it was worth, according to the *Valor*, £13 10s 0d.[49] In 1544 the rectory of Holywell worth

[46] J. Longland, *A Sermonde made before the Kynge his maiestye at grenewich* M.D. XXXVIII [1538], unpaginated.

[47] *L.P.*, XVI, no. 316.   [48] *Faculty Office Registers*, p. 128.

[49] L.A.O., Register 27, fo. 97; *Valor Ecclesiasticus temp. Henr. VIII* (6 vols, Record Commission, 1810–34), IV, p. 138. Flixborough was valued in 1526 at £10; *A Subsidy*, p. 31.

double that sum was vacant. Fyley had already paid the first fruits of Flixborough
to the king and by 1544 would have received from it only five years' income. He
took the risk of accepting Holywell and resigning Flixborough.[50] Death did not claim
him for several years so the gamble paid off. But Fyley was very fortunate. Holywell
was a valuable prize which had previously been held by John Dromyn who was
a chaplain to the Duke of Suffolk, and it was precisely the kind of living which a
licensed pluralist would want.[51] Unfortunately the visitation records are not
complete enough for it to be possible to see the date at which all livings of this kind
moved into the hands of pluralists, and there are problems in identifying both very
rich and very poor livings exactly since their valuations were apt to change
considerably between the subsidy of 1526 and the *Valor*. There had always been
a tendency for pluralism and non-residence to be concentrated in wealthier livings,[52]
but the act of 1529 accelerated and accentuated the concentration. By 1543, which
is the last date for which we have records of episcopal visitation before Longland's
death in 1547, we can detect a grouping of non-residents in livings valued at over
£15. In the deanery of Leightonstone in Huntingdonshire the rectories of Great
Catsworth, Coppingford, Hamerton and Buckworth, all valued at over £15, were
in the hands of non-residents.[53] Brington and Keyston, which were both nearer to
£30 in value, did not report a non-resident incumbent.[54] It is perhaps significant
that neither living had been vacant since the operation of the 1529 act: Brington
was held by Adam Bekensaw, who had been non-resident in 1518 but who was never
subsequently reported for being away,[55] and Keyston was given by Sir Thomas More
to John Palsgrave.[56] Palsgrave had several other livings, most of them secured for
him by More, but it seems that he spent the last years of his life in Huntingdonshire.[57]
In contrast to the pressure which a would-be pluralist might exercise to secure a
wealthy parish, there seems to have been much less use of the provision which
allowed of a plurality of livings whose total value (difficult though this is to assess)

[50] L.A.O., Register 27, fos. 82, 225; *Valor*, IV, p. 271. In the subsidy of 1526, Holywell was valued
    at £20; see *A Subsidy*, p. 191.
[51] L.A.O., Vj.12, fo. 4v; Vj.11, fo. 82.
[52] Bowker, *Secular Clergy*, pp. 92 *seq*. Because of the difference in valuations in the *Valor* and those
    given for the subsidy of 1526, *Valor* valuations are given in the text and those for the subsidy
    in the notes.
[53] L.A.O., Vj.12, fos. 8 *seq*.; *Valor*, IV, 259–60. In the subsidy Great Catworth was valued at £16,
    Coppingford at £20, Hamerton at £16 6s 8d, Buckworth at £19 6s 8d, *A Subsidy*, pp. 183,
    184 (*ter*).
[54] L.A.O., Vj.12, fo. 9; *Valor*, IV, p. 260 (*bis*). In the subsidy Brington and Keyston were valued
    at £24 and £18 respectively; *A Subsidy*, p. 184 (*bis*).
[55] *Visitations in the Diocese of Lincoln, 1517–31*, ed. A. H. Thompson (Lincoln Record Society,
    XXXIII, XXXV, XXXVII, 1940–7), I, p. 1; L.A.O., Register 23, fo. 382v.
[56] L.A.O., Register 27, fo. 234v.
[57] Emden, *Biographical Register of Oxford, 1501–40*, pp. 429–30.

did not exceed £8. Only three of the twenty parishes which reported non-residence between 1540 and 1543 in the archdeaconry of Huntingdon were valued at about £8.[58] In the archdeaconry of Buckingham only three out of fourteen parishes held in plurality were at about the £8 level.[59] In contrast some twenty benefices in the archdeaconry of Huntingdon could have been held in plurality on the grounds of value but do not appear to have been so held.[60] The act of 1529, therefore, seems to have concentrated the attention of the potential pluralist on the wealthy livings.

If the economic consequences of the 1529 act took some time to make themselves felt, the overall intention of the act was rather more immediate in its impact. It is not easy to arrive at accurate estimates of pluralism and non-residence.[61] For the diocese of Lincoln, though the material is extensive, it is uneven. We possess the records of the visitation of three archdeaconries, those of Bedford, Buckingham and Huntingdon for four different dates, namely 1518, 1530, 1540 and 1543.[62] The quality of the returns which have survived is not uniform. The returns for the archdeaconry of Buckingham in 1540 are poor and the returns for Bedford are formal in 1530; we have not got returns for the archdeaconries of Oxford and Lincoln for all the period and those of Northampton and Leicester are missing.[63] Yet the pattern revealed by the extant records is similar even though their individual defects vary. Non-residence fell between 1518 and 1530: all our records point to this conclusion, whether the very full ones which have survived for the archdeaconry of Lincoln or the staccato returns which characterise the other archdeaconries of the same date. The most dramatic fall was in the returns for the archdeaconry of Oxford and may reflect the stringent requirements of the act with regard to residence, and the more limited pluralism allowed to graduates below the ranks of doctor of divinity. But it is equally apparent that by 1540 things were reverting to their former course even though the actual problem of non-residence was to reassert itself less forcibly thereafter

---

[58] L.A.O., Vj.11, fos. 78–93, 130–59; Vj.12, fos. 1–22v. Hertford, St Nicholas was valued at £3 16s 0d in the *Valor* and £14 1s 4d in the subsidy; Throcking was valued at £8 in both and Radwell was valued at £13 6s 8d in the *Valor* and £8 in the subsidy. *Valor*, IV, pp. 277, 278 (*bis*); *A Subsidy*, pp. 173, 178, 179.

[59] L.A.O., Vj.11 fos. 55–75, 143–157v; Vj.12, fos. 38 *seq.* Great Hampden was valued at £10 in the *Valor* and £8 in the subsidy; Filgrave at £7 and £6 11s 8d and Walton at £9 and £8. *Valor*, IV, pp. 243, 244, 249; *A Subsidy*, pp. 226, 232, 233.

[60] *Valor*, IV, pp. 253–78. The subsidy valuations would suggest a figure of about thirty parishes which could have been so held: *A Subsidy*, pp. 171–91.

[61] There is an interesting discussion of my own figures and those drawn from the muster rolls in *The Certificate of Musters for Buckinghamshire in 1522*, ed. A. C. Chibnall (Buckinghamshire Record Society, XVII, 1973), pp. 12–13.

[62] *Visitations in the Diocese of Lincoln*, vols. I, II; L.A.O., Vj.11; Vj.12.

[63] We have records for the archdeaconry of Oxford until 1540; see *Visitations in the Diocese of Lincoln*; L.A.O., Vij.1, *passim*. The archdeaconry of Lincoln material is different from all the other visitation records used in that it is archidiaconal and dates from 1533 and not 1530.

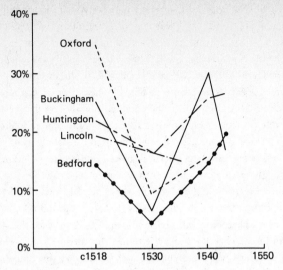

Graph 5 Percentage of non-residents to parishes visited in certain archdeaconries

(see Graph 5). The only explanation for the rise in the rate of non-residence in 1540 is that provided by both the central and diocesan records.

We know from the faculty office registers that the number of dispensations granted for plurality and non-residence increased between 1540 and 1549. Before 1540, it was usual for no more than fifty to be granted per annum to the elite, and no more than fifteen to the less privileged clergy. After 1540 the numbers rise: in 1546 as many as seventy were granted to the elite, though the numbers granted to the less privileged clerks continued to fall.[64] The diocesan material tells much the same story: there was a marked decrease in the number of non-residents who gave no reason for their absenteeism, but there was an increase after the act of those who simply alleged that they had another living (pluralists) and held a dispensation, and of those who claimed that they held chaplaincies at Court or served someone who, in the terms of the act, was allowed to have a chaplain who in his turn might possess two livings (see Graph 6). The numbers who used either episcopal service or scholarship as a reason for absence increased after 1540 when the number of pure pluralists or royal servants diminished. The long-term effect of the 1529 act was not only to concentrate pluralism on the wealthy parishes, it was to concentrate it yet more markedly in the hands of those who had enough favour at Court either to possess a chaplaincy or to command a dispensation which allowed of plurality beyond the terms of the act. But the act prevented, until 1540, the courtier priests taking more

[64] *Faculty Office Registers*, p. xxxvii.

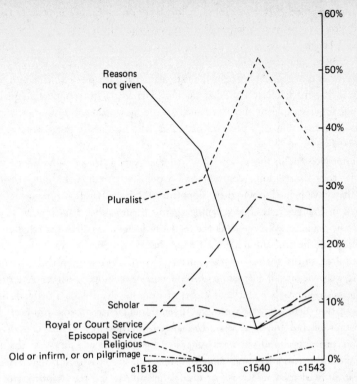

Graph 6 Reasons for non-residence given as a percentage of all non-residence

than their usual share of the benefice market, and after 1540 non-residence seems to have fallen slightly. It had prevented, in fact, the courtier priests filling an increasing number of vacant benefices, and the way was left open for the curates of former years to come into their own. They were not left to form a 'priestly proletariat', disappointed in its expectations of advancement, which might well have provided the nucleus of a movement of protest against religious change, as it had done in 1536.

For the unbeneficed priest, there are signs that after 1536, after the first dissolution of the monasteries with its effects on ordination, there were better times. Quite clearly, until other ordination lists are studied in detail, and the mobility of priests between dioceses is examined, it will be hard to know the extent to which the diocese of Lincoln benefited from a local shortage of priests, and the extent to which, as Fr Hughes suggested, and other ordination lists seem to confirm, there was a national shortage which was alleviated by the offer of obvious financial incentives in certain areas but not in others.[65] But we can see, within the diocese of Lincoln, that a change occurred after 1536. For the newly-ordained, few though they were, the chances of getting a benefice in ten instead of twenty years were greater. Of those ordained in 1537, eighteen per cent had a benefice by 1544, and of those ordained in 1538, twenty-two per cent had a benefice by the same date.[66] For the priest who had waited patiently in the market place, the last decade of Henry VIII's reign was equally rewarding. Of a sample of those ordained in the episcopate of Bishop Atwater (1514–21), we find that 44.5 per cent of priests who eventually got a benefice at all got one after 1536.[67]

The improvement in the prospects which the years 1536–47 provided for all priests, be they ex-religious, courtiers and would-be pluralists, or long-serving curates, may have helped to win their support for the Henrician Reformation. They acquiesced in changes instead of rebelling against them as they had done in 1536. But it seems unlikely from the evidence of the ordination lists that the religion of the statute book became the religion of men's hearts. Conviction was lacking and it showed itself in the absence of men offering themselves for the priesthood. But it was precisely the lack of conviction of some which gave hope to others. At a time when the possession of a rectory, of glebe, of tithe might provide a better hedge against inflation than a curate's meagre stipend could ever do, the prospects of advancement offered by these years had an effect. Moreover if the pattern of ordination, promotion and pluralism suggested by the evidence surviving for the Lincoln diocese is nationally applicable a further conclusion is inescapable. Unless conviction showed itself in a massive upsurge in ordinations, the chantries would have had to have been dissolved by 1560 to release the manpower necessary to the parishes. Their dissolution at an earlier date merely masked a mounting problem.

For those whose lives spanned the years 1521 to 1547, and particularly for a bishop like John Longland who had attempted some reform, the last decade of Henry VIII's reign must have been bitter indeed. The absence of ordinands, however welcome it might have been to curate and courtier, set back once more any hope of reversing

---

[65] We know that the dioceses of Winchester, Durham, Exeter, Chester and York exhibit a similar pattern to Lincoln. See Hughes, *Reformation in England*, II, p. 53 n. 1; Pill, 'Administration of the Diocese of Exeter', pp. 269–71. The evidence for Chichester suggests the same pattern though the ordination lists are lost: Lander, 'Diocese of Chichester', p. 189. Cf. C. Haigh, *Reformation and Resistance in Tudor Lancashire* (Cambridge, 1975), pp. 73–4. Dr Haigh suggests that in Lancashire the clergy were not declining in numbers, though it is unclear, from his text, whether this was because the Lichfield ordination figures kept high or whether new endowment enticed priests from elsewhere. The latter seems the more probable.

[66] L.A.O., Register 26, fos. 53v *seq.*; cf. Register 27, *passim*.

[67] L.A.O., Register 25, fos. 111 *seq.* Surnames beginning A–M have been used: cf. Register 27, *passim*.

the steady toll on the Church caused by unscrupulous non-residence.[68] The dissolution of the monasteries removed patronage yet further from episcopal control and made the chance of reforming the Church in its members yet more dependent on reforming the head. But for the Church in England as a whole, and particularly for the clergy, the bitterness of this pill was sugared by a prospect of advancement, and while there was still a benefice to be had, the Henrician clergy like their Puritan successors preferred an altar to silence, the parish to prison.[69]

[68] Not all non-residence was harmful, for some curates were as efficient as their beneficed counterparts, but prolonged absenteeism set up a grievance in a parish, and if priests were in short supply, there was no guarantee that the requirement that a non-resident would provide a deputy would be honoured. Bowker, *Secular Clergy*, pp. 105–9.

[69] I would like to thank the Leverhulme Trustees and the British Academy for grants which enabled me to pursue this research, and Professor A. G. Dickens and Mrs J. M. Horn for their helpful comments on the article itself.

5

POPULAR REACTIONS TO THE REFORMATION DURING THE YEARS OF UNCERTAINTY 1530–70

D. M. PALLISER

The Reformation provides perhaps the earliest instance in English history of conflicts over beliefs and attitudes in which ordinary people not only took sides in large numbers but also left those choices on record for posterity. Recent researches, especially at regional level, are beginning to show just how complex and fascinating those battles were. Gone is the commonplace assumption of nineteenth- and early twentieth-century historians that the battle was a simple one between 'Catholics' and 'Protestants', in which the 'True Church' was overthrown or revitalised according to one's prejudices; and gone too the assumption that almost everyone was passionately involved in the doctrinal issues at stake. There must have been many, lay and clerical, with the attitude of Vicar Aleyn of Bray, who kept his living from Henry VIII's reign to that of Elizabeth I. 'Being taxed by one for being a turncoat and an unconstant changeling, "Not so", said he, "for I always kept my principle, which is this, to live and die the vicar of Bray".'[1] Nevertheless, a Christian cosmological framework was accepted (outwardly at least) by almost everyone, despite the massive evidence for semi- or anti-Christian beliefs assembled by Keith Thomas and others. Given that framework, it is not surprising that the various ecclesiastical and doctrinal changes imposed by the Crown provoked strong feelings both of support and of opposition. Historians will always disagree how far the divisions reflected real doctrinal disagreement and how far they were provoked by the social, economic and political changes that were bound up with the successive church settlements; but the fact of a deeply divided country is incontrovertible.

If the 'official' Reformation may be taken for convenience to cover a series of statutes and other measures enacted between 1529 and 1559, the 'popular' Reformation has much vaguer chronological boundaries. But the period considered here is not an entirely arbitrary one. Before about 1530 small though influential groups of Lollards and Lutherans existed clandestinely in an overwhelmingly Catholic country, while after the 1570s a semi-reformed Church was accepted, willingly or

[1] T. Fuller, *The Worthies of England*, ed. J. Freeman (London, 1952) p. 23.

94

reluctantly, by the vast majority, and only small minorities openly dissociated themselves from it. Between those dates, however, 'the result was still unsettled and the theological positions not yet sharply and irrevocably defined; the disputants, in England at least, are neither integral Tridentines nor fully Protestant or Calvinist; they are indeed not wholly clear in their own minds where they stand, or whither the world is moving'.[2] The two generations unsure of themselves can be defined by their wills, many of which made provisions for religious rites 'if the law will suffer it'. Such bequests can be traced from 1529, immediately after the first statute affecting Catholic ritual, to at least 1572; by then the period of uncertainty was coming to an end.[3]

This chapter considers some of the evidence for the religious divisions of those years, as they are being revealed by recent researches. Older histories, in so far as they were concerned with religious dissent, concentrated heavily on those who became prominent by untypical means – martyrs, conspirators, refugees and rebels. It is now becoming possible, through research in local and diocesan records, to glimpse the opinions of much larger numbers of people, although many conclusions about the social, intellectual or geographical basis of religious disagreements must be very tentative. Much research remains to be done; and in view of the inarticulate nature of the 'silent majority' at all periods, dogmatic generalisations about popular attitudes will never be justified.

I

Since Lutheran books and ideas, and later Zwinglian, Anabaptist, Calvinist and other influences, entered England through London and the east-coast ports, it would be surprising if early Protestantism were not strongest in the south-east. A. G. Dickens has drawn attention to the importance of Lollard survival in the development of Protestantism, but the general pattern of early Protestantism can be explained largely in terms of accessibility to Continental influences. Areas receptive to the new ideas of the 1520s and 30s included London, East Anglia and Cambridge University, and (outside the south-east) districts centred on ports such as Hull and Bristol, which were, of course, in close touch by sea with the capital as well as with Europe. The bishop of Norwich said in 1530 that the gentry and commoners of his diocese were little affected by heresy, except for 'merchants and such as hath their abiding not far from the sea'. There was no geographical determinism in all this; in the south-east, Sussex and Hampshire remained almost unaffected, while Coventry and Yorkshire had their modest share of early Protestants. It may be significant, however, that one

---

[2] D. Knowles, *The Religious Orders in England*, III (Cambridge 1959) p. 436.
[3] *Historical Manuscripts Commission* 12th Report, Appendix, part IX, p. 534; C. Haigh, *Reformation and Resistance in Tudor Lancashire* (Cambridge, 1975), p. 220.

of the early Yorkshire heretics had brought back his ideas from contacts in Suffolk as a textile worker, just as the few early Lancashire Protestants can nearly all be shown to have travelled to areas of Protestant influence further south.[4]

Henry VIII's acquisition of control over the church in the 1530s provoked more opposition than was once believed. The royal supremacy was strongly resisted in both southern and northern Convocations and the Act in Restraint of Annates in the House of Lords. It is true that the abolition of papal supremacy provoked no open opposition in the country and that the fifty or so who may be called martyrs to the issue were drawn mostly from eight religious houses of strict observance. There may, however, be some truth in what apologists later said in Mary's reign, that many had consented to the new order only out of fear. G. R. Elton has drawn together evidence from many areas of men arguing in private about the supremacy and other issues and, since the evidence is only of those whose confidence was betrayed, such murmurings may have been even more widespread.

The attack on the religious houses touched more directly on everyday life, and one need not take a romantic view of them to see a close connection between their suppression and radical religious attitudes. As Latimer logically pointed out, 'The founding of monasteries argued purgatory to be, so the putting of them down argueth it not to be.' It is therefore not surprising that the first dissolutions in 1536 polarised opinion, and hostility to the suppressions can be taken as an indication of conservatism if not necessarily of articulate Catholicism. There may have been several such incidents as that in Exeter in 1537, where local women attacked the workmen suppressing St Nicholas's Priory. The strongest reaction to the dissolutions, however, occurred in the north.

The Pilgrimage of Grace has become an umbrella term for the five northern risings in the autumn and winter of 1536–7, but is more properly used of the main rising of October 1536, which was ostensibly a protest against royal policies and in defence of the Church; the rebels adopted the device of the five wounds of Christ as a banner. The rebellions were complex affairs, and some recent writers have emphasised social and economic grievances rather than religious motives and have suggested that the Lincolnshire and Yorkshire risings were instigated by discontented nobles, gentry and senior clergy rather than being, as was once thought, spontaneous mass protests. However, C. S. L. Davies has adduced weighty evidence that popular religious protest was a significant element; and J. J. Scarisbrick's judgement is that the Pilgrimage was an 'essentially religious' movement in 'the widest sense of that adjective'. Certainly contemporaries like John Hales and Robert Parkyn, on opposite sides of the religious fence, agreed that the cause had been the Crown's religious policies and the monastic suppressions. It is surely significant that at least

---

[4] A. G. Dickens, *The English Reformation* (London, 1964), p. 69; and *Lollards and Protestants in the Diocese of York* (Oxford, 1959), p. 48; Haigh, *Reformation and Resistance*, pp. 159–77.

sixteen of the fifty-five northern houses already suppressed were restored by the rebels.[5]

If this view is correct, how can the regional character of the revolt be explained? One of the Pilgrims' ballads exhorted the 'faithful people of the Boreal region' to overthrow the 'Southern heretics' and 'Southern Turks',[6] which must have made good recruiting propaganda, but there is no reason to think that a conservative north was facing a heretical south: the royal general, Norfolk, admitted that his own soldiers thought the Pilgrims' cause 'good and godly'. Without minimising the genuine religious zeal of some Pilgrims, one can agree with R. B. Smith and M. E. James that the crucial factor in the spread of the revolts was the attitude of the local nobles and gentry. For example, the central areas of the West Riding – dominated by the Percies and Lord Darcy – rebelled, whereas Hallamshire, the domain of the loyalist Earl of Shrewsbury, did not. Similarly the Earl of Derby was able to keep Lancashire quiet, though his authority did collapse north of the Ribble where the threatened monasteries were popular.

After the Pilgrims had been tricked into surrender, Henry encountered no more overt and widespread opposition to his religious policies, though G. R. Elton's evidence from the state papers shows that, in the later thirties at least, discontent from both right and left existed in all regions. The surrenders of the greater monasteries in 1537–40 passed off with the judicial murder of four abbots and one prior, and the Wakefield plot of 1541 was easily nipped in the bud. In the south-east significant numbers were keen to move in a Protestant direction, even after government policy became more conservative. Over 500 Londoners were indicted as hostile to the Act of Six Articles in 1539; at Chelmsford there is a picture of the people flocking to hear the newly installed Bible read out in the church; and a curious incident at Yarmouth in 1541 suggests that four leading merchants had already adopted radical 'sacramentarian' beliefs.[7] On the other hand, there is little sign of

5 For the Pilgrimage see M. H. and R. Dodds, *The Pilgrimage of Grace, 1536–37, and the Exeter Conspiracy, 1538*, 2 vols (London, 1915), a full narrative from a sympathetic standpoint. The social and economic interpretation was advanced by R. R. Reid, *The King's Council in the North* (London, 1921); see also A. G. Dickens, *Lollards and Protestants*, and 'Secular and Religious Motivation in the Pilgrimage of Grace', in *Studies in Church History*, IV, ed. G. J. Cuming (1967), pp. 39–64. Covert gentry leadership is cogently argued for in R. B. Smith, *Land and Politics in the England of Henry VIII* (Oxford, 1970), Chapter 5, and in M. James, 'Obedience and Dissent in Henrician England: The Lincolnshire Rebellion 1536', *P.&P.*, XLVIII (1970), pp. 3–78. A reassertion of the religous element is contained in C. Haigh, *Last Days of the Lancashire Monasteries and the Pilgrimage of Grace* (Manchester, 1969) *passim*; D. Palliser, *The Reformation in York 1534–1553* (Borthwick Paper, No. 40. 1971) pp. 7–12; and J. J. Scarisbrick, *Henry VIII* (London, 1968), pp. 339–46.
6 *Ballads from Manuscripts*, ed. F. J. Furnivall (Ballad Society, 1868–72), pp. 304–6.
7 Dickens, *English Reformation*, pp. 190, 193; *Narratives of the Days of the Reformation*, ed. J. G. Nichols (Camden Society, LVIII, 1852), pp. 349–51; R. A. Houlbrooke, 'Persecution of

Protestantism before 1547 in Devon, Cornwall or Lancashire, though A. G. Dickens has found a number of heresy prosecutions in Yorkshire.

One of the most voluminous sources for information about religious attitudes, if not always the easiest to interpret, is that of wills, which survive for large numbers of Tudor Englishmen (and women). Counting the frequency of bequests for religious purposes can give a rough idea of the relative popularity of a particular practice. W. K. Jordan's researches have shown, for instance, a decline in endowed prayers for the dead by the 1530s in Hampshire and Buckinghamshire, and their tenacious maintenance in Somerset, Kent, Norfolk, Lancashire and Yorkshire. Not all wills have bequests suitable for such analysis, but one feature of almost all Tudor wills, on which interest has more recently focused, is the 'bequest' of the soul to God as a first clause. Many such bequests are in a simple form which reveals nothing of doctrinal belief, but some testators made clearly traditional bequests – associating Our Lady and All Saints with God – or firmly Protestant statements, expecting salvation through faith in Christ alone. From the later 1530s such bequests vary socially and regionally in sufficient numbers to be worth using as evidence of religious change. Unfortunately the problems raised by analyses of will formulae are also considerable.[8] The most obvious difficulty lies in differentiating between personal statements of faith and those suggested to the dying man by the writer of the will, often a parish priest or clerk; though even in those cases local variations in will formulae still reflect differences of belief.

Analyses of wills of the later years of Henry VIII are not numerous enough to reveal a clear pattern. Published samples of wills from London and the north for 1537–47 are not dissimilar: the proportion of testators omitting the traditional mention of Mary and the saints was twenty-four per cent among Londoners and twenty-two per cent in Yorkshire and Nottinghamshire. In a comprehensive count of York citizens' wills in the same period, however, the proportion was only four per cent. The difference between the county and city figures may be due partly to a bias of the county sample towards wills of gentry, who included several early Protestants, and partly to early Protestantism among the textile workers of the West Riding; but in any case A. G. Dickens has rightly warned against presenting such results in a 'spirit of statistical pedantry'. Firmer guides to the growth of Protestantism are perhaps the wills of those who made bequests in solefideian form before this became common and who were plainly making personal declarations of faith. Such a man was Alderman Monmouth of London, who had been in trouble for heresy in 1528 and who in his will (November 1537) trusted in his salvation solely through the merits of Christ's passion. As if to make his views crystal clear, he also

Heresy and Protestantism in the Diocese of Norwich under Henry VIII', *Norfolk Archaeology*, xxxv (1973), p. 319.

[8] M. Spufford, *Contrasting Communities* (Cambridge, 1974), pp. 320–44.

left money for thirty-one sermons supporting the royal supremacy. A Bristol merchant's widow also made a Protestant will in 1537, and two men of Halifax (Yorkshire) in 1538, while several parishioners of Thornbury (Gloucestershire) did so in the 1540s, apparently influenced by their parish priest. On the other hand, no such will was made by any York citizen until 1547, and of five Cambridgeshire villages only one shows such wills as early as the 1540s.[9]

With the removal of Henry VIII's heavy hand in 1547, a Protestant party could emerge into the open and begin, with government support, to take the initiative. Thomas Hancock, preaching in Poole, Dorset, in 1548, found keen supporters: 'they were the first that in that part of England were called Protestants'. One indicator of religious radicalism was the destruction of images and stained glass, which was widespread in London, Essex and Norwich from the beginning of Edward's reign. Less radical areas took no action until the general order for removal of images in February 1548, while very conservative communities like Oxford and York seem to have made only a token compliance even then. Unfortunately the most recent study of iconoclasm raises the question of regional variations without answering it, and much local research is needed before it can be assessed.[10]

A partial, although not entirely satisfactory, picture of the most conservative areas can be drawn from the extent of the rebellions in 1549. Protector Somerset wrote on 11 June that rebels had assembled 'in the most parts of the realm...and first seeking redress of enclosures, have in some places by seditious priests and other evil people set forth to seek restitution of the old bloody laws'. In fact one revolt, in Norfolk, had almost purely economic motives, but that in the west country was in the main a protest against the first Edwardian prayer book. It engulfed much of Devon and Cornwall, besides attracting sympathy in Somerset and Dorset. The rebels, marching like the Pilgrims of Grace behind a banner of the five wounds of Christ, issued fifteen demands including the restoration of 'our old service' in Latin and the execution of heretics, and including only one non-religious clause. No other Tudor rebels made such overwhelmingly religious demands and the hostile eyewitness Hooker admitted that 'the cause thereof...was only concerning religion'. The same summer saw a serious Catholic rising in Oxfordshire as well as a limited revolt in East Yorkshire against the suppression of chantries. The Venetian ambassador referred obscurely to other rebels in 'Arvaschier' (Warwickshire or Derbyshire?) demanding the restoration of Henry VIII's religious settlement, and it may be that

---

[9] *Ibid.*, pp. 334–41; Dickens, *Lollards and Protestants*, pp. 171–2; Palliser, *Reformation in York*, pp. 19–21, 28, 32; K. G. Powell, 'Beginnings of Protestantism in Gloucestershire', *T.B.G.A.S.*, XC (1971), p. 144; J. Strype, *Ecclesiastical Memorials*, I (1721), pp. 316–19 and Appendix, pp. 249–52.

[10] J. Phillips, *The Reformation of Images: The Destruction of Art in England, 1535–1660* (Los Angeles, 1973), pp. 8, 187.

other local revolts have yet to be identified; one contemporary spoke of 'many more shires' rebelling in July 1549 'for maintenance of Christ's church'. The rebel areas were not solidly Catholic, as will be seen, and other areas which did not take the extreme step of rebellion were just as conservative as the west country. A Privy Councillor admitted that same year that 'the old religion is forbidden by a law, and the use of the new is not yet printed in the stomachs of eleven of twelve parts in the realm'.

There is abundant evidence of the strength of conservatism in Hampshire, Sussex and the Welsh marches in Edward's reign and well into that of Elizabeth. The north also remained generally conservative, despite pockets of Protestantism in the textile areas of Lancashire and the West Riding. The lack of a serious northern revolt in 1549 can be attributed partly to the savage repression of the Pilgrimage and partly to a subordination of religious to civic loyalties, but it does not indicate active support for the Edwardian reforms. A south Yorkshire priest testifed that in 1550 the region 'from Trent northwards' was lagging behind 'the south parts' in abolishing stone altars and Catholic ceremonial. A scheme for itinerant government preachers in 1551 shows clearly the unreliable areas – Devon, Hampshire, Wales, Lancashire, Yorkshire and the Scottish borders. At the other end of the religious spectrum, it is a fair assumption that in those towns which displayed zealous Protestantism almost as soon as Elizabeth ascended the throne – Coventry, Colchester, Ipswich, Leicester and others – Protestantism must have been firmly established before 1553.

Another rough index of religious sympathies is the incidence of clerical marriage. It was legalised in February 1549, though some early Protestant clergy in Suffolk had married as early as 1536–7. The numbers who took advantage of it between 1549 and 1553 can be approximately established by the deprivations of married clergy in Mary's reign. At one extreme was London, where nearly a third of the parish clergy married, followed closely by Essex, Suffolk and Norfolk with a quarter or more, and Cambridgeshire with one in five. In Lincolnshire and the diocese of York the proportion was only one in ten, and in Lancashire less than one in twenty.[11] As with will formulae, the figures should not be treated with too much respect, for the correlation between the religious outlook of the clergy and their propensity to marriage was not a close one. Nevertheless, conservative laymen were generally hostile to clerical marriage both in Edward's reign and later. In Cornwall and Lancashire married ministers were cold-shouldered throughout Elizabeth's reign, though such hostility was traditionalist rather than Catholic and was, of course, shared by the Queen herself.

[11] A.G. Dickens, *The Marian Reaction in the Diocese of York* (St Anthony's Hall Publication, No. 11, 1957), pp. 15–19 and *English Reformation*, p. 245; Houlbrooke, 'Persecution of Heresy', p. 317: Spufford, *Contrasting Communities*, p. 244; R. B. Walker, 'Reformation and Reaction in the County of Lincoln, 1547–58', *Lincolnshire Archaeological and Architectural Society*, IX (1961), p. 57; Haigh, *Reformation and Resistance*, p. 181.

The ease with which the Catholic Mary I succeeded to the throne in 1553 was, it is now accepted, owing to her legitimate hereditary claim and not to her religion. Early in the reign there was popular agitation in Kent and Essex for the restoration of Protestant worship; and Wyatt's rebellion in early 1554, though ostensibly a political protest, had a covertly Protestant aim, if some of his own remarks can be believed. He received strong support in Kent – though even there Canterbury, under a Catholic mayor, fortified itself against him – and his success was also said to be 'joyous to the Londoners', though he failed to take the capital. More important, his fellow conspirators completely failed to raise Devon, Herefordshire and the Midlands.[12] That may reflect loyalism rather than religious feeling, but studies of Lancashire and York suggest positive enthusiasm for the Queen's restoration of Catholicism. The York corporation hailed the accession of Mary as a 'godly' ruler – a term they did not repeat for her sister in 1558 – and there was even a rumour after the defeat of Wyatt that Mary would move her capital from London to York 'to be among Catholic people'.[13] After a generation of uncertainty, however, no area was homogeneous in its religious sympathies; Lancashire and Yorkshire both numbered small but dedicated Protestant minorities, like the 'busy fellows of the new sort' prosecuted at Leeds, and a large minority of A. G. Dickens's Yorkshire wills sample was non-traditional.

The best-remembered dissidents in Mary's reign are, of course, the exiles and the martyrs. Both were tiny minorities in a population of some three million, but they were highly influential and their geographical distribution is likely to be similar to that of the larger body of Protestants who did not carry their opposition so far. Christina Garrett counted 472 men, nearly all gentlemen, clergy or merchants, who fled to the Continent; of 350 whose residence she fairly firmly established, two out of five came from London and Middlesex, Kent, Sussex, Essex, Suffolk and Norfolk.[14] The 300 heretics burned between 1555 and 1558, mainly humbler folk, were even more concentrated; over three-quarters were burned in those six counties, through not all the victims suffered in their home county. The chief difference between the two groups, apart from their social composition, is that the exiles were drawn from a wider catchment area. There was no sizeable body of martyrs outside East Anglia and the Home Counties except at Bristol, where Foxe names seven but where recent research can confirm only four.[15] Devon and Cornwall, which contributed about thirty-five exiles, witnessed only one martyrdom; Lancashire and Yorkshire provided only one martyr but nearly forty exiles. The excessive

[12] D. M. Loades, *Two Tudor Conspiracies* (Cambridge, 1965), pp. 12–127, map opposite p. 284.
[13] *York Civic Records*, ed. A. Raine, 8 vols (York Archaeological Society, 1939–53), V, p. 92; P. F. Tytler, *England under the Reigns of Edward VI and Mary* (1839), II, p. 309 (translated).
[14] C. H. Garrett, *The Marian Exiles* (Cambridge, 1938).
[15] For doubts about the Bristol martyrs see K. G. Powell, *The Marian Martyrs and the Reformation in Bristol* (Bristol, 1972).

concentration of martyrs in the south-east probably reflects not so much the distribution of heresy as the zeal of ecclesiastical authorities. Pole of Canterbury and Bonner of London were proverbial for their hunting down of heretics, whereas other bishops like Tunstall of Durham and Heath of York were averse to persecution. Margaret Spufford, speaking of 'the depth of the reception of Protestant feeling' in Cambridgeshire, suspects that 'lenient administration of the diocese' was responsible for restricting the number of martyrs there to three.[16]

Episcopal zeal cannot, however, entirely explain away the special place of London and East Anglia in the story of early Protestantism. The capital, scene of sixty-seven burnings, was notorious for its sympathies. Pole complained to the Londoners 'that when any heretic shall go to execution, he shall lack no comforting of you, and encouraging to die in his perverse opinion'. Certainly London takes first place in the number of known underground Protestant congregations under Mary; and the next largest congregation recorded was in Colchester, a town notorious as 'a harbourer of heretics'. There is also the astonishing fact that four Essex parishes continued using the proscribed Edwardian services until 1555 without being disturbed.[17] The same geographical pattern was apparent when Elizabeth came to the throne. Iconoclasm in 1559, for instance, was most promptly and zealously pursued in London, 'with such shouting, and applause of the vulgar sort, as if it had been the sacking of some hostile city'. In the west country, on the other hand, the populace was devoted to the 'votive relics of the saints' and reluctant to destroy images.[18]

It is difficult to avoid writing history with hindsight. The religious opposition to Mary is often over-written because she died before her regime was firmly established; that facing Elizabeth I is perhaps still underestimated because her settlement ultimately endured. In 1562 the Bishop of Carlisle said that 'every day men look for a change', and a Yorkshire gentleman was confident 'that the crucifix with Mary and John should be set up again in all churches' before Christmas.[19] For the first decade of her reign Elizabeth moved warily, and only after the rising of the northern earls in 1569, a last, forlorn Catholic revolt, did she impose a tighter religious discipline. Like all the Tudors, she had to co-operate with the J.P.s who enforced law and order in the shires and they were very divided, as a series of reports on J.P.s' loyalties sent in by the bishops in 1564 reveals.[20] Roughly 431 J.P.s

---

[16] Spufford, *Contrasting Communities*, p. 248n.

[17] Strype, *Ecclesiastical Memorials*, III, Apendix, p. 248; Dickens, *English Reformation*, pp. 272–7; D. M. Loades, 'The Enforcement of Reaction, 1553–1558', *J.E.H.*, XVI (1965), p. 62.

[18] Hayward's Annals of the *First Four Years of the Reign of Queen Elizabeth*, ed. J. Bruce (Camden Society, VII, 1840), p. 28; *The Zurich Letters*, ed. H. Robinson (Parker Society, 1842), I, p. 44.

[19] P. McGrath, *Papists and Puritans under Elizabeth I* (London, 1967) p. 47; *York Civic Records* VI, p. 42.

[20] 'A Collection of Original Letters from the Bishops to the Privy Council, 1564', ed. M. Bateson, *Miscellany*, IX (Camden Society, new ser., LIII, 1895).

throughout England were described as favourable to the Elizabethan settlement; 264 as indifferent or neutral; and 157 as hostile. 'It was a sufficient majority among those who mattered', comments A. L. Rowse – but not in all counties. In Sussex there were only ten 'favourers' to fifteen 'mislikers'; in Staffordshire ten 'no favourers' out of seventeen; and in Lancashire six 'favourable' to eighteen 'not favourable'; four of the Lancashire non-favourers were still active justices as late as 1583. The benches in corporate towns were nearly all more conservative than the justices in the shires; the entire Hereford council was unfavourable or 'neuter', and all but two of the York aldermen. Widespread Catholic survivalism was revealed in diocesan visitations like those of York in 1567 and Chichester in 1569. In many places in Sussex chalices were kept 'looking for to have mass again'. Against these, there were radicals in other areas moving well to the left of the 1559 settlement. Independency was being tolerated in East Anglia as early as 1561, and what Patrick Collinson calls 'London's Protestant underworld' gave rise to a separatist church by 1567.[21]

By the 1570s the 'Established Church' was indeed firmly established, though assailed from both left and right. Even if Catholic recusancy of the Counter-Reformation type is beyond our brief, it is worth looking briefly at the tenacious maintenance of the older religious ways by a dwindling number of 'survivalists', who are not to be confused with the new Catholic recusants. These remained longest in what puritans were coming to call 'the dark corners of the land'. Chester, Boston, Wakefield and York, for example, kept up their medieval miracle plays until the 1570s, although so did Chelmsford in Essex. Many Catholic traditions were reported from the northern dioceses, and Archbishop Grindal found the northern province so conservative in 1570 as to seem 'another church, rather than a member of the reste'.[22] Gradually he and his ally the Earl of Huntingdon, Lord President of the Council in the North, enforced conformity, though Lancashire's exemption from the Council's jurisdiction made it something of a sanctuary for Catholics. The very last open cases of survivalism can be traced in wills – Catholic phraseology by the middle of Elizabeth's reign, by a dwindling number of testators mainly in the north, can indicate only their stubborn devotion to the old ways, coupled of course with a tolerance in the northern church courts towards registering such wills. Among the last testators known to have left their souls to God, the Blessed Virgin and the saints, in full medieval form, were an alderman of Newcastle (1582), Lady Wharton of Healaugh near York (1583), and a York alderman's widow (1585). The offending phrase has been deleted in the registered copy of the Newcastle will, but the two wills in the York register have been left uncensored. In 1575 a Duchy of Lancaster

[21] J. S. Purvis, *Tudor Parish Documents* (Cambridge, 1948), pp. 15–34; R. B. Manning, *Religion and Society in Elizabethan Sussex* (Leicester, 1969), pp. 42–6; C. Cross, *The Royal Supremacy in the Elizabethan Church* (London, 1969), p. 100; P. Collinson, *The Elizabethan Puritan Movement* (London, 1967), pp. 84–91.

[22] *The Remains of Edmund Grindal*, ed. W. Nicholson (Parker Society, 1843), p. 326.

official asked for prayers for his soul; in 1581 another Lancastrian left his parish priest 10s to pray for him; and in one Lancashire parish prayers for the dead were still recited at funerals in the 1590s.[23]

II

The evidence presented so far has partly confirmed the traditional textbook picture of a south and east more receptive to Protestantism during the period of uncertainty, and a north and west less so. As a crude generalisation, with many exceptions allowed, it may be acceptable. The inhabitants of London and the east-coast ports, after all, were in regular contact with the continental reformed churches, like Humphrey Monmouth and other London merchants who imported forbidden Lutheran books, or the Hull sailors who visited Bremen and Friesland in 1528 and witnessed Lutheran services. The west-coast ports traded more with the Catholic lands of Spain, Portugal and Ireland, though Bristol developed nevertheless into an early Protestant centre, as did landlocked Coventry. Something should be allowed too to T. M. Parker's claim that the greater prosperity of lowland England 'gave men more time for thought and bound them less to tradition, which always flourishes most where life is hard and experiment dangerous to existence'.[24] At any rate, some recent regional studies would appear to support the correlation: J. E. Oxley, M. Spufford and F. Heal have depicted Essex and Cambridgeshire as much more receptive than A. L. Rowse's Cornwall or Christopher Haigh's Lancashire. Many more such studies are needed for other areas, however, and it is clear that such a geographical correlation is a loose one at best. Christopher Haigh suspects that conservative Lancashire (apart from its south-east corner) was not so very different from other parts of England,[25] and Roger Manning's study of Sussex, with its strong conservatism until the 1570s, is certainly a warning against assuming that Protestantism could be easily enforced even in the south-east. Conversely, A. G. Dickens's studies showed some time ago that the north was far from being the uniformly reactionary region of popular tradition, and that Beverley, Halifax, Hull, Leeds, Rotherham and Wakefield all housed significant Protestant communities before 1558. As a further blow to geographical determinism, the radical Halifax was a clearly upland parish, whereas the city of York, in an outlier of lowland England, proved obstinately conservative. Furthermore, where highland areas did prove more difficult to control, administrative rather than physical barriers were often to blame. Much of the west midlands and the north formed before 1541 two huge dioceses, York and Lichfield, and though

[23] R. Welford, *History of Newcastle and Gateshead*, III (1887), p. 33; J. Hunter, *Hallamshire* (2nd edn. 1869), p. 82; B.I.Y., PROB reg. xxxiv, fo. 49; Haigh, *Reformation and Resistance*, pp. 220-1.

[24] T. M. Parker, *The English Reformation to 1558* (London, 1950), p. 24.

[25] Haigh, *Reformation and Resistance*, p. vii.

the creation of the see of Chester was a step in the right direction, Chester proved to be a most unsuitable centre, especially for controlling Lancashire, and was inadequately financed. Moreover, much of the north and west was divided into large parishes where detections of heresy and recusancy were inevitably difficult.

Perhaps the promising lines of future research are those concentrating on religious belief at the most local level, for regional studies have too coarse a mesh. Broad generalisations can be made about the distribution of conservatives and radicals but any determinist view based on geography or economic and social structure would ignore the vital role of committed individuals. The influence of Latimer in Bristol and Gloucester in the 1530s, or of Bernard Gilpin in County Durham in Elizabeth's reign, are but two examples of the enormous influence of dedicated clergy in changing the local religious climate. Indeed, it was similar zeal by committed laymen, in Claire Cross's view, which made impossible any return to religious uniformity at the end of the period of uncertainty. A small number of influential nobles and gentry used their patronage to present zealous Protestants to church livings in Suffolk, Leicestershire and other counties; and both Protestant and Catholic gentry retained as chaplains men unacceptable to the established ministry. 'In the last resort the state failed to compel the laity into uniformity because the zealots, both Catholic and Protestant, disregarding the parochial system, made their own households into centres of evangelism.' The negative influence of a local magnate could be equally crucial. The third Earl of Derby, who dominated Lancashire, played a waiting game in both 1536 and 1569, and though he did not in the event throw his considerable weight behind either rising, he did not actively work for the Crown either.[26]

Coupled with a realisation of the importance of the individual is a recognition that almost no area was entirely homogeneous in its religious beliefs between the 1530s and the 1570s: many villages were bitterly divided, while in the larger towns total uniformity was almost impossible to attain. G. R. Elton's survey of opinion in the 1530s identifies serious divisions between conservatives and radicals in Bristol, Rye and Gloucester as well as three Oxford colleges. Bristol remained deeply divided for another generation despite, or perhaps because of, the presence of zealous Protestants on the city council from an early date. The Catholic Roger Edgeworth, preaching at Bristol early in Mary's reign, said that, 'Here among you in this city some will hear mass, some will hear none... some will be shriven, some will not, but for fear or else for shame... some will pray for the dead, some will not, I hear of much dissension among you.' Similarly, when the married vicar of Orwell, Cambridgeshire, mocked the mass that he had to reintroduce he drew strong support from some parishioners but deeply offended others.[27]

London was large enough to hide a multitude of opinions and recorded dissent

[26] Cross, *Royal Supremacy*, p. 95–114; Haigh, *Reformation and Resistance*, entries indexed under Stanley, Edward.

[27] Powell, *Marian Martyrs*, pp. 8–9; Spufford, *Contrasting Communities*, pp. 244–5.

there may have been only the tip of the iceberg. True, most of it was radical dissent, from the bricklayer who annoyed his neighbours in the late 1530s by preaching from his window and his garden fence, to the exercises 'after Geneva fashion' being held in a church by 1559. Yet London, like Bristol, had its splits between right and left: when feasts were being abrogated by the government in 1549 and 1550 'some kept holy day and some none', and the same divisions were manifested when ʰhe festivals were restored in 1554. The Venetian ambassador clearly over-simplified when he said that the Londoners were the most disposed to obey the inconstant laws on religion, 'because they are nearer the Court'.[28] London's teeming population – it was at least ten times the size of any other English town – probably more than counteracted the pressure for conformity from the government at Westminster or the archbishop at Lambeth. After all, the capital of the northern province, York, showed no disposition to change its religion with its successive archbishops, despite the presence of their church courts in its midst, and remained as consistently conservative as London was radical.

The most vivid picture of urban division, if not the most objective, comes from the autobiography of Thomas Hancock, a Hampshire-born Protestant clergyman. In 1548 he preached against the mass in Salisbury, stirring up so much dissension that Protector Somerset forbade him to preach at Southampton. 'My lord said unto me that Hampton was a haven town, and that if I should teach such doctrine as I taught at Sarum the town would be divided, and so should it be a way or a gap for the enemy to come in.' Soon afterwards Hancock became curate of Poole in Dorset, where he found strong support, though his blunt attacks on the real presence again provoked violent controversy. A group led by a former mayor, 'a great rich merchant, and a ringleader of the Papists', attacked him in his church and the then mayor had to protect him physically. Such, at least, is what Hancock recorded long after the event, though his picture of zeal on both sides may have been magnified with distance. He proudly records a Salisbury draper's boast that 'a hundred of them would be bound in £100' as sureties for him, but his own artless testimony shows that their zeal was only moderate. When the chief justice reasonably preferred ten sureties of £10 each, the draper replied that 'it would grieve them to forfeit £10 apiece but in that quarrel to forfeit 20s apiece it would never grieve them'. Nevertheless, the picture of violent opposition to Protestant preachers in the region is corroborated from other sources: Bale, for instance, said in 1552 that attacks were being made on 'Christ's ministers' in many areas, 'chiefly within Hampshire'.[29]

Even further west, notorious to contemporaries as a region 'where popery greatly

---

[28] G. R. Elton, *Policy and Police* (Cambridge, 1972), pp. 162–4; McGrath, *Papists and Puritans*, p. 81; *Calendar of State Papers, Venetian*, v, p. 345; *Chronicle of the Grey Friars of London*, ed. J. G. Nichols (Camden Society, LIII, 1852), pp. 67, 89.

[29] *Narratives of the Reformation*, pp. 71–84, 315–16.

prevailed', Protestants were numerous enough to demolish any idea of uniform Catholicism. At Bodmin in 1548, schoolboys fought mock battles in gangs representing the old and new religions, and the western rising of 1549 received general but by no means unanimous support. Raleigh's father, who was alleged to have browbeaten an old woman near Exeter for telling her beads, was threatened with death by the rebels but rescued by 'certain mariners of Exmouth'. Exeter itself provides perhaps the best example of conflicting loyalties within a city. During the rising, according to Hooker's eye-witness account, the majority of citizens were Catholic, yet the city was firmly defended against the rebels because the magistrates, 'albeit some and the chiefest…were well affected to the Romish religion', put first 'their obedience to the King…and safety of themselves'. When, however, the city was tempted to join a Protestant rebellion five years later, the sheriff of Devon took no chances. Two aldermen known to be Catholics were given emergency powers to defend it, 'for as much as the mayor of Exeter and his brethren were of several religions'.[30] The precautions may have been unnecessary, for faced with a rebellion most town corporations thought of 'obedience' and 'safety of themselves' whatever their religious persuasion. Solidarity of the governing body was put before ideology, and, no doubt, one fear at the back of the aldermen's minds was the disorder and looting that might be unleashed by any surrender to a rebel army. Hence the London corporation held the city firmly against Wyatt, despite the widespread support he apparently enjoyed among lesser citizens, just as York held out strongly against the Catholic earls in 1569, although some of its leading aldermen had Catholic sympathies.

It should occasion no surprise that the reception of Protestantism, like that of any new belief or ideology, had an uneven impact; making its way in a complex society divided by rivalries between individuals, families, social groups and entire communities, it was almost certain to become entangled with existing dissensions. If one man or group adopted Protestantism, that might ensure that his or their enemies remained Catholic: or – which was not always the same thing – if one rebelled, another might be the more zealous in loyalty. Such considerations applied especially in districts where lords and their tenants did not trust one another. Some gentlemen might remain aloof from a rebellion out of prudence or out of contempt for the social status of the rebel leaders; both reactions can be seen among the Lincolnshire and Yorkshire gentry in 1536. Rebel commoners might use the cloak of revolt to work off grudges against their lords; or arrogant lords might use the opportunities of religious uncertainty to bully tenants. The purchaser of a monastic manor in Sussex was accused of harassing his tenants and boasting, 'Do ye not know that the King's Grace hath put down all the houses of monks, friars and nuns? therefore now is

---

[30] A. L. Rowse, *Tudor Cornwall* (2nd edn, London, 1969), p. 262; J. Hooker, *The Description of the Citie of Excester* (Devon and Cornwall Record Society, 1919), pp. 62–3, 67–8, 71.

the time come that we gentlemen will pull down the houses of such poor knaves as ye be', though it is fair to add that he denied the charge.[31]

The alignment of religious and social groups would depend on the local situation. At St Neots (Huntingdonshire) in 1547 conservative gentry confronted radical commoners: the parishioners removed images illegally, and the local gentlemen vainly ordered their restoration. In the west country the situation was often reversed: the 1549 rising had strong overtones of social protest by the Catholic rebels against the gentry. Likewise in Mary's reign it was the Cornish gentry who led opposition to her policies, while the 'stupid and backward-looking peasantry', to use A. L. Rowse's uncharitable phrase, remained loyal. An analysis of the abortive risings of 1554 suggests that the distinction between gentry and commons was more explicit in Devon than in any other area. One might conclude from studies like A. L. Rowse's that the gentry, with their superior education, were more open to new ideas than a stubbornly conservative peasantry, but this would be an unjustified inference. Commons as well as gentry could follow sophisticated arguments. Sir Francis Bigod, stirring an assembly of Yorkshire commons to renewed revolt in 1537, used technical arguments against the validity of the King's pardon which were obviously well understood. A Cambridgeshire husbandman travelled to Colchester about 1555 to discuss Pauline theology with fellow Protestants, and, on failing to satisfy his conscience, seriously considered travelling to Oxford to consult Ridley and Latimer.[32]

Social and economic grievances have also been emphasised as underlying the Pilgrimage of Grace. A. G. Dickens has drawn attention to several riots and quarrels in York just before the rising 'over issues unrelated to the ecclesiastical polity of the Crown', though at least one was apparently an accusation by one merchant against another for disloyalty to the royal supremacy. Aldermen and lesser freemen were certainly at odds over enclosures in May 1536, yet were apparently almost united in admitting the Pilgrims without resistance in October. However, York may not have been typical of northern communities and more research is needed on the Pilgrimage as a whole. In Lancashire it was indeed largely a religious protest, but the risings in Cumbria, and probably those in Craven and Richmondshire, had the characteristics of peasant rebellions.

Religious disputes could undoubtedly become an element in quarrels between rich and poor in town as well as countryside. At Rye, between 1533 and 1538, the vicar behaved in a provocative way – attacking 'heretics'; refusing to obey the new liturgical regulations; splitting the town into two factions; and, if his enemies can be believed, openly defending papal supremacy. Cromwell had for years to deal with

[31] *Tudor Economic Documents*, ed. R. H. Tawney and E. Power (London, 1924), I, pp. 20–1, 28.
[32] W. K. Jordan, *Edward VI: The Young King* (London, 1968), p. 150; Rowse, *Tudor Cornwall*, p. 318; Loades, *Two Tudor Conspiracies*, pp. 44–5; Dickens, *Lollards and Protestants*, p. 99; Spufford, *Contrasting Communities*, pp. 246–8.

the complaints of the rival factions, yet, when he finally stepped in, the vicar was only removed to another parish and no charges of treason were brought. The reason, apparently, was that he was strongly supported by the mayor and jurats and seventy-five 'worthy men' of Rye, whereas his enemies were 'very simple and of small substance'. 'It is clear enough', comments G. R. Elton, 'that the divisions here ran not only between adherents of the old and the new way in religion, but more especially also between the rulers of Rye and the poorer sort.' There are hints of a similar pattern at York forty years later, when Mayor Criplyng (1579–80) was in trouble with the authorities of Church and State for attacking the clergy and not presenting recusants. Criplyng, apparently a survivalist rather than a recusant, was hastily disowned by his fellow aldermen when his supporters put up 'filthy and lewd' posters in the streets, and there are indications that a group of committed Protestant merchants were taking over the city council, while Criplyng was supported by some of the poorer citizens.[33]

Criplyng's case is a reminder that Tudor rulers could enforce their policies only with the co-operation of unpaid officials in the localities. All statistics of religious offenders, therefore, reflect the zeal or success of those who presented them – clergy, churchwardens, J.P.s, gentry, private citizens – as much as the actual distribution of dissent. The justices were vital to the process of enforcing uniformity, certainly after 1559, and apparently there never was a thorough purge of Catholic J.P.s in Elizabeth's reign. In Yorkshire the J.P.s did not administer the oath of supremacy even to one another until 1562, and the Bishop of Winchester had great difficulty persuading his fellow justices to certify recusants. Much depended on the relationship of the bishop with the 'county community' of nobles and gentry. In Norfolk, Bishop Parkhurst (1560–75) deferred to the conservative Duke of Norfolk (d. 1572) as long as he lived, but in the last three years of his life was able to follow his own inclinations and to pack the bench with radical Protestants. His successor Bishop Freake (1575–85), however, appointed J.P.s 'backward in religion' to control the puritans. Richard Curteys of Chichester (1570–82), the first bishop to make real inroads into the ingrained conservatism of Sussex, attempted to do for that county what Parkhurst had done for East Anglia, but his 'fanaticism and inquisitorial methods clashed with the attitude of pratical tolerance that the Sussex gentry felt was dictated by the special conditions of local politics'. He attacked a group of crypto-Catholic justices, only to find that the bench united against him despite their religious divisions. When he pressed some of them to swear that they 'kept no company with any that were backward in religion' they replied that 'we cannot take knowledge of every man's religion and conscience that cometh into our company'.[34]

Diversity of opinion was true of the nobles and gentry throughout the period of

[33] Elton, Policy and Police, pp. 20–1, 85–90; D. Palliser, Tudor York (Oxford, 1979).
[34] J. H. Gleason, The Justices of the Peace in England, 1558–1640 (Oxford, 1969), pp. 68–72; R. B. Manning, 'Elizabethan Recusancy Commissions', H.J., xv (1972), p. 25; A. Hassell

uncertainty, though the approximate statistics in recent studies relate only to the end of the period. It has been estimated that of sixty-six peers in 1580, twenty-two were committed Protestants, twenty recusants and twenty-four relatively indifferent; that among office-holding gentry in Sussex in the 1560s known Catholics outnumbered Protestants two to one; and that of 567 families of Yorkshire gentry in 1570, 368 (sixty-five per cent) were still Catholic.[35] Given such divisions, and the common preference for social solidarity among the gentry over religious opinions, the lukewarm prosecution of successive settlements in many counties is scarcely surprising. The gentry not only dominated the commissions of the peace but were also prominent on the mixed lay–clerical ecclesiastical commissions favoured by Elizabeth as instruments of religious uniformity. Christopher Haigh has shown that in Lancashire, at least, the ecclesiastical commission and the bench of justices were both unreliable instruments, including crypto-Catholic gentry and even open recusants. Nor should one neglect the lesser lay officials, the churchwardens, whose office it was to enforce church attendance. Over half the recusants returned in Cheshire in 1578 lived in nine parishes where the wardens had not been imposing the statutory fines for non-attendance.[36] In fact several recent studies suggest that the visitation procedures could cope only with minority problems: if a group of offenders were generally supported by the other parishioners, they would be unlikely to be presented. That suggests the depressing possibility that the records indicate only the distribution of small minorities of dissenters and that areas of widespread dissent might often pass unrecorded. There must have been strong social pressure on churchwardens not to betray their neighbours; and it is remarkable how often heretics presented were immigrants from other parts of England or from overseas. Given the parochial loyalties of the age, a 'foreigner' must always have stood more danger of arrest than a native.

The role of the senior clergy was, of course, equally vital in enforcing the successive settlements. Mary and Pole are often criticised for dying with five sees vacant, so making Elizabeth's settlement easier; it is less often remarked that Elizabeth unwisely left many more sees vacant after the Marian bishops were deprived, both to save money and to bargain for advantageous land exchanges with the bishops elect. Of the twenty-two English sees, sixteen were unfilled at the end of 1559 and nine were still vacant a year later; Oxford, the last, was not filled until 1567. Some of the longer vacancies were in the north and west and they gave Catholic survival

Smith, *County and Court: Government and Politics in Norfolk 1558–1603* (Oxford, 1974), pp. 206–8, 226–8; Manning, *Religion and Society*, pp. 61–125.

[35] L. Stone, *The Crisis of the Aristocracy 1558–1641* (Oxford, 1965), p. 741; Manning, *Religion and Society*, p. 259; J. T. Cliffe, *The Yorkshire Gentry from the Reformation to the Civil War* (Oxford, 1969), p. 169.

[36] K. R. Wark, *Elizabethan Recusancy in Cheshire* (Chetham Society, 3rd ser., xix, 1971), pp. 16–17.

or revival precious extra time to become more firmly established. Lichfield was not filled until March 1560, when Bishop Bentham found Catholic furnishings still retained in many Shropshire churches. At York 'the hard core of the central ecclesiastical administration' was shattered in 1559 and not repaired for two years, a crucial delay in the view of Hugh Aveling. Chester (which included Lancashire) was administered by a Catholic commissary until February 1561. Even when bishops were at last appointed – Young to York and Downham to Chester – both proved very weak instruments of uniformity. Archbishop Parker saw the danger of vacant sees clearly and complained that 'whatsoever is now too husbandly saved will be an occasion of further expense of keeping them down if (as God forfend) they should be too much Irish and savage'.[37] The position would have been worse if the Queen had accepted a scheme to keep Chester permanently vacant and pocket its revenues; she contented herself with an eighteen-year vacancy at Ely, a safely Protestant see. Nor should one neglect the vital importance of the right cathedral appointments to assist the bishops in enforcing conformity. Indeed, in Dr James's view, it was the Durham cathedral chapter which successfully established Protestantism in a very conservative diocese. These zealous graduates were theological elitists, chiefly concerned to win over the educated. Bernard Gilpin, for instance, remained unmoved when he offended 'the plebeians' by his opinions, commenting that he 'never desired the love of the vulgar'. Contempt for the religious opinions of humble folk, for which Foxe castigated the Marian bishops, was no monopoly of Catholic clerics.

Still more important than the senior clergy as moulders of opinion must have been the mass of parish clergy and unbeneficed chaplains. Despite widespread anticlericalism and a growing tendency of parishioners to form their own theological opinions, the parish priest was the most literate and knowledgeable man in many rural communities, with the possible exception of the lord of the manor, and the character and example of both must have been crucial in many villages. It is clear that every settlement was hampered by the incumbency of clergy appointed under a previous regime. The 9000 parish priests suffered no major purges except for perhaps 2000 in 1554 (many of whom were simply transferred to other parishes after abandoning their wives) and a few hundred in 1559. Admittedly, the continuity of personnel was maintained because most clergy, like Aleyn of Bray, conformed outwardly to every settlement. A revealing anecdote from Exeter tells how in Edward's reign the rector of St Petrock's vowed never to say mass again; yet in 1554 his friend Mayor Midwinter – a Protestant – found him robed for mass. Midwinter 'pointed unto him with his finger remembering as it were his old

[37] M. R. O'Day, 'Thomas Bentham', *J.E.H.*, XXIII (1972), p. 145; J. C. H. Aveling, *Catholic Recusancy in the City of York 1558–1791* (Catholic Record Society, 1970), p. 20; Haigh, *Reformation and Resistance*, p. 210.

protestations... but Parson Herne openly in the church spake aloud unto him, "It is no remedy, man, it is no remedy"'.[38] Or there was the ex-friar who as late as 1583 was a parish priest in Berkshire, when he was reported for saying that 'if ever we had mass again he would say it, for he must live'.[39]

Yet if most priests did not openly defy successive settlements, the presence of many traditionalist priests under Edward, of crypto-Protestants under Mary and crypto-Catholics under Elizabeth must have been a strong influence in hampering uniformity. Such was Thomas Dobson, the Cambridgeshire priest already mentioned. He conformed to Mary's restoration of the mass but 'before he came to the altar, he used himself unreverently, saying "We must go to this gear" with laughter'; despite this and other offences he was merely transferred to a neighbouring parish after being disciplined. A survivor of the opposite type was Robert Parkyn, the south Yorkshire vicar. He conformed with great inner reluctance under Edward (continuing to say prayers for the dead in secret); welcomed the Marian reaction joyfully; but conformed again to the 1559 settlement and retained the living till his death in 1570. There were many like-minded priests in conservative areas.[40]

The presence and character of the manorial lord must, in the countryside, have been almost as crucial as that of the priest. Alan Everitt has suggested that later non-conformity can often be correlated with a weak manorial structure or with settlements without a resident lord. Margaret Spufford agrees, though she points out that the difference between large and small settlements was perhaps the crucial factor, small settlements usually having a stronger manorial structure and being easier to control; and she warns against determinism in this as in other areas.[41] No similar study has yet been made for the sixteenth century, but it would be surprising if the pattern of lordship did not prove to be of major importance.

One larger question concerns the extent of continuity in popular religious beliefs. Was there, for instance, continuity in certain areas from Lollardy to Protestantism and later to separatism, or in other areas from late medieval orthodoxy to Catholic recusancy? A. G. Dickens has drawn attention to a correlation between Lollard and puritan areas in Yorkshire, especially in the ports and textile towns, though R. Knecht has suggested that an entrenched native heresy might actually be a repellent to Protestantism.[42] There are similar difficulties in making connections between pre- and post-Reformation Catholicism, though Lancashire seems to furnish a textbook

[38] W. T. MacCaffrey, *Exeter 1540–1640* (Cambridge, Mass, 1958), pp. 191–2.

[39] W. H. Jones, *Diocesan Histories: Salisbury* (London, 1880), p. 194.

[40] Spufford, *Contrasting Communities*, pp. 244, 249; A. G. Dickens, 'Robert Parkyn's Narrative of the Reformation', *E.H.R.*, LXII (1947), pp. 58–83; Haigh, *Reformation and Resistance*, pp. 212, 217–18.

[41] Spufford, *Contrasting Communities*, pp. 306–15.

[42] Dickens, *Lollards and Protestants*, p. 247; R. J. Knecht, 'The Early Reformation in England and France', *History*, LVII (1972), p. 7.

example. Both Jordan and Haigh point as an explanation to the backward state of the county, so that Catholicism was still a vital, almost missionary, influence there when it had already become stereotyped and mechanistic in other areas. Hence Protestantism was able to make little headway 'especially as the political and social structure of the county was as underdeveloped as its religion'.[43] Outside Lancashire, however, continuity on a large scale has yet to be proved, and to expect it in many districts would be to lack faith in the possibility of conversions in large numbers. A. G. Dickens is sceptical of continuity between late medieval orthodoxy and Elizabethan recusancy, or between Marian heresy and Elizabethan puritanism: 'New leaders and new ideas bulk larger than old survivals.'[44]

The need for many more local studies has, it is hoped, been amply demonstrated. Not only is too little known of popular opinion, but also of its variety, which can only with difficulty be forced into the strait-jacket of 'Catholic' and 'Protestant' labels. How does one classify the testators who bequeathed their souls in full Catholic form but then added their hope of salvation solely through the merits of Christ's passion?[45] How far can one allocate the Yorkshire cases of 'tavern unbelief' to Protestant heresy and how far to age-old scepticism? Keith Thomas emphasises the oft-forgotten facts that not all Englishmen went to church, 'that many of those who did went with considerable reluctance, and that a certain proportion remained... utterly ignorant of the elementary tenets of Christian dogma'. The story of the popular Reformation, when it can eventually be properly retold, will probably be much more complex than can yet be imagined.

[43] Haigh, *Reformation and Resistance*, p. 139.

[44] A. G. Dickens, 'The First Stages of Romanist Recusancy in Yorkshire', *Yorkshire Archaeological Journal*, xxxv (1940–3), pp. 180–1, and *Marian Reaction*, ii, p. 14.

[45] Such wills have been observed between 1549 and 1586; the latest noted in York is B.I.Y., PROB reg. xxiii, fo. 223.

6

THE LOCAL IMPACT
OF THE TUDOR REFORMATIONS

RONALD HUTTON

In recent years, our understanding of the Tudor religious changes has been considerably increased by local studies, each concerned with a particular city, county or region and employing a range of different sources for the task.[1] This essay is concerned instead with one of the principal varieties of material used in such studies, the accounts kept by parish churchwardens, and attempts to make a national survey. By taking the surviving accounts from across the whole of the country, with supporting information from visitation returns, sermons, official correspondence and literary sources, it is possible to examine issues which cannot be considered convincingly in local studies, and so to offer a different perspective to earlier work on the subject.

Most of the churchwardens' accounts are incomplete, and several of those surviving give mere annual totals of income and expenditure without individual entries. In large part these faults are the work of time and personal inclination respectively, but they also reflect the tensions prevailing in the period as detailed sets of accounts often break off or become summary (infuriatingly) as the religious changes commence. Contentious items were erased as regimes and policies altered:

[1] During the past ten years before writing, the principal examples have been C. Haigh, *Reformation and Resistance in Tudor Lancashire* (Cambridge, 1975); F. Heal, 'The Parish Clergy and the Reformation in the Diocese of Ely', *Proceedings of the Cambridge Antiquarian Society*, LXVI (1975–6), pp. 141–63; P. Clark, *English Provincial Society from the Reformation to the Revolution* (Hassocks, 1977), and 'Reformation and Radicalism in Kentish Towns', in *The Urban Classes, the Nobility and the Reformation* (German Historical Institute, 1979); D. Palliser, *Tudor York* (Oxford, 1979), Chapter 9; R. Whiting, 'The Reformation in the South-West of England' (University of Exeter Ph.D. thesis, 1977), 'Abominable Idols', *J.E.H.*, XXXIII (1982), pp. 30–47, and 'For the Health of My Soul', *Southern History*, V (1983), pp. 69–94; A. M. Johnson, 'The Reformation Clergy of Derbyshire', *Journal of the Derbyshire Archaeological and Natural History Society*, C (1980), pp. 49–63; G. Williams, 'Wales and the Reign of Mary I', *Welsh History Review*, X (1980–1), pp. 334–58; E. Sheppard, 'The Reformation and the Citizens of Norwich', *Norfolk Archaeology*, XXXVIII (1981–3), pp. 44–55; and G. Mayhew, 'The Progress of the Reformation in East Sussex', *Southern History*, V (1983), pp. 38–67.

Thus, of the 198 sets used for this study, being the great majority of those extant,[2] only eighteen cover *all* the years between 1535 and 1570, in detail.[3] Furthermore, they are geographically limited. The third of England north of the Trent is reflected by only a thirteenth of the accounts, and the four northernmost counties and the whole of Wales have yielded only one set each. The total represents about two per cent of the parishes of the age.

Nevertheless, the value of such a survey ought to be considerable. The accounts provide our principal evidence for the ritual and ornamentation employed in parochial worship. The sample collected reflects communities of all sizes, terrains and economies, scattered widely across the southern two-thirds of England with a few examples from other regions. A systematic exploitation of this source might at least extend the debate over the English Reformation.[4]

One immediate conclusion results from the study: that whether or not the English and Welsh were Protestant at specific points of the Tudor period, they certainly were *governed*. A crucial aspect of the religious changes was that churchwardens had repeatedly to receive or attend upon representatives of Crown, bishops and archdeacons, who instructed and cross-examined them. The churchwardens of Yatton in north Somerset had to attend visitations at Chew Magna in 1547–8, Bedminster and Wells in 1548–9, and Axbridge and Wells in 1549–50. In the single financial year 1550–1, the wardens of Stoke Charity, in the Hampshire downs, had to report twice to royal commissioners and once to the archdeacon. The villagers of Great Packington, Warwickshire, succeeded in preserving their rood loft intact for a year after Queen Elizabeth ordered such lofts to be cut down; then they were faced by a furious representative of the local archdeacon, and it was removed immediately.[5] Such typical examples indicate the considerable degree of enforcement which Church and State put behind their policies. Whether or not the Reformation came from 'above' or 'below', the presence of external authority was something with which most local people had to reckon in these years.

Another immediate impression is gained from the accounts: the consensus of recent historians, that pre-Reformation religion was a flourishing faith, is amply confirmed. For the years 1500–35, the entries record continual embellishment:

[2] For reasons of space, a full list of the accounts used cannot be given here.

[3] St Lawrence, Reading; Stratton; St Mary-on-the Hill, Chester; St Michael, Oxford; Thame; Holy Trinity, Chester; Great Witchingham; St Margaret, Westminster; St Martin-in-the-Fields; Worfield; Leverton; Morebath; Ashburton; St Petrock, Exeter; Badsey; Boxford; St Mary, Bungay; and Wing.

[4] Recently fuelled not only by the works quoted in n. 1, but by J. J. Scarisbrick's general survey, *The Reformation and the English People* (Oxford, 1984). For a discussion of the debate, see Chapter 1 above.

[5] Bishop Hobhouse, *Churchwardens' Accounts* (Somerset Record Society, 1890), pp. 160–2; J. F. Williams, *Early Churchwardens' Accounts of Hampshire* (1913), p. 79; Warwickshire R.O., DR 158/19, p. 10.

churches were enlarged, rood lofts built or redecorated, windows reglazed, side altars added, new images of saints bought and existing ones decorated more richly, obits, lights and guild chapels multiplied, and additional rituals, popular customs and dramatic productions were instituted. Too often, the Church of the early Tudors is spoken of as a static entity, whether healthy or ailing. It is important to stress that many of the decorations and activities outlawed during the various Reformations had been present for only a generation, and that parish religion in 1530 was an intensely dynamic and rapidly developing phenomenon. From the churchwardens' accounts, one has the impression that to the average parishioner what was most disturbing about the local church was the chance that it might become too over-decorated to allow of further elaboration.[6] The remainder of this essay will be devoted to explaining, chronologically, what happened instead.

The first great acts of the Henrician Reformation, the establishment of the royal supremacy, the Injunctions of 1536 and the dissolution of the religious houses, made little discernible impact upon *parish* religion. The payment of Peter's Pence vanished punctually from all sets of accounts, while an occasional parish church benefited from the dissolution of a nearby monastery. The record scoop was at Halesowen, where the rood, organ, images and pictures were obtained from the abbey.[7] The first great alteration in local worship was made by the Injunctions of 1538, which instructed each parish to purchase a Bible; to extinguish all lights in the church except those on the altar, in the rood loft and before the Easter sepulchre; to remove any images which had been 'abused with pilgrimages or offerings'; to regard the surviving representations of saints simply as memorials and to be prepared for the removal of more later; and to reject the veneration of relics. The last direction affected only those few parishes which had relics to venerate, in our sample Halesowen and All Saints, Bristol, where they were promptly delivered to the bishop for destruction. The single positive Injunction, to buy a Bible, was also the most widely flouted, for most of the accounts in the sample do not record a purchase by the end of 1540. Of those which do, the majority derive from London and diocesan capitals, though a few rural communities did comply.[8]

The greatest consequence of these Injunctions for parish churches, however, was the snuffing out of the lights. In most a candle had been kept burning constantly

---

[6] I intend to substantiate this in detail in my forthcoming book, *The Stations of the Sun.*

[7] F. Somers, *Halesowen Accounts* (Worcestershire Historical Society, 1957), p. 78. Sherborne also obtained an image, from Cerne Abbey: Dorset R.O., P155/CW/19.

[8] St Margaret, Westminster; St Martin-in-the-Fields; St Lawrence Pountney; St Mary Magdalen Milk Street; All Hallows Staining; St Petrock, Exeter; St Dunstan, Canterbury; Great Dunmow; Dartmouth; Yatton; All Saints, Bristol; Sheriff Hutton; and Thame did. Wing; St John, Peterborough; Leverton; Morebath; Cratfield; Bethersden; St Michael, Oxford; Ashburton; Badsey; Halesowen; Sherborne; Holy Trinity, Chester; Stratton; Culworth; Swaffham; and Boxford did not.

before the image of a favourite saint, supported by special collections. Some had as many as thirteen such votive lights, while in arable districts of East Anglia and the East Midlands a 'plough light' had been maintained to bring blessings upon tillage. It was paid for by a gathering made on Plough Monday, the second after Epiphany, each year, solicited by the youth of the community going from door to door dragging a plough.[9] When the Injunction against them was published, all such candles were apparently promptly extinguished in the parishes in the sample.[10] In a few,[11] the Plough Monday collection went on, the proceeds going to the general church fund, but elsewhere, if it continued, it ceased to relate to religious matters. The Injunctions had achieved in this case an effect which the Protestant reformers were later to make general: the dissociation of many folk rituals from formal religion. The sample covering 1538 represents none of the rural parishes of the north, nor any in Wales. But, given that it includes some of the more remote parts of southern and, central England, the acquiescence in the royal will is striking, especially as it was not imposed by visitors and commissioners with the thoroughness of later changes.

None of the accounts record the removal of images, for most of those associated with pilgrimage were housed in their own shrines. But the Injunctions had a tremendous effect of a different kind: after 1538 only one *new* image was erected in any of the parishes in the sample, until the Marian reaction.[12] This probably resulted from the threat to existing statues and pictures which one Injunction had made. It probably also signified that if saints were henceforth to be regarded only as good human beings, rather than as powerful intercessors whose presence was in some fashion embodied in their images, then parishioners were just not so interested in them. This latter explanation is also suggested by the decline in the number and importance of parish guilds which followed the Injunctions. These fraternities,

---

[9] Mentioned in the accounts of St John, Peterborough; Leverton; Sutterton; Wigtoft; Great Witchingham; Great St Mary, Cambridge; Shipdam; St Mary, Bungay; Holy Trinity, Bungay; Brundish; and Denton. Boxford and Cratfield had the collection but no light.

[10] The 'stock' light was still burning at St Thomas, Salisbury, in 1546–7, but may have stood on the altar or rood loft: H. Swayne, *Accounts of St. Edmund and St. Thomas Salisbury* (Wilts. Record Society, 1896), p. 274. In 1542 a gift was made for St Giles's light to the university church at Cambridge, but there is no mention of the light itself: J. Foster, *Accounts of St. Mary the Great* (Cambridge Antiquarian Society, 1905), p. 98. In 1546–8 a St Mary candle was burned at Prescot, Lancashire, but this seems to have stood in for the paschal candle made in every church for Easter: F. Bailey, *Prescot Churchwardens' Accounts* (Lancashire and Cheshire Record Society, 1953), pp. 24–7.

[11] Boxford; Swaffham; Tilney; Brundish; Cratfield.

[12] St Lawrence, Reading, had an image of Jesus glued to a desk in 1541, but this may have been a repair: C. Kerry, *History of the Municipal Church of St Lawrence, Reading* (1883), p. 32. So the only certain exception is the erection of a St Clement at St Nicholas, Bristol, in this same year: E. Atchley, *Transactions of the St Paul's Ecclesiological Society*, VI (1906), p. 62.

supernatural insurance schemes whereby members paid a subscription in life to ensure
prayers for their souls, may well have suffered from Protestant criticism of the
doctrine of Purgatory; but Purgatory was upheld by the Act of Six Articles in 1539.
Instead, it may be significant that most guilds had taken a patron saint, and the attack
upon these intercessors may have weakened belief in the efficacy of the organisations.
Certainly, those which collapsed fastest tended to be those dedicated to minor
saints.[13] Thus, to an almost uncanny degree, the Henrician Reformation had inflicted
effective blows upon a flourishing popular religion. The only part of the Injunctions
commonly ignored was that which Protestants had hoped would supply a faith to
replace that demolished: the order for the purchase of parish Bibles.

During the remainder of Henry's reign, some minor reforms were made in
religion. One resulted from a royal proclamation of 1541,[14] ordering churchwardens
to obtain a Bible or pay fines: under this pressure, virtually all parishes in the sample
obeyed within three years, though a few took longer.[15] Between 1542 and 1545 also,
a majority of the churches in the sample acquired the new processional in English,
the first break in the monopoly of Latin in services.[16] Yet when the London parishes
are excluded, the majority almost vanishes, and it is probably misleading. Some
country churches *did* obtain the processional, and some in London did not, but most
of the parishes which failed to make the purchase were in remoter provinces, and
the small number of accounts surviving from such communities produces an
imbalance in the picture. Overall, the pattern indicates once more the limited interest
in the positive aspects of Reformation unless parishes were coerced. In 1541 another
proclamation carried the negative process further by abolishing the custom whereby
children were dressed as saints or prelates, adding interest to certain feasts and another
means by which money could be collected for pious purposes. The most celebrated
of these figures was the Boy Bishop, who had officiated in certain cathedrals, religious
houses and parish churches during the Christmas season. Prohibition was a marginal
change in habits of popular piety, for the great majority of parishes had never
introduced the custom and it had reached its peak of popularity a generation earlier.

---

[13] The guilds and their history have been well treated by Whiting, in *Southern History*, 1983, and
Scarisbrick, *Reformation*, Chapter 2, and the south-western sources used by Dr Whiting are
by far the best parish records for this sort of institution. I differ from him only in suggesting
that prayers for the dead and saints may have been closely inter-related.

[14] P. L. Hughes and J. F. Larkin, eds., *Tudor Royal Proclamations* (New Haven, 1964), I, no. 200.

[15] Like Cratfield (1547), Tarring (1547), St Peter-in-the-East, Oxford (1545–6); and St Mary
Woolnoth (1545–6).

[16] Bramley; Yatton; St Margaret, Westminster; St Michael Spurriergate, York; St Andrew,
Lewes; Ashburton; Badsey; St Martin Outwich; Stogursey; St Nicholas, Bristol; Long Sutton;
St Martin, Oxford; St Mary, Bungay; All Hallows Staining; St Dunstan-in-the-West; and St
Mary Magdalen Milk Street bought it. Boxford; Crondall; St Michael, Worcester; Morebath;
Leverton; Ludlow; Thame; Woodbury; St Mary Woolnoth; and St Michael Le Quern
apparently did not.

In those places where it still endured, it was terminated promptly in obedience to the royal will.[17]

Apart from the alterations enforced by law, however, the surviving accounts show that most of the rituals and ornaments of the 1520s remained in English churches in Henry VIII's last years. The images of saints were washed, utensils, banners, veils and vestments mended or replaced, and endowed obits sung for the dead. Six churches in the sample sold some service equipment,[18] but those things that went were usually old and certainly second-best, and such sales to raise ready cash had been made before.

The dramatic changes began with Henry's death in January 1547. It was marked by obsequies on a scale far greater than those accorded his two successors, and indicates something of the impact he had made on his subjects' imagination. Parishes in London, Leicester, Cambridge, Norfolk, Worcester, Salisbury and Devon held dirges and dead-masses for him. The corporations of Shrewsbury and Norwich paid for such services, the latter placing 120 candles and six escutcheons around the catafalque.[19] During the first seven months of Edward VI's reign, in the 'ritual half' of the Christian year, the old ceremonies were carried out as before, but there were a few signs of change. The wardens of St Botolph, Aldgate, bought six books of psalms in English, though the curate refused to use them. Those of another London parish removed all images, including the rood, and painted texts from Scripture on the walls, but were rebuked by the Privy Council after a protest by the bishop and the Lord Mayor. Images were apparently broken at Portsmouth.[20] Against such incidents must be set the number of provincial churches which continued to invest in the old order, replacing the cords which drew up rood cloths and lenten veils, buying new altar cloths and vestments, mending the rood or rood loft and painting banners.[21] A Radnorshire man even set up alabaster stelae in his church carved with scenes from the life of Becket, the saint proscribed ten years before.[22]

[17] Evidence for the period 1530–41 survives from Boxford, Sherborne and St Andrew, Lewes. The much greater material for the preceding epoch will be cited in *The Stations of the Sun*. The proclamation is in Hughes and Larkin, *Proclamations*, I, no. 202.

[18] St Lawrence, Reading; Great St Mary, Cambridge; North Elmham; St Martin Outwich; St Mary Woolnoth; and Tarring.

[19] St Michael, Worcester; St Martin, Leicester; Great St Mary, Cambridge; Mickfield; Ashburton; St Thomas, Salisbury; North Elmham; Wandsworth. C. Wriothesley, *A Chronicle of England*, ed. W. D. Hamilton (Camden Society, 1875), I, p. 181; H. Owen and J. B. Blakeway, *A History of Shrewsbury* (London, 1875), I, p. 341; Blomefield, *The County of Norfolk* (London, 1806), III, pp. 216–17.

[20] Guildhall R.O., MS. 9235/1, 17 July 1547; *A.P.C.*, II, pp. 25–6; *The Letters of Stephen Gardiner*, ed. J. A. Muller (Cambridge, 1933), pp. 273–6.

[21] Eg. Halesowen; Ludlow; Winterslow; Stratton; Thame; Great Hallingbury; Christ Church, Bristol; Wandsworth; Marston; St Mary-on-the-Hill, Chester; Bletchingley; Ashburton.

[22] B.L., Add. MS. 25460, fo. 70 (deposition by New Radnor parishioners).

It was in this context that the government of Protector Somerset issued its Injunctions on 31 July. They ordered the destruction of all 'shrines', paintings and pictures of saints and all images which had been offered to or had candles burned before them; limited the lights in the church to a couple upon the high altar; forbade processions in or around the church when mass was celebrated; and repeated the instruction to purchase the Bible and added one to buy the *Paraphrases* of Erasmus. To enforce these, the realm was divided into six circuits, Archbishop Cranmer and the Privy Council naming from four to six visitors for each. All the men chosen were either Protestants or reliable servants of the regime: a carefully selected handful of activists. Their activity is recorded in all the surviving accounts during the rest of the year and the next, including those for Lancashire and Cumberland. It was frequently felt heavily. Some Salisbury churchwardens had to produce two bills for the visitors, one certifying the condition of the church before their coming and the other detailing the changes that had been made since. Yorkshire and Somerset parishes had to return a second bill after their first was rejected, while one in Shropshire had to send in eight bills. At Hull, the visitors broke the statues in the church in person. At St Paul's Cathedral, they destroyed most of the images in September, and pulled down all the remainder two months later, at night to avoid a commotion. They generally made wardens present evidence upon oath, and sometimes summoned other parishioners in addition, to obtain alternative information.[23]

Even while the visitation was proceeding, government policy evolved. In September 1547, in response to uncertainty on the part of the corporation of London, the Privy Council reaffirmed that images which had not been cult objects could remain – unless the priest, the churchwardens *or* the visitors decided upon their removal.[24] On 6 February a royal proclamation forbade four important ceremonies of the old Church: the blessing of candles at Candlemas, ashes upon Ash Wednesday and palms upon Palm Sunday, and the adoration of the rood upon Good Friday, popularly called 'Creeping to the Cross'.[25] Two weeks later, the council ordered the removal of *all* remaining images from churches, on the grounds that their

[23] The visitors are discussed in W. K. Jordan, *Edward VI: The Young King* (London, 1968), pp. 163–6. Details of their activities are in Swayne, *St. Edmund and St. Thomas*, pp. 274–5; Somerset R.O., D/P/ban. 4/1/1, year 1546–7; H. Walters, 'Accounts of Worfield', *Transactions of the Shropshire Archaeological and Natural History Society*, VII (1903–9), p. 239; J. Purvis, 'Sheriff Hutton Accounts', *Yorkshire Archaeological Journal*, XXXVI (1944), p. 184; G. Hadley, *History of Kingston-upon-Hull* (Hull, 1788), pp. 88–9; R. Howlett, ed., *Monumenta Franciscana* (Rolls Series, 1882), pp. 214–15; Wriothesley, *Chronicle*, II, p. 1; C. B. Pearson, 'Accounts of St Michael, Bath', *Somersetshire Archaeological and Natural History Society Proceedings*, XXVI (1877–80), p. 118.

[24] Corporation of London R.O., Journal 15, fo. 322, and Letter Book Q, fos. 210v and 214.

[25] E. Cardwell, *Documentary Annals of the Reformed Church of England* (Oxford, 1844), I, p. 42.

continued presence was causing dispute and disorder.[26] In the autumn of 1547, two acts of Parliament had carried the Reformation further, one instructing that the laity should take communion in both kinds, and the other decreeing the seizure by the State of the endowments of chantries, religious guilds and perpetual obits, on the grounds that the doctrine of Purgatory was false.

The impact of this campaign upon the parish records is profound, but blurred by the fact that few accounts dated individual items, so that the precise chronology of change is usually irrecoverable. Two parishes show unmistakable evidence of Protestant zeal: Rye, where the images were removed before September 1547 and called 'idols', and St Botolph Aldgate, where the congregation got rid of their curate in October after a fierce tussle with the Lord Mayor, and adopted an English service.[27] All observers agree that images were cleared from the churches of London by the end of that year,[28] and the surviving accounts bear this out. The process seems an orderly one, the statues and panes of glass being removed by workmen paid by the wardens rather than shattered privately. It was a very formal sort of iconoclasm. In the provinces it was virtually complete by the end of 1548, in most cases as a consequence of the royal visitation, and in the autumn of 1547 the Privy Council punished two cases of resistance, at St Neots and High Wycombe.[29] The last recorded clearances of images took place at St Dunstan, Canterbury, in 1549, and at Worfield, Shropshire, and Ashburton, Devon, in 1549–50. The surviving Lancashire account does not mention the removal of images by name, but after the visitation the wardens sold much brass, pewter, and iron, which probably marks the same process. The surviving account from York records that the statues were taken away in 1547, and the curate of a living near Doncaster stated firmly that all in the county were plucked down early in 1548.[30] At Stratton, Cornwall, the rood and 'pageants' were removed in 1548, replaced during the rebellion of 1549, and then taken down again.[31] Thus it looks as if the campaign against representations of saints had triumphed all over England within about three years. In the same period, most of the churches in the sample were reglazed and coated with white lime on the interior, almost certainly to obliterate images in stained glass and wall-paintings. In seventeen parishes out of the ninety-one in the sample for these years, the rood lofts themselves, upon which

[26] J. Strype, *Ecclesiastical Memorials* (Oxford, 1822), II (ii), p. 125.
[27] East Sussex R.O., Rye Corporation Records 147/1, fo. 111v; Guildhall, R.O., MS. 9235/1, 5 Oct.–23 Dec. 1547.
[28] *Calendar of State Papers, Spanish*, IX, p. 148; *Monumenta Franciscana*, II, pp. 214–15; *Wriothesley Chronicle*, II, p. 1.   [29] *A.P.C.* II, pp. 140–1, 147.
[30] J. Cowper, 'Accounts of St. Dunstan', *Archaeologia Cantiana*, XVII (1886–7), pp. 111–12; A. Hanham, *Accounts of Ashburton* (Devon and Cornwall Record Society, 1970), p. 124; Walters, 'Worfield', p. 114; Bailey, *Prescot*, pp. 25–7; B.I.Y., PR Y/MS. 3, fo. 217v; A. G. Dickens, 'Robert Parkyn's Narrative', *E.H.R.*, LXII (1947), p. 66.
[31] B.L., Add. MS. 32243, fos. 48–9.

some of the principal images had stood, were demolished. No provision for this had been made in the official instructions: in some of the urban parishes reforming zeal seems an obvious reason, but some of the provincial demolitions remain mysterious.[32]

The same success attended the government's action against chantries, gilds and obits. For this task it employed county commissions, numbering between five and thirteen and mixing officials of the Court of Augmentations with local gentry. More than the visitors, therefore, they represented action by the central government through a filter of provincial notables. But the contrast can be exaggerated, for these men were not a cross-section of shire leadership but individuals hand-picked for the job. How much sensitivity they displayed in preserving the educational and charitable functions of the institutions they dissolved varied from county to county, but all worked with remarkable speed and efficiency. They began their surveys in February 1548 and the expropriations after Easter.[33] All the obits and almost all the gilds vanish from the surviving accounts during that year, and the last gild is mentioned at Stratton in 1549. In the same period the common custom of tolling bells for the repose of all souls in Purgatory upon the evening of All Saints' Day died out in every parish in the sample. All that was left of the great number of institutions and rituals concerning the dead was the occasional burning of candles at the burial of a parishioner.[34]

All the four ceremonies prohibited by the government in February 1548 were forsaken that year in every church in the sample. With them went others of universal importance: the burning of a paschal candle from Easter Eve until Ascension Day, and the blessing of new fire and the hallowing of the font upon Easter Eve.[35] Many churches in large towns had adopted the ritual of carrying the consecrated host beneath a canopy in procession upon Corpus Christi Day. Although not specifically forbidden by statute or proclamation, this had incurred the bitter hostility of Protestants, who regarded it as idolatry, and had ceased everywhere by 1548.[36] Another rite not specifically condemned by the government was that of lodging the

---

[32] Boxford, 1547; St Ewen, Bristol, 1547–8; Morebath, 1551; St Martin, Leicester, 1548–9; Wandsworth, 1548–9; Rye, 1547; Badsey, 1552–3; St Martin-in-the-Fields, 1552–3; St Michael, Cornhill, 1548; Banwell, 1548; St Mary Redcliffe, Bristol, 1550; All Saints, Bristol, 1549–50; St Nicholas, Bristol, 1548; Tilney, 1548; St John Bow, Exeter, 1549; South Littleton, 1552–3; St Michael, Gloucester, 1550–1; St Mary-at-Hill, London, 1547–8.

[33] W. K. Jordan, *Edward VI: The Threshold of Power* (London, 1970), Part VI; C. J. Kitching, 'The Chantries of the East Riding', *Yorkshire Archaeological Journal*, XLIV (1972), pp. 178–85; N. Orme, 'The Dissolution of the Chantries in Devon', *Transactions of the Devonshire Assocation*, CXI (1979), pp. 75–123; Scarisbrick, *Reformation*, Chapter 6.   [34] At Wandsworth.

[35] The last in the sample to use them being Ludlow and Prescot, at Easter 1549.

[36] Recorded in 1545–7 at St Dunstan, Canterbury; Holy Trinity, Chester; Ashburton; Sherborne; and all the Bristol and London churches in the sample. The decline of the rite in London is chronicled in *Monumenta Franciscana*, II, pp. 217, 220, 228.

host in an Easter sepulchre upon Good Friday and 'resurrecting' it upon Easter Day. This was attacked by Archbishop Cranmer in his visitation articles of 1548, and by lesser prelates thereafter.[37] Despite the fact that all the parishes in the sample, save some small rural communities, had practised this ceremony in the mid-1540s, its survival is only recorded in one place from 1549 until the death of Edward.[38] Yet another very common ritual, especially in urban churches, had been the reading or singing of the Passion upon Palm Sunday, often by performers in costume. This was apparently forbidden by nobody, but by 1549 it survived in only two parishes in the sample, and it ended in that year.[39] All these ceremonies were formally legal but disliked by Protestants: it is unclear whether they were forsaken because they were denounced by royal or ecclesiastical visitors, or whether the proscription of related rites caused their spontaneous abandonment in a mood of confusion and disorientation.

With these ecclesiastical rituals crashed a whole world of popular custom which had been associated with the parish church. In communities across most of southern England, the principal source of parish funds had been the holding of church ales by the wardens, usually in Whitsun week. During the mid-1540s such ales were regular occurrences in seventeen parishes in the sample, but after 1549 they continued in only five of these.[40] Some reason for this decline is provided by the chance survival of one document:[41] a letter from the royal visitors of the West Country in 1547, forbidding such ales upon the grounds of the 'many inconveniences' arising from them. The choice of a practical rather than a religious objection to the custom is significant, for the charge of 'inconvenience' was to be levied at such popular gatherings repeatedly over the next hundred years. Already, the alliance between Protestant Reformation and the regulation of folk recreations in the name of order had been formed. That this was the attitude of most, but not all, of the sets of visitors is suggested by the fact that four of the five parishes where ales survived were in the southern Midlands, where official policy was apparently more lenient.

Almost certainly as part of the same process, the remaining Plough Monday gatherings vanish from the sample after 1547. In 1547-8 Wandsworth parish sold its maypoles, and the great pole which had stood in Cornhill was hacked to pieces in 1549 after a Protestant preacher called it an idol.[42] Another item which vanished

---

[37] Cited in A. Heales, 'Easter Sepulchres', *Archaeologia*, XLII (1867), p. 304.

[38] At Minchinhampton in 1551 (printed in Heales, 'Easter Sepulchres', p. 304).

[39] St Lawrence, Reading, and St Nicholas, Bristol.

[40] Boxford; Wing; Crondall; Morebath; Yatton; Ashburton; Worfield; St Michael, Oxford; Sherborne; Halse; Ilminster; Marston; Pyrton; Norton-by-Daventry; Thame; Winsford. The last five were those where ales survived.

[41] Historical Manuscripts Commission, *Dean and Chapter of Wells MSS*, II, pp. 264-5.

[42] C. Davis, 'Accounts of Wandsworth', *Surrey Archaeological Collections*, XV (1900-2), p. 90; J. Stow, *A Survey of London* (ed. C. L. Kingsford, 1908), p. 144.

from the accounts after 1547–8 was 'hocking', the collection of money, on the Monday and Tuesday after Easter Week, by gangs of men or women who captured members of the opposite sex in the street and made them pay forfeits.[43] With this disappeared the mysterious 'hognels' or 'hogglers', groups of parishioners who went about in the winter season apparently collecting for parish funds.[44] The Injunctions of 1547 only forbade the holding of processions about church and churchyard, and need not have halted the most important processions of all, those around the parish in Rogation Week with cross and banners to ask blessings upon it. Yet in each parish in the sample this custom also lapsed in 1547–8.[45] Still another casualty was the habit of decking churches, like private houses, with greenery at certain feasts: thus those of London were festooned with holly and ivy at Christmas, box on Palm Sunday and birch at Midsummer. Such trappings were abandoned in every community represented by the accounts before the end of 1548. Like so many of the rites and customs described above, they were not specifically prohibited in Injunctions, acts of council or visitation articles, but could be subsumed under the general headings of 'superstition' or 'idolatry'.

Alongside this immense process of demolition, the reformers laboured to inculcate their new faith, but with much less success. In 1547 the government sponsored the publication of the *Book of Homilies*, sermons on key topics and doctrines which could be read by a clergy incapable of preaching. During the reign of Edward, this was purchased by only nineteen out of the ninety-one parishes in the sample,[46] and the majority of those which did not obtain the volume were precisely those provincial or rural communities where the priest would most need it. The government had more success with the English translation of Erasmus's *Paraphrases*: of the parishes in the sample, forty-one had bought it before the end of 1548, and another twelve by the end of Edward's reign. How far this lively but scholarly work was read or understood by parishioners is, however, a different matter, and some of the entries recording the purchase do not encourage optimism. In the accounts of Yatton, Somerset, the book is called 'The Paraphrases and Erasmus', in those of St Dunstan,

---

[43] Like the Boy Bishop, this was in decline by the 1540s, when it features in the accounts from Wing; St Andrew, Canterbury; St Thomas, Salisbury; St Lawrence, Reading; and Thame.

[44] Recorded in the mid-1540s at Hawkhurst; Wandsworth; Bletchingley; Banwell; Chagford; and Nettlecombe.

[45] It was particularly important at Christ Church, Bristol; St Ewen, Bristol; St Michael, Oxford; St Thomas, Salisbury; Holy Trinity, Chester; Long Sutton; and in the London parishes in the sample. Robert Parkyn noted that it ceased generally in Yorkshire after 1549: Dickens, 'Narrative', p. 67.

[46] By Bramley; St Ewen, Bristol; St Martin, Leicester; Pyrton; Yatton; Wandsworth; Tarring; St Andrew Hubbard; St Edmund, Salisbury; St Mary, Dover; Thame; Great Hallingbury; Crediton; All Hallows Staining; St Margaret Pattens; St Alphage London Wall; St Botolph Aldgate; St Dunstan-in-the-West; St Lawrence Pountney.

Canterbury, 'Parasimus', and in those of Sheriff Hutton, Yorkshire, 'Coloke of Herassimus'.[47] Of the sample, twenty parishes employed the cruder but probably effective educational technique of having texts from Scripture painted upon the walls, the rood loft or a cloth hung from the loft. The greatest positive step taken by the regime was the publication of the first Book of Common Prayer, prescribed by the parliamentary Act of Uniformity of 1549. With this legal provision behind it, the book was obtained by *every* parish in the sample by the specified date, Whit Sunday 1549. In December of that year, however, a royal proclamation complained that many priests were failing to use it, and attempted to eliminate competition by ordering the delivery of old service books to the bishops for destruction.[48] Seventeen parishes in the sample obeyed, and most of the remainder combined compliance with the spirit of the order with fund-raising, by selling off the volumes condemned. Hence, whatever priest or congregation may have thought of it, the Protestant service seems to have been conducted across most, and perhaps all, of the realm by 1550.

The regime of Protector Somerset has been regarded by Protestants at the time, and historians since, as relatively moderate and willing to compromise in the work of reform. Yet its impact was devastating: the great majority of the decorations and rites employed in and around English churches in early 1547 had gone by late 1549. As far as the churchwardens' accounts tell the story, all that the succeeding 'radical' administration of Northumberland had to do was to 'mop up' by revising the Prayer Book, replacing the altars with communion tables and confiscating the obsolete church goods. The new service was introduced in every parish in the sample within the prescribed period in 1552–3, and the other reforms were just as thoroughly carried out, although over a longer period. In fourteen parishes in the sample, altars were removed under Somerset, apparently a token of local Protestant zeal: a third of these were in the capital, but nine counties are also represented.[49] In April 1550 Nicholas Ridley, the new Bishop of London, instituted a campaign to take down the rest, and by the end of the year this had happened – not merely in every church in his diocese for which accounts survive, but in all those in the sample from Bristol and some from a range of shires including Devon, Worcestershire and Yorkshire.[50]

---

[47] Hobhouse, *Churchwardens' Accounts*, p. 161; Cowper, 'St. Dunstan', p. 111; Purvis, 'Sheriff Hutton', p. 185.

[48] Hughes and Larkin, *Proclamations*, I, no. 353.

[49] St Benet Gracechurch; St Lawrence, Reading; Wimborne Minster; Rye; St Andrew Hubbard; St Michael Cornhill; Winterslow; Holy Trinity, Chester; Holywell; Harwich; Tilney; St John Bow, Exeter; St Botolph Aldgate; and St Stephen Walbrook. In addition, the altars at St Leonard, Eastcheap, were broken up by private persons in October 1548: Corporation of London R.O., Letter Book Q, fo. 250v; Repertory 11, fo. 473v.

[50] Boxford; Wing; St Nicholas, Warwick; St Martin, Leicester; Yatton; Banwell; Halesowen; St Mary, Devizes; Sheriff Hutton; Louth; St Mary, Bungay; Woodbury; St Michael, Bath.

Thus, when in November the Privy Council wrote to the bishops that most of the altars in the country had been taken down, and that the remainder should now be removed to avoid disputes,[51] they could have been exaggerating only slightly, if at all. The order, doubtless driven home by the ecclesiastical visitations recorded in the accounts, was complied with by virtually all the remaining parishes in the sample within the year: only Thame, in Oxfordshire, managed to postpone the work until December 1552.[52]

The Privy Council had been interested in the fate of church goods since 1547, when it ordered the bishops to ensure that inventories were made in each parish. In 1549, complaining of sales and misappropriations, it instructed sheriffs and justices to take fresh inventories, retaining copies, and to prosecute those who had disposed of equipment. Three years later, commissioners were appointed to repeat this process, and in January 1553 another set of commissions was issued with instructions to seize all the surviving goods except linen, chalices and bells. Plate, money and jewels were to be sent to London, while robes, cloths and base metals were sold locally and the proceeds sent up.[53] The activities of the bishops are mostly lost in the usual entries of reports to ecclesiastical visitations, but all the accounts register the activities of the county commissioners. Those of 1552–3 were, like the men who dissolved chantries and gilds, local worthies selected for their obedience or enthusiasm, and they did their work well. The churchwardens of Harwich had their initial inventory rejected, and the acceptance of their second was postponed until the whole commission was present. The vicar of Morebath, Devon, was interrogated four times over. After visiting the commissioners for the North Riding five times and writing to them once, the wardens of Sheriff Hutton had to attend the Council of the North to obtain a stay of confiscation of some of their church goods.[54] The parish accounts also show that the government's fear of disposal and misappropriation was justified, for sixty-nine of the ninety in the sample record the sale of ornaments and vestments between 1547 and 1552. The majority of sales had occurred in London and the neighbouring counties, both more Protestant and, arguably, more conscious of a need to profit from the goods before the government did. The sums raised were often comparatively large, such as the £32 from one sale at St Stephen Walbrook or £43 9s at the other City church of St Alphege, London Wall. Yet they often represented only a percentage of the goods' original value, a glaring case being at St Lawrence, Reading, where the gilding of just two tabernacles in 1519 had cost

[51] A.P.C., III, pp. 168–9.
[52] Oxfordshire R.O., Par. Thame b. 2, p. 104.
[53] All entered conveniently in W. Page, ed., *Inventories of Church Goods* (Surtees Society, 1896), pp. xii–xv.
[54] Essex R.O., T/A/122/1, fos. 32–3; J. E. Binney, *Accounts of Morebath* (Exeter, 1904), p. 175; Purvis, 'Sheriff Hutton', p. 187.

£1 but all the tabernacles and some other fittings were sold in 1547 for 2s 8d.[55] Clearly, many parishes were determined to turn the religious changes to financial advantage, and almost certainly were hurrying to sell their goods before confiscation set in.

A sample of the surviving visitation returns and church court records for Edward's reign bears out the impression left by the accounts. In Kent in 1548 people from three parishes were accused of having failed to deface images removed from churches, and one rector summoned for having continued the ceremonies of paschal candle and sepulchre at Easter. In late 1550, before altars were proscribed by the Privy Council, members of fourteen Kentish parishes were in trouble for not destroying them with sufficient speed and two priests were excommunicated till this was done, while seven priests were accused of having kept old service books. In Lancashire in 1552, four parishes admitted to having failed to remove altars, and in Wiltshire in 1553, one parish confessed to having an altar. In the archdeaconry of Norwich in 1549, none of the thirty-one parishes admitted to preserving images, tabernacles or the old ceremonies. In the diocese of Ely during the whole of Edward's reign, visitations aroused some concern about the quality of the clergy and their performance of the Protestant service, but none about the adaptation of the churches for Protestant worship.[56] For Wales there exist no such records, but evidence of a sort is provided by the lament of a Glamorgan poet written near the end of the reign, describing the churches as universally empty of altars, roods, pyxes and holy water stoops.[57] Such sources reinforce the impression of compliance with the reforms and (in the case of Kent) of the ruthlessness with which the Protestants who had taken over the ecclesiastical machinery would enforce that compliance, running ahead of declared government policy.

Long before Edward's commissioners had completed the task of turning obsolete church goods into public money, the goods had ceased to be obsolete. The King was dead, Mary on the throne, and the Reformation halted and then reversed. The new monarch took power in July 1553, and decreed a temporary toleration of both creeds. In December Parliament repealed the reforming statutes of Edward's reign and restored the service of 1546, and the Queen ordered every parish to build an altar, obtain a cross, and hallow ashes on Ash Wednesday, palms on Palm Sunday and water on Easter Eve. In March she issued Injunctions for the restoration of all

[55] Guildhall R.O., MS. 59312, years 1549–50, and MS. 1432/1, fo. 101; Kerry, *St. Lawrence*, p. 68.

[56] Haigh, *Lancashire*, p. 144; C. E. Woodruff, 'Original Documents', *Archaeologia Cantiana*, XXXI (1915), pp. 95–105; Wiltshire R.O., Salisbury Diocesan Records, Detecta Book 1, fos. 106–35; Norfolk R.O., ANW 1/1; Cambridge University Library, EDR B12/3.

[57] G. Williams, 'The Ecclesiastical History of Glamorgan, 1527–1642', in G. Williams, ed., *Glamorgan County History*, IV (1974), pp. 218–19.

processions and all 'laudable and honest ceremonies'.[58] The fact that most wardens did not date individual entries vitiates attempts to assess the choices of parishioners and priests during the period of 'liberty' from July to December, but there are some indications. At Stratton, Cornwall, vestments were repurchased, a canopy for the sacrament made and tapers bought as soon as Mary took power. The wardens of Stanford-in-the-Vale, Berkshire, sold the communion table with a reference to the past 'wicked time of schism'. At Harwich the high altar was made, and at Halse, Somerset, the mass restored, by October. In the London church of St Dunstan-in-the-West both altar and old service were back before the end of September.[59] These hints bear out the picture presented by the literary sources,[60] of a slight spontaneous revival of Catholicism in the capital and a more pronounced one in the provinces. It was a distinctly more impressive anticipation of policy than Edward's Reformation had received in early 1547, but the Protestants in those months, unlike the Catholics in late 1553, had had no legal freedom to act.

Once the administrative machinery had been captured by the proponents of Counter Reformation, it was worked with all the vigour that Protestants had given it. Metropolitan, episcopal and archidiaconal visitations and royal commissioners passed through the provinces, and wardens were constantly returning inventories and statements to them. In December 1553 the Privy Council imprisoned a Maidstone man who had sponsored a petition for Protestantism in his parish, while in March it made four Essex gentry give bonds to erect altars in their respective churches. The wardens of one London parish, St Pancras Soper Lane, were ordered by Cardinal Pole's commissioners in 1555 not merely to rebuild a rood loft but to make it five feet long, with images, and to complete the work in six weeks. Those of another, St Botolph Aldgate, imposed a rate to raise money for extensive rebuilding, on the command of Bishop Bonner. The metropolitan visitors instructed those of St Neots in 1556 to rebuild every altar which had stood in their church in King Henry's time, within one month. Those of Bromfield, Essex, were excommunicated in 1558 because their church contained no images, while during two months in 1554 the wardens of Harwich had to return three successive bills to the Queen's commissioners.[61]

[58] Strype, *Memorials*, III (i), p. 34; Hughes and Larkin, *Proclamations*, I, nos. 390, 407.
[59] B.L., Add. MS. 32243, fo. 53; W. Haines, 'Accounts of Stanford', *The Antiquary* (1888), p. 118; Essex R.O., T/A/122/1, fo. 62; Somerset R.O., D/P/hal. 4/1/4, fo. 21; Guildhall R.O., MS. 2968/1, year 1552–3.
[60] *The Diary of Henry Machyn*, ed. J. Nichols (Camden Society, 1848), p. 42; C. H. Cooper, *Annals of Cambridge* (Cambridge, 1842), III, p. 82; Dickens, 'Narrative', p. 80; *Narratives of the Days of the Reformation*, ed. J. G. Nichols (Camden Society, 1859), p. 81; *Monumenta Franciscana*, II, pp. 242–7; Wriothesley, *Chronicle*, II, pp. 101–5.
[61] *A.P.C.*, IV, pp. 375, 411; J. P. Malcolm, *London Redivivum* (London, 1802), II, p. 169; Guildhall R.O., MS. 9235/1, year 1554–5; H. Pollard, 'Cardinal Pole's Visitation', *Transactions of the Cambridgeshire and Huntingdonshire Archaeological Society*, IV (1915–30), pp. 81–7; Essex R.O., D/P 248/5/1, p. 6, and T/A/122/1, fo. 71.

Accounts survive from 134 parishes in the sample for Mary's reign, and show a considerable homogeneity in the process of Catholic restoration. By the end of 1554, all had rebuilt a high altar, and obtained vestments and copes, some or all of the utensils and ornaments of the mass (a crucifix, holy water stoop, chalice, pyx, pax, patten, sacring bell, chrismatory, cruets, censers and candlesticks) and some or all of the necessary books (a mass book, processional, psalter, manual, coucher, hymnal, antiphonal, legend, breviary and grail). During the remainder of the reign, they added to this equipment, and most acquired a rood with flanking figures of Mary and John, some images or paintings of saints, a side altar, rood lights, and altar cloths, rood hangings, banners and a canopy. All those parishes which had removed their rood lofts under Edward now rebuilt them. Where the purchase of items is not recorded, this may often mean that they were brought out of hiding, and the frequent entries for mending old ornaments bears this out. In many parishes, a wooden crucifix was bought at first, to be replaced by a silver or gilded one, and the rood, Mary and John were painted on a cloth until carved wooden figures could be paid for. The process slackened only slightly after the first year, and most of the parishes in the sample were carrying out further embellishments until the moment of Mary's death. The majority of these acquisitions were compulsory: the high altar and mass were prescribed from December 1553, while rood lofts, and the rood, Mary and John that they carried, were necessary by 1555 and images of patron saints of parishes by 1556.[62] Yet most of the parishes in the sample decorated their churches more than the legal minimum required.

All this activity posed a serious financial problem: the meagre expenses of reformation had easily been covered by selling church goods, but restoration cost a great deal. The Privy Council ordered ten of Edward's commissions to return to parishes those ornaments they had received which were as yet intact, but this procedure was of benefit to only three of the churches in our sample.[63] In nineteen cases, the accounts record that parishioners presented the parish with goods (in many cases probably bought from it under Edward) or money to obtain them.[64] (On the other hand, records of church courts under Mary abound with suits against people who failed to disgorge ornaments or cloths when pressed to do so.[65]) In many churches items were apparently brought out of store. But the accounts make it clear that the great bulk of the work of restoration had to be paid for, by rates and compulsory gatherings among the congregation or from accumulated funds. A

[62] Wriothesley, *Chronicle*, II, pp. 105, 131, 134.
[63] Prescot; Ashburton; and All Saints, Bristol. The council orders are in *A.P.C.*, IV, pp. 338, 344, 348, 354–5, 360–1, 371, 376; V, pp. 112–13; VI, pp. 267–8.
[64] Morebath; Great Dunmow; Eltham; Stanford-in-the-Vale; Wandsworth; St Petrock, Exeter; St Botolph, Aldgate; St Martin, Leicester; St Nicholas, Warwick; St Martin-in-the-Fields; St Mary-at-Hill; Banwell; Halesowen; St Mary-on-the-Hill, Chester; Shipdam; Crediton; Woodbury; St Dunstan-in-the-West; and Tintinhull.
[65] E.g. Woodruff, 'Original Documents', pp. 107–10.

multiplicity of local solutions was found: at South Littleton in Worcestershire, for example, the priest agreed to pay for the necessary books on being given the right to cull and sell the pigeons which lived in the steeple.[66] The financial problem amply explains why the process of restocking the churches was so gradual, and more so in rural parishes where the Reformation had presumably taken least hold. It is small wonder that in every case the new decorations and utensils were less imposing and expensive than those disposed of under Edward.

The restoration of ritual was fairly complete. Every church in the sample readopted the paschal candle, the blessing of new fire and the hallowing of the font, while the Easter sepulchre reappeared in the same proportion of churches (the great majority) where it had existed before the Reformation. The blessing of palms and reading of the Passion of Palm Sunday,[67] the hallowing of candles at Candlemas,[68] 'Creeping to the Cross',[69] the Corpus Christi processions,[70] the Boy Bishop[71] and the ringing of bells upon All Saints' Day[72] feature as often in the Marian accounts as before the Reformation. Celebrations of the reconciliation of England to the Papacy are mentioned in only three cases,[73] probably an accurate reflection of the traditional lack of interest of most parishioners in the distant pontiff. Customs connected with the parish church, such as ales,[74] Hocktide gatherings,[75] Plough

[66] Worcestershire R.O., 850/1284/1, p. 12.
[67] At St Benet Gracechurch; St Andrew, Canterbury; Chagford; St Martin-in-the-Fields; St Peter Cheap; St Matthew Friday Street; St Michael Cornhill; Ludlow; Thame; Coldridge; All Hallows Staining; St Margaret Pattens; St Alphage London Wall; Halse; St John, Bristol; St Botolph Aldgate; St James Garlickhithe; St Dunstan-in-the-West; St Mary Woolnoth; and St Peter Westcheap.
[68] At Strood; Bethersden; St Andrew, Lewes; Mere; Thame; Holy Trinity, Cambridge; Swaffham; Crediton; Woodbury; All Saints, Bristol; St Mary Woolnoth; and Bridport.
[69] Recorded at Great St Mary, Cambridge; Tarring; and St Thomas, Salisbury. Wriothesley, *Chronicle*, II, p. 105, states that it was universally restored in London.
[70] Recorded at Holy Trinity, Chester; Wing; Strood; Lambeth; Wandsworth; Ashburton; Louth; Ludlow; St Mary, Dover; St Mary, Bungay; Holy Trinity, Cambridge; and in all the Bristol and London accounts.
[71] At St Mary-at-Hill. Machyn, *Diary*, pp. 77–8, 121, 160, and Stow, *Annals*, pp. 121, 160, agree that most other London parishes revived the custom.
[72] At St John, Peterborough; Strood; Stanford-in-the-Vale; Bethersden; Ashburton; Long Sutton; Thame; St Mary, Bungay; Swaffham; Tilney; Dartington; Woodbury; Christ Church, Bristol; All Saints, Bristol; St Botolph Aldgate; St Mary Woolnoth; and St Michael le Quern.
[73] Stanford-in-the-Vale; Sheriff Hutton; and South Littleton.
[74] Recorded in Mary's reign at Crondall; St John, Winchester; St Nicholas, Warwick; Morebath; Yatton; Stanford-in-the-Vale; Marston; Pyrton; Thame; St Michael, Oxford; Ashburton; Badsey; St Edmund, Salisbury; Mere; St Mary, Dover; Sherborne; Woodbury; and Halse.
[75] At St Andrew, Canterbury; Bramley; Stoke Charity; St John, Winchester; St Lawrence, Reading; St Michael, Oxford; Lambeth; St Edmund, Salisbury; and St Thomas, Salisbury.

Monday collections,[76] the hognels or hogglers,[77] May games,[78] Rogationtide processions[79] and decking of churches with plants, underwent a complete revival, becoming as common as they were in the last years of Henry VIII. Most of these activities were not encouraged by the Marian regime, and in 1555 the Privy Council forbade all May games in Kent on the grounds that 'lewd practices' of 'vagabonds and other light persons...are appointed to be begun at such assemblies'.[80] Clearly, the popular culture associated with the old Church retained considerable ebullience, and the impulse to regulate it more severely in the name of public order crossed the confessional divide.

Amid such enthusiastic revival, it is interesting to note what was *not* restored under Mary. The abiding casualties of the preceding Reformations seem to have been the cult of the saints and the provision for souls in Purgatory. Only one set of accounts, from Prescot, Lancashire, records the purchase of more than three images, other than those of the rood loft. Most wardens only obtained those made compulsory, the loft statues and that of the patron of the parish. Where one or two more were added, they tended to be those of the Virgin or the better-known Apostles rather than of saints who had inspired local cults before the Henrician attack. Only at Prescot, again, do lights seem to have been burned before any images, save those upon the high altar or rood loft, and private donations of statues or pictures, or embellishments to those existing, appear in only five sets of accounts (out of the 134).[81] Only four parishes in the sample definitely rebuilt more than two of the side-altars at which saints had been honoured,[82] in contrast to the large number found in pre-Reformation churches, especially in towns. A small minority of the parish guilds and fraternities which had flourished in the early 1530s were restored, and most of these were the 'high' guild or store of their communities, unconnected with a particular patron, or dedicated to the Virgin. Nor does it appear that all those revived had intercessory functions, some now being fund-raising organisations.[83] In contrast with the almost ubiquitous references in pre-Reformation accounts to obits, bede rolls, dead-masses

---

[76] At Leverton; St Mary, Bungay; Holy Trinity, Bungay; and Swaffham.
[77] At Molland; Ashburton; Launceston; Banwell; Coldridge; Winkleigh; Minchinhampton; Halse. Curiously, while thriving in the west under Mary, they do not seem to have reappeared in the south-east.
[78] At Crondall; St John, Winchester; St Lawrence, Reading; and Thame.
[79] At Holy Trinity, Chester; Snettisham; St Martin, Leicester; Strood; Lambeth; Wandsworth; St Edmund, Salisbury; St Thomas, Salisbury; Ludlow; Mere; Long Sutton; Melton Mowbray; St Michael, Bath; and all Bristol and London parishes in sample.
[80] *A.P.C.*, v, p. 151.
[81] St Nicholas, Warwick; Morebath; St Botolph Aldgate; St Martin, Leicester; and St Martin-in-the-Fields.
[82] St Lawrence, Reading; St Mary, Devizes; St Dunstan-in-the-West; Prescot.
[83] Whiting, 'For the Health of My Soul', pp. 82–3; Scarisbrick, *Reformation*, pp. 36–8.

and burial rites employing a cross and tapers, these forms of intercession for individual souls feature in only thirty-two of the Marian accounts in the sample.

Such alterations should not be over-emphasised. After all, the work of centuries could not be repeated in five years. The attention of resources of devout parishioners would be employed under Mary in restoring the essential (and compulsory) trappings of Catholic worship. Perhaps the absence of an obvious Catholic successor to the throne in the event of Mary's demise discouraged individual investment in ornaments, rituals and fraternities. Yet the continuity with the decline of both these great forms of belief during the later years of Henry is striking. Had devotion to personal patron saints and conviction of the need to secure prayers for the repose of one's soul been as strong as they had obviously been in the 1520s, they should have left more impression on the accounts. The hiatus of Edward's reign might even have added urgency to the need to express them. But Marian Catholicism seems both less 'personalised' and less 'localised' than the faith of the old Church.

Visitation records, again, bear out the picture of restoration presented by the accounts. In Wiltshire in 1556, only two parishes admitted to having no altars and two others to lacking a rood, Mary and John. In Lancashire in 1554, only one of thirty-one churches and chapels visited had no altar, one no images and seven no ornaments; by 1557, three out of thirty-four had less than the full complement of books and ornaments and all had altar and images. Under Elizabeth, when exaggeration would have been politic, out of 153 Lincolnshire parishes, only four claimed to have had no rood under Mary, one no side-altars, eight no vestments, ten no candlesticks and five no mass books. Of 242 Somerset parishes visited in late 1557 and early 1558, twenty-one admitted to having no pyx, six to having no rood, twenty-two to having no Mary and John, two to having no rood loft and one to having no crucifix. The slowest progress was recorded in Kent. There, thanks to a mixture (impossible to quantify) of more thorough reformation, more widespread Protestantism and more searching visitation, in 1557 out of 243 parishes, forty-five had no holy water stoops, fifty-three no rood light, twenty-two no rood, sixty no crucifix, forty-three no candlesticks, fifty-three no pyx, forty-seven no high altar and ninety no side-altars, while sixty-one lacked some of the necessary books.[84] All told, however, it was not a bad achievement for so few years. Putting the whole body of evidence together, it looks as if, had Mary reigned for as long as Elizabeth did, the religion of her realm would have been emphatically Catholic, but still rather different from that of her grandfather's: more uniform in its patterns of piety, more subject to direction from the centre, much less remarkable for local and personal

---

[84] Wiltshire R.O., Salisbury Diocesan Records, Detecta Book 2, fos. 1–21; Haigh, *Lancashire*, p. 202, E. Peacock, *English Church Furniture* (London, 1866), *passim*; Somerset R.O., D/D/Ca/27; *Archdeacon Hapsfield's Visitation, 1557*, ed. L. E. Whatmore (C.R.S., LXV–VI, 1950–1).

cults. It would not have been just the old Church revived, but neither was the Counter Reformation Church upon the Continent, and the differences were more or less the same in the European case as those suggested here for England.

The death of Mary in November 1558 put religion into limbo yet again. A proclamation by Elizabeth in December ordered that the existing rites be continued pending a settlement, save that the Creed could be pronounced in English. When private persons attacked fittings, vestments and books in a church in Sussex and one in London, the Privy Council ordered their punishment. Not until April 1559 did Parliament pass a statute prescribing use of a new Protestant liturgy, by Midsummer Day, with the ornaments and vestments which had been legal in 1548, unless the Queen directed otherwise.[85] It is thus hardly surprising to find that the Catholic rituals were maintained in virtually every church in the sample until after Easter 1559. Only at Rye, a strong centre of Edwardian Protestantism, was any spontaneous move made towards reform, when the wardens removed the altars before Easter. By contrast, some parishes in early 1559 behaved as if Mary's religion was going to endure, such as St Andrew, Canterbury, where the crucifix was mended, Marston, Oxfordshire, where a bequest was made to purchase one, and Ludlow, where a new canopy was made for the host.[86]

In July, Elizabeth issued a set of Injunctions and a set of commissions for a visitation to enforce them. The Injunctions promised a Protestant Reformation rather more moderate than that of Edward: they instructed parishes to obtain the Bible and the *Paraphrases*; forbade processions on a practical ground – that they caused parishioners to compete acrimoniously for places, but exempted those of Rogationtide provided that they were a mere beating of parish boundaries without cross and banners; left the decision between an altar or a communion table to the parish or to the visitors; and ordered the destruction of monuments 'of feigned miracles, pilgrimages, idolatory and superstition' while not specifically forbidding the retention of images.[87] This impression of compromise is contradicted by the nature and work of the royal visitors. On paper they numbered 125, divided between six circuits, and included many peers and leading gentry. In practice, the majority of these notables failed to serve, and the work was apparently done in each area by four or five individuals, mostly lawyers or clerics. They were led by men who had been in exile during Mary's reign, and represented some of the most determined Protestants in Elizabeth's

[85] Hughes and Larkin, *Proclamations*, I, no. 451; *A.P.C.*, VII, pp. 76–7; *Statutes of the Realm*, IV (i), pp. 355–8.
[86] East Sussex R.O., Rye Corporation Records, 147/1, fo. 154v; C. Cotton, 'Accounts of St. Andrew', *Archaeologia Cantiana* (1917–22), p. 51; F. Weaver and G. Clark, *Churchwardens' Accounts* (Oxfordshire Record Society, 1925), p. 22; T. Wright, *Ludlow Churchwardens' Accounts* (Camden Society, 1869), p. 92.
[87] Hughes and Larkin, *Proclamations*, I, no. 460.

realm.[88] It is thus not surprising that, in the bulk of the 127 sets of accounts in the sample surviving wholly or partly for the first twelve years of her reign, the arrival of the Injunctions and visitors is followed promptly by the removal of altars and images.

The 1559 visitors were as exacting as any of the previous royal and ecclesiastical enquiries. Several sets of churchwardens had to re-submit reports to them, and those of Steeple Ashton, Wiltshire, had to attend them six times and to hand in bills thrice.[89] In London the commissioners produced a trail of bonfires of roods and images, and sometimes of vestments, cloths, Easter sepulchres, banners and ornaments as well. At Exeter they forced the citizens who had most venerated the images under Mary to throw them into the flames.[90] At Yatton, Somerset, the wardens begged for a reprieve for their church's Mary and John, to no avail.[91] The temper of the Queen's agents may well have been summed up by a sermon delivered by one of those in the northern circuit, Edwin Sandys, glorifying his monarch for defacing 'the vessels that were made for Baal', breaking down 'the lofts that were builded for idolatory' and demolishing 'all polluted and defiled altars'.[92] Like Edward's government, Elizabeth's had been restrained in its declarations, ruthless in its actions.

In fact, the impression of a clean sweep given in Sandys's sermon is fallacious, and Elizabeth's Reformation seems to have been rather slower and less effective than Edward's had been. At Crediton, Devon, the priest was still blessing Candlemas candles in the year after the visitation and the smashing or burning of most of his church's ornaments. In two York churches, the altars were taken down only in 1561, and the images remained in one of these until 1562.[93] The altars survived at Wing, Buckinghamshire, Stanford-in-the-Vale, Berkshire, and Worfield, Shropshire, until 1561, at Stoke Charity, Hampshire, till 1561–2, at St Mary-at-Hill, Chester, until 1562, and at Thame, Oxfordshire, until 1564. At Morebath, Devon, the high altar was simply covered with a board.[94] In most of these cases, the authorities had to

[88] W. P. Haugaard, *Elizabeth and the English Reformation* (Cambridge, 1970), pp. 136–8; Wriothesley, *Chronicle*, II, p. 145; G. Williams, 'The Elizabethan Settlement', in *Welsh Reformation Essays* (Cardiff, 1967), pp. 141–53.
[89] Wiltshire R.O., 730/97/1, year 1559.
[90] Machyn, *Diary*, pp. 206–9; Wriothesley, *Chronicle*, II, p. 146; Devon R.O., Exeter Corporation Records, John Hooker's Commonplace Book, fos. 352–3. The accounts for St Andrew, Holborn, make clear that the immolation of the rood, Mary and John was on the direct orders of the visitors: Malcolm, *Londinium Redivivum*, II, pp. 186–7.
[91] Hobhouse, *Churchwardens' Accounts*, pp. 170–1.
[92] E. Sandys, *Sermons*, ed. J. Ayre (Parker Society, 1841), p. 250.
[93] Devon R.O., 1660A/PW1/V, years 1559, 1560; B.I.Y., MS. Y/MCS 16, pp. 43–65, and R.XII Y/HTG 12, p. 13.
[94] Buckinghamshire R.O., PR/234/5/1, years 1561–2; Haines, 'Stanford-in-the-Vale', p. 168; Williams, *Early Churchwardens' Accounts*, p. 87; Walters, 'Worfield', p. 134; Cheshire R.O., St Mary-on-the-Hill, year 1562; Oxfordshire R.O., Par. Thame b. 2, p. 160; Binney, *Morebath*, pp. 210, 238.

exert considerable pressure to secure compliance – but secure it they did. The Elizabethan ecclesiastical visitation and court records bear out this picture. In Kent by 1569 the process of reformation had been very effective, leaving only a few holy water stoops and one crucifix undefaced. In the Norwich diocese in that year the physical changes were also more or less complete, though the bishop had great trouble stopping parishes ringing bells on All Saints' Day. In Essex in 1565–6 one church still had an altar, and two still had images. In Lincolnshire, 153 parishes claimed in 1566 to have removed all trappings of Catholic worship, but the process had taken the full seven years, and the altars and images were still in place at Belton-in-Axholme until just before the account was rendered. The metropolitan visitors of the diocese of Lichfield in 1560–1 had to order wardens from at least four Staffordshire villages to destroy altars. A church in Holderness in 1567 had retained altars and images, and another its images. Statues of saints survived in several Lancashire churches in 1563–4, and one altar remained until 1574. In 1567 the Bishop of Bangor reported that he had recently found, in this most remote and mountainous of all dioceses, images with candles burned before them, altars, and relics which were carried in procession at feasts: a cross-section of all the structures and ceremonies condemned by Protestants since 1538.[95]

This was still a relatively rapid and complete destructive reformation, and if comparable records had survived for the north and North Wales from Edward's reign, they would probably show at most the same degree of conformity. But when evidence is available for comparison, the reforms of 1559 appear to have been delayed and resisted to a somewhat greater degree than those of 1547–50. Four reasons may account for this: that the early Elizabethan machinery of enforcement was weaker than that of Edward; that Mary's regime had left Catholicism a stronger faith than before; that after the reversal of 1553 parishioners were reluctant to destroy their churches' fittings until a Protestant succession to the throne was secured; and that the ability of the Tudor State to make its subjects alter their religious habits on demand had slightly declined. There is no evidence in favour of the first of these, and much against, but the relative importance of the remaining three cannot be determined from the sources employed in this study. The case of rood lofts, however, indicates that the last two may have been the most significant.

The Protestant objection to the lofts was that articulated by Sandys: their purpose had been to support images, to which they might function as memorials. It is likely that, once stripped of statues, their religious significance for most parishioners was minimal, but they were large and beautiful structures upon which much money and

95 Essex R.O., D/AEA/23 and D/AEV/1; Peacock, *Church Furniture*, *passim*; A. Hussey, 'Archbishop Parker's Visitation, 1569', *Home Counties Magazine*, VI (1904), pp. 109–14; Norfolk R.O., VIS/1/1569; L.J.R.O., Lichfield Diocesan Records, B/V/1/3; B.I.Y., IR. VI. A.2; Haigh, *Lancashire*, pp. 114, 210–20; P.R.O., S.P. 12/4/27.

pride had been lavished. In 1560 the new Bishop of London, Edmund Grindal, encouraged the Protestant parishioners of St Michael le Quern to insist on the demolition of theirs. This course was taken by their fellow believers in nearby St Mary Woolnoth,[96] and in the same year by most of the other city parishes in the sample and nine in the provinces, almost all of these being either in towns or in East Anglia.[97] In October 1561, using the now traditional excuse for a further step in reform, Elizabeth ordered that to prevent contention all remaining lofts were to be cut down to the beam.[98] This direction was followed within the year in most of the remaining southern and midland parishes in the sample, and in a few in the north also, but there are signs of considerable reluctance. In seven cases the accounts record serious pressure exerted by diocesan officials to secure compliance, and in three of these the parishioners were excommunicated.[99] In the province of York, most of the parishes in the sample ignored the order, until in 1570–1, in the aftermath of the Revolt of the Earls and the translation of Grindal to York, a comparable effort of enforcement was mounted.[100] During the next two decades, most visitations resulted in the discovery and destruction of one or two more lofts, and many parishes, either from choice or coercion, further cut down the remnants of theirs.[101] Even so, pre-Reformation rood lofts, apparently unrestored, exist today at North Weald, Essex, and in three churches in Somerset, five in Wiltshire, three in Yorkshire and ten in Wales, and more were removed during the last century. They illustrate the extent to which a community could resist relatively peripheral aspects of the Reformation if it were very determined and very lucky. By contrast, only one pre-Reformation rood, Mary and John survives in an English or Welsh church (at Betws Gwerfyl Goch, near Corwen), and not a single stone altar.

Nor did popular pastimes succumb to Elizabeth's Reformation as completely as to Edward's. Most of the parishes in the sample which held church ales under Mary continued to do so into the new reign. The same is true of May games, while Hocktide gatherings went on in three parishes in the sample,[102] hognel or hoggler

---

96 Guildhall R.O., MS. 2895/1, fo. 169; MS. 1002/1, fo. 99.

97 St Peter Westcheap; St Stephen Walbrook; St Mary Magdalen Milk Street; St Mary Woolchurch Haw; St Dunstan-in-the-West; St Botolph Aldgate; St Margaret Moses (at command of Lord Mayor); St Andrew Hubbard; St Benet Gracechurch; Boxford; St Martin, Leicester (on orders of mayor); Halesowen; Holy Trinity, Coventry; Thame; Chelmsford; Bromfield; Heybridge; and Tilney.

98 W. H. Frere, *Visitation Articles and Injunctions* (Alcuin Club Collections, 1910), III, pp. 108–10.

99 Stoke Charity; Stanford-in-the-Vale; Prescot; Great Packington; Worfield; Stratton; and Cornworthy. Excommunication was employed at the last three places.

100 See Holy Trinity, Chester; Holy Trinity Goodramgate, York; Masham; and Sheffield.

101 A typical example being Ashburton, where the loft was 'pulled down' in 1563–4, 1571–2, and 1579–80. Five other Devon parishes made further reductions in the 1570s, and the pattern holds for other counties.

102 Bramley; St Edmund, Salisbury; and St Thomas, Salisbury.

collections in three,[103] and Plough Monday collections in two others.[104] Decking of churches with vegetation ceased in most parishes in the mid-1560s, but continued in three of the sample much later.[105] All this argues for some restrictive impact upon traditional festivities by the early Elizabethan reformers, and certainly the drives for reformation of religion and of manners were frequently to be associated later in the reign (and ever since). But the contrast with the almost total collapse of the same customs in 1547–8 is still marked, and puzzling.

As in the reign of Edward, the positive aspects of the Reformation are less apparent in the accounts than the negative. Certainly, virtually all those in the sample record the new Prayer Book within a year of its issue, and most of those which do not seem to be incomplete. But only thirty-three of the 127 enter the purchase of a new Bible, while two payments for mending an old one suggest that an unknown number were brought out of hiding. The *Paraphrases* were definitely obtained by twenty-six parishes, and, again, may have been restored to others by private hands, while the purchase of the revised *Book of Homilies* appears in twenty-three sets of accounts. The erection of a board written with the Ten Commandments is recorded for thirty-four parishes in the sample. The probability that the Bible and *Paraphrases* were restored informally to churches makes it difficult to compare the success of Edward's regime in propagating Protestant views with that of Elizabeth during its first six years; however, in both cases it can be said that the removal of Catholic decorations was more easily achieved than the substitution of Protestant texts. At the visitation of Kent during 1569, no parish admitted to preserving an altar, image or rood loft, but forty of the 169 returns recorded the absence of either the Bible or the *Paraphrases*:[106] and this was the most perfectly-reformed county of the decade, and one with good visitation records.

To conclude: the evidence of the churchwardens' accounts bears out the assertions of Dr Haigh and Professor Scarisbrick, that the great majority of the English and Welsh peoples did not want the Reformations of Henry, Edward and Elizabeth. Catholic practices retained their vitality in the parishes until the moment they were proscribed, and there were few anticipations of official instructions. Indeed, the accounts suggest that Tudor parishioners were reluctant to implement any religious changes. If it be asked then why they got them, the answer is that they were forced to conform. The machinery of coercion and supervision deployed by the government was so effective that for most parishes passive resistance was simply not an option. When active resistance was employed, by the Pilgrims of Grace, the western rebels

[103] Molland; Launceston; and Minchinhampton. They were active at Dursley, Gloucestershire, until 1626: Gloucestershire R.O., P124/CW/2/4.
[104] Leverton and St Mary, Bungay.
[105] St Ewen, Bristol; Lambeth; and St Dunstan-in-the-West.
[106] Hussey, 'Archbishop Parker's Visitation', *passim*.

of 1549 and the followers of the Northern Earls, it proved disastrous. The absence
of comparable violent opposition to Mary's religious policy argues for its relative
popularity, the rebellion of Wyatt being far less clearly related to religious
developments than were the conservative risings. Yet it is arguable from the accounts
that her counter-reform, too, would not have achieved as much as it did without
considerable pressure by the authorities. Furthermore, these records testify to the
power of the Tudor regime to compel the minds of its subjects as well as their bodies.
It appears that the English and Welsh of the early sixteenth century had a limited
capacity to sustain any beliefs attacked both by leading churchmen and by the
Crown. They had great difficulty in digesting Protestantism, but they lost faith in
precisely those aspects of the pre-Reformation Church which had been most
dynamic, most personal and most localised. There are signs by the accession of
Elizabeth of a slight growth in reluctance to comply with each new royal demand,
but it cannot be proved that this was any more than the parochial equivalent of
war-weariness, rather than heightened religious belief.

In essence, churchwardens' accounts suggest that the English Reformation has been
treated too much as a confessional struggle and not sufficiently as an episode in the
history of the secular British polity. The association had been there from the
beginning, for Christianity was after all imposed in these islands by a series of royal
decisions. In this sense the Protestant Reformation was indeed a harking back to the
primitive Church, though not in the way that the reformers intended.

7

REVIVAL AND REFORM IN
MARY TUDOR'S CHURCH:
A QUESTION OF MONEY

R. H. POGSON

In explaining the failure of Mary Tudor's plans for Catholic revival during her reign, it is customary to dwell on her manifold errors of judgement. No one can deny her ardent desire to restore the love for Rome among her subjects – she declared that her people's souls meant more to her than ten kingdoms;[1] but she is remembered for burning heretics and thus providing English Protestantism with much-needed martyrs and respectability, rather than for inspiring Counter Reformation zeal. The most obvious reason for this failure was Mary's early death, which left her little time for long-term policies; but in addition emphasis must be placed on her misunderstanding of her subjects' prejudices and confusion after the schism. She disgusted the strong Henrician national feeling by marrying a foreigner and delighting openly in her Spanish blood; she showed no sympathy for the financial worries of influential subjects who had obtained monastic property and had no wish to surrender it; she instigated a persecution which aroused distaste even in minds accustomed to sixteenth-century suffering and punishment; and she embarked on an unpopular war and lost Calais disastrously. Moreover, she reposed greatest trust in Reginald Pole, the papal legate, another leader who failed to comprehend the bitterness of English xenophobia and the strength of anticlericalism and heresy. Pole assumed that anti-Roman sentiments were the short-lived results of schismatic sin and would fade with the orderly restoration of Roman rule; and so he did not even begin to build a militant organisation which could have tried to resist Elizabethan Protestantism.[2] It is an impressive catalogue of mistakes.

But it is too simple to indulge in this orgy of criticism and then leave it as a

---

[1] J. Foxe, *Actes and Monuments*, ed. S. R. Cattley (London, 1837–41), VII, p. 34.

[2] For Mary's policies, see A. G. Dickens, *The English Reformation* (London, 1964); D. M. Loades, *The Oxford Martyrs* (London, 1970). Pole's assessment of his task in England is the main theme of R. H. Pogson, 'Cardinal Pole: papal legate to England in Mary Tudor's reign' (University of Cambridge Ph.D thesis, 1972); cf. W. Schenk, *Reginald Pole: Cardinal of England* (London, 1950).

complete explanation. Mary and Pole may, indeed, have made political errors and misjudged English opinion, but they also made some impressive preparations for Catholic reform. Mary arranged a series of meetings in 1555 between Pole and her other leading councillors to make the legate familiar with problems which had arisen during his exile and to draw up long-term ecclesiastical and secular plans.[3] Pole called a legatine synod in the winter of 1555–6 and there issued detailed decrees for the restoration of Roman authority, law and ceremonial, the removal of clerical abuses and the re-establishment of Catholic preaching and education;[4] and in pursuing those aims he gathered an efficient group of lawyers and advisers and bombarded his bishops with instructions.[5] Together, Mary and Pole chose bishops of pastoral and scholarly experience, trying to avoid the dangers of an episcopate too closely associated, as Henry VIII's had been, with the interests of secular administration.[6]

That these plans for reform came to nothing cannot be explained simply in terms of the political ineptitude of the Marian regime. Before they could formulate realistic policies, Mary and Pole had to sort out colossal administrative problems of a complexity which would have baffled any politician. These problems occupied them throughout the short reign and carry some of the blame for the absence of action to follow up Pole's plans. Some of the best illustrations of this administrative difficulty can be found in the financial confusion in the Marian Church. If the Roman Church was to recover its traditional authority in England, it had to recover also the wealth which it had surrendered in the schism; but an appalling shortage of information, as well as the expected anticlerical hostility, prevented Mary, Pole, the popes and the bishops from making any rapid progress. Before they could even contemplate the recovery of lost wealth, they had to find how much had been lost, where it was, whether anyone knew anything at all about it, and how many people were laying claim to it. We shall take some examples of this confusion, for they should enable us to gain a fairer picture of Mary's failure; and they should also help to illustrate the governmental difficulties which she inherited from the schism, and give some background to the problems of the Elizabethan Church.

---

[3] P.R.O., S.P. 14/190 (20 fos. from end); B.L., Cotton, Titus B II, fo. 160, for a meeting of 29 August 1555.

[4] The decrees were printed in Rome in 1562 and reprinted in facsimile: *De Concilio Liber* and *Reformatio Angliae* (London, 1962).

[5] Pole brought some of his most trusted friends from Italy, notably Nicolo Ormanetto, who, to judge from marginal notes, seems to have supervised the writing of Pole's legatine register; he used his namesake, David Pole, with Nicholas Harpsfield, Thomas Stemp and Henry Cole as legal advisers in legatine and archiepiscopal courts (Pole's legatine register, Douai Municipal Library (L.P.L. on microfilm), I, fos. 60–1; Pole's archiepiscopal register, L.P.L., fos. 15–6, 27–31). These registers will hereafter be referred to as Leg. Reg. and Arch Reg. For the use made of these lawyers, see Pogson, 'Cardinal Pole: Papal Legate to England in Mary Tudor's reign', pp. 224–9.

[6] Cf. P. Hughes, 'A Hierarchy that fought', *Clergy Review*, XVIII (1940), pp. 25–39.

The schism had cost the Church in England vast sums: the dissolution of the monasteries had brought Henry VIII some £160,000 each year before his son added the proceeds of the chantries.[7] Of this sum, about three-quarters came from lands which had been administered by religious houses in a manner no different from lay landlords, and Henry forfeited some of that income when he parted with land to the gentry and aristocracy in the 1540s. The remaining quarter consisted of spiritual income from impropriated benefices to which the monasteries had acted as rectors − perhaps as many as two-fifths of all English livings − and which the Crown took over in the same capacity; many of these rights also were sold.[8] Added to all this was the profit from plate and ornaments − perhaps over one million pounds − and the collection of taxes such as first-fruits which had originally gone to Rome. A levy of one-tenth had been imposed annually on the clergy by Henry's government as a kind of income tax.[9]

The recovery of lost wealth was of vital importance to Pole's plans for Catholic revival. His letters and the decrees of his synod reveal that he aimed at a restoration of traditional Roman order, custom and discipline in the English Church rather than a vigorous, new-style Counter Reformation campaign of preaching. He wanted to inspire affection and respect for Roman ritual and law by reviving Catholic ceremonial, providing highly-qualified clergy for the parishes, restoring the monasteries, and removing the financial abuses which had aroused anticlericalism.[10] But he could not bring back the beauty of holiness in the Catholic ritual without the vestments which had been removed and the ornaments which had been sold or stolen during the schism. He could not re-endow many monasteries without the confiscated monastic lands. Furthermore, he could not raise the quality of large numbers of the clergy or eliminate the abuses of pluralism and absenteeism without reforming the entire system of impropriations. These had long been a millstone round the necks of ecclesiastical reformers. Before the breach with Rome the monasteries had taken the income from their impropriated benefices, paying a fixed stipend to a resident

---

[7] Dickens, *English Reformation*, pp. 147–8.

[8] C. Hill, *Economic problems of the Church, from Archbishop Whitgift to the Long Parliament* (Oxford, 1956), p. 4; cf. M. Bowker, *The Secular Clergy in the Diocese of Lincoln, 1495–1520* (Cambridge, 1968), p. 129, where one third of the parishes in Lincoln diocese before the breach with Rome are seen to be impropriated; D. Wilkins, *Concilia Magnae Britanniae et Hiberniae* (London, 1737), IV, p. 95, for the bitter complaints of the lower house of the 1554 Convocation about lay impropriators.

[9] Hill, *Economic Problems of the Church*, p. 3: Hill estimates the gain from plate and valuables to have been £1–1½ millions, and the first-fruits and tenths to have brought in perhaps £40000 each year; cf. F. C. Dietz, *English Government Finance, 1485–1558* (London, 1964), p. 212: he puts that last figure as low as £25000.

[10] Pole's letters are edited by A. M. Quirini, *Epistolae Reginaldi Poli* (Brescia, 1744–57), in five volumes, including in the fifth volume the biography of Pole by his secretary Beccatelli. See above, p. 139 n, for references to Pole's English aims.

vicar. The result was that in many parishes the priest who actually came into contact
with the people had to be content with an income which was only adequate because
of help and concessions offered by the personnel of the monastery. And this meant
in turn that few clerics with good qualifications were tempted into the local pastoral
work which Pole considered so important. Moreover, without a redistribution of
income from some wealthy to some very poor livings, many clergy had to become
pluralists in order to survive at the level expected of them. Greed and corruption
can explain some of the Church's abuses, but genuine poverty has to be taken into
account also. This series of connected problems was already serious, then, before the
breach with Rome; during the schism the situation worsened in at least three ways:
impropriated livings fell into the hands of laymen who were naturally delighted with
their new profits and were even less prepared than abbots to redistribute their income
in the interests of impoverished parish clergy; the monasteries were no longer
available to supplement vicars' stipends in kind; and the inflation of the 1540s and
1550s was likely to hit the holders of small benefices and fixed stipends worst of
all.[11] Pluralism, absenteeism and a substandard local clergy would remain problems
unless Pole could establish legatine control over the income from hundreds of
impropriated benefices. From this viewpoint, his entire spiritual vision of reform in
the Marian Church depended heavily upon successful financial negotiation.

Such negotiation was not Pole's strong suit. He was on very good terms with Mary,
so that bargaining between Church and Crown offered few terrors for him;[12] but
much of the property which Pole needed was in other lay hands. He came towards
England in 1553 and 1554 expressing the opinion that Englishmen who wished to
appear sincere in their devotion to the pope should automatically want to surrender
ill-gotten monastic gains; they should simply rely on Pole's good judgement of what
should and what should not be recovered.[13] To judge by the legatine powers which
Pole was bearing, Mary's councillors and M.P.s showed no such confidence in the
competence of the legate. For Pole's original commission carefully divided his powers
for dealing with the Church's movable property from those concerned with

[11] The problems discussed in this paragraph are dealt with fully in Bowker, *Secular Clergy*, esp.
pp. 142–3 on the effects of inflation, and P. Heath, *English Parish Clergy on the Eve of the
Reformation* (London, 1969), esp. p. 166 on the necessity of pluralism.
[12] Michiel, the Venetian ambassador, reported that Pole often spent hours in consultation with
Mary and was chief advisor: *Calendar of State Papers, Venetian*, VI, pp. 1056, 1070, 1071.
[13] MSS. from Bibliotheca Vaticana, Rome, housed in the Bodleian Library Oxford (hereafter
Bodleian, Biblio. Vat.), Vat. Lat. 5968, fo. 99 – Pole told Parliament that when they thought
of their sin, a 'horryble feare' should come over them; Archivio Vaticano, Rome (hereafter
Arch. Vat.), *Nunziatore Diversae*, 145, fo. 211 – Pole accused Englishmen of fearing that they
should ever have to part with one farthing; Bodleian, MS. Smith 67, p. 36 – Pole told Mary
in August 1554 that Englishmen must 'have confidence in the person of the legate' on the issue
of lands.

land.[14] Pole could give absolution to those who had 'wrongfully obtained' movable goods from churches, or spent the proceeds of their sale; presumably Julius III felt that ornaments purloined twenty years before were untraceable and not worth the fuss of investigation. But the pope clearly assumed the recovery of many church estates. In the bull of extraordinary faculties issued in August 1553, Pole was empowered to delay dispensation for possession of movable goods until lands had been restored to the Church.[15] By the powers invested in him by another bull at his first commission, Pole could allow a layman to sell the church estates which he possessed, but only if the sale benefited the church or monastery to which the land had once belonged.[16] Julius III added airily that Pole must do all that he thought 'right and necessary'.

These powers underline the extent to which the papacy had lost contact with English opinion and events during the schism. There was never any prospect that English landowners would accept this version of Pole's role in England, but a great deal of valuable time was lost before the dispute was resolved. Julius III merely confirmed the original powers in May 1554, but this led Mary to accuse Pole of expecting 'parfettnes'[17] and Gardiner to assure him that without some change in his faculties he could not enter England.[18] By June even Pole and Julius had realised the problem, and on 28 June the pope made concessions.[19] After the confusion of the schism, he said, he was anxious to hold out the hope of papal mercy to sinners; Mary had interceded for the holders of monastic property, and the pope announced that he would place reconciliation with England before quibbles over money.[20] This time Pole was empowered to absolve Englishmen for their sins of holding both land and ornaments, and dispense them to continue to do so. But a saving clause was added, by which those cases which seemed to Pole of great importance and requiring a higher authority could be referred to Rome. This prevented the new brief from easing English fears, for it held out the daunting prospect of a tribunal at Rome which might decide the fate of lands which English families had come to think of as their own. Again, Pole's judgement was the key factor and again it was insufficient guarantee. There followed an autumn of considerable tension, with a

---

[14] C. Dodd, *The Church History of England from 1500 to the Year 1688*, ed. M. Tierney (London, 1839–43), II, pp. cx–cxvii: a number of bulls issued on 5 August 1553 are printed. Arch. Vat., Arm. 41: 70, fos. 223–6: the confirmation in March 1554 of the bull of extraordinary legatine faculties of 5 August 1553.

[15] Arch. Vat., Arm. 41:70, fo. 224.   [16] Dodd, *Church History*, II, p. cxv.

[17] Bodleian, Biblio. Vat., Vat. Lat. 5968, fo. 83: 'fragment towching disposition of the goods of the church'.

[18] B.L., Add. MS. 25425, fo. 241.

[19] Quirini, *Epistolae*, IV, 434: Julius III to Pole, 28 June 1554; Dodd, *Church History*, II, p. cxix, for the new papal ideas.   [20] B.L., Add. MS. 25425, fos. 285–6.

flow of letters from Mary, her council, Charles V, his ambassadors, and eventually even Pole's own household, in an effort to persuade the pope that further concessions would have to be made.[21] Pole seems to have been the slowest to realise that official sanction would have to be given to laymen, allowing them without reservation to keep their church lands, but interviews with Granvelle and English agents in Brussels made him recognise that he must climb down if he was ever to see England.[22] Over a year had passed since Mary's accession and the English Church remained unreconciled to Rome. So in October 1554 Pole was moved to a frenzy of letter-writing (unusual in him)[23] and on 7 November Morone, Pole's closest link with the Curia, wrote to tell him that the new powers had just left Rome.[24] By 24 November Pole was discussing those new powers with Philip and Mary in London.

Pole had thus been committed to signing away much of the church property which he wanted for Roman revival; his ignorance, and that of Julius III, of events in England since 1530 had left him unprepared for the extent of the blow. As soon as he reached England he received an even clearer indication of the determination of English landowners to retain their monastic estates. In the council meeting of 21 December 1554, faced by men with whom he would have to co-operate closely in his plans, he struggled vainly to keep the discussion of land separate from the debate about the reconciliation of an erring nation to Rome.[25] Pole felt that the English return to Roman obedience must not be a mere bargaining counter, to be offered in return for the pope's dispensation to those with monastic land, but must be a sincere statement of penitence in its own right. But many councillors seem to have been quite prepared to shelve the reconciliation until they had organised the full reassurance that the land was safe in lay hands. After bitter recrimination, Pole issued the dispensation, contenting himself with a refusal to acknowledge specifically the usurpers' title to the lands and some dark references to the fate of Cyrus, who

---

[21] Mary had long conversations with Penning, one of Pole's agents, in September 1554 (Arch. Vat., *Nunziatore Diversae*, 145, fo. 125); Charles V's ambassadors pointed out to the emperor the inadequacy of Pole's powers (*Calendar of State Papers, Spanish*, XIII, p. 28); Ormanetto and Mary's Councillors, from their very different viewpoints, made the same urgent demands for changes in Pole's faculties (Arch. Vat., *Nunziatore Diversae*, 145, fos. 99, 117).

[22] Pole described his interview with Granvelle to the pope in Arch. Vat., *Nunziatore Diversae*, 145, fos. 90–6.

[23] *Ibid.*, fos. 90–6, 107, 108–11, 113–6; B.L., Add. MS. 25425, fos. 325–30: letters to Julius III, Philip and Mary, Morone, Penning and Holland.

[24] Quirini, *Epistolae*, IV, 171. It is clear from Pole's letters that Morone took every chance to explain English affairs to the pope, and it was after Paul IV turned against Morone in Rome that Pole's relations with the pope became particularly difficult. Cf. D. Fenlon, *Heresy and Obedience in Tridentine Italy: Cardinal Pole and the Counter Reformation* (Cambridge, 1972), pp. 269–71.

[25] B.L., Add. MS. 41577, fos. 161 ff.: Priuli's account of the meeting. Cf. J. H. Crehan, 'The return to obedience: new judgements on Cardinal Pole', *The Month*, N.S. XIV (1955), pp. 221–9.

desecrated the Temple of the Lord.[26] This was not practical retaliation; the impoverishment of the schism had been largely perpetuated, and it had cost more than a year of the mission to reach that defeat.

At least Pole could hope that Mary, sharing his views on obedience to Rome, would quickly restore to the Church those spiritual revenues which remained in the Crown's hands. But even here he was confronted by a serious administrative obstacle; it was not a question of straightforward transfer. With the best will in the world Mary could not surrender money until she had a clear idea what she was surrendering and had straightened her accounts. Pole called for an immediate surrender of first-fruits and tenths by the Crown,[27] but in doing so was underestimating the backlog of debts and accounts which Mary had inherited. When she came to the throne, the unprecedented scale of taxation and inflation in the previous reigns had left a number of bishops deeply in debt: eighteen of them owed £9825 10s 5¼d which should have been paid at Christmas 1552.[28] With the change of regime in the summer of 1553, the issue was immensely complicated by deprivations: Holgate, the Edwardian Archbishop of York, was carefully examined because of the possibility that he had stolen property from his see, and those who were deprived had to seek exemption from their debts.[29] Bishops who served under Mary were given time to pay – Thirlby and Hopton had five years' grace and later Thirlby was completely exonerated.[30] Even after Pole's arrival the council was writing round to bishops demanding that they should pay their first-fruits to the Crown.[31] Clearly, any change-over from royal to legatine and papal control had to be negotiated over a period of time.

Mary was nonetheless anxious to make some speedy reparation on behalf of the Crown. Although Julius III had rejected the idea of chasing all the ornaments and movables lost from the parish churches, Mary, with the Crown's financial interests as well as those of the Church at stake, embarked on the arduous task of following up Edward VI's many commissions for confiscating and collecting church goods. Three officials of the Court of Augmentations, William Berners, Thomas Mildmay and John Wiseman, spent much of Mary's reign in this frustrating pursuit.[32] It was

---

[26] Crehan, op. cit., p. 228; Bodleian, Biblio. Vat., Vat. Lat. 5968, fo. 205: Pole to Philip and Mary on the reconciliation.

[27] Bodleian, Biblio. Vat., Vat. Lat. 5968, fo. 82: a 'fragment towching disposition of the goods of the church'.

[28] P.R.O., S.P. 11/1, fos. 3–4: arrears of tenths.

[29] P.R.O., S.P. 11/6, fo. 131; 11/4, fos. 62–7.

[30] P.R.O., E 337/1, nos. 20, 21; E 337/2, fo. 252.   [31] A.P.C., v, p. 111.

[32] P.R.O., E 117/14: a series of documents on their inquiries. We also have a number of royal authorisations to these three men to examine previous commissions – the quantity of bell-metal and lead due to the Crown since 1536, or how much silver from chantries since 1547: Calendar of the Patent Rolls, Philip and Mary, III, pp. 114–15.

clear from their researches that the Crown had not received its due from the confiscation of church goods by the time Edward died. For all the parishes of Norfolk and Suffolk, for instance, the assessed value of the goods taken by the commissioners from each church, and the amount received, differed by several pounds.[33] The answer was to work back over the two previous reigns to find where the Crown had been defrauded or inefficient, investigating particularly the Edwardian commissions. The old commissioners were asked: 'what therin hathe byn done by youe?' and the answers were not always satisfactory and often demanded lengthy investigation. A commissioner for Lincolnshire asserted that he had been given no episcopal inventories for reference, and so produced inaccurate figures:[34] John Cary of Bristol said that he had no record of lead which he had removed because the other commissioners had taken away his book.[35] This was a good example of Mildmay's problem; there had been so many commissions in Edward's reign that the Marian investigators did not always know whether they were chasing the books and agents of the second or seventh commission of the previous reign.[36] What could have been discovered if Edward had lived much longer defies even speculation.

Even when they found the men they wanted, Mary's agents were often thwarted in their search for information. Fear of reprisals, greed and perhaps resentment of probing by the central government were all likely to lead ex-commissioners and witnesses to be obstructive. At one monastery, one William Hever was reported to have removed large quantities of lead without showing his authority, and no one seemed able to assist in a search for it.[37] Others were either unlucky to be questioned or else expertly slippery, for they said, in effect, that Mildmay had got the wrong man: 'nor enie of us receavid...enie commission', they said, or 'any commyshon in any suche matter ther cam never noon to my hands'.[38]

This tangled evidence delayed and frustrated the Queen's admirable intention of returning as many valuables as possible to deprived parishes. Good beginnings were made: as early as April 1555 it was estimated that of 4545 ounces of silver obtained from churches in the archdeaconries of Taunton and Wells, 1178 had been restored in the form of unspoiled chalices; and the chancellor of the diocese of Norwich was asked to provide a list of the plate which had been 'redelivered ageyne' to parishes.[39] But this was likely to be a drawn-out process; and the visitation records of Salisbury, Bath and Wells and Canterbury in the middle of the reign reveal lists of devastated churches and in many cases little or no improvement from the opening of the reign.[40]

[33] P.R.O., E 315/167.
[34] P.R.O., E 117/14, 48(2), 20 April 1556.   [35] P.R.O., E 117/14, 33, 11 May 1556.
[36] E.g. the search for suspected commissioners in P.R.O., E 117/14, 64.
[37] P.R.O., E 117/14, 158.
[38] P.R.O., E 117/14, 13 and 19.   [39] P.R.O., E 117/14, 192; E 117/13, 17.
[40] Somerset R.O., D/D/Ca 18, 27: visitations of Bath and Wells in 1554 and 1557; V.C.H., Wiltshire, III, p. 31, with reference to the visitation of Salisbury in 1556; L.P.L., VC III/1/2: Pole's visitation of Canterbury, 1556.

Even in the cathedrals, considerable restoration was necessary, and Tunstall's injunctions to the dean and chapter of Durham allowed for the restitution of ornaments in the cathedral only by 1558 – and that was probably optimistic.[41] All this shows that it was not simply a question of efficient restoration of confiscated goods, huge though that problem threatened to be; the question had first to be asked, what confiscations had occurred, and who had possession of the goods?

During this struggle for information, and in spite of the obstacles, Mary was trying to push ahead also with the big step of surrendering the Crown's spiritual revenues to the Church. The meetings which she arranged between Pole and other councillors in the spring and summer of 1555 were intended to explain to the legate the implications of schismatic events and to formulate policy. Finance was high on the agenda; in August, for instance, Pole met Gardiner, Paulet, Arundel, Pembroke, Thirlby, Paget, Rochester and Petre, and finance was the first topic for discussion.[42] The deep differences over church property and obedience to Rome cannot have made these gatherings particularly cordial, but at least Mary was striving to arrange long-term policies. In spite of the loose ends which remained, a statute was drafted by the autumn of 1555 for the royal renunciation of first-fruits, tenths and the spiritual income from impropriated benefices which remained in royal hands.[43]

If this was intended as a spur to the feelings of laymen who held monastic property, it appears to have been a failure. There were some signs of piety, genuine or conventional, and a few expressions of remorse: Petre and Berkeley, for instance, both invested money which they had gained from the dissolution in chapels and pensions,[44] and Petre confessed to Cecil that he thought they were worshipping Mammon rather than God.[45] But, with a few notable exceptions like these, the gentry and aristocracy seem to have been content to view Mary's generosity from afar without associating themselves with it. Mary's reputation with her parliaments, for instance, did not stand so high that she could expect self-sacrificial enthusiasm because she called for it; and the royal generosity was partly tarnished by the continued sale and lease of monastic estates by the Crown.[46]

In the meantime, Mary and her legate had sufficient problems in the administration of the royal surrender without worrying about future generosity. The most immediate effect of the transfer of property from Crown to Church from Pole's point of view was a further headache. Now that the Crown had divested itself of

[41] *Visitation Articles and Injunctions of the Period of the Reformation*, ed. W. H. Frere and W. P. M. Kennedy (Alcuin Club Collections, XIV–XVI, 1908), II, p. 412.

[42] B.L., Cotton, Titus B II, fo. 160.

[43] *Statutes of the Realm* (London, 1810–28), IV, pp. 275–9, 2/3 Philip and Mary, c. 4.

[44] Kent Archives Office, Maidstone, Rochester Register 1546–1639, fo. 82, with Pole's authorisation of Petre's endowing of pensions; Leg. Reg., VI, fo. 171, for Lord Berkeley's gesture.

[45] J. E. Oxley, *The Reformation in Essex to the death of Mary* (Manchester, 1965), p. 253.

[46] E.g. B.L., Cotton MS. Titus B. XI., fo. 434: Mary to Sussex, 6 August 1558, agreeing to a compromise between two claimants for the temporal estates of a monastery.

tenths, tithe, glebe and so on, it had also handed on to the Church the attendant
responsibility for the payment of pensions to ex-religious who had lost their
vocations – willingly or unwillingly – at the dissolution. Pole was not yet in the
position to provide many re-endowed monasteries, and so he had to provide the
pensions instead.[47] But it was not just that the job had to be done; it was once again
the absence of information on which to base it which was disturbing. Pole inherited
a large and confused administrative task which the Edwardian and Marian
governments had been trying rather unsuccessfully to sort out before his arrival. Lay
commissioners for Edward in 1552 and episcopal and archidiaconal visitors for Mary
in 1554 produced lists of those still receiving and still eligible for pensions from the
Crown, and tried to detect abuses and frauds in the system.[48] This last worry was
natural, for Edward's total spending on these pensions and annuities in 1550–1 had
been £44 861, and by 1552 he had been forced to postpone payment.[49]

Mary and Pole clearly needed their own definitive list of obligations which the
Church was taking over; and this was completed by February 1556.[50] It was arranged
under counties and then under the religious houses in those counties; at the end was
a list of other annuities which the Church clearly undertook to pay in addition.
The surviving Exchequer document is a magnificent record, beautifully drawn up
on a large scale; the pensions recorded in it are on a grand scale also, adding up
to £36 372 6s 2¼d for fifty-three counties.[51] This book demonstrates the problems
which Pole experienced in his search for accurate figures. For, although some of the
trends in the figures for 1550, 1552, 1554 and 1556 are as we should expect – the
total sum for Pole's list was about one fifth lower than that for 1550, presumably
through death and other disqualifications[52] – there were peculiarities. For example,

[47] In May 1557, the Venetian ambassador mentioned seven restored houses of strict observance:
D. Knowles, *The Religious Orders in England* (Cambridge, 1959), III, p. 438.

[48] A. G. Dickens, 'Edwardian Arrears in Augmentations Payments and the Problem of the
Ex-Religious', *E.H.R.*, LV (1940), pp. 384–418; G. A. J. Hodgett, *The State of the Ex-religious
and former Chantry Priests in the Diocese of Lincoln, 1547–74* (Lincoln Record Society, LIII, 1959)
pp. 26–74, 75–126; G. Baskerville, 'Married Clergy and Pensioned Religious in Norwich
Diocese, 1555', *E.H.R.*, XLVIII (1933), pp. 199–228; G. Baskerville, 'The Dispossessed Religious
in Surrey', *Surrey Archaeological Collections*, XLVII (1941), pp. 12–28, especially p. 13 for reference
to abuses of the system.

[49] Dietz, *English Government Finance*, p. 213; Dickens, 'Edwardian Arrears', p. 386. Cf. Wilkins,
Concilia, IV, p. 97, where the lower house of Canterbury Convocation in 1554 is recorded as
petitioning for the efficient payment of pensions.

[50] P.R.O., E 164/31: the Exchequer copy of Pole's certificate of pensions; the list for Lincolnshire
from that list is printed by C. W. Foster in *Associated Architectural Society Reports and Papers*,
XXXVII, p. ii.

[51] P.R.O., E 164/31, fo. 77: the sum recorded in the book is £36 808 0s 10½d., but the sum of
the totals for each county is the figure in the text above.

[52] Dietz, *English Government Finance*, p. 213. In 1552 there were 216 pensioners in Nottinghamshire, whereas Pole had 195 in 1556: Dickens, 'Edwardian Arrears', p. 398, and P.R.O., E 164/31,
fos. 62–3, to take just one example.

nine pensioners in the diocese of Lincoln listed as dead in 1552 reappeared in Pole's list; and ex-religious who had been detected as 'married' in 1554 were still included in Pole's 'boke' in spite of that most heinous Marian crime.[53] It seems, then, that Pole's certificate of pensions was a compilation of all obligations which might be charged to the Church, without comment on the irregularities or anomalies; some of the sums recorded in 1556 would clearly never have been paid.[54]

This presupposed a complex and often tedious investigation of disputed claims for pensions and decisions on a recipient's right to remain on the list; this was over and above the task of seeking fraud, which Edwardian officials had found quite difficult enough. For the precise checking of pensioners' rights, Pole appointed a committee, consisting of the Lord Chancellor, Lord Treasurer, Lord Privy Seal, and two judges, and they were instructed to mark on the list the name of anyone whom they disqualified.[55] In fact, there are no such cancellations in the Exchequer copy of the list, so it seems that this colossal document was not in full administrative use. This was only one small aspect of the full range of Pole's financial problems, and in the short time of his mission he had obviously only just come to terms with it. Complex tangles like these had to be cut before Pole could formulate policies.

Although in the detail of this massive book it is easy to lose sight of the fact, all the work on pensions was intended simply as a preliminary to using the rest of the surrendered income for the improvement of impoverished livings. The negotiations between Pole and Mary for the transfer of royal income coincided with the meeting of the legatine synod in London in the winter of 1555–6, and Pole took advantage of the synod to place on the shoulders of the bishops the responsibility for collecting the money and discovering where it was most needed. The bishops were granted all 'suitable' powers for collecting first-fruits and tenths and paying pensions to the ex-religious, and told to draw up their accounts for audit by Michaelmas 1556.[56] The instructions to Pate of Worcester, one of Pole's closet colleagues, added the interesting point that the accounts should be entered under counties, presumably to provide comparison with Exchequer accounts.[57] Bonner's register for London enables us to see the local effect of Pole's orders in an efficient diocese; within six days of Pole's letter Bonner had organised his archdeacons for the collection of tenths and payment of pensions.[58] At the same time Pole called for diocesan visitations to discover the details of hardship in the localities, so that he could plan the redistribution of the money which was not required for pensions.

[53] Hodgett, *Ex-religious in Lincoln*, pp. xviii, 28–30, 116; P.R.O., E 164/31, fo. 9.
[54] Cf. Dickens, 'Edwardian Arrears', p. 390.
[55] P.R.O., E 164/31, fo. 1, and Arch. Reg. fos. 5–6, for the indenture between Pole and Mary clinching their arrangement.
[56] Guildhall MS. 9531/12 (Bonner's register), fo. 399; *The registers of...G. Bourne, Bishop of Bath and Wells, L.V*, ed. H. Maxwell-Lyte (Somerset Record Society, 1949), p. 143.
[57] Worcester Diocesan R.O., Register 2648: 716.093, 9(IV), 47 (Pate's register).
[58] Guildhall R.O., MS. 9531/12, fo. 399.

Pole asked shrewd and detailed questions, as we see from the reminder which he sent to Turberville of Exeter in March 1557.[59] He wanted to know the state of buildings, the value of benefices, the names and numbers of parishes without resident priests, the wealth of parishioners and their capacity to help in restoration, the parishioners' opinions of the needs of their churches, and so on. Ideally, then, Pole hoped to have reliable information by the autumn of 1556 on the pension list, the surplus remaining from the collection of tenths, and the urgent requirements of the dioceses. Partly with this in mind, the synod, prorogued for Lent 1556, was summoned to reassemble the following November.[60] The accumulation of that information would have been a long step towards a coherent ecclesiastical policy.

In June 1556 Pole was still hoping to meet the clergy in November, but by 31 October he had admitted defeat and extended the prorogation until the following May.[61] The size of the dioceses and the scale of the investigation had prevented the collection of all the information. We can sense Pole's frustration as he found the impossibility of taking short-cuts through this forest of administrative confusion. He pleaded with the clergy to prepare themselves for May 1557 so that the reforming work of the synod could be completed without delay; he urged them to send their findings in writing to speed up the collection of information.[62] But, even so, the year 1556 passed without even the appointment of an auditing committee for all the bishops' accounts.

In February 1557, only five months before the revocation of Pole's powers by Pope Paul IV, we at last find the appointment of a central committee of audit for episcopal accounts.[63] Bonner, Thirlby of Ely, Griffith of Rochester, Henry Cole and William Pye were named, and in the autumn of that year, after the official end of his mission, Pole at last received some valuable information. If Mary had not had the foresight to arrange that the archbishop of Canterbury could continue the work if the legate failed to complete it, the revocation would have been an even greater administrative upset than in fact it proved.[64] Even as it was, the information came much too late to be of great value in the remaining months of the reign. We are seeing that ineptitude alone was not the reason for the absence of policy.

Not surprisingly, it was discovered that some bishops enjoyed a large surplus after they had collected the first-fruits and paid the pensions, while others were struggling with a deficit. Early in 1557 Pole had suggested as a stop-gap measure that the

---

[59] Wilkins, *Concilia*, IV, pp. 149–50.

[60] Leg. Reg. VI, fo. 134: 'prorogatio synodi'.

[61] *Calendar of State Papers, Venetian*, VI, p. 500; Leg. Reg. VI, fo. 134.

[62] *Ibid.*, fo. 134; V, fos. 96–7.

[63] *Ibid.*, V, fos. 7–8, 98–9. The commission appears twice in the register in identical form; this may have been a confirmation or a response to a query or request for clarification. The instructions sent by Pole to collectors in 1557 ordered them to send their audited books to this committee (Leg. Reg. V, fos. 96, 99, 181).   [64] P.R.O., E 164/31, fo. 1.

Archdeacon of Llandaff should give some of his surplus for the payment of the debts of the see of St David's,[65] and in the spring of 1558 this was converted into a general policy.[66] Whereas previously absence of figures had forced Pole to advise collectors to hold their surpluses or make good losses from diocesan funds, now he knew enough to organise redistribution. Collectors could give half their surplus to a neighbouring diocese, or otherwise send it to the central committee for allocation. Specific arrangements were made: some of the colossal bills of London diocese, where the ex-religious of Syon alone cost £856 8s 8d, were paid by £400 from the surplus of Norwich; there is a long list of these financial acrobatics in Bonner's register. And Pole could also begin to think of easing the burden of poverty in some livings; for the moment all he could do was to lessen taxation on impoverished benefices. This he did in the closing months of 1557 by releasing from the payment of tenths all benefices with less than twenty marks; and in April 1558, presumably in the light of long-awaited figures from the committee, he halved all taxations of a tenth on the clergy. Money collected wrongly in 1557 was to be returned in 1558.[67]

This was a start; but without the income lost to laymen Pole could not meet the needs of local hardship. Bishop Turberville reported one example for Totnes in Devon.[68] There the priory had been the impropriator before the break with Rome, and the vicar's stipend had been eight pounds, supplemented with meals at the priory and wood from priory land; in dealing with 1,400 parishioners, he had the assistance of a chantry priest. The Crown had taken over at the dissolution, and the vicar found himself without monastic, and soon without chantry, assistance, and paying increased taxation in a period of inflation. Turberville recognised that Mary's government stood for the return of 'devoute' services for the people's benefit; but without money or the priory's support the priest was desperately handicapped in providing those services. The full income could be given to a resident rector who could then work with an assistant, and because the pious monarchs were still the impropriators such a solution was possible. But there remained the damage done by the schism in hundreds of similar parishes, many of them beyond the reach of Pole and Mary; where could they recover the traditional beauty of holiness which Pole felt was the key to revived Catholic enthusiasm?

The sad story of Totnes emerged from an episcopal report, a report demanded by Pole in the long list of instructions to the bishops. It is worth remembering at this point that Mary's bishops, like the legate and the Crown, were inundated with complications, worries and delays. Just as Pole fulminated against delays in the collection of information, so the bishops struggled in vain to speed up that collection.

[65] Leg. Reg. v, fo. 99.
[66] Guildhall R.O., MS. 9531/12, fo. 439; Pole to Bonner, 1 April 1558.
[67] B.L., Lansdowne MS. 980, fo. 239 (from Exeter episcopal registers); Guildhall R.O., MS. 9531/12, fo. 439. [68] B.L., Additional Charters, 24705.

In August 1558 Tunstall at Durham was complaining that 'I shall scant geat money for to paye the pencons and annuities' because his collection of tenths was proceeding so slowly.[69] Oglethorpe in Carlisle at last received a royal warrant restoring some ecclesiastical revenues gained by the Crown to the use of the bishop on 14 November 1558, only a few days before the deaths of Queen and legate.[70] All this burden of administration was added to their own personal and financial worries. Humiliating though it was for Henrician and Edwardian bishops to ask forgiveness from a legate who had been condemned as a traitor under Henry VIII, the members of Mary's episcopate who had erred in the schism had to seek Pole's absolution. Their cases were treated with meticulous care, and Pole's response varied with the seriousness of the backsliding; even Bonner and Tunstall had to gain personal absolution through the legate.[71] On the top of this personal difficulty of settling into the Marian regime came the bishops' financial hardships; an effort had to be made to revive the sees after the despoiling of Edward's reign, for inflation and taxation had by no means exempted bishops from their damaging effect. As well as the heavy debts of taxation which many of them owed to the Crown, the bishops had suffered severe loss of ornaments and vestments, for cathedrals, like parish churches, had been a target for confiscation, official and unofficial; and Tunstall of Durham, for one, was still not expecting anything like full recovery by 1558.[72] Again, the bishops, like Pole, suffered from a shortage of information: in Winchester, for example, the accounts of the treasurers of the diocese did not cover the whole of the decade before Mary's accession, with the result that irregularities were difficult to see and follow up.[73] In Pole's legatine register we find five bishops appealing to Pole for dispensations to hold benefices *in commendam* in other dioceses to tide them over in the difficult time of recovery.[74] And Paul IV, though anxious to recommence taxation of the English Church, was unexpectedly generous and recognised in July 1555 that the English clergy needed time to recover. He permitted Pole to use all episcopal first-fruits to meet the needs of the Church in England rather than the demands of the pope in Rome.[75] Furthermore, Paul IV eased the burden of biennial visitation which was

[69] P.R.O., S.P. 11/13, fo. 114: Tunstall to Pole, 16 August 1558.
[70] V.C.H., Cumberland, II, p. 60.
[71] Pole imposed new oaths of loyalty to the pope on ex-abbots who had become Henrician bishops (Leg. Reg. I, fos. 65–72); the absolutions to Tunstall and Bonner were Leg. Reg. I, fos. 43–4, 113–5.
[72] Frere and Kennedy, Injunctions, II, p. 412.
[73] Arch. Vat., Instr. Misc. 4008, an inquiry into the 'true value' of English sees, undertaken by Pole for the pope.
[74] Leg. Reg. I, fos. 100–1; II, fos. 77–8; IV, fos. 50–1, 106; V, fo. 176. The bishops were Stanley, Griffith, Turberville, Brooks and Oglethorpe.
[75] Arch. Vat., Arm. 42:6, fo. 130. The pope received a very grateful letter from Pate of Worcester thanking him for the concession (Arch. Vat., AA Arm XVIII 6540, fo. 170).

expected of the English bishops and asked only that they should visit their dioceses every six years; he obviously felt they had worries enough.[76]

For the papacy itself these years of Mary's reign were as much a reconnaissance into the unknown of the English Church as they were for Mary, Pole and the bishops. Paul IV, as we have seen, expressed a genuine concern for the poverty of the English sees, but he was not a man to allow permanent loss of money which was owing to him. The problem was, however, that Rome had little conception of English episcopal finances after twenty years of schism and inflation, and Paul had to know whether the 'old taxes' could be paid. In July 1555, in the same month as his financial concession, the pope instructed Pole to examine the 'true value' of English dioceses, so that Rome could make fair tax assessments.[77] In August Paul followed this up by appointing Ormanetto, one of Pole's closest friends and ablest advisers, as collector of taxes for the papal see.[78] The pope was thus adding another large administrative task to the anxious search for information which was already the characteristic of the mission. In May 1556 Ormanetto decided to take advantage of vacancies at Winchester and Chester to put those sees under close scrutiny, and he conducted searching interviews to discover the wealth of the dioceses as well as the virtues of the proposed new bishops. Stemp of the legatine court and David Pole and John Christopherson, two of Pole's strongest supporters, were all questioned.[79] Presumably because he was reluctant to waste such industry, Pole chose Winchester as the first see for his large-scale investigation for Paul IV; he apologised that he could not lead the enquiry himself – we have seen enough of his problems to absolve him of laziness – and delegated Heath of York and Thirlby to carry out the task.

They showed great thoroughness, and the results of their labours were beautifully recorded by John Clerk, one of Pole's leading notaries and agents.[80] But the enquiry encountered a series of problems which were typical of Pole's difficulties. The chancellor and treasurer of the diocese could produce records for only eight of the previous ten years. Paul IV had demanded the accounts of the whole decade to give an indication of Winchester's true situation. Thirteen major witnesses were called to the chapel of Sir Richard Sackville in Salisbury Place, and the information which they supplied frequently required interpretation. The effects of inflation, for instance, proved baffling, and a Florentine merchant was asked to hold forth on the relative

[76] Arch. Vat., Arm. 42:6, fo. 99.

[77] Arch. Vat., Instr. Misc. 4008. This is the record of the inquiry into the wealth of Winchester, in response to Paul IV's orders; Pole gave the pope the details of his plan for finding the 'true value' in Instr. Misc. 4010 in the same collection of documents.

[78] Arch. Vat., Arm. 42:6, fos. 265–6.

[79] Arch. Vat., Arm. 64:28, fos. 319–27. Ormanetto's inquiries into Winchester and Chester.

[80] Arch. Vat., Instr. Misc. 4008. A large and elaborate record for Rome's benefit; at times Pole's administration was meticulously efficient.

values of the pound and the angel in the schismatic period. Again, the investigators were in great need of other figures for comparison, and the treasurers of other dioceses were called in. By September, Pole was arranging for another batch of figures, this time for Durham; and on this occasion he trusted Tunstall and his dean, Thomas Watson, sufficiently to authorise them to look into the annual revenue of their own see for the previous ten years and send their findings to Rome to ensure accurate assessment for taxation.[81] We have no more examples of this search for the 'true value' in the remaining nine months of the mission, but of course Pole's relations with Paul IV became increasingly strained. The pope had, in any case, given Pole many years of administration in this project alone.

In the twelve months between the summers of 1555 and 1556, then, Pole was planning and carrying through the transfer of land, money and colossal responsibilities from the Crown to the Church, preparing for and holding the great legatine synod, then organising widespread visitations to discover the local needs of the Church. Meanwhile, Paul IV was bombarding Pole with instructions and requests. To all this we can add the vast diplomatic task which Julius III had given to Pole in 1553 and which lies outside the immediate scope of this paper; Pole had received powers to mediate between Habsburg and Valois in their European wars, and even when the synod was actually sitting Pole had to find time to send streams of letters in an effort to bring Henry II and Charles V together for talks.[82] When we remember, too, that Pole was always justifiably fearful of Pope Paul IV's bitterness towards him, it seems extraordinary that he even formulated plans.[83] The financial obstacles alone were sufficient to hold him up, and they were only a part of the difficulties of a hectic year.

These financial obstacles were all the more daunting because they heightened tension in many other important issues. The quarrel over the ownership of land accentuated political divisions on the Council and in parliament; the argument could rapidly lead to ideological statements of loyalty to the idea of a united Christendom, on the one side, or to a national Tudor feeling, on the other.[84] That kind of bitterness was dangerous to any government's stability. Secondly, in his search for information Pole had to place great burdens on the bishops; and since many of them had grown accustomed to hating Pole for his writings against the Henrician Church, these already delicate relationships were likely to be strained still further by constant central

---

[81] Leg. Reg. VI, fos. 123–4.

[82] B. L., Add. MS. 41577, fos. 216–9: 20 November, 18 December, 27 November 1555 and 25 January 1556. Four important letters on the subject of peace while the synod was in session.

[83] Cf. Fenlon, *Heresy and Obedience*, pp. 243–50, for Pole's long and difficult relationship with Caraffa.

[84] This confrontation occurred in the Council meeting of 21 December 1554: B.L., Add. MS. 41577, fos. 161 ff. Cf. note 25. For the bitterness which the question of land aroused in Mary's parliaments, see J. E. Neale, *Elizabeth I and her Parliaments* (London, 1965 edn.), I, p. 22.

interference in episcopal affairs. Rome began to receive complaints and requests for Pole's removal, and it may not have been merely administrative difficulty which delayed some of the local information which Pole needed so badly.[85] Thirdly, the legate could not look for massive Catholic support in the parish churches, for until the money had been recovered and used, the dilapidations and inadequacies of local worship remained, and there was little visible evidence of the orderly, harmonious revival which Pole was seeking.[86] Indeed, the struggle for land ownership was repeated on a small scale in many localities as priests and parishioners fought ingloriously over rights to ornaments, lead and tithes; the financial confusion of the schism was thus a likely cause of that Tudor nightmare, local disorder.[87] And, finally, the government's interest in the lost wealth of the Church laid them open to the renewed attacks of heretics and anticlericals that Catholics wanted only money: 'such pickpurse matters is all the rabble of your ceremonies', Robert Smith told the Catholic bishops who were interrogating him.[88] Pole and Mary devoted much time to financial headaches in their attempt to restore order, and so they surrendered the pulpit to their articulate opponents and gave them texts for their sermons.

It could be argued that Pole and Mary added to their own problems by an obsession with the Church's former worldly glories; but it is unrealistic to expect them to have forgotten centuries of Roman tradition. Catholics and Protestants alike recognised the strength of the visual appeal of the Roman Church;[89] even if Pole had placed emphasis on, say, an evangelical campaign, he would still have been forced to work for the financial recovery of the Church in England if Rome was to regain anything resembling its former influence. And so he and Mary were committed to an ecclesiastical policy demanding the recovery of wealth which seemed irretrievable. Overshadowing all were two problems: ignorance of the true local state of the

[85] For two separate reports of clerical resentment of Pole's efforts, see P.R.O., S.P. 11/7, fo. 15; S.P. 69/11, fo. 119. Gardiner is reported to have never wanted Pole in England in the first place: *Calendar of State Papers Spanish*, XI, p. 202.

[86] Pole's visitations: of Canterbury, 1556 – L.P.L., VC III/1/2; of Lincoln – J. Strype, *Ecclesiastical Memorials* (London, 1822), III (pt. II), p. 389. Harpsfield's visitation of Canterbury, 1556–7, in *C.R.S.*, XLV–I (1950–I), ed. L. Whatmore. The episcopal visitations of Bath and Wells, 1554 and 1557 – Somerset R.O., D/D/Ca 18, 27. All these records tell the story of dilapidation; Pole visited 146 churches in 1556, and ninety were in urgent need of basic structural repair.

[87] E.g. the cases in P.R.O., Sta. Cha. 4, 5/36, with disputed tithes in the parish of Therfield, and past and present vicars quarrelling over them.

[88] Foxe, *Actes*, VII, p. 351.

[89] Chedsey at the Essex heresy trials said that the heretic Hawkes was 'against the ceremonies of the church' and so 'denieth the order of the catholic church': Foxe, *Actes*, VII, p. 107; Cheke on the Protestant side saw 'superstition' as one of the Roman strengths: *Original Letters, relative to the English Reformation*, ed. H. Robinson (Parker Society, 1856), p. 141; Pole was expert in explaining the spiritual significance of ceremonies: e.g. Quirini, *Epistolae*, v, p. 37 and Bodleian MS. Biblio. Vat., Vat. Lat. 5968, fo. 384.

churches, and the system of impropriations, complicated by the lay determination to retain schismatic winnings. Both these problems were to check plans for ecclesiastical reform for decades – the latter even for centuries – after Mary's death. In his questions to the bishops in 1556, Pole spoke hopefully of gaining a 'perfect understanding' of the Church's financial problems;[90] we have seen why that understanding was denied him, and how without it he could not begin to introduce the necessary reforms.

[90] B.L., MS. Lansdowne 989, fo. 57: Pole on taxation and tenths, 1 April 1558.

8

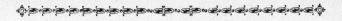

BONNER AND
THE MARIAN PERSECUTIONS

GINA ALEXANDER

Edmund Bonner was Bishop of London during the reign of Mary Tudor, and his name has always been linked with hers in the history of the persecution. More than one-third of all the victims of the Marian reaction were indeed burnt within his diocese, but Bonner's prominent place in the record rests primarily on Foxe's identification of him as one of the arch-villains of Mary's reign. Foxe's *Acts and Monuments* launched 'Bloody Bonner' into history as the epitome of evil and injustice. He included in his book not only many documents but also episodes which had been passed to him by word of mouth. Such was the story of Tomkins, a weaver from Shoreditch 'endued with God's mighty spirit'.[1] When Bonner summoned him for examination, Tomkins remained steadfast in his faith, which so enraged Bonner that he seized Tomkins's hand and held it directly over the flame of a candle until the flesh blistered. Foxe did not invent this story. The Spanish ambassador had heard of Tomkins's ordeal before the end of March 1554/5, but his version emphasised Tomkins's bravado in voluntarily testing how much pain he could bear. Foxe did not probe as to who had initiated the candle episode. He was concerned to tell the history of the age-long conflict between the true and the apostate Church and so would not blur the picture he had drawn of the main protagonists. Tomkins was the holy martyr, Bonner the 'persecutor of the light and a child of darkness'.[2] The Elizabethans accepted Foxe's picture unhesitatingly and later historians have accepted it or modified it usually according to their own religious persuasion. Bonner himself was aware of his reputation: 'they report me to seek blood, and call me "Bloody Bonner": whereas God knoweth I never sought any man's blood in all my life'.[3] Bonner's role in the Marian persecutions cannot be evaluated without Foxe's evidence; but that evidence can be used to establish how far Bonner's actions were

---

[1] J. Foxe, *The Actes and Monuments*, ed. J. Pratt and J. Stoughton (London, 1877), VI, p. 718.
[2] *Calender of State Papers, Spanish*, XIII, p. 148; Foxe, *Actes*, VIII, p. 669.
[3] J. E. Neale, *Elizabeth I and her Parliaments*, I (London, 1953) p. 180, and P. Collinson, *The Elizabethan Puritan Movement*, (London, 1967), pp. 265, 378; Foxe, *Actes*, VII, p. 349.

determined by the decisions of the Queen and her government and the pertinacity of the Protestants.

On 5 August 1553 Bonner received Queen Mary's pardon and was discharged from the Marshalsea prison where he had been since the autumn of 1549. The Greyfriars chronicler wrote that as Bonner came to St Paul's 'the pepulle range the belles for joye'.[4] Such enthusiasm, if indeed it did correspond with popular feeling, may have been at the prospect of a return to the old ways rather than as a token of appreciation for Bonner. The bishop was not particularly spiritual or gentle, neither a preacher[5] nor a theologian. A lawyer, originally discovered by Wolsey, Bonner had served Cromwell loyally, acting as ambassador in Rome, Hamburg and France. Cromwell protected Bonner from the wrath which his insolence and tactlessness aroused in fellow-ambassadors and in the King of France. During the 1530s Bonner was firmly identified with the King's anti-papal policy, writing a violent preface to Gardiner's *De Vera Obedientia* in 1536 and conducting the long drawn-out process of getting the government-sponsored translation of the Bible printed on French presses in 1539. After Cromwell's fall Bonner was more clearly identified as a conservative in religion, but he gave no hint that he would welcome the reintroduction of papal authority in England. Many years later Bonner was reported to have said that during Henry's reign 'fear compelled us to bear with the time'.[6] Perhaps, but it was at that time that he reached the episcopate and collected numerous profitable preferments.

Bonner was never an easy or equable person, and as the years passed he seems to have grown more violent. Foxe wrote a long and circumstantial story describing an incident which occurred during Bonner's visitation of his diocese in October 1554. Bonner lost his temper and struck out at the rector of Hadham. Feckenham, Dean of St Paul's, exclaimed: 'Bear with my lord; for truly his long imprisonment in the Marshalsea, and the misusing of him there, hath altered him, that in these passions he is not ruler of himself, nor it booteth any man to give him counsel until his heat be past; and then...my lord will be sorry for those abuses that now he cannot see in himself.' Bonner once analysed his rages, admitting that to be 'something overhasty...is a natural disease to some men. And surely they are not the worst natured men: for I myself shall now and then be hasty but mine anger is soon past.'[7] His comment, both defensive and complacent, was typical of the man who was at the centre of events in London from 1553 to 1558.

When Bonner was formally restored to this bishopric in September 1553 he faced a confused and rapidly changing political and ecclesiastical situation. His main experience as a servant of the Crown had been in the years after Henry VIII and

[4] *Chronicle of the Grey Friars of London*, ed. J. G. Nichols (Camden Society LIII, 1852), p. 82.
[5] Foxe, *Actes*, VII, p. 100.
[6] *Ibid.*, VIII, p. 110.   [7] *Ibid.*, VI, p. 563; VIII, p. 477.

Cromwell had withdrawn England from the papal jurisdiction. Now the Queen was anxious to turn back the clock not merely to 1547 but to 1529. Mary wanted to make England a Catholic country as quickly as possible: to reintroduce the pope's authority, to repeal those parliamentary statutes which had so radically altered the relationship of Church and State and to restore to the Church its Catholic doctrine and services. Nothing was to be allowed to stand in her way. No murmurings among the people, no riots or rebellions or intrigues, not even the advice of the Spanish ambassador to make haste slowly[8] could deflect the Queen from her purpose.

One of Mary's main concerns in the first eighteen months of her reign was the restoration of the legal position of 1529. To accomplish that, the repeal of the Edwardian and Henrician legislation was accompanied by the revival of the medieval statutes against heresy. Mary has been accused of excessive legalism in her endeavours to bring England back into the Catholic fold, but she could hardly have achieved her objectives peacefully without first getting Parliament to make fundamental changes in the law. Mary may have seen the restoration of the heresy laws simply as a necessary part of her endeavour to restore the legal position of the Church in England, or she may deliberately have decided on a policy of persecution. Just as her exact motives remain obscure, it is not clear whether the initiative for the re-enactment of the heresy statutes came from the Queen herself, perhaps influenced by her Spanish confessors, or from her Chancellor, Stephen Gardiner.[9]

Mary's first parliament in the autumn of 1553 repealed the Edwardian legislation after considerable dispute, and it required two parliaments in the spring and autumn of 1554 to reverse the Henrician legislation and to re-enact the three medieval statutes against heresy. These statutes, of 1382, 1401 and 1414, had re-enforced the Church's own powers to deal with heretics, and had also closely involved the secular authorities in the pursuit and execution of religious offenders. Death by burning at the hands of the sheriffs became the penalty for those who, convicted of heresy in the church courts, refused to recant. If Mary had repealed the Henrician legislation without reviving the medieval statutes she would have forfeited the government's right to present heretics to the bishop for examination and also the use of secular punishments. At the same time the bishops' powers would have been those of 1381 and not 1529. Mary could not withdraw the support of the secular authorities from the Church: to have done so would have meant abdicating her responsibilities as a Catholic ruler towards the Church and her people.

[8] *Calendar of State Papers, Spanish*, XIII, pp. 138–9.

[9] Gardiner has been described as the initiator of the persecution, but he was an ineffective and unwilling inquisitor. It is more likely that he pressed for the re-enactment of the heresy statutes in 1554 because of his desire to restore the full jurisdiction of the bishops. See D. M. Loades, 'The Enforcement of Reaction, 1553–1558', *J.E.H.*, XVI (1965), p. 58; Foxe, *Actes*, VII, p. 157; and see the important letter from Renard to the emperor of 21 December 1554 in *Calendar of State Papers, Spanish*, XIII, p. 124.

Bonner as Bishop of London sat in the Lords in Mary's parliaments but he had little influence on the Queen or her government. He was never a member of the council and he did not help to formulate the Queen's policy. Bonner did however agree with the policy of persecution; and he was prepared to declare publicly that that policy was dictated by love of God. In July 1555 Bonner rewrote the homily on Christian love which had originally appeared in Cranmer's first book of homilies in 1547. He declared 'to love our enemies is the proper condition onely of them, that be the children of God, the folowers of Christ'. He asked 'If charity requyre to thinke, speake, and doo well unto every man, bothe good and evyl, how can magystrates execute iustice upon malefactours?' Charity commands that all governors should correct offenders within their jurisdiction '... those that be evil, of love, we ought to procure unto them theyr correction'. He summed up his argument with this analogy: he who is in authority must be 'as a good surgeon (who) cutteth away a putryfied and festred member, for the loue he hath to the hole body, least it infecte other members adioynynge to it'.[10] Foxe thought that Bonner was motivated by cruelty; Bonner declared he acted out of love. In the first years of Mary's reign the majority of Bonner's contemporaries probably saw nothing strange in using the stake as the ultimate weapon to impose uniformity of belief: some may even have been able to understand Bonner's declaration that he was driven by love.

The Crown provided the impetus and initiative in restoring the legal framework in which the diocesan bishops could act against heresy, so the government made sure that all the forces it could muster were engaged in seeking out suspected heretics and presenting them to the ecclesiastical officers. In the months before the statutes were re-enacted the Queen made clear to the bishops the religious policies she wished them to pursue. The proclamation of 4 March 1553/4 included detailed injunctions for religion and authorised the bishops to deprive clergy who had married in Edward's reign.[11] After the reconciliation with Rome and the revival of the justices' rights to inquire into heresies according to the act of 1414, Mary felt it necessary to issue a proclamation in May 1555 to spur on the justices to execute the law 'with diligence'.[12] At the same time the King and Queen reprimanded Bonner in a letter which made their attitude to his episcopal authority startlingly plain: his jurisdiction

---

[10] *Homelies sette forth by...Edmunde Byshop of London* (London, 1555), fos 25, 25v, 26v–27, and cf. *Certayne Sermons or homilies* (London 1547), sig. L. III.

[11] P. L. Hughes and J. F. Larkin, *Tudor Royal Proclamations*, II (New Haven, 1969), pp. 35 ff., and see also Bonner's letter to the Archdeacon of Essex of 6 March 1553/4 in his episcopal register: Guildhall R.O., MS. 9531/12, fo. 341v.

[12] Hughes and Larkin, *Proclamations*, II, p. 53. See also the letter from the King and Queen to the justices in March 1554/5 reminding them to send suspects to the bishops: B.L., MS. Cotton, Titus. B.II, fo. 100 (printed in *History of the Reformation of the Church of England by Gilbert Burnet*, ed. N. Pocock, v, (London, 1865) p. 427).

had been restored to him in order that he should execute government policy without delay.[13] Although eight heretics had been burnt in London between 20 January when the statutes came into force and 24 May when this letter was written, there were also five more who had been condemned but not burnt and at least sixteen suspects in London prisons who had not been tried in the ecclesiastical courts. Bonner, whose every action was noted by the Queen and her council, had little choice. He ordered Dr Chedsey to preach at Paul's Cross so that the people of London might know what instructions he had received,[14] and in June and July another thirteen heretics were condemned in the consistory court of London.

The council, a large, divided and changing body which rarely spoke with a united voice, nevertheless daily exercised direct control over the actions of the bishops. The council understandably took action to ensure that, when convicted heretics had been handed to the sheriffs by the ecclesiastical authorities, there were sufficient well-wishers present to ensure that burnings took place without risk of riot or disturbance, but it was also constantly on the alert to see that the bishops carried out their responsibilities properly. Three times, between 1554 and 1556, the council specifically instructed Bonner to send his preachers, chaplains or commissaries into Essex. The council ordered the arrest of individual suspects such as John Rough and Cuthbert Simpson and intervened directly in at least ten other cases. Men already in prison were to be sent to Bonner for examination of their religious beliefs. Bonner was 'to order' suspects according to the laws:[15] he could hardly refuse. Individual councillors also took it upon themselves to tell the Bishop of London what he must do. In June 1555 both Sir Richard Southwell and the Marquis of Winchester were pressing Bonner to examine suspected heretics 'since they be come to London; and so I pray they may be, and I certified of your proceedings, that I may follow; which I shall do'.[16]

Southwell and Winchester were friendly enough but there was no mistaking who was directing religious policy and who saw to its prompt execution by the ecclesiastical authorities. Another and even clearer example of the close control which the council exercised over Bonner's day-to-day activities arose in 1556. In August 1556 the Council ordered the Essex justices to send twenty-two suspects whom they had apprehended at prayer meetings at Dovercourt and Harwich to Bonner for further examination.[17] Bonner had recently displeased Cardinal Pole[18] and he now

---

[13] Foxe, *Actes*, VII, p. 86.   [14] *Ibid.*, VII, pp. 647, 286.

[15] *A.P.C.*, V, p. 30; VI, pp. 216, 276; Foxe, *Actes*, VIII, pp. 444–5; VII, p. 739.

[16] *Ibid.*, pp. 322, 371, and see *A.P.C.*, V, p. 135.

[17] *Ibid.*, p. 334. See the distraught letter from John Kingston, Bonner's commissary in Essex about these twenty-two suspects: Foxe, *Actes*, VIII, pp. 304 ff.

[18] Three heretics excommunicated by Bonner on 13 June 1556 were absolved by Pole, who procured a royal pardon for them: Foxe, *Actes*, VIII, p. 154, P.R.O., C. 85/127, fo. 21, *Calendar of the Patent Rolls, Philip and Mary*, III, p. 516.

wrote to Pole for direction. Possibly at the Cardinal's suggestion, he presented the twenty-two Essex suspects with a shortened form of submission which they felt able to sign. The council may have connived at this gentle treatment but if so it had second thoughts. In November the council sharply rebuked Bonner for his leniency and ordered him to recommence proceedings against two of the suspects.[19]

Mary did not only rely on her own exhortations and the vigilance of the council. She saw no ambiguity in renouncing the Royal Supremacy while maintaining the prerogative Henry had established in issuing royal commissions to deal with religious matters. Royal commissioners were vigorously inquiring after, seizing and examining suspected heretics during 1555, and in February 1556 commissioners were appointed by letters patent to inquire into heresies and seditions. These commissions were directed to the bishop and the leading clergy and laymen in each diocese. Bonner and his colleagues were given a larger commission than the other diocesans. Even the commission to the archdiocese of York was made subordinate to that of London.[20] The following year another royal commission was issued to Bonner, members of the council and other prominent clergy, laymen and lawyers. Their powers were wider than those given to the diocesan commissioners in 1556, for as well as examining offenders, they were also authorised to search out all who refused to go to church and to examine churches and vicarages for dilapidations.[21]

Unfortunately no records of the commissioners' proceedings have been found, and only odd references in Foxe show how they went about their inquiries. At least fifteen men and women eventually excommunicated by Bonner were sent to him by the commissioners. Dr John Story was the most zealous of the commissioners working in London. John Philpot, Archdeacon of Winchester, wrote reports of the long and numerous examinations which he endured between October and December 1555. From Philpot's record it is clear that Bonner, using both guile and threats, worked hard to reconcile him. Story however was impatient to be done: he had no time for Philpot and little respect for the office or the person of the bishop. On one occasion Story did not deign to wait to speak to Bonner, but asked 'one of you tell my lord that my coming was to signify to his lordship that he must out of hand rid this heretic away'.[22]

The royal commissioners also concerned themselves closely with the internal administration of the diocese of London. On 2 April 1557 they issued an order to all parsons, curates and churchwardens in the diocese of London to search out those

---

[19] Foxe, *Actes*, VIII, pp. 383, 387, 390; *A.P.C.*, VI, pp. 18, 19. See also P.R.O., C. 85/127. fo. 24.

[20] Foxe, *Actes*, VI, p. 593; VII, pp. 151, 329, 342–3, 371, 605; *Calendar of the Patent Rolls, Philip and Mary*, III, p. 81. The Bishop of Exeter and his colleagues were specifically instructed to refer difficult cases to the Bishop of London: D. Wilkins, *Concilia Magnae Britanniae et Hiberniae*, IV (London, 1737), p. 142; R. W. Dixon, *History of the Church of England*, IV (London, 1891), pp. 573–4n.

[21] *Calendar of the Patent Rolls, Philip and Mary*, III, pp. 281–2.   [22] Foxe, *Actes*, VII, p. 628.

who did not go to church, make their confession or receive the sacrament. A year later they published a little book of Interrogatories to be answered by all churchwardens, inquiring about the marital status of the clergy, their doctrinal views, and ordering them to check the existence of 'heretical, naughty or seditious erroneous' books, Bibles or Testaments.[23] We do not know when the commissioners acted on their own, or with juries of twelve men, or when they relied on evidence laid before them by individual informers. If the booklet of Interrogatories is any guide, the London commissioners conducted a visitation of the city, if not of the whole diocese, relying on information supplied by the churchwardens. Because Bonner was appointed a royal commissioner both in 1556 and 1557, and indeed according to Foxe was a chief commissioner as early as the spring of 1554,[24] it is difficult to know when he was acting as a diocesan or as a commissioner. Commissioners acting without Bonner conducted many preliminary examinations of suspected heretics whom they sent on to him for formal trial in consistory, but they also sat with him there. One of Bonner's own officials regarded his authority as a commissioner as greater than his authority as bishop of London.[25]

Once the statute of 1401 had been re-enacted Bonner, like other diocesans, had the right to arrest suspected heretics. Foxe believed that Bonner personally sent out his apparitor-general, Richard Cloney, to arrest Londoners, and he told the story of Margaret Mearing, who, knowing that Cloney was looking for her at her house, deliberately returned home courting arrest.[26] Cloney was responsible for seeing that offenders were present at the church courts when they were supposed to be, and there are references to his activities in the act book which records those sessions of the consistory court held by the vicar-general, Nicholas Harpsfield, in the winter of 1554–5.[27] Cloney's powers of summons were not the same as the justices' powers of arrest; he could not compel attendance on those willing to risk excommunication for non-appearance. Apart from Foxe's hints there is no evidence that Bonner deliberately sent out his officials to arrest suspected heretics. The three people who are recorded as appearing before Harpsfield and who were eventually martyred were not sent to Bonner as a result of Harpsfield's investigations or Cloney's summons. The commissioners sent them to the bishop.[28] As Bishop of London Bonner had

[23] Guildhall R.O., MS. cit., fo. 419; *Interrogatories upon which ... the churchwardens ... shall be charged withall set forth by the King and Queen's majesty's commissioners* (London, 1558): see especially articles 2–5, 7.
[24] Foxe, *Actes*, VIII, p. 623.
[25] See the letter from Chedsey, Archdeacon of Middlesex, of 21 April 1558 at B.L., Harl. MS. 416, fo. 74.
[26] Foxe, *Actes*, VIII, p. 451. See also pp. 551–2.
[27] G.L.R.O, MS. D.L.C./6/614, fos. 7, 7v, 8.
[28] Thomas Fust, George Tankerville and Isabella Foster were examined by Harpsfield in November and December 1554. Fust and Tankerville were sent by the Commissioners to Bonner in July 1555, and Isabella Foster appeared before Bonner in January 1555/6: Guildhall R.O., MS. cit., fos. 4, 21, 36, 16v; Foxe, *Actes*, VII, pp. 342, 344, 748.

little personal control over the way in which suspected heretics were sent to him for examination.

Like the royal commissioners, justices of the peace were directly answerable to the Crown, and subject moreover to the constant vigilance of the council. A statute of Mary's first parliament authorised justices to arrest religious offenders reported to them by constables and churchwardens and to keep them in custody until they repented. Eight men examined by Bonner in the summer of 1554 had probably been arrested by the justices in accordance with this statute of 1553. When the statute of 1414 came into force on 20 January 1555, justices of the peace were empowered to initiate inquiries into heresy and to arrange the arrest of suspects. A number of justices acted with particular energy from January 1555 until the summer of 1558, personally examining suspects and supervising arrests made by the local bailiffs and constables or by their own men. The activity of the justices varied greatly from one county to the next, and within the diocese of London there was no uniform pattern. In these three and a half years justices sent Bonner more than forty suspects who were later excommunicated and handed back to the secular authorities to be burnt. Other suspects were also sent by the justices to the Lord Chancellor or to the royal commissioners and were later dealt with by Bonner. Those who were eventually excommunicated and burnt were probably only a small proportion of all the suspects sent to the bishop by the justices. Unfortunately evidence for the activity of the Marian justices is scanty,[29] and once again we are thrown back on the evidence Foxe has left us.

Like the royal commissioners the justices had no doubts about their ability to determine orthodoxy. On 2 March 1556, two of the Essex justices, John Mordaunt and Edmund Tyrrel, wrote to Bonner about three suspects 'not conformable to the orders of the church, nor to the real presence of Christ's body and blood in the sacrament of the altar' and asking Bonner 'to use your lordship's pleasure with them as you think good, committing your good lordship to the tuition of the Almighty God'. Mordaunt and Tyrrel reminded Bonner of his fallibility. They did not admit that they also might err, yet not one of these three particular suspects was eventually martyred. James Harris for example was persuaded by Bonner to make his confession and then, said Foxe, the bishop 'of his accustomed devotion, took the poor lad into his garden, and there, with a rod, gathered out of a cherry-tree, did most cruelly whip him'. Having undergone his penance young James also disappears from view.[30]

[29] In the fifteenth century commissioners of oyer and terminer returned their indictments to the King's Bench and this evidence has been used in assessing the strength of late fifteenth-century Lollardy. Indictments of this kind have not survived for the Marian period. Nor do the reports from the justices of the peace of their sessions in the counties placed at the end of the Coram Rege rolls in King's Bench contain any records of the justices' investigations into heresy: J. A. F. Thomson, *The Later Lollards* (Oxford, 1965), p. 7 n4, p. 67 n2; see P.R.O., K.B. 9/984–7, 588–90, and K.B. 27/1174–82, esp. K.B. 27/1178, rr. 16, 28.
[30] Foxe, *Actes*, VIII, pp. 141–2, 526.

The Essex justices seem to have been exceptionally active, especially Anthony Brown, the Tyrrel brothers and Lord Darcy. The council knew them to be zealous supporters of the policy of persecution, and they worked with enthusiasm. Foxe's stories show that at least sixty of the heretics condemned in the London diocesan courts came from Essex, while only thirty were Londoners, one was from Hertfordshire and one from Middlesex. There may well have been fewer non-conformists in Hertfordshire and Middlesex, but did Essex have twice as many active Protestants as the city of London? Is this discrepancy explained by the greater energy with which the Essex justices set to their task?

The justices could ensure that some suspected heretics were sent to Bonner, but they had to have the full co-operation of the jurors who were sworn to give information about suspected criminals and heretics in their own districts. The justices, meeting at Colchester or Chelmsford, relied on jurors' reports for knowledge of heretical activity in more distant areas of the county, such as Harwich. Bonner's official, John Boswell, complained to him of the conduct of the inquests: 'I do see by experience, that the sworn inquest for heresies do, most commonly, indict the simple, ignorant, and wretched heretics, and do let the arch-heretics go; which is one great cause that moveth the rude multitude to murmur, when they see the simple wretches (not knowing what heresy is) to burn.'[31] Of all the Essex martyrs, only three are described by Foxe as gentlemen: Thomas Cawston, Thomas Higbed and Thomas Hawkes, who were all probably arrested in 1554. Cawston and Higbed were first imprisoned in Colchester Castle, and 'Bonner...perceiving these two gentlemen to be of worshipful estate, and of great estimation in the country, lest any tumult should thereby arise, came thither himself...thinking to reclaim them to his faction and fashion: so that great labour and diligence was taken therein.'[32] To no avail. After long, frequent and patient examinations by the bishop and his chaplains, Hawkes was excommunicated on 9 February 1555 and Cawston and Higbed a month later. They did not only lose their lives. Cawston and Higbed were of sufficient worth to have their property subject to an *inquisition post mortem*. Another commission was also sent to the Tyrrels, Anthony Browne, and others on 2 April 1555, instructing them to inquire which Essex men had fled abroad and to ascertain what goods they had. They were also to conduct an inquisition into the goods and land within the county of Essex and the town of Colchester belonging to Cawston and Higbed, and four others who had also been burnt at the end of March. The commissioners were to make an exact inventory and send it to Chancery: all the goods, lands and property of these executed heretics were forfeit to the Crown.[33]

[31] J. Oxley, *The Reformation in Essex* (Manchester, 1965), pp. 189–90; *A.P.C.*, v, p. 334; Foxe, *Actes*, VIII, p. 388 and see p. 383.
[32] *Ibid.*, VI, pp. 729, 724; VII, p. 98; VI, 730.
[33] P.R.O., C. 85/127, fos. 4, 5, 7; Foxe, *Actes*, VI, p. 737; VII, pp. 114–15; P.R.O., C. 142: 102/66, 53; C. 142: 107/48(2); P.R.O., C. 202/H/68, fo. 14.

Cawston, Higbed and Hawkes were not the only Protestants to be found among the Essex gentry. At least a dozen more fled abroad. Others with like convictions may well have moved to counties where the justices were less vigorous. For those who remained, the added threat of penury for their families may have reinforced a natural fear of the stake and ensured their conformity. Yet the question suggested by Boswell's remark remains: did the Essex justices leave the more affluent and more powerful alone? Artisans and craftsmen – tanners, weavers, fullers and the like – make up sixty per cent of those convicted heretics in the diocese of London whose social status is known to us, and this pattern is similar to that which prevailed in other parts of the country.[34] Were those with the skill and opportunity to acquire a trade more liable to heretical views than members of other classes of society? Did they at the same time lack the social connections necessary to avoid arrest? These are some of the questions to which there are at present no answers. All that can be said with certainty is that in the diocese of London many of the Essex justices consistently and loyally supported the government's policy to stamp out heresy by force. Local gaolers and lesser officials may not always have felt the same loyalty or sympathy, but the justices' allegiance was the significant factor. They could rely not only on the town constables,[35] but on their own men in the event of any disturbance. Theirs was the task of arresting heretics, and it was they who kept the bishops' courts busy.

Bonner blamed both the council and the heretics for his reputation as 'Bloody Bonner',[36] and indeed as Bishop of London he was caught between the upper and the nether millstone. The Queen assembled all the powers of the state to fulfil her fervent desire 'to restore the Mass and religion'. At the same time Bonner was in charge of a diocese which in twenty-five years had accepted three major changes of religion with equanimity and in some cases with enthusiasm. Nowhere in the kingdom had there been a greater circulation of Protestant ideas of many varieties, nowhere had Protestant modes of worship taken firmer root than in the diocese to which Bonner was restored in September 1553. The kingdom might be officially reconciled to Rome and the ancient ecclesiastical jurisdiction re-established, but Londoners had not automatically returned to Catholic orthodoxy. Many may have echoed the enthusiasm of the Greyfriars Chronicler, many more were no doubt indifferent and willing enough to accept the dictates of the Queen, but there were others whose hearts and spirits had gloried in the doctrines of the Edwardian church and who were

---

[34] C. H. Garrett, *The Marian Exiles* (Cambridge, 1938), pp. 73, 124, 126, 128, 137, 165, 243, 260, 271, 303, and also pp. 72, 157, 312, 334; D. M. Loades, 'The Essex Inquisitions of 1556', *B.I.H.R.*, xxxv (1962), pp. 87–97. K. G. Powell, *The Marian Martyrs and the Reformation in Bristol* (Bristol, 1972), p. 15.

[35] Oxley, *Reformation in Essex*, p. 188.

[36] Foxe, *Actes*, VII, pp. 738–9, 746; VIII, p. 416.

unconvinced that the accession of their ageing half-Spanish Queen proved the superiority of Catholicism.

Ralph Allerton, when he was examined by Bonner in April 1557, analysed the religious situation: 'there are in England three religions'. When Bonner asked him 'Which be those three?' Ralph replied: 'The first is that which you hold; the second is clean contrary to the same; and the third is a neuter, being indifferent – that is to say, observing all things that are commanded outwardly, as though he were of your part, his heart being yet wholly against the same.'[37] The government and the bishops were of like mind in wishing to re-impose Catholicism in England. The number of those prepared with great courage to prove themselves 'clean contrary' at the stake was relatively few and not as united as Allerton suggested. The number of those who conformed only outwardly was far greater than the government had anticipated.

Although Foxe was interested in describing the lives and sufferings only of the martyrs, even from his pages it is clear that the 113 men and women martyred in London were only the most determined and stalwart of a large number of people disinclined to accept the new religious orthodoxy. He mentions at least another seventy suspects who were also sent to the Bishop of London. They were either reconciled by him or his officers before formal proceedings began, or they submitted and were released at their trials, or they died in prison before their trials or executions could take place. Foxe also described the Christian congregation in London which numbered 'sometimes forty, sometimes a hundred, sometimes two hundred'. This was not the only group of courageous non-conformists in Marian London, for there was also the group of 'freewillers' under the leadership of Henry Hart, and other smaller Protestant cells in London itself, as well as the congregations in Essex, at Dedham and Colchester.[38] The Protestant underground remains indistinct, but two things can be said with certainty: it contained men of sharply differing views and it survived. The Marian system of persecution rested on information given to the council, to the commissioners and to the justices. Informers there were, but the sympathetic silence of the majority of their neighbours ensured the survival of the non-conformist communities.

Bonner was aware that his diocese contained both committed Protestants and a large number of waverers and doubters. He was willing enough to co-operate with the government in its policy of persecution, but he had also a clear awareness of his responsibility to those who, not committed to Protestant doctrine, had been confused or excited by the varieties of religious belief in Edwardian London. But Bonner had only the old disciplinary tools of the ecclesiastical courts and the

[37] Foxe, *Actes*, VII, p. 407.
[38] *Ibid.*, pp. 559, 458, 384. See also *ibid.*, p. 164, and A. G. Dickens, *The English Reformation* (London, 1964), pp. 273–4.

visitation. His most dramatic measure was to initiate the visitation of his diocese in 1554. He began the visitation before England had been formally reconciled to Rome and without the consent of Queen or council. On the contrary the Spanish ambassador wrote that Bonner had published his visitation articles 'without the knowledge of the King, Queen or Council. When asked how he ventured to do so, he replied that it was a matter pertaining to his own post. He well knew that if he had told the Council about it there would have been opposition and he had acted out of his zeal for God's service.'[39]

Bonner's visitation articles were more numerous and more detailed than those Ridley had issued in 1550. Bonner began with thirty-seven articles directed to the clergy inquiring about their morals, preaching and marriages as well as their orthodoxy. There were eleven articles inquiring about the conduct of the archdeacons, sixteen concerning the churches and their ornaments and forty-one articles for the laity. The bishop wanted to know who had spoken against holy ceremonies, or in favour of predestination or justification by faith alone, who had failed to make a Lenten confession, or refused to participate in processions or Latin services. Finally came eight articles for schoolmasters, six for midwives and five for the patrons of benefices, making a total of 133 articles in all. They provided the framework for a thorough and searching inquiry into the morals, practices and beliefs of his people.[40]

The visitation began on 3 September 1553 and lasted until October the following year. In October 1554 Bonner and his officials travelled around the diocese visiting each deanery.[41] At a central place Bonner personally read out the articles and summoned the incumbents and churchwardens of each parish to appear before him. They were given a month in which to study the articles; then they were to appear before the vicar-general or one of the commissaries to make complete answer to the bishop's inquiries. For months afterwards the vicar-general's court was busy dealing with cases revealed by the visitation. Sixty-three sessions of the consistory court took place between 9 November 1554 and 20 June 1555. Between November and March Nicholas Harpsfield, the vicar-general, and his deputies prosecuted about 450 people resident within the archdeaconry of London for offences revealed by the visitation. Cases involving seventeen people from the other archdeaconries took place in consistory in May and June 1555.[42] Other offenders from Middlesex, Essex, Colchester and St Albans may have been examined in the archidiaconal courts, in the commissaries' courts or in later sessions of the consistory court.

[39] *Calendar of State Papers, Spanish*, XIII, pp. 66, 68.
[40] E. Cardwell, *Documentary Annals of the Reformed Church of England*, 1 (London, 1844), pp. 136–67.
[41] *Injunctions geven in the visitatio(n) of the Reverend father in God Edmunde*...(London, 1555), frontispiece; Guildhall R.O., MS. 9537/1. See also the expense and receipt book of the Dean and Chapter of St Paul's which records the expenditure of 26s 8d 'at the finyshyng of my lorde of Londons vicitacion' on 8 October 1555: St Paul's MS., W.A. 60a, fo. 19.
[42] G.L.R.O., MS. *cit.*

Few of the people accused before the vicar-general can be considered committed Protestants. Fifty-three were summoned for offences against the marriage laws, with adultery, or with laxity in paying tithes. More than double that number were accused of failing to attend church on Sundays or holy-days. These were all offences of commission or omission likely to have been revealed by any earlier visitation. Many other cases can be specifically related to Bonner's visitation articles. For instance, in the thirty-second article of inquiry directed to the laity Bonner had urged the churchwardens to identify 'any that at the sacring time, do hang down their heads, hide themselves behind pillars, turn away their faces, or do depart out of the church'. For behaving in this manner, parishioners from St Mary Magdalen, St Stephen Walbrook and St Augustine appeared before the vicar-general.[43] One hundred and five men and women were explicitly accused of doctrinal errors: of being 'sacramentaries'[44] or with publicly condemning the mass. Even these charges do not reveal firm Protestant commitment. The vast majority of the accused either denied the charges brought against them and brought witnesses to swear their innocence, or they were penitent and returned within a few weeks with a certificate from their parish priest that they had performed the penances laid on them by the vicar-general. Only on three occasions does the act book record that lengthy conversations or sermons were necessary to persuade the accused that the doctrine or practices they had followed in Edward's reign were false. Of the 470 accused by the incumbents and churchwardens in these consistory court hearings only three were later to figure among the martyrs, a tiny proportion of convinced Protestants to the far greater number of waverers and doubters. The answer of three men of St Botolph may stand for many: 'before the Quenes reigne that nowe ys, they were mainteyners and favorers of suche doctryne, as then was putt forth, but not syns'.[45]

We do not know what non-conformity the ordinary proceedings of the archidiaconal courts revealed or whether the archdeacons' visitations of Essex in 1556 and of St Albans in 1557 inquired after heresy.[46] Only one archidiaconal act book has survived, for St Albans, recording twenty-seven sessions of that court between February 1556 and March 1558. The sessions were short and were mainly concerned with defamation, tithe and marriage cases. There are however two entries which show that rural Hertfordshire had its share of non-co-operation in the last year of Mary's reign, but once again there is no evidence of entrenched Protestantism. Although Bonner's Injunctions had commanded that all church furnishings should be restored by Christmas 1555, two years later, on 4 December 1557, the Archdeacon

---

[43] Cardwell, op. cit., p. 160; G.L.R.O., MS. cit., fos. 23v, 26.
[44] Ibid., fo. 59. See also M. Jagger, 'Bonner's Episcopal Visitation of London, 1554', B.I.H.R., XLV (1973), pp. 306–11, esp. p. 307.
[45] G.L.R.O., MS. cit., fos. 36, 39, 47v; ibid., fo. 64v., printed in W. H. Hale, A Series of Precedents and Proceedings...extracted from Act-Books of Ecclesiastical Courts (London, 1847), p. 144.
[46] Foxe, Actes, VIII, p. 383; Hertfordshire Record Office, MS. A.S.A. 7/3, fo. 22.

of St Alban's had to order the churchwardens of Bushey to fix a light before the rood and restore the image of their patron. In March 1558 two parishioners from Redbourne were charged before the archdeacon that at Candlemas they had failed to offer their candles but had contemptuously thrown 'theyr candle into the rood lofte to the evell example of that that where present'.[47] The men and women of Hertfordshire were like the Londoners indicted before Harpsfield: they were of Allerton's third group, neuters ready to conform outwardly once a little pressure had been applied by their appearance in consistory or archidiaconal court.

The visitation was a wide-ranging inquiry thoroughly carried out. In parish after parish offences against morals, ancient custom and Catholic doctrine had been revealed by the testimony of the churchwardens and responsible parishioners. It was an old and well-tried method of exercising episcopal discipline but in the ferment of Marian London it was not enough. Bonner now knew the full diversity of practice and belief within his diocese; the visitation revealed the urgent necessity of re-educating the people of London. In July 1555 Bonner arranged for the publication of thirteen homilies including his own conribution on the nature of Christian love, in order to provide a manual of sermons for his clergy. In the absence of a licensed preacher one of the homilies was to be read out to the people every Sunday and every holy-day. Two months later a new definition of faith appeared called the *Profitable and Necessary Doctrine*, which was a long and serious attempt to restate Catholic orthodoxy with explanation, argument and quotation. It was modelled closely on the King's Book of 1543, the last and most conservative definition of doctrine put forward in Henry's reign. As in 1543, the 1555 formulary began with an exposition of the nature of faith, and continued with an explanation of the creed, of the sacraments, the ten commandments, the Lord's Prayer and the Ave Maria. The section on faith was identical with that in the King's Book. The explanation of the creed was an adaptation of the 1543 formula: certain paragraphs were rewritten, others included as they stood. In the section on the sacraments the King's Book had omitted a detailed explanation of the sacraments of confirmation and unction; in 1555 both were accorded full analysis and defence. Similarly the long explanation of the sacrament of the altar in the *Necessary Doctrine* differed markedly from 1543 in order to emphasize the doctrine of the sacrifice of the mass. The *Necessary Doctrine* made a few references to the 'late schism' but it was not violent or controversial; it was an intelligent and reasoned restatement of faith.

In every section Bonner and his chaplains developed their arguments using long quotations taken from the gospels, from St Paul and from St Augustine, St Cyprian and St Ambrose, to justify their assertions. It is unlikely that Bonner himself wrote a great deal of the *Necessary Doctrine*, for during the spring and summer of 1555

---

[47] *Injunctions*, sig. B.1; Hertfordshire R.O., MS. A.S.A. 7/3, fos. 23v, 27v.

he was increasingly occupied with the examination of suspected heretics. Yet it was on his initiative that the formulary was produced and it was very soon granted semi-official status as a definition of Catholic faith. The injunctions set forth at the conclusion of the Cardinal's legatine visitation of 1556[48] declared that if no sermon could be preached the clergy should read part of the *Necessary Doctrine* and ordered all churchwardens to procure a copy of it for their churches.

The *Necessary Doctrine* was designed for the clergy and educated laity. To complement it, Bonner, in January 1556, published a little catechism for children, called *An honest godlye instruction*, and ordered that this ABC should supersede all other primers and catechisms in use in the diocese. The *Instruction* began with the alphabet, and then continued with the Lord's Prayer, the creed, the responses at the mass and the commandments, ending with lists of the seven virtues, the seven sacraments and the seven deadly sins. Printed in red and black to make greater impact on the children using it, the *Instruction* was a small handbook written without explanation. It was a guide for schoolmasters to use with their young pupils; adults, as Bonner explained in his preface, had already been provided with the *Necessary Doctrine*.

At the conclusion of his visitation in October 1555, Bonner published a list of Injunctions which was a comprehensive list of instructions to clergy, laity and archdeacons directly related to the visitation articles and to what had been revealed by the consistory court hearings. One example must suffice of the way in which the bishop hoped to deal with both apathy and non-conformity. He knew that some of his flock visited alehouses or went hawking on Sundays while others stayed secretly at home in order to avoid attendance at mass. The bishop ordered that from now on all men and women over the age of fourteen were to attend their parish church on Sundays and 'to remayne in praier and godly meditations all the tyme of divine service'.[49]

Bonner realized that inquiry and re-education must supplement the government's policy of repression. The visitation had revealed apathy and varieties of Christian observance; with the homilies, the *Necessary Doctrine* and the catechism, as well as with the injunctions, Bonner intended to provide the means to bring the wavering majority back to the Catholic faith. But the execution of the injunctions and the effective use of his publications depended on the quality of his clergy. There was nothing to distinguish the clergy of his diocese in Mary's reign from the clergy he had had during the first half of his episcopate. Even among the upper clergy the zealots were in the minority. Harpsfield and Chedsey were able and conscientious, but Bonner's diocesan team also included his old friend Edward Mowle and his nephew John Wymmisley, who, appointed to their archdeaconries by Bonner in

[48] Wilkins, *Concilia*, iv, pp. 146, 148.   [49] *Injunctions*, sig. B.1 (verso).

1543, had there remained undisturbed during Ridley's episcopate. Bonner himself, an old-fashioned career cleric, a violent anti-papalist in Henry's reign, was a poor model to arouse among his clergy a burning confidence in their faith similar to that which so characterised the martyrs. Nor did the manuals provided by Bonner reinterpret the faith in a new or vibrant way: they were declarations and pronouncements. Even the *Necessary Doctrine*, the most ambitious of Bonner's writings, was too long and complicated for the average parish priest or parishioner. It was so closely modelled on the King's Book that it could be taken for simply another government publication, an official instruction to the people once more to change the manner and content of their faith. Bonner might instruct his clergy to read it; in 1542 his injunctions had charged them to read that earlier formulary, the reformist Bishops' Book of 1537.[50] To rekindle the Catholic faith in the hearts of Englishmen, a clarion call was needed. Bonner did not have the men or the spiritual resources to provide it.

Bonner nevertheless provided action, and throughout Mary's reign the diocese resounded with one investigation after another: the visitation of 1554–5, the commissioners' inquiries of 1557 and 1558, the archidiaconal visitations of Essex and St Albans and the special commission sent to Essex in 1557[51] to examine suspects arrested by the justices. Above all there were the examinations and trials of heretics conducted by Bonner and his officials in the consistory court. The register of the heresy trials has been lost, but Foxe used it extensively, enabling us to assess Bonner's day-to-day behaviour as an ecclesiastical judge and administrator. Although Bonner occasionally heard a case which reached consistory because of the visitation,[52] he delegated the major part of these proceedings to Harpsfield and his deputies. For a time two parallel inquiries were conducted in consistory: the vicar-general's and the bishop's. Bonner's concern was the heresy trials, and there is no doubt that he was closely involved in all the proceedings against suspected heretics which took place in his diocese. Bonner kept an exceptionally tight grip on the minutiae of the proceedings and was himself active at every stage, from the first informal examination of a suspect to the final despatch of a signification to Chancery that a heretic had been excommunicated.

The formal examinations and trials in consistory form a large part of Foxe's narrative. He used the descriptions written by the martyrs themselves and also the entries in the court register. The basic form of the trials before Bonner varied very little. Articles or interrogatories were administered to the suspects who were usually examined on their answers to these questions. If they refused to accept orthodox Catholic doctrine they were pronounced impenitent heretics, excommunicated and sentenced to be handed to the secular authorities. Occasionally depositions were also

[50] Wilkins, *Concilia*, III, p. 864.   [51] Foxe, *Actes*, VIII, pp. 452–3.
[52] *Ibid.*, pp. 139, 377, 411; G.L.R.O., MS. *cit.*, fo. 34v.

taken from witnesses.⁵³ This form of examination was extremely flexible. The accused might appear once, twice or many times before the assembled court. The suspect's answers to the interrogatories could last a short time or a long time depending on the calibre of the accused and the interest of the judge. The endless examinations of leading Protestants like Bradford and Philpot show that in certain cases at least the suspect's submission was of more importance to the bishop and his officers than a speedy end to the examinations.

Ralph Allerton, who had made a full recantation at Paul's Cross in January 1556/7, relapsed in April 1557 and was once again sent to Bonner.⁵⁴ He was examined eight times before he was excommunicated on 10 September. As with so many of the martyrs, Allerton's arguments with Bonner were about the nature of the true Church and the sacrament of the altar. To Ralph, Bonner represented 'the bloody church, figured in Cain the tyrant', and was 'not of the church of Christ'. Allerton would not accept transubstantiation but insisted 'when the worthy receivers do take and eat, even then are fulfilled the words of Our Saviour unto him, or every of them that so receiveth'. Bonner, swearing by St Mary, by St Augustine, by the Blessed Sacrament of the Altar, or vigorously denouncing Allerton as a 'whoreson varlet and pricklouse', was deeply anxious to convert him. Bonner's analogies were down-to-earth if not always suitable. Allerton argued that Christ's words at the last supper 'take, eat, this is my body' should be interpreted in a symbolic manner, but Bonner replied with a parable: 'If I should set a piece of beef before thee, and say "eat, it is beef"; and then take part of it away, and send it to my cook, and he shall change the fashion thereof, and make it look like bread, what! wouldst thou say that it were no beef, because it hath not the fashion of beef?' Yet Bonner was no fool; on occasion he would cite appropriate texts from the Fathers or canon law with ease. Bonner cajoled, bullied, threatened, bribed and swore, trying to force his beliefs on the men and women appearing before him. But there were many he could not touch and Allerton was one of that constant band who welcomed martyrdom.⁵⁵

The consistory court was Bonner's arena. Other bishops, royal commissioners, secular officials like the mayor and sheriffs of London sat with him at various stages of the examinations and trials of different heretics, but his was not only the general jurisdiction, but the personal control which he exercised not only in St Paul's, but in his palace nearby, or at Fulham. Bonner personally conducted the vast majority⁵⁶ of the examinations in consistory and he was not only prosecutor, but also judge and jury. The accused believed that their opponents' aim was to trick and muddle

⁵³ Foxe, *Actes*, VIII, p. 439.   ⁵⁴ *Ibid.*, pp. 405–17.
⁵⁵ *Ibid.*, pp. 407, 408–9, 410, 414, and see VII, pp. 614, 618, 622, 625, 640, 643.
⁵⁶ It was only towards the end of the reign that Bonner delegated the conduct not only of the preliminary examinations but of the trials themselves to his officers: *ibid.*, VIII, pp. 454, 467–8, 638.

them with 'many words'.[57] Bonner had little need of wiles. The system which he
and his colleagues were operating made it inevitable that they would appear harsh.
The terms of submission were laid down by the bishop, and the accused could choose
between submission and death. As the years passed Bonner grew more cautious about
the public spectacle which the heresy trials in St Paul's presented to the people of
London. Occasionally he had pronounced sentence in his chapel at Fulham Palace
and in July 1558 he wrote to Pole suggesting that he should use the parish church
at Fulham where he might proceed 'very quietly and without tumulte'.[58] In this
letter Bonner expressed no doubts about the actions he should take; he was simply
suggesting a different venue. One hundred and thirteen men and women were found
guilty of heresy in the diocese of London: Bonner himself personally pronounced
the awesome judgement of excommunication on at least eighty-nine of them.

Bonner's involvement with the convicted heretics continued after he had
sentenced them in consistory. Chancery required the bishop to send a signification
of those he had excommunicated before it issued the writ *de heretico comburendo* to
the sheriff. The sheriff in turn had to have the writ before he could proceed with
a burning.[59] Of the 113 heretics condemned in Bonner's courts the significations sent
by the bishop to Chancery have survived for ninety-nine.[60] There are only sixty-nine
significations of excommunication for heresy for all the other dioceses of the
kingdom of Mary's reign. This disproportion partly reflects the greater number of
excommunications for heresy in London than in any other diocese, and it may be
due to no more than chance survival within Chancery records. It may also reflect
the great care for administrative procedures shown by Bonner and his registrar,
Robert Johnson. Another example of Bonner's personal attention to detail is that
all the London significations except one bear his signature. Indeed this one may have
been considered defective by Chancery officials, for a second, signed by Bonner, was
sent for the same heretic three weeks later.[61] Although strictly the bishop had no

---

[57] *Ibid.*, p. 187.

[58] *Ibid.*, p. 155; Inner Temple Library, Petyt MS. 538/47, fo. 3.

[59] This procedure was developed during the fifteenth century when the use of the writ *de
excommunicato capiendo* in the case of heretics was supplemented by use of the writ *de heretico
comburendo*: F. D. Logan, *Excommunication and the Secular Arm in Medieval England* (Toronto,
1968), pp. 69–70. See Foxe, *Actes*, VII, pp. 31–2.

[60] Foxe's accuracy about time and place is attested again and again by the London significations,
but although in other dioceses significations give full details of heretics' views (P.R.O.,
C. 85/64, 12, 16), in London the significations make only a formal and standardised statement
of the heretics' disbelief in transubstantiation.

[61] P.R.O., C. 85/127, 18, 20. Bishops in other dioceses occasionally signed a signification but
in no other diocese is this a regular practice. Bonner signed the signification even if he had
not personally pronounced the excommunication. On one occasion one of Bonner's officials
made an error in the surname of a convicted heretic in a signification which was repeated in
the writ and resulted in a delay in the burning of an Essex heretic: Foxe, *Actes*, VIII, pp. 387–93;
P.R.O., C. 85/127, fo. 24; Foxe, *Actes*, VIII, pp. 421–3; *A.P.C.*, VI, p. 144.

further concern for a heretic once he had been excommunicated and handed to the secular authorities, the bishop could and did expedite the issue of the writ *de heretico comburendo*. In July 1558 he arranged with Pole that when the six 'obstinate hereticks that doo remayne in my house' had been excommunicated on the 12th, they should be executed very quickly thereafter. They were burnt at Brentford on the 14th.[62] Bonner took great interest in all the stages of the condemnation of heretics in his courts; once suspects had been handed over to the bishop of London very few were lost in the interstices of his administrative machinery.

The vast majority of Bonner's flock were wavering, uncertain and ignorant, buffeted one way and another as varieties of religious belief were imposed on them from above. The policy of repression which sought out the active Protestants, and ensured that the full ecclesiastical discipline was used against them, turned those waverers against the Queen and her religion. The government inspired and controlled every aspect of the persecution. The council, not the Cardinal-legate, was Bonner's daily master. In the complicated relationship of Church and State in Marian England, the Crown was the dominant partner, giving the Church the wrong weapons and forcing it to use them in a fight it could not win. In a few other spheres is it possible to see so clearly how royal policies were carried out in the localities: the history of the persecution is not just of the edicts of Queen and Council, but of the active co-operation of the respectable and responsible members of society carrying out government decisions. Bonner's courts were filled with suspected heretics because the council, the commissioners, the justices and the jurors placed them there.

Bonner has a central role in the mythology of the persecution although he had no responsibility for initiating the policy of repression and he was not the sadistic villain whom Foxe described. Out of his mind with rage one moment, he could show extraordinary patience and guile with a stubborn opponent the next. He was well aware of his own spiritual limitations. He knew the people of London needed leadership and spiritual renewal yet by his own nature he was incapable of supplying more than a frantic activity. He is central to the story because the London persecutions depended on his competence and energy. The fate of a suspected heretic was determined at his trial before Bonner in St Paul's. Bonner had not set him there; Bonner had no choice but to act once he was there, but Bonner was the judge who personally ensured that 113 men and women of the diocese of London were burnt to death for their religious beliefs.

[62] Inner Temple, MS. *cit.*; P.R.O., C. 85/127, fo. 30; Foxe, *Actes*, VIII, pp. 479–82. Another example of Bonner personally seeing to the despatch of the writ may have occurred in June 1557: *ibid.*, pp. 391, 421, but see also *A.P.C.*, VI, p. 135.

9

THE CONTINUITY OF CATHOLICISM
IN THE ENGLISH REFORMATION*

CHRISTOPHER HAIGH

When rebuked for her recusancy by judges at Oxford in 1581, Cecily Stonor retorted:

> I was born in such a time when holy mass was in great reverence, and brought up
> in the same faith. In King Edward's time this reverence was neglected and reproved
> by such as governed. In Queen Mary's time, it was restored with much applause;
> and now in this time it pleaseth the state to question them, as now they do me, who
> continue in this Catholic profession. The state would have these several changes,
> which I have seen with mine eyes, good and laudable. Whether it can be so, I refer
> it to your Lordships' consideration. I hold me still to that wherein I was born and
> bred; and so by the grace of God I will live and die in it.[1]

Cecily Stonor was one of the large number of Catholics who claimed consistency
in the religion, who claimed continuity in their own persons with an earlier Catholic
tradition, and who accused the Protestants of mutability and dangerous innovation.

But such a view of post-Reformation English Catholicism as a survival through
the sixteenth century of traditional religion has been ably challenged by modern
historians. The evidence of Elizabethan visitations prompted A. G. Dickens to
formulate an influential distinction between 'survivalism' and 'seminarism': conservative attachment to old traditions soon declined, and later there arrived a new
brand of post-Reformation Catholicism, a dynamic foreign importation brought by
missionary priests. More recently, Aveling has argued that English medieval
Catholicism died between 1534 and 1570, and thereafter a combination of
spontaneous revival in England and missionary effort from the seminaries abroad
created a new Catholic body. Most strongly of all, John Bossy has insisted that the
post-Reformation English Catholic community was created by the seminary priests

---

* The development of the ideas contained in this paper owes much to discussions with John Bossy,
Margaret Bowker, Susan Brigden, Tim Curtis, Geoffrey Dickens, Geoffrey Elton, John Miller,
Paul Slack and Keith Thomas, who commented on an earlier version.
[1] H. Clifford, *Life of Jane Dormer, Duchess of Feria* (London, 1887), pp. 38–9.

and Jesuits after 1570, and owed nothing to what had gone before.[2] Such assertions of an absence of organic continuity between medieval and recusant Catholicism can be placed within a more general argument on the relationship between medieval popular religion and post-Reformation disciplined Christianity. It has been suggested that pre-Reformation religion was primarily a matter of customary observance, in which those aspects of official religion which had relevance to the cycle of birth, maturity, reproduction and death were pursued in an automatic, ritualised fashion, but there was no widespread commitment to anything which could be seen as authentically 'Catholic'. The Reformation and the Counter Reformation saw, it is argued, the construction of two new religions of individual choice and involvement, a bibliocentric and evangelical Protestantism and a reformed and regulated Catholicism.[3] We may, in summary, observe that historians have detected both 'organic discontinuity' and 'spiritual discontinuity' between medieval and modern Catholicism.

The discontinuity argument seems to have its origins in the polemical needs of post-Reformation writers. Its appeal to Protestant lawyers and theologians is clear enough, while among Catholics, though it received moderate support from William Allen and Augustine Baker,[4] it began as a propagandist Jesuit version of Tudor Catholic history. When the Jesuits came to England in 1580, many Catholics responded with fear and suspicion: it was thought that the order would provoke harsher persecution, and the Jesuits were 'looked on as meddlesome innovators' by some older priests.[5] The novelty of the order and its methods were justified by criticism of the spiritual inadequacy of the parish clergy, proved by their spineless conformism under Edward and Elizabeth and their lack of fervour under Mary. The clearest expositions of such a view came from Robert Parsons, whose contrast

[2] A. G. Dickens, 'The First Stages of Romanist Recusancy in Yorkshire, 1560–1590', *Yorkshire Archaeological Journal*, XXXV (1941), esp. pp. 157–8, 180–1; J. C. H. Aveling, *The Handle and the Axe: The Catholic Recusants in England from Reformation to Emancipation* (London, 1976), pp. 19, 27, 43 ff., 49, 52, 56–61, 65; J. Bossy, *The English Catholic Community, 1570–1850* (London, 1975), pp. 4–5, 11–12, 106–7, 147.

[3] For the general argument, see J. Delumeau, *Catholicism between Luther and Voltaire* (London, 1977), pp. 160–1, 167, 171–96, 190–201, and for its application to the British Isles, J. Bossy, 'The Character of Elizabethan Catholicism', *P.&P.*, XXI (1962), p. 41; J. Bossy, 'The Counter-Reformation and the People of Catholic Ireland, 1596–1641', *Historical Studies*, VIII (1971), pp. 155–69; G. Williams, *Welsh Reformation Essays* (Cardiff, 1967), p. 21. For a wide-ranging examination of changes in Catholicism, see J. Bossy, 'The Counter-Reformation and the People of Catholic Europe', *P.&P.*, XLVII (1970), pp. 52–4, 62–7.

[4] [*First and Second*] *Douai Diaries*, ed. T. F. Knox (London, 1878), pp. xxii–xxiv; *Memorials of Father Augustine Baker*, ed. J. McCann and H. Connolly (C.R.S., XXXIII, 1933), pp. 16–18, 20.

[5] 'The Memoirs of Father Robert Persons', I, ed. J. H. Pollen, in *C.R.S. Miscellanea*, II (C.R.S., II, 1906), pp. 176, 178; J. Gerard, *The Autobiography of an Elizabethan*, ed. P. Caraman (London, 1951), p. 29.

between the failures of the supine hierarchical pre-Reformation church and the successes of the Elizabethan missionary priests was part of his long struggle with conservatives and later Appellants, who wished to preserve the traditional structure and customs of the Church.[6] The Parsons version of the origins of English recusancy was given powerful support by Jesuit reports from England, which stressed the number of committed new Catholics, and by John Gerard, who emphasised the quality of Jesuit-inspired lay spirituality.[7] Some Catholics were thus using the discontinuity argument to disown the ramshackle medieval Church and to present a new, improved version of their religion which could attract the articulate laity. But if there was a 'Counter Reformation' in England, it was less a spiritual crusade and more a series of adjustments to the fact of disestablishment.

It will be suggested here that there was much more continuity in England than those who have distinguished between 'medieval Catholicism' and 'Counter Reformation Catholicism' have allowed, and that emerging English recusancy owed much to what had gone before: the English Reformation was not a precise and dramatic event, it was a long and complex process. In 1559 Catholicism lost its hierarchical structure and its churches, and it has been assumed that in the shift from prescribed orthodoxy to prohibited deviation it lost the mere conformists and kept only the committed few. But such a view much exaggerates the real impact of the legislation of 1559 and ignores the transitional period of the 1560s and 1570s. It is clear that the Church of England was not immediately protestantised in its clergy, furnishings, services and the beliefs of its people: the government did not dare to enforce the Elizabethan Settlement rigorously, and bibliocentric Protestantism proved unattractive to the rural masses.[8] Away from the cathedral cities and the main towns, official Protestantism made little real progress: Bishop Sandys of Worcester reported in 1569 that 'I have long laboured to gain good will. The fruits of my travail are counterfeited countenances and hollow hearts: this small storm [the Rising of the Earls] maketh many to shrink. Hard it is to find one faithful.'[9] There was,

---

[6] 'The Memoirs of Father Robert Persons, I, ed. Pollen, pp. 54–7, 60–2; *Letters and Memorials of Father Robert Persons*, I, ed. L. Hicks (C.R.S., XXXIX, 1942), pp. 46, 57–8. At times, however, Parsons found it useful to argue that Catholics had vigorously opposed the Reformation, and that there was a continuity of resistance: R. Parsons, *A Treatise of Three Conversions*, 3 vols (St Omer, 1603–4), II, pp. 240–1, 244, 258–9, 264–5.

[7] *Letters and Memorials of Father Robert Persons*, ed. Hicks, p. 179; H. Foley, *Records of the English Province of the Society of Jesus*, 7 vols (London, 1877–84), v, p. 988; VII, pp. 985–6, 1095, 1098; Gerard, *Autobiography*, pp. 27–9, 32, 150. See also P. Caraman, *Henry Garnet and the Gunpowder Plot* (London, 1964), pp. 109–11.

[8] Even Richard Greenham, the most active of pastors, had little success in Cambridgeshire. See S. Clarke, *A General Martyrology* (London, 1677 edn.), pt. 2, pp. 12–15. For less surprising failures, see my 'Puritan Evangelism in the Reign of Elizabeth I', *E.H.R.*, XCII (1977), pp. 30–58.

[9] V. Burke, 'Catholic Recusants in Elizabethan Worcestershire' (University of Birmingham M.A. thesis, 1972), p. 24. See also R. B. Manning, *Religion and Society in Elizabethan Sussex*

in the early years of Elizabeth's reign, considerable uncertainty over the future of English religion: it was widely believed that Catholicism would be restored once again, and many parishes retained altars and images to avoid further heavy expenditure.[10] In 1563 Lord Keeper Bacon complained that the common people 'seldom' attended services, and Augustine Baker noted that in areas such as his own south Wales a religious vacuum developed in these years: the laity, 'as they knew not the Catholic verities, so neither knew they the contrary thereof, being heretical conceits, but rather remained in a kind of heathenism'. From this neutral state, Baker thought, it was easy to make the people into Catholics, and Robert Parsons evidently thought the same since he wanted priestly resources concentrated where Protestantism had failed to make an impact.[11]

There were, however, features of the unprotestantised Church of England which were even more promising from a Catholic point of view. Marian Catholicism was linked to recusant Catholicism by the complex phenomenon now known as 'survivalism' or 'post-Catholicism':[12] the early part of the reign of Elizabeth should not be seen as an unfortunate gap in the history of English Catholicism, but as the period in which the constituency from which later recusants could be recruited was substantially maintained. It is essential for an understanding of these years to avoid a restrictive definition of Catholicism which stresses union with Rome and conscious rejection of a heretical Church of England. At the parish level the issues were blurred, and it is more helpful to recognise that for the peasantry the old religion was a complex of social practices, many of which remained available. The altars, images, holy water, rosary-beads and signs of the cross, which visitations from many parts of the country show remained prominent in the churches, kept aspects of Catholic

(Leicester, 1969), pp. xiii, 39–41, 43–6; H. N. Birt *The Elizabethan Religious Settlement* (London, 1907), pp. 311–12, 427–30; J. E. Paul, 'The Hampshire Recusants in the Reign of Elizabeth I' (University of Southampton Ph.D. thesis, 1958), pp. 6–7, 13, 28–32; W. P. M. Kennedy, *Elizabethan Episcopal Administration*, 3 vols (Alcuin Club Collections, XXV–XXVII, London, 1924), I, pp. cxciv–cxcv; *V.C.H. Durham*, II, p. 39; C. Haigh, *Reformation and Resistance in Tudor Lancashire* (Cambridge, 1975), pp. 209–24; N. Sander, *The Rise and Growth of the Anglican Schism*, ed. D. Lewis (London, 1877), p. 265.

[10] H. Aveling, 'The Catholic Recusants of the West Riding of Yorkshire, 1558–1790', *Proceedings of the Leeds Philisophical and Literary Society* (Literary and Historical Section), X (1963), pp. 195, 205; H. Aveling, *Northern Catholics* (London, 1966), pp. 20–2; Haigh, *Reformation and Resistance*, pp. 208, 216–20; M. D. R. Leys, *Catholics in England, 1559–1829: A Social History* (London, 1961), p. 7; M. Spufford, *Contrasting Communities: English Villagers in the Sixteenth and Seventeenth Centuries* (Cambridge, 1974), pp. 242–3.

[11] J. E. Neale, *Elizabeth I and Her Parliaments*, 2 vols (London, 1953–7), I, p. 96; *Memorials of Father Augustine Baker*, ed. McCann and Connolly, pp. 16, 18; *Letters and Memorials of Father Robert Persons*, ed. Hicks, pp. 98, 108. It was noted in the Jesuit 'annual letter' for 1615 that conversion of those brought up in heresy was very difficult, but 'wanderers' of uncertain religion were easy to influence. See Foley, *Records of the English Province*, VII, pp. 1076, 1095.

[12] Dickens, 'First Stages of Romanist Recusancy', p. 181; Aveling, *The Handle and the Axe*, p. 39.

worship in the public arena, and many clergy made the Prayer Book services as much like masses as circumspection allowed.[13] Other 'conforming' clerics provided the official sacraments in their churches and Catholic ones in secret, to the horror of Allen and Rishton,[14] and some incumbents were vigorous propagandists for Catholic ways: the vicar of Whalley, Lancashire, in 1575 called the Church of England 'a defiled and spotted Church' and encouraged his parishioners to pray 'according to the doctrine of the Pope of Rome', while in 1580 the rector of Bonnington in Lincolnshire told his people that only those who confessed to Catholic priests would be saved.[15] Clergy such as these surely did as much towards the survival of Catholicism in England as did the firmest recusant priest or the bravest seminary missioner, for they held the loyalty of their flocks to as much of the old faith as circumstances permitted, until official pressure, personal frustration and a clarification of issues made more laymen willing to move into recusancy. The conservative parish clergy thus fulfilled an essential bridging role between the Marian Church and separated Elizabethan Catholicism. Some historians have regarded the contribution of 'survivalism' to post-Reformation Catholicism as negligible,[16] but such a view seems not to take account of the chronology and geography of conservatism and recusancy.

Many years ago A. G. Dickens argued, from the evidence of the Elizabethan visitations of the diocese of York, that there was virtually no chronological overlap between 'survivalism' and 'seminarism', that conservatism in the parish churches had almost died out by 1575 but significant recusancy did not begin until 1577.[17] Since he wrote, however, the discovery and analysis of the records of the York ecclesiastical commission have demonstrated that recusancy was well-established before 'survivalism' disappeared, and it is also clear that there were overlaps in the dioceses of Chester, Norwich and Winchester.[18] Though the evidence will not permit

[13] Birt, *Elizabethan Religious Settlement*, pp. 326–8, 349–50, 396–7, 428–9. See also the instructive case of Weaverham in Cheshire, where it is clear that by 1578 few concessions, in either the decoration of the church or the behaviour of the people, had been made to the 1559 settlement: K. R. Wark, *Elizabethan Recusancy in Cheshire* (Chetham Society, 3rd ser., XIX, 1971), p. 16. As late as 1586, eleven Cornish benefices were held by men who seem to have been active conservatives. See *The Second Parte of a Register*, ed. A. Peel, 2 vols (Cambridge, 1915), II, pp. 98–110.

[14] Burke, 'Catholic Recusants in Elizabethan Worcestershire', p. 39; Haigh, *Reformation and Resistance*, pp. 218–19; B.I.Y., HC.AB 3, fos. 118, 176, 182; *Unpublished Documents Relating to the English Martyrs*, ed. J. H. Pollen (C.R.S., v, 1908), p. 72 (a Suffolk rector still saying masses in his house in 1584); *Douai Diaries*, ed. Knox, p. xxiii; Sander, *Rise and Growth of the Anglican Schism*, p. 267.

[15] Haigh, *Reformation and Resistance*, p. 218; R. Simpson, *Edmund Campion* (London, 1896), p. 219.

[16] Dickens, 'First Stages of Romanist Recusancy', pp. 180–1; Aveling, *Northern Catholics*, p. 35.

[17] Dickens, 'First Stages of Romanist Recusancy', pp. 165–7.

[18] There was certainly a good deal of recusancy among the Yorkshire gentry by 1571–2, as demonstrated by B.I.Y., HC.AB 6, fos. 13, 39v, 40, 43, 51v, 103, 112v, 143, 182v. For the

convincing proof, there are several examples which suggest that recusants were recruited from among conservatives and 'mislikers', and that 'survivalism' could be a stage towards recusancy as well as a malady of old women. In Essex, some of those returned in the recusants list of 1577 had been known for their conservatism since as far back as 1561; in Hampshire, two men who were before the courts in the 1560s for criticizing the Elizabethan services were recusants by 1577; and in Worcestershire several of the 'adversaries' and 'indifferent' of the bishop's report in 1564 were later recusant leaders.[19] In the dioceses of Chichester and Exeter, a number of those reported as opponents of the Elizabethan settlement in 1564 were recusants by 1577, and in almost every county, but particularly Lancashire and Yorkshire, the 1564 lists of hostile J.P.s name men who were later to be prominent recusants.[20] There is also a reasonably close geographical correspondence between the areas of marked 'survivalism' and those of densest recusancy: bishops had major difficulties in enforcing the provisions of the reformed liturgy in south-east Hampshire, west Sussex, south Wales, Worcestershire and Herefordshire, the Derbyshire Peaks, south and west Lancashire, and the northern edges of both the North Riding and the West Riding,[21] and these districts were to produce substantial numbers of recusants. A correspondence between the geography of conservatism and that of recusancy can also be observed at a local level. In Yorkshire, parishes such as Hemingborough, Kirkby Malzeard, Masham, Ripley and Ripon show a steady

other dioceses, see Haigh, *Reformation and Resistance*, pp. 216–22, 249–62; R. Houlbrooke, *Church Courts and the People during the English Reformation, 1520–1570* (Oxford, 1979), pp. 246–52; Paul, 'Hampshire Recusants', pp. 28–32, 36, 39, 47–8, 412.

[19] M. O'Dwyer, 'Catholic Recusants in Essex, *c.* 1580–*c.* 1600' (University of London M.A. thesis, 1960), pp. 19–20; Houlbrooke, *Church Courts and the People*, pp. 249–50; Burke, 'Catholic Recusants in Elizabethan Worcestershire', pp. 67–8. The work of the Lancashire recusant priest John Lee, otherwise known as 'Old Beggar', between 1578 and 1591 is a good illustration of the link between recusancy and survivalism: in addition to his priestly activities for recusants, he provided medical and veterinary care, recommending to his human patients fasts on the eves of saints' days, attendance at thirteen masses, recitation of psalms and the use of holy water in food – he came to be regarded as a saint and his methods were still in use in 1607. See B.I.Y., HC.AB 9, fos. 171, 173v; HC.AB 11, fos. 309, 330; Foley, *Records of the English Province*, II, p. 114; A. Jessopp, *One Generation of a Norfolk House* (London, 1913), pp. 43–4.

[20] 'Letters from the Bishops to the Privy Council, 1564', ed. M. Bateson, in *Camden Miscellany*, IX (Camden Society, new ser., LIII, 1895), pp. 5–6, 7, 10, 27, 32, 36, 38, 63, 69–72, 77–80; 'Diocesan Returns of Recusants for England and Wales, 1577', in *C.R.S. Miscellanea*, XII (C.R.S., XXII, 1921), pp. 76, 80–1.

[21] Paul, 'Hampshire Recusants', pp. 28–32; Manning, *Religion and Society in Elizabethan Sussex*, pp. 43–6; Foley, *Records of the English Province*, IV, p. 441; *Memorials of Father Augustine Baker*, ed. McCann and Connolly, pp. 16–20; Burke, 'Catholic Recusants in Elizabethan Worcestershire', pp. 43, 58–9; 'Letters from the Bishops', ed. Bateson, pp. 14, 19–21; *The Catechism of Thomas Becon*, ed. J. Ayre (Parker Society, 1844), pp. 421–2; Haigh, *Reformation and Resistance*, pp. 211, 217, 219–20; Aveling, 'Catholic Recusants of the West Riding', pp. 195, 201; Aveling, *Northern Catholics*, pp. 20–2.

progression from 'survivalism' to heavy recusancy,[22] and, in the North Riding, parishes in trouble between 1559 and 1572 for offences such as failure to remove images from church were twice as likely as other parishes to have large recusant groups by 1604.[23] Even Holderness, which, with widespread conservatism displayed in the 1567 visitation but little recorded Elizabethan recusancy, seemed to show that 'survivalism' and separated Catholicism were unrelated, appears to fit our pattern: Holderness was a major recusant centre by 1640, and there may have been undetected recusancy earlier.[24]

The birth of post-Reformation English Catholicism has been presented as the withdrawal of Catholics from the parish church to the gentry household,[25] and this is a suggestive and helpful model. But the separation of Catholics from the worshipping village community was a very slow process, which began early with non-communicating, took the next step in refusal to attend regular services, but achieved severence in baptism, marriage and burial much later.[26] We need not see 'becoming a recusant' as a specific, conscious, individual decision to reject the State religion: a family, a group, even a hamlet or village, may gradually change the form of its Catholicism, moving in stages from conservative practices within the parish church to total withdrawal, so that Catholicism may remain the social norm and individuals may move into recusancy by conformity to community standards. It is not necessarily true that inertia and social pressures worked in favour of conformity to the Church of England: in 1578 a man from Boroughbridge in the North Riding justified his recusancy on the grounds that 'he doth see that no such number now come to church as did in the time of Latin service', and in 1602 a Lancashire

---

[22] T. Burton, *The History and Antiquities of the Parish of Hemingbrough*, ed. J. Raine (Yorkshire Archaeological Society, 1888), pp. 107–8, 297, 314, 318n.; Aveling, 'Catholic Recusants of the West Riding', pp. 195, 207, 221, 222–3; A. G. Dickens, 'The Extent and Character of Recusancy in Yorkshire in 1604', *Yorkshire Archaeological Journal*, xxxvii (1948), pp. 45, 46. For Masham and Ripon, see pp. 183–4 below.

[23] A comparison of the North Riding parishes in trouble for keeping images and similar objects in 1559–72 with those parishes with fifteen or more recusants in 1604 shows that though fourteen per cent of all parishes had fifteen or more recusants in 1604, thirty per cent of the parishes which had retained images had fifteen or more; fifteen per cent of all parishes were in trouble over images, but twenty-four per cent of the parishes with fifteen or more recusants had kept illegal images (and eight more parishes with images are not in the surviving 1604 lists, one of which had had seventeen recusants even in an imperfect return of 1596). Cf. Aveling, *Northern Catholics*, pp. 20–1; *A List of Roman Catholics in the County of York, 1604*, ed. E. Peacock (London, 1872), *passim*.

[24] Dickens, 'First Stages of Romanist Recusancy', pp. 161, 180–1; H. Aveling, *Post-Reformation Catholicism in East Yorkshire, 1558–1790* (East Yorkshire Local History Ser., xi, 1960), pp. 13, 35; K. J. Lindley, 'The Lay Catholics of England in the Reign of Charles I', *J. E. H.*, xxii (1972), p. 202.

[25] Bossy, 'Character of Elizabethan Catholicism', pp. 40–2.

[26] Bossy, *English Catholic Community*, pp. 108–44.

preacher complained of local Catholics who said 'It is safest to do in religion as most do'.[27]

The process by which a small group or community retained Catholic norms during a movement from conformist conservatism into recusancy will, in the nature of things, be largely unrecorded, since official documentation means outside interference and the disruption of the process we are seeking to trace. But there is suggestive evidence for Yorkshire, which shows that sections of a local population could maintain Catholic customs publicly during a move towards recusancy. At Tickhill in 1569 many of the parishioners had already abandoned the church, but attended masses at the surviving chapel of the Maison Dieu, where the altar was still standing. At a parish near York in the mid-1570s there was an almost unanimous withdrawal from services at the church, and the minister regularly locked up the building when none responded to the call of the bell.[28] At Masham the trends which were to make the parish a considerable recusant centre by 1604 were well under way in 1570–2: images from the church had been hidden away, the rood-loft had not been taken down, and there was a good deal of scuffling and threats when the 'monuments' were burned on the orders of the ecclesiastical commissioners. Deprived Marian priests lived with local people and were active in the parish, the curate had been ill-treated by conservatives, hosts were made for use in masses, the churchwardens failed to report those who refused to attend church, and two influential local gentry were non-communicants or worse.[29] Ripon, with ten clergy in trouble for various conservative offences in 1567–70, provides a well-documented example. In 1567 three priests were operating a mass-centre in the church's 'Lady loft', which they had crammed with images, and they offered masses and churchings to rival the official services in the chancel. A recusant priest lived locally and the parish clerk, a frequent critic of established religion, was busy making hosts. In the following year images were still being concealed and there was bell-ringing with the customary collections on All Hallows' Eve, while during the rebellion of 1569 there was a full restoration of the mass with processions. The attention given to Ripon by the York commissioners in these years appears to have had little effect, for in 1577 curates were again in trouble for conservatism, two laymen were dealt with for 'papistry' and assaulting ministers, and the archbishop found that recusancy was already a serious problem.[30] In 1580 we can observe growing recusancy and

[27] B.I.Y., HC.AB 9, f. 164v; W. Harrison, *A Brief Discourse of the Christian Life and Death of Mistress Katherine Brettergh* (London, 1602), 'A Postscript to Papists', sig. N.
[28] B.I.Y., HC.AB 4, fo. 89v; *Chronicle of the English Augustinian Canonesses*, ed. A. Hamilton, 2 vols (Edinburgh, 1904), I, p. 167.
[29] B.I.Y., HC.AB 5, fo. 147; HC.AB 6, fos. 32, 47v, 48, 54v, 55, 167; HC.AB 7, fo. 43v; Aveling, *Northern Catholics*, pp. 21, 42, 45, 169; Dickens, 'Extent and Character of Recusancy', p. 46.
[30] Aveling, 'Catholic Recusants of the West Riding', pp. 195, 201; B.I.Y., HC.AB 3, fos. 176, 182, 185, 189, 190; HC.AB 4, fos. 11v, 19, 24, 29, 33v; 39v; HC.AB 5, fo. 114; HC.AB 9,

widespread observance of traditional customs side by side: the ecclesiastical commission complained that 'many undutifully and unchristianly abstain and refrain from church, divine service, preaching and receiving of the sacraments', while 'a great number superstitiously given do still, contrary to all good order, solemnly keep and observe, by refraining from their usual and daily work, old superstitious holy days and fasting days long since abrogated and forbidden'. When the commissioners attempted to proceed against offenders, the presentment of recusants was inadequate and the jurors had to be asked for a further certificate. There were 120 known papists in the parish by 1604, and, as there was no substantial gentry leadership, we should probably ascribe the strength of recusancy to an administrative isolation which allowed a survival of Catholic norms, within which a development from conservatism to recusancy could easily take place.[31]

For the diocese of Chester, with its less active ecclesiastical commission, the evidence is less detailed, but there too conservative customs were common and the road to recusancy could be an undramatic one. In Cheshire only two parishes, Bunbury and Malpas, developed substantial recusant groups, and in both cases this seems to have been due to the work of parish clergy who became recusant priests and led some of their people out of the Church of England.[32] In the deanery of Blackburn in Lancashire, there must have been a strong impression of continuity: there half a dozen former chapel-curates were active recusant priests by the spring of 1571, providing masses for their erstwhile parishioners. Loyalty to the ex-curates was presumably one reason for the developing recusancy of the chapelries, but the borderline between official Church and separated Catholicism was far from clear when the recusant priests were sheltered by their conforming former colleagues and forbidden feasts were observed in Whalley parish church.[33] The extent to which Catholicism remained a local norm, which could be followed from habit rather than deliberate choice, in many parts of Lancashire is shown by two much later examples. In 1624 John Layton, an effective Jesuit preacher, was holding masses and sermons in an enlarged and decorated barn, to which he attracted not only committed recusants but nominal 'Anglicans' and occasional conformists. On the major festivals the nearest church was deserted except for the parson's family and a few others, but Layton's barn was full.[34] In the 1620s and 1630s the Benedictine Ambrose Barlow had a public status equal to that of his near-neighbour, the rector of Leigh, as 'the very parson of the parish': he visited his flock openly, his congregation met for services at the same times as those at the parish church, and he had a considerable

fos, 119, 124, 125, 127v; Dickens, 'First Stages of Romanist Recusancy', pp. 162–3; 'Diocesan Returns of Recusants, 1577', pp. 32–4.

[31] B.I.Y., HC.AB 10, fos. 18, 39v, 63, 75–8; Dickens, 'Extent and Character of Recusancy', pp. 42, 45; Aveling, 'Catholic Recusants of the West Riding', pp. 221, 222–3

[32] Wark, Elizabethan Recusancy in Cheshire, pp. 132, 133, 176.

[33] B.I.Y., HC.AB 6, fos. 64v, 65v, 67v, 114v; Haigh, Reformation and Resistance, pp. 254–9.

[34] Foley, Records of the English Province, VII, p. 1108.

reputation as an exorcist and reconciler of quarrels. The Catholics of Leigh, led by Barlow, were not a secretive, persecuted sect; indeed, Barlow criticised the gentry who did not like to be seen publicly at mass; they formed instead an open denomination, playing their part in the life of the parish.[35] In many local communities, the surviving traditions of popular culture provided a framework within which families could be Catholic, even recusant, without flouting convention.

But the argument for Catholic continuity does not depend upon the suggestion that what some have dismissed as mere conservatism in fact contributed to the rise of recusancy. Even if we adopt the strict test of organic unity with and obedience to the See of Rome, the continuity of English Catholicism was fractured only briefly. By mid-1564 a committee of the Council of Trent and the Holy Office had declared firmly that English Catholics might not attend the services of the Church of England, and faculties had been issued to four priests to reconcile to Rome those who had fallen into schism. In 1566 Pius V in consistory forbade church attendance, and the former warden of Manchester College was sent into England with the instruction. Though he encountered some initial doubts, Vaux's mission was a considerable success in south-west Lancashire, and a number of leading gentry, served by recusant priests, moved into strict recusancy.[36] It seems that Vaux was less influential elsewhere, and his authority was challenged: in 1567 the Holy Office confirmed the necessity of recusancy and the powers of the priests deputed to reconcile, and notarial attestations of this decree were soon circulating in England.[37] From the 1566 mission of Vaux at least, there existed in England the concept of a separated Catholic Church united with Rome, into which priests and laity were received by reconciliation. William Holmes told a packed congregation in Durham cathedral during the revolt of 1569 'that he had authority to reconcile men to the Church of Rome, willed all that was disposed to be reconciled to kneel down, whereupon he pronounced a *forma absolutionis* in Latin, in the name of Christ and Bishop Pius of Rome'. At the church of St Helen in Bishop Auckland, George White said mass, and 'when he had preached against the state of religion established in this realm, he willed them [the people] to revert to the Church of Rome, and thereupon he read absolution in the Pope his name to all the people'.[38] In May 1571 a Yorkshire gentleman told the

---

[35] R. Challoner, *Memoirs of Missionary Priests*, ed. J. H. Pollen (London, 1924), pp. 394–7; 'The Apostolical Life of Ambrose Barlow, O.S.B.', ed. W. E. Rhodes, in *Chetham Miscellanies*, new ser., II (Chetham Society, new ser., LXIII, 1909), pp. 4–5, 6, 10, 12. Cf. Bossy, *English Catholic Community*, p. 126.

[36] C. G. Bayne, *Anglo-Roman Relations, 1558–1565* (Oxford, 1913), pp. 163–71, 177–80; J. H. Pollen, *The English Catholics in the Reign of Queen Elizabeth* (London, 1920), pp. 104–6; Haigh, *Reformation and Resistance*, pp. 249–50.

[37] A. O. Meyer, *England and the Catholic Church under Elizabeth* (London, 1915), pp. 475–8; W. MacCaffrey, *The Shaping of the Elizabethan Regime* (Princeton, 1969), p. 204.

[38] *Depositions and Other Ecclesiastical Proceedings from the Courts of Durham*, ed. J. Raine (Surtees Society, XXI, 1845), pp. 143–4, 181.

ecclesiastical commissioners 'that he was one of that Church whereof the pope had always been taken and was supreme head and vicar general under Christ in earth', and in the following year a reconciled minister asserted 'that the pope, the bishop of Rome, is supreme head of the Catholic Church, and that he would stick in that opinion until death, by God's grace'.[39] There were self-consciously *Roman* Catholics in southern England, too; in 1577 an Essex tailor was 'sure the true and right religion was and still is at Rome, even as it was left there by St. Peter. But what manner of religion we have here in England I know not, for that preachers do preach their own inventions and fantasies, and therefore I will not believe any of them.'[40] The work of the English exiles at Louvain must have emphasised the catholicity of the Church to which the English opposition claimed to belong: by 1564 Louvainist attacks on the Church of England were in circulation, and by 1568-9 there were collections for the support of the exiled scholars.[41]

In deliberately joining themselves to a body of English recusant priests and laymen identified as part of the international Catholic church, Elizabethans rejected the Church of England as schismatic, lacking the authentic priesthood and liturgy. In 1563 Sir Robert Brandling, a former mayor of Newcastle, left vestments to local churches, 'provided always that those vestments shall not be given except the old accustomed service be used according to the Catholic usage of the Church'.[42] In 1572 William Tessimond of York told the ecclesiastical commissioners

> that he did not communicate nor come to the church to hear divine service this two or three years, and that the cause thereof was his misliking of the order of the service, for that it is not like unto the order of the service of the Catholic Church and for that sacrifice is not offered in the same for the sins of the quick and the dead.

In 1573 Thomas Awdcorne, also of York, admitted that he had been a recusant for eighteen months, 'and that his conscience hath been since and is persuaded that the religion now established is not according to God's word nor is not Catholic, and that he is persuaded that after the consecration the body of Christ is really present in the Sacrament'. Robert Bayarde, from a village near Doncaster, said in 1574 'that the religion in this realm established is not the true religion nor of the Catholic religion'.[43] By 1576 there was a considerable group of Catholics in York who rejected the Church of England on similar grounds. Isabel Porter said 'she cometh

[39] B.I.Y., HC.AB 6, fo. 13; HC.AB 7, fo. 39.
[40] O'Dwyer, 'Catholic Recusants in Essex', p. 47.
[41] J. C. H. Aveling, *Catholic Recusancy in the City of York, 1558–1791* (C.R.S., monograph ser., II, 1970), p. 32; 'Letters from the Bishops', ed. Bateson, p. 67; W. R. Trimble, *The Catholic Laity in Elizabethan England* (Cambridge, Mass., 1964), p. 39; Birt, *Elizabethan Religious Settlement*, pp. 427-8.
[42] E. Walsh and A. Forster, 'The Recusancy of the Brandlings', *Recusant History*, x (1969), p. 37.
[43] B.I.Y., HC.AB 7, fos, 40, 104; HC.AB 8, fo. 38v. Professor Dickens tells me that Bayarde was a friend of the conforming conservative Robert Parkyn: another blurred boundary!

not to the church because her conscience will not serve her, for things are not in the church as it hath been aforetimes in her forefathers' days', and some forty others gave much the same answer:

> William Bowman, locksmith, sayeth he refuseth to come to the church because he thinketh it is not the Catholic Church, for there is neither priest, altar nor sacraments...

And:

> Dorothy Vavasour, wife of Thomas Vavasour, doctor of physic, sayeth she comet not to the church because her conscience will not serve her so to do, for she sayet she will remain in the faith she was baptised in.[44]

There existed in York an informed and separated Catholic group, two years before the first seminarist missioner reached the city.[45] Nor were such clear distinctions between churches and liturgies confined to the north: in 1577 George Binkes, brother of the Essex tailor already quoted, had been telling those whom he tried to convert to Rome:

> that the mass is good and *confiteor* is good, and that he will believe as long as he liveth. Item, that the images are good and ought to stand in the church to put men in remembrance that such saints there were, and that the crosses in the church and in the highways ought to stand, to put men in remembrance that Christ died upon the cross; and desireth and would be called by the name of a papist.[46]

By the time the seminary mission and later the Jesuits had an impact upon England, there already existed the essential concept of a separated Catholic church, and there was a recusant priesthood providing sacraments for lay people who regarded themselves as Catholics. Recusant priests were active by 1564 in the diocese of Hereford, Lichfield, Peterborough and Worcester, and the Bishop of Hereford was able to name a dozen priests, 'mortal and deadly enemies to this religion', who were travelling around gentry houses and saying masses.[47] In all, over 150 'Marian priests', who had withdrawn from the official English Church and seem to have regarded themselves as members of a distinct Catholic body, were active in Yorkshire, and about seventy-five in Lancashire. No other counties are, as yet, known to have such impressive concentrations, though the Welsh marches and the west midlands remain possibilities: Lancashire and Yorkshire were fairly safe areas in which to work and

---

[44] J. Morris, *The Troubles of Our Catholic Forefathers*, 3 vols (London, 1872–7), III, pp. 248–58, quotations at pp. 248–50.

[45] 'Diocesan Returns of Recusants', p. 18; Aveling, *Catholic Recusancy in the City of York*, pp. 41–5.

[46] O'Dwyer, 'Catholic Recusants in Essex', p. 47. It is possible that the Binkes brothers had been influenced by seminary priests, but George's defence of images and crosses rings of traditionalism.

[47] 'Letters from the Bishops', ed. Bateson, pp. 3, 19, 34, 40.

were presumably regarded as promising recruiting-grounds for recusants, since in each case roughly two-thirds of the recusant clergy were attracted from outside.[48] We also know something of the work of such priests in Northumberland and Durham, Worcestershire, Hampshire and Sussex, though in southern counties their attentions may have been concentrated upon the gentry, who were able to provide shelter and financial suppport.[49] The recusant clergy were a varied group: some were former church dignitaries, who settled in gentry households; others were university scholars, who became itinerant proselytisers; others were former chapel-curates, who served their former congregations on a free-lance basis; and still more may have been made redundant by the contraction of the official demand for clergy in 1559, and set themselves up in competition with their beneficed former colleagues.[50] They were, perhaps, better suited to meeting the differing spiritual needs of the various Catholic social groups than the seminary priests were to be, for the latter formed a more homogeneous and intellectual band. The role of the recusant clergy in the creation of networks of Catholic households and circles was of great importance in some areas: in 1571 a dozen of them were at work in Richmondshire and Claro, reconciling schismatics, and in that year thirty-eight priests were reported to be active in Lancashire. At least thirty-one recusant clergy were busy in Lancashire in 1580, outnumbering the seminary men by more than two to one, and even in 1590 a quarter of that county's Catholic clergy were Marians.[51] The Jesuit Holt thought in 1596 that there were still forty or fifty recusant priests in England, and Hugh Ile, ordained by Bishop Tunstall in 1559, was apparently still working in the North Riding in 1611.[52]

It was the Marian clergy who initiated lay recusant Catholicism, which was already well established before the mission from the Continent could have had any real effect.[53] It is possible to trace a number of cases of recusancy back to the Elizabethan settlement or just after,[54] but it is usually assumed that these were merely isolated

[48] Aveling, *Northern Catholics*, p. 34; Haigh, *Reformation and Resistance*, pp. 255–7; M. Hodgetts, 'Elizabethan Priest-Holes: I', *Recusant History*, XI (1972), p. 280.

[49] A. Forster, 'Bishop Tunstall's Priests', *Recusant History*, IX (1967), pp. 178–9, 189, 191–4; Burke, 'Catholic Recusants in Elizabethan Worcestershire', pp. 37–9; Paul, 'Hampshire Recusants', pp. 171–2; Birt, *Elizabethan Religious Settlement*, pp. 427–9.

[50] Aveling, 'Catholic Recusants of the West Riding', pp. 198, 200, 208; Haigh, *Reformation and Resistance*, pp. 215–16, 248–51, 254–7, 266. It seems that the counties which produced most recusant clergy were those with larger-than-average parishes: it was easier for dissidents to operate outside the single-township, squire-dominated parishes of eastern England, and the larger parishes appear to have shed some of their clergy in 1559.

[51] Aveling, 'Catholic Recusants of the West Riding', p. 208; B.I.Y., HC.AB 6, fos. 64–119; Haigh, *Reformation and Resistance*, p. 256.

[52] *Douai Diaries*, ed. Knox, p. 378; Forster, 'Bishop Tunstall's Priests', p. 193.

[53] See Humphrey Ely's comments, quoted in *Douai Diaries*, ed. Knox, p. lxii.

[54] Birt, *Elizabethan Religious Settlement*, p. 518; A. Gibbons, *Ely Episcopal Records* (Lincoln, 1881), p. 49; Burke, 'Catholic Recusants in Elizabethan Worcestershire', pp. 63, 177; A. Davidson,

individuals and that a substantial growth in recusancy came only with the arrival of the missioners.[55] The rise of recusancy is extremely difficult to chart, since our evidence is dependent upon official detection and therefore upon official effort. In the 1560s the Elizabethan regime tried to avoid provoking conservative resistance, and there was little serious attempt to enforce church attendance: only at times of political crisis, such as the approach of the papal envoy Martinengo in 1561, were dissidents harried.[56] But when officials were forced to look, they usually found recusants. We have little concrete evidence of recusancy in Lancashire until, in 1567, some worrying rumours reached the privy council and the bishop of Chester was ordered to investigate: he found an already established circuit of gentry households providing shelter for at least seventeen mass-priests, mainly in south-west Lancashire.[57] From 1569 the political situation grew more dangerous for William Cecil and his supporters, with the Norfolk marriage project, the Revolt of the Earls, *Regnans in excelsis* and the Ridolfi Plot: action against Catholics, which had hitherto seemed so dangerous, now became less of a risk than inaction, and a few days after the outbreak of the 1569 rebellion the council challenged the conservative gentry by ordering J.P.s to subscribe to the Book of Common Prayer.[58] Thereafter, bishops in dangerous coastal dioceses, often under pressure from the centre, moved against the hitherto undetected recusants. After complaints from the council about his slackness, Bishop Parkhurst held a visitation of the archdeaconry of Norwich and uncovered 180 recusants and non-communicants. After the death of Bishop Barlow, a metropolitan visitation of the diocese of Chichester found a score of recusant

'Roman Catholicism in Oxfordshire, from the late Elizabethan Period to the Civil War, *c.* 1580–*c.* 1640' (University of Bristol Ph.D. thesis, 1970), p. 611; Aveling, *The Handle and the Axe*, p. 47; Wark, *Elizabethan Recusancy in Cheshire*, pp. 5–6; Haigh, *Reformation and Resistance*, p. 248; Paul, 'Hampshire Recusants', pp. 131–2.

[55] P. McGrath, *Papists and Puritans under Elizabeth I* (London, 1967), pp. 100, 111–13; P. Hughes, *The Reformation in England*, 3 vols (London, 1963 edn.), III, pp. 303–4; A. G. Dickens, *The English Reformation* (London, 1964), p. 311.

[56] Although there were some official attempts to remind churchwardens of the duty to fine absentees from church (see, for example, W. P. M. Kennedy, 'Fines under the Elizabethan Act of Uniformity', *E.H.R.*, XXXIII (1918), pp. 522–6), it is clear that there was widespread failure and that recalcitrant wardens seem not to have been harried, especially where recusancy was a real problem. See P. Tyler, 'The Ecclesiastical Commission for the Province of York, 1561–1641' (University of Oxford D. Phil. thesis, 1965), p. 234; F. X. Walker, 'The Implementation of the Elizabethan Statutes against Recusants, 1581–1603' (University of London Ph.D. thesis, 1961), pp. 6–8, 53–5; Haigh, *Reformation and Resistance*, p. 264. For 1561, see MacCaffrey, *Shaping of the Elizabethan Regime*, pp. 77–80.

[57] P.R.O., S.P. 12/44, fos. 116 r–v; 12/48, fos. 73–4, 75–6; Haigh, *Reformation and Resistance*, pp. 222–4.

[58] E. Rose, *Cases of Conscience* (Cambridge, 1975), pp. 37–8. There was also a drive against papists in the inns of court: see G. de C. Parmiter, *Elizabethan Popish Recusancy in the Inns of Court* (*B.I.H.R.*, Supplement XI, 1976), pp. 9–12.

gentry, and 'except it be about Lewes and a little in Chichester, the whole diocese of Chichester is very blind and superstitious'.[59] The Winchester consistory dealt with sixteen recusants and seventy-one non-communicants from Hampshire in 1569, but then pressure intensified and in only eight months of 1570 116 recusants and 128 non-communicants were cited.[60] Further north, the authority of the Bishop of Chester was inhibited after complaints of inactivity, and a special metropolitan visitation in 1571 found fifty-four lay recusants, forty of them gentry, twenty-three non-communicants and thirty-eight active recusant priests in Lancashire. In the province of York as a whole, the ecclesiastical commission began to move systematically against Catholic gentry: the frequency of sessions was increased, and in 1572-4 about fifty gentlemen were dealt with.[61]

This considerable increase in the incidence of detected recusancy has been variously explained as a response to the papal bull of 1570 and as the result of a spontaneous Catholic revival, and it is certainly possible to show individuals moving into recusancy about 1570.[62] But it is much more likely that there was no dramatic growth in actual recusancy in these years, and that more vigorous investigation revealed a Catholic separatism which had been developing for some time. The same suggestion might be made about the increase in recusancy which is thought to have followed the arrival of the missionary priests. It is true that evidence of recusancy mounts from 1577, but this was the product of greater official concern with the Catholic problem. From 1574 the Privy Council embarked upon a more systematic attack on papist gentry, and at times, as in Staffordshire in 1575 and Norfolk in 1578, the council itself proceeded against groups of gentlemen.[63] At home and overseas the Catholic threat seemed to grow: from 1576 there were plans for an 'Enterprise of England', and Sander's attempt to raise Ireland in 1579 was a stage in the fulfilment of an Elizabethan nightmare; the work of the missionary priests sapped England's ability to resist attack, and the French marriage project in 1578-9 put the committed Protestants on the council in a weak position, as the French ambassador sought support among conservative nobles and court Catholics.[64] Under this pressure, the

[59] Houlbrooke, *Church Courts and the People*, pp. 246, 252; Birt, *Elizabethan Religious Settlement*, pp. 427-30.
[60] Paul, 'Hampshire Recusants', pp. 39, 47-8, 412. The 1569 visitation of Worcester diocese focused upon aspects of the Catholic problem: see Burke, 'Catholic Recusants in Elizabethan Worcestershire', pp. 43, 58-9.
[61] Haigh, *Reformation and Resistance*, pp. 223-4, 254-5; B.I.Y., HC.AB 5, fos. 139v-41v, 164v, 169, 200; HC.AB 6, fos. 64-119; Tyler, 'Ecclesiastical Commission', pp. 150, 236.
[62] W. Camden, *The History of the Most Renowned and Victorious Princess Elizabeth* (London, 1675), p. 245; *Calendar of State Papers, Domestic, Elizabeth I, Addenda, 1566-1579*, pp. 321-2; Leys, *Catholics in England*, p. 22; Aveling, *The Handle and the Axe*, pp. 43-9, 52. 64-5.
[63] Trimble, *Catholic Laity*, pp. 68-9, 71-2; *A.P.C.*, IX, pp. 13, 15, 17, 46-7, 57; X, 310-13; Jessopp, *One Generation of a Norfolk House*, pp. 106-9.
[64] McGrath, *Papists and Puritans*, pp. 123-4; J. A. Bossy, 'English Catholics and the French Marriage, 1577-81', *Recusant History*, v (1959), pp. 4-7.

Protestants on the council struck out: in October 1577 the bishops were instructed to conduct the first full census of recusants, and some of those reported were called to London; the executions of seminary priests began in November 1577 and continued in the following February; and Protestant councillors took advantage of a progress through Norfolk and Suffolk in the summer of 1578 to move against prominent East Anglian recusants.[65] For reasons which have much to do with factional conflicts at Court, there was a general drive against Catholics in the late 1570s: often under instruction from the centre, local officials took action in the dioceses of Exeter, Winchester, Chichester, Norwich, Worcester, Bangor, St Asaph and York,[66] and no doubt elsewhere too. It is therefore not surprising that these dioceses produced more evidence of recusancy.

But the documentation created by this flurry of activity does not suggest that recusancy was the result of the work of the missioners. A hastily conducted official survey, which concentrated mainly upon gentry recusants and known malcontents,[67] listed 1500 recusants in the autumn of 1577: only thirty seminary priests had been sent to England by the summer, and two of them had been arrested almost immediately.[68] Though the counties of Worcestershire, Herefordshire, Staffordshire and Shropshire produced 230 recusants in the return, it seems that no seminarians had worked in these areas, though two may have passed through. The considerable Lancashire recusancy shown by a visitation in 1578 reflects the distribution of recusant rather than seminary clergy: 128 of the 304 detected recusants were in the deanery of Warrington, where twenty recusant clergy had worked but which was not the base of a seminary priest until 1583, and the three earliest Lancashire seminary priests seem to have concentrated upon Amounderness, which produced only seventy-two recusants and had had only four recusant priests.[69] We know that recusancy was

[65] Walker, 'Implementation of the Elizabethan Statutes', pp. 46–9; McGrath, Papists and Puritans, pp. 117–19; A. H. Smith, County and Court: Government and Politics in Norfolk, 1558–1603 (Oxford, 1974), pp. 201–3, 207–25, shows the co-operation between Privy Councillors and committed Norfolk Protestants in an attack on the rival Catholic and conservative faction in East Anglia.

[66] A. L. Rowse, Tudor Cornwall (London, 1969 edn.), pp. 343, 347, 355; Paul, 'Hampshire Recusants', pp. 47–9; Manning, Religion and Society in Elizabethan Sussex, pp. 80–6, 130; Smith, County and Court, pp. 216, 218; Burke, 'Catholic Recusants in Elizabethan Worcestershire', pp. 58–9, 60–1; E. G. Jones, 'The Lleyn Recusancy Case, 1578–81', Transactions of the Honourable Society of Cymmrodorion (1936), pp. 98–100, 104; P. Williams, The Council in the Marches of Wales (Cardiff, 1958), pp. 91–3; Haigh, Reformation and Resistance, pp. 263–4; Walker, 'Implementation of the Elizabethan Statutes', pp. 69–70; Tyler, 'Ecclesiastical Commission', pp. 242–6, 254–61.

[67] 'Diocesan Returns of Recusants', pp. 2, 3, 6–9, 11, 54, 65, 71; Parmiter, Elizabethan Popish Recusancy, pp. 25, 27–8.

[68] The movements of priests are calculated from Douai Diaries, ed. Knox, and G. Anstruther, The Seminary Priests, 1 (Ware, n.d.).

[69] B.I.Y., Vis. 1578–9/CB3, fos. 34–103v; HC.AB 9, fos. 168v–75; Haigh, Reformation and Resistance, pp. 263–4.

established before the arrival of the seminary priests in the North Riding, the West Riding, Lancashire, Cheshire, Staffordshire, Herefordshire, Worcestershire, Hampshire, Sussex, Essex and Norfolk, and that many of the families which were to lead English Catholicism already had recusant members by 1574, when the mission began.[70]

Popular Catholicism was thus not driven from the parish churches by the 1559 legislation, and recusancy was soon established as one Catholic response to the Elizabethan Settlement. The first decades of Elizabeth's reign therefore formed a significant transitional period, and we should avoid any sharp distinction between a monopolistic 'church' Catholicism destroyed in 1559 and a new 'sect' Catholicism created by the mission. For though the trained missionary clergy are a striking novelty in post-Reformation English Catholicism, they are not a sign of a break in continuity and of the Counter Reformation come to England. The colleges at Douai and Rome were influenced less by the Trent decree on clerical training than by William Allen's changing perception of the future needs of Catholicism at home. Douai was founded as a refuge for exiled scholars and as a college for the clerical leaders who would be needed when England returned to the faith: the mission was an accident and an afterthought.[71] Whatever the original intention, Douai became a missionary college and sent a steady supply of priests to England, but we should examine the recruitment and objectives of the seminarians before we conclude that their arrival led to the creation of a new form of English Catholicism.

Though the new priests came to England from the Continent, they had first, in the main, been recruited from the existing English Catholic body. Some of the early recruits were converts (though, as we shall see, it is important to distinguish 'conversion' from the more common 'reconciliation'), but in general the first wave was composed of Catholic university scholars and students anxious to escape from the heretical Church of England, and thereafter the trainees were the sons of the Catholic gentry and yeomanry of England.[72] It is not possible to establish with

---

[70] Aveling, *Northern Catholics*, p. 88; Aveling, 'Catholic Recusants of the West Riding', pp. 205, 208; Aveling, *Catholic Recusancy in the City of York*, pp. 39, 41, 42–4; Haigh, *Reformation and Resistance*, pp. 247–68; Wark, *Elizabethan Recusancy in Cheshire*, pp. 5–6, 10, 14–17; W. N. Landor, *Staffordshire Incumbents and Parochial Records, 1530–1680* (William Salt Archaeological Society, Collections for a History of Staffordshire, 1916), p. 367; 'Letters from the Bishops', ed. Bateson, p. 19; Burke, 'Catholic Recusants in Elizabethan Worcestershire', pp. 61, 67, 105; Paul, 'Hampshire Recusants', pp. 36, 38, 39–40, 47–8, 412; Manning, *Religion and Society in Elizabethan Sussex*, pp. 45, 130, 154; O'Dwyer, 'Catholic Recusants in Essex', pp. 18–20; Houlbrooke, *Church Courts and the People*, pp. 246, 250–2.

[71] W. Allen, *An Apology and True Declaration of the Institution and Endeavours of the Two English Colleges* (Rheims, 1581), fos. 21–26v; *Douai Diaries*, ed. Knox, pp. xxvi, xxviii, xxxiv–xxxv; 'Memoirs of Father Robert Persons', ed. Pollen, I, p. 190; Bossy, *English Catholic Community*, pp. 13–14, 18–20.

[72] *Ibid.*, pp. 12–17, 198–200.

precision the background of recruits until the *responsa* of the English College at Rome begin in 1598, but it is likely that most came from Catholic families. The geographical origins of the men who entered Douai in its first ten years were remarkably similar to the origins of the recruits to the seminaries both in the reign of Elizabeth as a whole and in the years 1603–59: Lancashire and Yorkshire, for example, each consistently contributed about one-sixth of the students.[73] Catholic teachers in England were soon operating 'feeder' schools which served Douai: Nicholas Garlick, master of the Derbyshire school founded by the Marian Bishop Pursglove, sent three of his pupils to the college in the 1570s, before crossing over to train as a priest himself.[74] Laurence Yate, the Church-papist master at Burnley from 1571 and later at Blackburn, sent nine of his students to train as priests, and five of them had been received into the seminary by the middle of 1580. Later, Thomas Somers, a Westmorland schoolmaster, persuaded several students to train for the priesthood before, like Garlick, following his former pupils to Douai.[75] From 1598 the *responsa* of those entering the seminaries show that over half, and later three-quarters, of them came from families in which both parents were clearly Catholic: between 1598 and 1621 recruits from the more conservative areas of England, where Catholic continuity was more likely, were more apt to come from Catholic backgrounds than were those from districts where Protestantism had made substantial progress.[76] Jesuits, too, were often from Catholic families: even in the 1560s the young Thomas Fitzherbert operated a harsh fasting regime and was reluctant to meet Protestants, while in the 1570s John Gerard was taught Latin by a conservative tutor and Greek by a Marian priest.[77]

It would be unwise to distinguish sharply between the 'old priests' of the traditional Church and the 'seminary priests' of the new dispensation, since William Allen tells us that some recusant clergy were invited to Douai for 'refresher courses'

[73] *Douai Diaries*, ed. Knox, pp. 3–9; Anstruther, *Seminary Priests*, I, pp. 398–405; II (Great Wakering, 1975), p. 406. For convenience, I refer to the college as 'Douai' even for the few years of the transfer to Rheims.

[74] Challoner, *Memoirs of Missionary Priests*, pp. 129–30; Foley, *Records of the English Province*, III, pp. 224–5; J. M. J. Fletcher, 'Bishop Pursglove of Tideswell', *Derbyshire Archaeological Journal*, XXXII (1910), pp. 19–20.

[75] Haigh, *Reformation and Resistance*, pp. 278–9; Challoner, *Memoirs of Missionary Priests*, pp. 321–2.

[76] Bossy, *English Catholic Community*, p. 157n.; A. C. F. Beales, *Education under Penalty* (London, 1963), p. 85; *The Responsa Scholarum of the English College, Rome, 1598–1621*, ed. A. Kenny (C.R.S., LIV, 1962), *passim*. Seventy-six per cent of recruits from Lancashire had always been recusants or church papists, and seventy-three per cent of those from Yorkshire, sixty-seven per cent from Warwickshire and from Hampshire, and sixty per cent from Staffordshire and from Norfolk.

[77] Foley, *Records of the English Province*, III, p. 210; Gerard, *Autobiography*, p. 1. For Jesuit recruitment, see B. Basset, *The English Jesuits, from Campion to Martindale* (London, 1967), pp. 15, 18.

and we know that at least two priests from the north took the opportunity.[78] The priests sent on the mission, especially in the early years, were not always impressionable young men, who might have been moulded into agents of Tridentine reform; they were often older inheritors of an established English tradition. Indeed, the career of one of these, set out in his deposition of 1586, is a fine demonstration of the continuity of Catholicism:

> Thomas Bramston saith he hath taken no degrees in schools. He saith he was brought up in his young years in the grammar school in Canterbury under old Mr. Twine. From Mr. Twine he went to Westminster and there continued a year and was a novice in the abbey. From thence he went to Mr. Roper of Eltham, where he continued about a year. From thence he went to Oxford to St. John's College where he continued about three or four years and was fellow of that college. From thence he went to wait upon Dr. Feckenham who was in the Tower, where he continued so about two years. From thence he went to serve Sir Thomas Tresham, to whom he did belong, coming and going, about ten years and was schoolmaster to his house until such time as the Act of Parliament was made that none should teach either publicly or privately but such as would conform themselves to the religion now established, which as he thinketh was about the 18th year of the Queen's Majesty's reign. From Sir Thomas Tresham's service he went over sea, and, confessing that he is a priest, he will not answer to any question, neither when he went over, but saith that he was no priest when he was schoolmaster in Sir Thomas Tresham's house, which was ten or eleven years since.[79]

This quotation is so apposite, in its mingling of 'traditional' and 'Counter Reformation' influences, that it might have been invented to serve the case: Bramston went from Pole's Canterbury to the restored Westminster Abbey, to Thomas More's son-in-law, to a fellowship at a new Catholic foundation with Edmund Campion, to the last Abbot of Westminster in the Tower, to one of the leading recusant gentry, to a seminary and finally to the English mission.

If the recruitment of the missionary priests does not represent a break with traditional Catholicism, nor does their objective. The English mission, if indeed 'mission' is an appropriate term,[80] was not an evangelical movement but a pastoral organisation: its objective was not the conversion of heretics but the care of Catholics.[81] It is essential to distinguish the clerical rhetoric of 'mission' and 'conversion' from the reality of the seminary priests' historical function. To sustain

[78] *Douai Diaries*, ed. Knox, pp. xxxix, xli, 104; Haigh, *Reformation and Resistance*, pp. 250, 251; Forster, 'Bishop Tunstall's Priests', p. 194.

[79] Anstruther, *Seminary Priests*, I, p. 47. See also Foley, *Records of the English Province*, III, pp. 224–5; Challoner, *Memoirs of Missionary Priests*, pp. 66–7, 129–30.

[80] J. Berington, *The Memoirs of Gregorio Panzani* (Birmingham, 1793), p. 42.

[81] See Meyer, *England and the Catholic Church under Elizabeth*, pp. 61–2; T. H. Clancy, *Papist Pamphleteers* (Chicago, 1964), p. 146; Davidson, 'Roman Catholicism in Oxfordshire', pp. 480–2.

their fervour in training and their courage in the field, students and priests gave their task a cosmic significance. It was reported of the young men at the English College in Rome in 1582 that:

> They ever bear in mind that they are a remnant snatched from the ruin of their country, and gathered together here by a special favour of Divine Providence to fit themselves by virtue and learning to free England from the yoke of heresy, even though the sword of the foe bar their path and their own life-blood be the price they have to pay for ransoming souls from the dark captivity of falsehood and error.[82]

But their leaders and the more perceptive observers were more realistic: Allen, Baker, Gerard and Parsons make it clear that the task of the missioners was the reconciliation of schismatics, the turning of already-Catholic church-papists into recusants, rather than the conversion of heretics.[83] Henry Shaw, one of the first men from Douai to be sent into England, found that he was so busy absolving Catholics from schism that he had no time to think of other tasks. John Gerard admitted that he had little success with heretics, and that his main achievement was to stiffen the resolve of conforming Catholics: when Gerard writes of 'conversion' he means what others call 'reconciliation', as in his comment on Sir Francis Fortescue, 'a schismatic (that is, a Catholic by conviction), but there was no hope of converting him'.[84]

The 1580 instructions for the Jesuit mission forbade the priests to approach heretics, encouraged them to deal with reconciled Catholics whenever possible and stressed that their aim was 'the preservation and augmentation of the faith of the Catholics of England'.[85] Allen wrote that the secular priests went into England 'to serve them whose hearts God shall touch to admit spiritual comforts and to prefer salvation before worldly commodities, and to minister unto them all sacraments necessary for the life and grace of their souls', and John Bost and Edmund Campion announced that they came to preach the Gospel and provide sacraments.[86] The training given at Douai was designed to produce pastors, not controversialists or evangelists: Allen remarked that 'Our students, being intended for the English harvest, are not required to excel or be great proficients in theological science', and in most parts of the country the most useful men were the less academic, though

---

[82] Foley, *Records of the English Province*, VI, p. 82.
[83] Aveling, *Post-Reformation Catholicism*, p. 28. See also R. Southwell, *An Humble Supplication to Her Majesty*, ed. R. C. Bald (Cambridge, 1953), p. 11.
[84] *Douai Diaries*, ed. Knox, p. 98; Gerard, *Autobiography*, pp. 25, 32–3, 166; Basset, *English Jesuits*, p. 130.
[85] *Letters and Memorials of Father Robert Persons*, ed. Hicks, pp. 319–21; Basset, *English Jesuits*, pp. 40–1.
[86] Allen, *Apology and True Declaration*, fo. 25v; Morris, *Troubles of Our Catholic Forefathers*, III, p. 199; R. Simpson, *Edmund Campion* (London, 1896), p. 226.

since all the labourers we send are employed in administering the sacraments and above all things in hearing confessions (for the people have hardly any pastors now but them) we take care that they are most carefully instructed in the whole catechism and in pastoral matters, and are not ignorant of ecclesiastical penalties and censures, or of the way to deal with their people in such cases.[87]

The priests were sent not to create a new Catholicism, but to provide pastoral care for a pre-existing Catholicism. In 1580, at the 'synod of Southwark', a meeting of Jesuits, seminary priests and recusant clergy decided that the mission should concentrate upon three areas: Lancashire and the north, which had already demonstrated its Catholicism; Wales, where a Catholic population was declining into ignorance for want of priestly care; and East Anglia, where the radical influence of Cambridge had to be combated.[88] Even the Louvain controversialists came to recognise that the task was preservation rather than conversion. Richard Hopkins noted that in 1568 Thomas Harding had persuaded him to translate Spanish spiritual works, from which more good would result 'than by books that treat of controversies in religion'. The first of seven Elizabethan editions of Laurence Vaux's highly conservative *Catechism* appeared in 1568, and the 1570s and 1580s saw the publication, often in several editions, of numerous devotional works for English Catholics.[89]

Thus the Elizabethan mission did not break from the Catholic past in either its recruitment or its objectives. But what of its achievement? It is difficult to assess the impact of the early missionaries upon either the number of Catholics or the nature of their response to the Church of England, because of the character of the evidence and because the first decade of the mission coincided with a number of other influences upon Catholics. We have already seen that recusancy was well established before the arrival of the seminary priests, and if the number of recusants really did increase in the 1570s this was partly because conformism became less attractive as ex-Marian clergy died and Protestant bishops drove conservative practices from the parish churches. As we shall see, the cases of Wales and the far north-west of England demonstrate that seminary priests were a pre-requisite for the long-term survival of Catholicism, but at least in the short term they had a remarkably slight impact on the structure of English Catholicism. We know where sixty-one of the priests dispatched to England and Wales by the end of 1580 worked, and it is possible to compare their geographical distribution with the distribution of recorded recusancy

[87] *Douai Diaries*, ed. Knox, pp. xxxviii–xlii.
[88] *Letters and Memorials of Father Persons*, ed. Hicks, p. 108; R. Parsons, 'Of the Life and Martyrdom of Father Edmond Campion', *Letters and Notices*, XII (1878–9), p. 38.
[89] J. R. Roberts, ed., *A Critical Anthology of English Recusant Devotional Prose, 1558–1603* (Pittsburgh, 1966), pp. 4–5; A. F. Allison and D. M. Rogers, 'A Catalogue of Catholic Books in English, 1558–1640', *Recusant History*, III (1956), *passim*.

at about the same time.[90] If we exclude the priests arrested on arrival in England or while still apparently in transit, fifty-one per cent of the remainder seem actually to have worked in London and the Thames valley, in a belt of counties stretching from Essex westwards through Middlesex, Hertfordshire, Buckinghamshire, Berkshire and Oxfordshire: but in *circa* 1580 these counties contained only nineteen per cent of the Catholics recorded by the government. Only eighteen per cent of the priests worked in the six northern counties, but thirty-eight per cent of known recusants were in the north, and the true proportion was certainly higher since detection was especially poor in the large-parish counties.[91] It seems that not one of the priests had worked in the west midland counties of Worcestershire, Herefordshire, Warwickshire, Staffordshire, Shropshire and Derbyshire by the end of 1580, but twenty per cent of the recusants were in these counties.

From even a preliminary analysis, two things seem clear: the growth of recusancy was not dependent upon the impact of this mission; and an intensive missionary drive could not significantly alter a prevailing religious disposition – the seminarists could not make the Thames valley as Catholic as west Lancashire. I hope to argue elsewhere that the geography of allegiance to the pre-Reformation church, measured in a number of ways, prefigured the distribution of later recusancy, and that the geographical structure of post-Reformation Catholicism remained fairly constant, at both local and national levels, until the pattern was broken by population mobility in the Industrial Revolution. There was thus a stability in the geography of English Catholicism, which the Reformation and the seminarist and Jesuit missions did little to change. The distribution of the missionary priests, who were concentrated in southern and eastern England, did not result in a reconstruction of English Catholicism, and the geography of recusancy was maintained despite, not because of, the logistics of the mission. We do not find that close relationship between the distribution of priests and that of recusants which would have existed if the mission had built a new Catholic community or had been decisive in altering the form of Catholicism from 'survivalism' and church-papistry to recusancy.

If the new priests did not create post-Reformation Catholicism, they were nevertheless essential for its continued existence: Catholicism could only be sustained after the death of the conservative and recusant clergy by an adequate and properly distributed supply of seminary priests and regulars. There was, in 'survivalism' and early recusancy, a massive potential for future Catholicism, especially in peripheral

---

[90] The distribution of priests is calculated from Anstruther, *Seminary Priests*, I, *passim*; the distribution of recusants is drawn from a conflation of returns for 1577 ('Diocesan Returns of Recusants', pp. 6–9) and 1582 (P.R.O., S.P. 12/156, f. 78).

[91] Haigh, *Reformation and Resistance*, pp. 22–3, 269–72; A. D. Gilbert, *Religion and Society in Industrial England* (London, 1976), pp. 98–100.

England and in Wales, but without a continuing supply of priests this would decline to mere superstition, as happened in the Isle of Man.[92] But by 1580 there was already a serious maldistribution of clergy: the ratio of detected recusants to priests in the north was twice that in the Thames valley, and the real position was even worse. When Robert Parsons came to England in 1580, no seminary priests had penetrated Wales or the four most northern English counties, though there was then an attempt to remedy the position. In 1586 Robert Southwell reported that 'in three or four shires together there is not one priest, though desired of many', and 'the priests actually at work here make for one or two counties, leaving others without shepherds', but he was guilty of the error he condemned, abandoning a peripatetic mission in Hampshire and Sussex for the Countess of Arundel's house in London.[93] It is clear that, as a Capuchin visitor observed in 1632, the missioners preferred comfort and security in the houses of the gentry to risking poverty and arrest by working in the open: Bishop Challoner noted as unusual men those who chose to work with the poor, and one Worcestershire priest left his poor penitents to become tutor and chaplain to the Sheldons.[94] The missionary priests probably had some sense of their social and clerical dignity, for half of them were drawn from the gentry and they were, as Allen pointed out, very much better educated than the medieval parish clergy.[95] William Anlaby spend his first four years on the Yorkshire mission working with the poor, travelling on foot and in simple clothes, but in 1582, 'humbly yielding to the advice of his brethren', he acquired a horse and improved his dress. Robert Southwell thoroughly disapproved of itinerant priests, telling a colleague, 'I am much grieved to hear of your unsettled way of life, visiting many people, at home with none. We are all, I acknowledge, pilgrims, but not vagrants; our life is uncertain, but not our road.'[96] The implication of these clerical preferences was that the missioners would concentrate upon the houses of the lowland gentry, to the neglect of the peasants of the northern uplands, and from 1586 Weston and Garnet were busy establishing a network of 'fixed residences' in gentry households, primarily in southern England.[97] By 1590 there may have been a glut of priests in the Thames valley, and Thomas Stransham left Oxfordshire 'for want of harbour and entertainment' and moved north. But at the same time priests in Hampshire

[92] J. Miller, *Popery and Politics in England, 1660–1688* (Cambridge, 1973), p. 15; Bossy, *English Catholic Community*, p. 111.

[93] *Letters and Memorials of Father Robert Persons*, ed. Hicks, p. 108; *Unpublished Documents Relating to the English Martyrs*, ed. Pollen, p. 309; Foley, *Records of the English Province*, I, p. 330; C. Devlin, *The Life of Robert Southwell, Poet and Martyr* (London, 1956), pp. 133–5.

[94] G. Albion, *Charles I and the Court of Rome* (London, 1935), pp. 111–14; Challoner, *Memoirs of Missionary Priests*, pp. 232, 275, 300, 322, 359, 394; *Unpublished Documents Relating to the English Martyrs*, ed. Pollen, pp. 347–8.

[95] Bossy, *English Catholic Community*, p. 415; *Douai Diaries*, ed. Knox, p. xlvi.

[96] Challoner, *Memoirs of Missionary Priests*, p. 232; Foley, *Records of the English Province*, I, p. 338.

[97] W. Weston, *Autobiography of an Elizabethan*, ed. P. Caraman (London, 1955), pp. 72, 77, 79; Caraman, *Henry Garnet*, pp. 32–6, 44–5.

and Yorkshire had more work than they could cope with, and the laity had only intermittent contact with priests.[98]

It is likely that there was a good deal of 'leakage' from Catholicism in areas such as west Lancashire, Cleveland, south Herefordshire and east Monmouthshire, due to inadequate clerical support, while elsewhere the potential for long-term Catholic survival was lost. There were no regions of significant recusancy which had not earlier exhibited traditionalist predilections, but there were some 'survivalist' regions which did not generate substantial recusancy. The cases of north Wales and the far north-west of England do not demonstrate that mere conservatism had little to contribute to the future of Catholicism, only that conservatism by itself was not enough. In 1567 the Bishop of Bangor reported that there were still altars and images in the churches of his diocese, and that the people still made pilgrimages and used relics and rosaries, and in 1589 another observer noted similar 'gross idolatry'.[99] From the mid-1570s, this conservatism began to develop into committed recusancy, with the efforts of active and imaginative missioners supported by gentry families in Lleyn and Creuddyn, but with official drives against the Owens in 1579 and the Pughs in 1587 the growth of separated Catholicism was arrested.[100] Thereafter, though there were pockets of recusancy in Caernarvonshire, the county did not have the widespread popular recusancy which had seemed to be developing in the middle of Elizabeth's reign. Of the explanations offered for this failure, the shortage of gentry, the tainting of Catholicism by treason and the low levels of literacy may be discounted, as they did not prevent popular recusancy elsewhere. It is probable that, in an area of weak ecclesiastical government, bishops could do little to prevent conservative practices in the churches, and recusant Catholicism may have been less attractive to the laity than in relatively better-governed dioceses. But the key to the failure of recusancy in north Wales appears to lie in the scarcity of missionary priests, perhaps as a result of the anti-Welsh coup at the English College, Rome, in 1578–9: although the dioceses of Bangor and St Asaph produced forty-six Elizabethan recruits for the seminaries, only five of them returned to work in their home districts and most went to south Wales or to England.[101] It is significant that the largest recusant groups in north Wales were to be in the neighbouring parishes of Bodffari, Tremeirchion and Holywell, where shrines attracted pilgrims and, more importantly,

---

[98] Davidson, 'Roman Catholicism in Oxfordshire', pp. 416–17; Challoner, *Memoirs of Missionary Priests*, pp. 595–6; Aveling, *Northern Catholics*, pp. 191–2. I have discussed the distribution of clerical resources more fully in my 'From Monopoly to Minority: Catholicism in Early Modern England', *T.R.H.S.*, 5th ser., XXXI (1981), pp. 129–47.

[99] D. Mathew, 'Some Elizabethan Documents', *Bulletin of the Board of Celtic Studies*, VI (1931), pp. 77–8; Jones, 'The Lleyn Recusancy Case', pp. 108–9.

[100] *Ibid., passim*; A. H. Dodd, *A History of Caernarvonshire, 1284–1900* (Caernarvon, 1968), pp. 59–60; Williams, *Welsh Reformation Essays*, pp. 55–8; Williams, *Council in the Marches*, pp. 92–3, 97.

[101] D. A. Thomas, *The Welsh Elizabethan Catholic Martyrs* (Liverpool, 1971), pp. 32, 36–9; Dodd, *History of Caernarvonshire*, pp. 56, 58, 172.

priests who ministered to local Catholics.[102] Where a continuing supply of priests
was available, and perhaps where a shrine could serve as a focus for Catholic loyalty,
'survivalism' could be converted into long-term recusancy, but in the absence of
priests it degenerated into crude superstition: in 1589 bullocks were being sacrificed
to St Beuno in Clynnog, home of the first rector of the English College in Rome.[103]

Another instructive region, where the transition from traditionalism to committed
recusancy was frustrated and organised Catholicism declined after a promising start,
was Cumberland, Westmorland and the Furness district. There, the Church of
England probably made less progress in the early part of Elizabeth's reign than
anywhere else in the country: the Bishop of Carlisle complained in 1561 and 1562
that the 1559 Settlement had barely been enforced.[104] By 1571 there was an
interesting fragmentation: progress had been made in some parishes by the removal
of recalcitrant clergy, but there were villages 'amongst whom is neither fear, faith,
virtue nor knowlege of God, nor regard of any religion at all'; 'survivalism'
remained vigorous in other parishes, with forbidden feasts, ornaments, vestments,
beads and mass books, and conservative alterations to the Prayer Book services; and
separated Catholicism was emerging with the work of 'roving popish priests',
ominously supported by some of the parish clergy.[105] At the 1578 visitation a score
of recusants were returned in some scrappy presentments for the deanery of Furness,
most of them living in one chapelry, and by 1589 there was something approaching
an organised Catholic group, with two seminary and two recusant priests active in
Furness and perhaps a hundred lay recusants there. But signs of weakness were already
present: official fear that Spanish invaders might land in Furness led to frequent
searches for priests, and three of the priests were very old men.[106] By the 1590s
recusancy in the far north-west was clearly in decline, and a careful survey of 1596
found only 102 recusants, seventy-three of them gentry and their servants, in the
diocese of Carlisle and three Chester deaneries: popular recusancy, which had been
growing rapidly in the 1580s, had all but disappeared.[107] Bishop Robinson of Carlisle,

---

[102] T. Richards, 'The Religious Census of 1675', *Transactions of Honourable Society of
Cymmrodorion* (1925–6), pp. 101–2; E. G. Jones, 'Catholic Recusancy in the Counties of
Denbigh, Flint and Montgomery, 1581–1625', *Transactions of the Honourable Society of
Cymmrodorion* (1945), pp. 120–1, 126–31; Thomas, *Welsh Elizabethan Catholic Martyrs*,
p. 45; Leys, *Catholics in England*, pp. 80–1.

[103] Jones, 'Lleyn Recusancy Case', pp. 108–9.

[104] Birt, *Elizabethan Religious Settlement*, pp. 311–12; C. Dodd, *Church History of England*, ed.
M. A. Tierney, 5 vols (London, 1839–43), II, p. cccxx.

[105] Birt, *Elizabethan Religious Settlement*, p. 315; J. Nicholson and R. Burn, *The History and
Antiquities of the Counties of Westmorland and Cumberland*, 2 vols (London, 1777), I, pp. 496, 507;
II, pp. 89–90, 114, 127, 381, 463; B.I.Y., HC.AB 6, fos. 63v, 64, 69v.

[106] *Ibid.*, Vis. 1578–9/CB3, fos. 64–6; *Calender of State Papers, Domestic, Elizabeth I, 1581–1590*, p.
633; *Unpublished Documents Relating to the English Martyrs*, ed. Pollen, pp. 180–2, 221.

[107] J. S. Purvis, *Tudor Parish Documents of the Diocese of York* (Cambridge, 1948), pp. 79, 81;
Miscellanea: Recusant Records, ed. C. Talbot (C.R.S., LIII, 1960), pp. 62–6, 105–7. Cf. Holtby's

in a perceptive report of 1599, noted that the recusant gentry were moving out of his diocese, and the main problem he faced was not popery but the ignorance of the people due to the shortage and poor quality of his clergy. Bishop Snowdon confirmed this view in 1617: the diocese had about eighty recusants, as against almost 62000 Anglican communicants, and organised Catholicism was confined to a few gentry families.[108] The reason for this failure was the death of the old priests and the absence of replacements: the gentry moved to better-served areas. The far north-west produced few recruits for the seminaries, and attracted fewer to work in inhospitable territory far from the usual landing-places. Thomas Somers, a Westmorland Catholic schoolmaster, encouraged his pupils to go to Douai, 'so they might one day return again to their own country to assist the souls of their neighbours', but when he became a priest himself he chose to work among the poor of London.[109]

It has been suggested by some that we should see the Elizabethan mission as a major success, which created a new Catholic community after the medieval church had succumbed to the Reformation attack, and it has become usual to see the seminary priests as selfless crusaders fighting against heavy odds. But if it is accepted that a radical discontinuity between pre- and post-Reformation Catholicism cannot be supported, then the mission must in some respects be judged a failure. Through the social exclusiveness of the clergy[110] and the selfishness of the gentry,[111] priests came to concentrate their attentions on south-east England, an area with little missionary potential, and opportunities elsewhere were missed: the seminary priests lost north Wales and the north-western corner of England for their faith. Catholics slipped into conformity where there were too few priests to maintain their solidarity and provide the saving sacraments. In Suffolk in 1621–2 peasant Catholics had to wait up to six months to have access to a priest, and in 1632 it was reported that, though priests were getting in each other's way in the London area, elsewhere people were dying without the sacraments.[112] No doubt there seemed little to commend

account of the problems Catholics faced in the north-east in these years: Dodd, *Church History of England*, III, pp. 76, 87–109.

108 *Calendar of State Papers, Domestic, Elizabeth I, 1598–1601*, p. 362; R. S. Ferguson, *Diocesan Histories: Carlisle* (London, 1889), pp. 132–3; B. Magee, *The English Recusants* (London, 1938), p. 83.

109 Anstruther, *Seminary Priests*, I, p. 394; II, p. 406; Bossy, *English Catholic Community*, p. 227; Challoner, *Memoirs of Missionary Priests*, pp. 321–2. See also J. A. Hilton, 'The Cumbrian Catholics', *Northern History*, XVI (1980), pp. 41–7.

110 See, for example, *Letters and Memorials of Father Robert Persons*, ed. Hicks, pp. 320, 361–2; Gerard, *Autobiography*, p. 33; and the fuller discussion in Haigh, 'From Monopoly to Minority', *passsim*.

111 See, for example, Morris, *Troubles of Our Catholic Forefathers*, III, pp. 453–4; M. J. Havran, *The Catholics in Caroline England* (London, 1962), p. 78, and the discussion in Haigh, 'From Monopoly to Minority', *passim*.

112 M. C. E. Chambers, *The Life of Mary Ward*, 2 vols (London, 1882–5), II, pp. 28, 35; P. Hughes, *Rome and the Counter-Reformation in England* (London, 1942), p. 410.

a religion which stressed the role of priests in the scheme of salvation, and then failed to provide them where they were needed.

The mission, therefore, changed the structure of Catholicism only in the limited and negative sense that it failed to sustain the potential for recusancy in all parts of England and Wales. But perhaps the mission had a more significant impact on the spirit of traditional Catholicism: was a reformed and revitalised religion, produced by the Council of Trent and the associated revival, brought to England by the new priests? There is some evidence that recusant clergy and some lay Catholics thought the Jesuits were bringing in a new-fangled religion,[113] and there was certainly some trouble in the early 1580s over fasting rules. Catholics brought up securely within local customs wished to maintain the strict English traditions, while the Jesuits and some seminarists, especially those trained in Rome, wanted to observe the laxer Roman fasting. This was an important issue, since it went to the heart of a family's expression of its religious allegiance, and the significant fact is that, despite a face-saving formula, the 'modernists' lost the argument and the traditionalists triumphed. In 1580 the dispute was sorted out without difficulty by a meeting of Jesuits, seminary priests, recusant clergy and laymen, and it was agreed that each part of the country would follow its own traditional practices.[114] This settlement was disrupted in 1584, when a group of younger priests, led by the cross-grained Jesuit Jasper Heywood, tried to bring the laity into line with Rome: one scandalised layman threatened to hand Heywood over to the Privy Council, and the Jesuit was, in due course, recalled from England.[115] The issue of church attendance was also raised in 1580, and there is no doubt that Parsons pressed the need for recusancy, but some historians have interpreted the paper war between Parsons and Alban Langdale as part of a wider dispute between 'new' and 'old' priests.[116] There was a division over church attendance, but despite Parsons's presentation of the case the conflict was not between representatives of a weak-kneed traditional English Catholicism and those of a vibrant Counter Reformation: the argument on this issue was as much within the ranks of the missionary priests, and it continued at least until 1606.[117]

[113] *Letters and Memorials of Father Robert Persons*, ed. Hicks, p. xix; 'Memoirs of Father Robert Persons', ed. Pollen, I, p. 178; A. Morey, *The Catholic Subjects of Elizabeth I* (London, 1978), p. 176.

[114] Parsons, 'Of the Life and Martyrdom of Father Edmond Campion', pp. 32–8; 'Memoirs of Father Robert Persons' ed. Pollen, I, pp. 27, 176; Basset, *English Jesuits*, pp. 46–7.

[115] 'Memoirs of Father Robert Persons', ed. Pollen, I, p. 177; 'The Memoirs of Father Robert Persons', ed. Pollen, II, in *C.R.S. Miscellanea*, IV (C.R.S., IV, 1907), pp. 105, 107; Foley, *Records of the English Province*, I, pp. 394–8; *Douai Diaries*, ed. Knox, pp. 354–5.

[116] 'Memoirs of Father Robert Persons', ed. Pollen, I, pp. 61–3, 178–81; II, pp. 4–5, 7; R. Parsons, *A Brief Discourse Containing Certain Reasons Why Catholics Refuse to Go to Church* ('Douai', 1580), esp. fos. 3v–6; Trimble, *Catholic Laity*, pp. 102–3.

[117] Caraman, *Henry Garnet*, pp. 157, 172, 224; *The Wisbech Stirs*, ed. P. Renold (C.R.S., LI, 1958), p. 205; Foley, *Records of the English Province*, IV, pp. 371–4.

Post-Reformation English Catholicism was 'post-Tridentine' in little more than a chronological sense. The Douai seminarians' study of the Trent canons was confined to the dogmatic decrees, and their ecclesiastical law was learned from Lyndwood's *Provinciale*.[118] Probably in law and certainly in fact, the Trent disciplinary decrees did not apply to England: it is clear that the decree *Tametsi* on marriage did not apply, since it was to come into force after a promulgation which did not take place in England, and the Jesuits argued that the other disciplinary decrees were inoperative for the same reason.[119] It is, indeed, arguable that English Catholicism and post-Tridentine Catholicism were, in some respects, moving in opposite directions in the sixteenth and seventeenth centuries. It has been argued that Tridentine Catholicism meant the substitution of a disciplined, regular, parish-centred religion for the more relaxed medieval religion of family, hamlet and confraternity.[120] But the Reformation and its aftermath saw a loosening rather than a tightening of discipline for English Catholics: it seems that parochial discipline had been stricter in pre-Reformation England than on the Continent,[121] and thereafter English Catholicism had no structure of parishes and courts through which discipline could be exerted. Though the imposition of the Trent decrees on Catholic Europe raised the authority of bishops and priests, when Richard Smith asserted his episcopal powers under a Trent decree, between 1625 and 1631, he was hounded out of the country by an alliance of gentry and regular clergy.[122] In England, furthermore, there could be no regularity of sacramental observance for any but those gentry with resident chaplains, and in many areas of the country it was difficult to obtain sacraments even for the dying.[123] Finally, though Tridentine reform shifted the focus of religion from the household to the parish church, the English Reformation forced Catholic piety from the parish to the family: the Council of Trent banned masses

---

[118] *Douai Diaries*, ed. Knox, p. xlii; Hughes, *Rome and the Counter-Reformation*, p. 172.

[119] *Canons and Decrees of the Council of Trent*, ed. H. J. Schroeder (London, 1941), p. 185; H. Aveling, 'The Marriages of Catholic Recusants, 1559–1642', *J.E.H.*, XIV (1963), p. 69; J. Bennett, 'Narratio Historica', in *C.R.S. Miscellanea*, XII (C.R.S., XXII, 1921), p. 164; E. Gee, *The Jesuit's Memorial* (London, 1690), pp. 14–15.

[120] Bossy, 'Counter-Reformation and the People of Catholic Europe', pp. 51–62; J. Bossy, 'Blood and Baptism: Kinship, Community and Christianity in Western Europe from the 14th to the 17th Centuries', in D. Baker, ed., *Studies in Church History*, X (Oxford, 1973), pp. 129–43.

[121] This is a complex subject which requires detailed treatment, but the point seems reasonably established by a comparison of John Bossy's comments in 'Counter-Reformation and the People of Catholic Europe', p. 53, with Ralph Houlbrooke's rather different picture of the early Tudor dioceses of Norwich and Winchester (*Church Courts and the People*, pp. 222–3) and the careful supervision exercised in so unpromising an area as the forest uplands of east Lancashire: *Act Book of the Ecclesiastical Court of Whalley, 1510–38*, ed. A. M. Cooke (Chetham Society, new ser., XLIV, 1901), *passim*.

[122] Hughes, *Rome and the Counter-Reformation*, pp. 336–90; Bossy, *English Catholic Community*, pp. 53–9.

[123] See, for example, Wark, *Elizabethan Recusancy in Cheshire*, pp. 42–4; Hughes, *Rome and the Counter-Reformation*, p. 410.

in private houses,[124] but the domestic mass was to be the key feature of Catholic worship in post-Reformation England. There were practical adjustments to the fact of 'disestablishment' in 1559, but there was no breach in the continuity of English Catholicism and there was no Tridentine Counter Reformation in England.

There was, however, more to the Counter Reformation than the decrees of the Council of Trent and, superficially at least, it seems that Delumeau's contrast between pre- and post-Reformation religion may usefully be applied to England and Wales. Perhaps the habitual, mechanical observance of local customs which passed for religion among medieval laymen was replaced by the informed and involved religion of the recusant household: perhaps Catholics were converted by the missionaries to regular confession, frequent communion and an all-embracing life of piety.[125] Among the Babthorpes at Osgodby, the Montagues at Battle and the Wisemans at Braddocks, in Dorothy Lawson's house near Newcastle and in the partnership of John Mush and Margaret Clitheroe at York,[126] there was an intense religious life which contrasts sharply with the superstitious magic of the pre-Reformation villages. Such piety was related to the spiritual training given to priests in the seminaries, to the *Spiritual Exercises* and to the new ideal of frequent confession and communion under the guidance of a spiritual director, but it was also the product of post-Reformation circumstance in England. There was, perhaps, something of the fanaticism of the persecuted, and a claustrophobic atmosphere generated within the single-household chaplaincies characteristic of lowland England. Such households are the foundation upon which accounts of post-Reformation piety are built, but in response to the contrast between their intensity and the conventionality of pre-Reformation religion two comments must be made.

First, the domestic piety of the post-Reformation Catholic household was not new, and it owed more to the invention of printing than to the Counter Reformation. The introduction of printing and the expansion of education made possible and necessary an increasing lay involvement in personal religion which preceded the Reformation, and handbooks such as Richard Whitford's *Work for Householders* met a growing demand for guidance in an ordered family piety on the model of the More household. Individual religious commitment was in the ascendancy in the years preceding the break with Rome, and there was a ready market for the *Hours of the*

[124] *Canons and Decrees of the Council of Trent*, ed. Schroeder, p. 151.
[125] Delumeau, *Catholicism between Luther and Voltaire*, pp. 160–1, 167, 171–6, 180–201; K. Thomas, *Religion and the Decline of Magic* (London, 1973), pp. 27–57, 179–206; Bossy, *English Catholic Community*, pp. 126–9. John Gerard prided himself upon the number of lax Catholic families he had turned into pious communities: *Autobiography*, pp. 27–9, 32, 150, 169.
[126] Morris, *Troubles of Our Catholic Forefathers*, III, pp. 390–4, 467–8; *An Elizabethan Recusant House: The Life of Lady Magdalene, Viscountess Montague*, ed. A. C. Southern (London, 1954), pp. 47–50; *Chronicle of the English Augustinian Canonesses*, ed. Hamilton, I, pp. 80–2; W. Palmes, *Life of Mrs Dorothy Lawson*, ed. G. B. Harrison (Newcastle, 1851), pp. 33–40.

Blessed Virgin, psalters, primers and other devotional aids.[127] The central role which the household was to play in post-Reformation English Catholicism was no novel departure, and it is difficult to resist the conclusion that the Elizabethan shift of Catholic focus from church to household was so smooth because it was the dramatic conclusion of an existing process. There was certainly much continuity in the pious literature of the sixteenth-century Catholic family, and the key text here is perhaps the *Jesus Psalter*, one of the best-sellers of early modern English religion, which, after becoming popular before the Reformation, was reprinted on the Continent for English Catholics forty-one times, alone or with other pious works, between 1570 and 1640.[128] New works such as Robert Parsons's *Christian Directory* and translations of Luis de Granada were influential in some quarters, but most of the primers printed for Catholics were conservative commentaries on the old Sarum use and the most widely used catechism was by a Marian priest and had a distinctly traditionalist tone.[129] For much of the reign of Elizabeth, domestic piety must have been based upon surviving copies of old devotional works, and recusant households seem to have preserved such books with care: we know that Margaret Clitheroe's main devotional reading, in addition to the Rheims New Testament, was the *Imitation of Christ* and William Peryn's *Spiritual Exercises* (1557), and she learned by heart the Latin of Our Lady's matins.[130]

The second caveat on post-Reformation domestic spirituality is that it was not, and could not be, typical of English Catholicism as a whole. The homiletic recording of exemplary lives and self-defensive propaganda by Jesuits have led to an over-representation of the pious in the annals of Elizabethan and Stuart Catholicism, and historians, like the missionaries, have focused their attention upon the gentry. But the piety of the gentry household was parasitic, possible only because the gentry arrogated to themselves the clerical resources of the Catholic community: in 1635 an aged Essex priest complained of the ignorance of poor local Catholics, and blamed

---

[127] H. S. Bennett, *English Books and Readers, 1475–1557* (Cambridge, 1952), pp. 57–8, 65–70, 74–5; C. S. L. Davies, *Peace, Print and Protestantism, 1450–1558* (London, 1977), pp. 143–9; J. Rhodes, 'Private Devotion in England on the Eve of the Reformation', 2 vols (University of Durham Ph.D. thesis, 1974), I, pp. 6–7, 176–96; II, pp. 98–9.

[128] Roberts, *Critical Anthology of English Recusant Devotional Prose*, pp. 36–40, 52, 53, 54; Rhodes, 'Private Devotion', I, p. 385; II, p. 369; Allison and Rogers, 'Catalogue of Catholic Books', pp. 58, 77–8, 92–5, 144–5, 153–4.

[129] *Ibid.*, pp. 157–9; E. H. Burton, *The Life and Times of Bishop Challoner*, 2 vols (London, 1909), I, p. 128; *A Catechism, or Christian Doctrine, by Laurence Vaux*, ed. T. G. Law (Chetham Society, new ser., IV, 1885), pp. xciv–xcvii, 48–9; H. Davies, *Worship and Theology in England, 1534–1603* (London, 1970), pp. 162, 164.

[130] *Ibid.*, pp. 414–15; Paul, 'Hampshire Recusants', p. 140; G. Anstruther, *Vaux of Harrowden* (Newport, 1953), pp. 150–2; J. J. N. McGurk, 'Lieutenancy and Catholic Recusancy in Elizabethan Kent', *Recusant History*, XII (1973), p. 158; Morris, *Troubles of Our Catholic Forefathers*, III, pp. 393–4.

the gentlemen who kept priests within their own houses.[131] For the illiterate, the book-based piety of the gentry household was impossible, and, for the Catholic peasants of upland England in particular, contact with a priest was too irregular and brief to sustain intensive devotion. There was a further fragmentation of Catholic lay piety, which had begun with printing, and we may observe at least three varieties of lay religion: that of the gentry household with regular access to a priest, where the round of frequent confession and communion could be followed; that of the isolated Catholic family, in which religion was expressed through the cycle of feast and fast and the reciting of Latin prayers; and that of the partly Catholic areas, such as east Monmouthshire, south Herefordshire, the High Peak, west Lancashire, the borders of the West and North Ridings and coastal Cleveland, where a more public Catholic culture survived.

In parts of late Elizabethan and Jacobean Herefordshire, Lancashire and Yorkshire, where Protestant services were disrupted, officials were driven out and church attendances were often poor, the Church of England was still an alien intruder upon established local customs: the gentleman who took a minister to Pately Bridge after there had been no sermons for twenty years was told he 'had brought Antichrist into Nidderdale'.[132] In these peripheral districts, popular culture seems to have changed hardly at all. In Lancashire in 1590 those attending church services worshipped the communion bread and used Latin prayers, the sign of the cross and the knocking of the breast; traditional festivals were observed with the old celebrations, and there were 'popish rites' at baptisms, weddings and funerals.[133] In Lancashire and the North Riding there were church ales, dancing and piping on Sundays, often led by known papists – customs which were identified as 'popery' for two reasons; first because they were survivals from medieval parish-religion and second because they were thought to be used by Catholics to draw villagers from the services of the official church.[134] In Lancashire, Cheshire and north Wales, and even in Buckinghamshire and Staffordshire, exorcisms were used to publicise the powers of the Catholic priesthood more widely, and the vigour of the Protestant counter attack suggests that the priest was a powerful magical figure in the popular imagination.[135] Within such a conservative cultural framework, Catholics were not segregated from their neighbours into a rigid body of strict recusants with an easily

[131] Havran, The Catholics in Caroline England, p. 78.
[132] R. Mathias, Whitsun Riot (London, 1963), pp. 2, 5–6, 14–15, 22–3, 81; Haigh, Reformation and Resistance, pp. 245, 275–8, 327–30; M. Hodgetts, 'Elizabethan Priest-Holes: V', Recusant History, XIII (1976), pp. 263–4; C. Howard, Sir John Yorke of Nidderdale (London, 1939), pp. 17–20.
[133] 'The State, Civil and Ecclesiastical, of the County of Lancaster', ed. F. R. Raines, in Chetham Miscellanies, v (Chetham Society, old ser., XCVI, 1875), pp. 2, 4–7.
[134] Haigh, 'Puritan Evangelism', pp. 51–4; Aveling, Northern Catholics, p. 289.
[135] Historical MSS. Commission, Salisbury MSS., VIII, pp. 213–14, 293; Foley, Records of the English Province, II, pp. 6, 17–23; III, p. 446; F. Peck, Desiderata Curiosa (London, 1779), pp. 105, 113;

defined membership: Catholicism was a varied and amorphous phenomenon, and individuals drifted in and out of formal recusancy while always regarding themselves as Catholics and retaining Catholic habits.[136] If the broader popular culture remained traditionalist, the religious culture of peasant Catholics in these safer regions was barely influenced by Reformation and Counter Reformation: Catholicism still meant masses and rites of passage, Latin prayers learned by rote, protective magic and village pipers, plays and pilgrimages. The Catholics used charms, relics and holy water for protection and cures after the Reformation as before, and the curative elements in popular Catholicism became even more significant as miracles at Holywell and exorcisms in Lancashire became increasingly common.[137] There was even Catholic drama, and in the North Riding a group of Catholic players moved round the recusant centres, guying Puritan clergy and laymen, at least between 1609 and 1616, and perhaps from 1595.[138] The relaxed, peasant Catholicism of the dales and the Fylde was a far cry from the piety of John Gerard's reformed households, but it was close to the religion of *The Lay Folk's Mass Book* and its character was little influenced by the work of the missionary priests. It was also much more typical of post-Reformation Catholicism, at least in the pre-Civil War period, than the more publicised devotion of the gentry families.

Separated English Catholicism, with its important church-papist penumbra,[139] was not a new post-Reformation creation of missionaries from the Continent; it was a continuation of traditional English Catholicism shaped by the circumstances of the Reformation in England. The deepest foundations of post-Reformation Catholicism were medieval, in both its piety and its structure: it will be argued elsewhere that there is a close correspondence between areas of pre-Reformation Catholic strength and areas of densest recusancy. The immediate foundations of recusant Catholicism were Marian: the Marian bishops seem to have fostered lay religion and they gave an early example of resistance; lesser Church dignitaries and academics became exiled

B. Rich, *The True Report of a Late Practice Enterprised by a Papist* (London, 1582), *passim*; S. Harsnet, *A Declaration of Egregious Popish Impostures* (London, 1605), *passim*; J. Gee, *The Foot Out of the Snare* (London, 1624), pp. 48–55.

[136] C. Haigh, 'The Fall of a Church or the Rise of a Sect?: Post-Reformation Catholicism in England', *H.J.*, xxi (1978), pp. 184–5; Challoner, *Memoirs of Missionary Priests*, p. 240; Historical MSS. Commission, *Kenyon MSS.*, p. 585; Foley, *Records of the English Province*, vii, p. 1106. See especially the comments in Gerard, *Autobiography*, pp. 32–3.

[137] Thomas, *Religion and the Decline of Magic*, pp. 33–4, 84; 'Documenta de S. Wenefreda', *Analecta Bollandiana*, vi (1887), pp. 305–51; D. Thomas, 'St Winifred's Well and Chapel, Holywell', *Journal of the Historical Society of the Church in Wales*, viii (1958), pp. 20–2; Foley, *Records of the English Province*, ii, pp. 17–23, 565–6; iv, pp. 534–5; vii, pp. 1098, 1122.

[138] Aveling, *Northern Catholics*, pp. 193, 289–90; Howard, *Sir John Yorke*, pp. 21–6.

[139] Despite the views of Parsons and the rigorists, church-papistry was not the limp reaction of a weak and defeated old Church to the Elizabethan settlement, soon to be replaced by the muscular recusancy of a vibrant Counter Reformation: it was a long-term feature of post-Reformation Catholicism, and a realistic response to persecution.

propagandists against the Elizabethan Church; Marian Privy Councillors and officials became the mainstays of East Anglian recusancy; and both university scholars and parish clergy became recusant priests and led the laity into separation. By the arrival of the seminary priests, the essential features of separated Catholicism had already been formed, with a concept of a Catholic Church distinct from the State Church, an independent priesthood offering saving sacraments, and a laity which had begun to withdraw from the parish churches. There was, it is true, a long process of transition, between the monopolistic medieval Church and a separated group which was, in some senses, 'sectarian'. But the 'parish-church Catholicism' of the 1560s and later church-papistry should not be dismissed as mere 'survivalism', since they provided an organic link between Church and sect and a reservoir of potential recusants. Catholicism survived through the Reformation and was properly called 'the old religion' by its adherents. The Catholic clergy had therefore to sustain, and it was the Protestants who had to convert: it was the Church of England, not that of Rome, which needed to be a missionary Church.

CONCLUSION

Revisionism has challenged the traditional version of English Reformation history. The essays collected in this volume argue or imply interpretations which differ sharply from conventional textbook accounts. The late-medieval Church was not a corrupt and repressive institution whose abuses demanded radical reforms. There was very little popular demand for Reformation, so official changes were implemented without enthusiasm and Protestantism spread only slowly. The reign of Mary saw a vigorous and quite imaginative programme of restoration, and, despite difficulties, the prospects for an established Catholic Church seemed good. Widespread attachment to Catholic beliefs and rituals survived both State repression and Protestant evangelism, and popular conservatism remained strong well into the reign of Elizabeth I. The English Reformation, therefore, was not a joyous national rejection of outmoded superstition: it was a long drawn-out struggle between reformist minorities and a reluctant majority, and the victory of the reformers was late and limited. Only in the 1570s and after did the officially-Protestant Church of England acquire the missionary manpower and organisation for a campaign of conversion, and even then its impact was restricted. Conscious Catholic commitment remained entrenched in many parts of England, and there was stubborn resistance to some central Protestant tenets.[1] The Reformation did not produce a Protestant England: it produced a divided England.

The Reformation, then, was unpopular – but it did *happen*, even if it happened slowly, and it happened without civil war. It was suggested in the 'Introduction' that the fortunes of politics and the strength of conservatism made the Reformation piecemeal, and therefore enforceable in small portions. But even the imposition of Reformation by instalments implies, as Professor Scarisbrick has noted, that the Tudor State had a formidable coercive capability.[2] It is, however, difficult to see

[1] See C. Haigh, 'The Church of England, the Catholics and the People', in *The Reign of Elizabeth I* (Basingstoke, 1984), pp. 195–220.

[2] J. J. Scarisbrick, *The Reformation and the English People* (Oxford, 1984), p. 81.

the Tudor monarchs as unbridled despots oppressing a disciplined people. Neither at the centre nor in the localities did the Tudors have the bureaucratic and policing institutions needed to enforce unacceptable policies. Tudor government was not quite government by consent, but it was at least government by collaboration. The Crown could rule effectively only if it could secure the co-operation of those with influence in the counties and parishes. Such co-operation might be obtained in a number of ways: the prestige of the monarchy, expanded by pageantry and propaganda, might overawe nobles and gentlemen, and the patronage network might buy their assistance.[3] But the Reformation could hardly have been enforced against universal hostility, and even its limited successes needed some enthusiastic proponents. The Reformation required reformers.

The essays in this volume consider mainly those who ejected or reluctantly endured Reformation, but there would have been no Reformation had it not appealed to some. The risk in a revisionist approach is that in minimising the forces of change it appears to eliminate them. We may redefine anticlericalism and diminish Protestantism, but we cannot *quite* write them out of Reformation history altogether. The unbalanced whig version of the Reformation should not be replaced by a countervailing revisionist imbalance, which sees everything Catholic in the best of Catholic worlds. The vast majority of late-medieval English men and women may have been more or less content with their Church and the religion it purveyed, and the vast majority of their children may have disliked the Reformation imposed upon them, but this cannot have been true of all. The official Reformation was made by princes and politicians manoeuvring to their own advantages, but it became effective only because it gained the support of some local notables – and alongside the legislative Reformation was the Reformation of belief by genuine conversions, which was slow but real. The Reformation appealed to minorities – but the minorities cannot be ignored.

Although we may dispute the importance of possible long-term causes of the Reformation, this does not mean that there were no preceding conditions to make Reformation acceptable. It was suggested in Chapter 3 that shifts in the patterns of court business predisposed lawyers towards criticism of ecclesiastical jurisdiction, and the increasing number of common lawyers looked jealously at the work of Church courts.[4] But it would be too cynically reductionist to stop there, for the pretensions of lawyers were accompanied by a developing theory of national sovereignty and common law supremacy. Lawyers argued both that external authorities should not infringe territorial dominion, and that internal ecclesiastical jurisdiction should not infringe the sphere of common law.[5] The crucial issue, of course, was where the

---

[3] P. Williams, *The Tudor Regime* (Oxford, 1979), pp. 351–74.

[4] See above, p. 65.

[5] J. H. Baker, ed., *The Reports of Sir John Spelman* (Selden Society, 1977), II, pp. 65–8.

boundary between the spiritual and temporal spheres lay – and lawyers showed an increasing willingness to redefine the temporal sphere at the expense of the spiritual. By the 1520s, Christopher St German was allocating property matters to the common law, and seeking to restrict ecclesiastical jurisdiction to narrowly sacramental and spiritual affairs. In 1531 he propounded a theory of parliamentary sovereignty which subjected clerical activity to the control of statute and envisaged a parliamentary reform of canon law.[6] St German himself was one of the influences which gave Henry VIII a radical solution to his marital difficulty, but the wider attitudes which he exemplified made that radical solution acceptable – perhaps even desirable. In the 1530s Henry VIII seized powers which lawyers had claimed he should hold, and he imposed on the clergy limitations which the lawyers had advocated.

Chapter 3 disputes the existence of the widespread anticlericalism which is supposed to have made the English Reformation possible. There is little evidence for a general lay hostility towards Church and priests, and there are few sound reasons for it to have existed. There were, however, *specific* groups with grievances against churchmen, and the lawyers were the most obvious and influential. Lawyers were well-represented in the Commons of the 'Reformation Parliament', and they staffed its committees. Common lawyers played an increasing role on the king's Council and in royal administration: they drafted legislation and they supervised its enforcement. Lawyers argued cases in the courts and, as judges, decided them. And some legal education became more and more characteristic of the English gentleman and country justice.[7] So legal attitudes were pervasive among the rulers of England, and in some respects legal attitudes were anticlerical. It is true there remained a strong Catholic element in the legal profession, and the inns of court were not safely Protestant even in the reign of Elizabeth,[8] but their assertion of common law supremacy predisposed lawyers to value national sovereignty above papal authority, and parliamentary jurisdiction above ecclesiastical independence. The Henrician Reformation was thus acceptable to lawyers – especially when the suppression of the monasteries generated an expansion of land-litigation! The Reformation appealed to minorities, it is true – but one of the minorities was the legal profession, and its general adherence was crucial.

The arguments which Henry VIII and his propagandists offered in defence of the

---

6 J. A. Guy, 'The Tudor Commonwealth: Revising Thomas Cromwell', *H.J.*, XXIII (1980), pp. 684–87; 'Thomas More and Christopher St. German: the Battle of the Books', *Moreana*, XXI (1984), pp. 7–12.

7 E. W. Ives, 'The Common Lawyers in Pre-Reformation England', *T.R.H.S.*, 5th series, XVIII (1968), pp. 153–57; W. R. Prest, *The Inns of Court under Elizabeth I and the Early Stuarts, 1590–1640* (London, 1972), pp. 5–7, 21, 23.

8 G. de C. Parmiter, *Elizabethan Popish Recusancy in the Inns of Court* (*B.I.H.R.* Supplement, 1976), *passim*.

royal supremacy over the Church had much to commend them. Even conservative bishops recognised the claims of monarchical rights and national unity – and some wrote in support of them. It was possible to vindicate the Henrician reforms as the purification of a still-Catholic Church, in which the essentials of the faith were maintained against the challenges of ignorance and heresy;[9] but the Reformation under Edward VI posed a clearer threat to the core of the old religion: it came piecemeal, but for the observant the implications of the pieces were far-reaching. The *Homilies* taught justification by faith; the Injunctions forbade images; the Chantries Act denied the efficacy of prayers for the dead; the 1549 Prayer Book put the mass into ambiguous English; the 1550 Ordinal turned a sacramental priesthood into a preaching ministry, and for emphasis the altars were taken down; in 1552 the Church was given a Protestant liturgy, and in 1553 a Protestant theology – as Edward VI lay dying, the old vestments and service equipment were being confiscated from parish churches. Those changes which affected the localities were usually implemented obediently, but the speed of reversal in the next reign suggests a general aversion.[10] Except for those laymen who got chantry lands and those clergy who got wives, Edward's Reformation brought few real gains – but for the Protestants it brought something close to true religion.

Professor Dickens has argued that any version of the English Reformation which ignores the dynamic impact of early Protestantism remains incomplete and unconvincing[11] – and he is right. For some, Protestantism came as a liberating creed, which released them from the thraldom of the priests. The doctrine of justification by faith alone freed tender consciences from the oppression of the penitential system and tender pockets from the cost of prayers for souls. The doctrine of predestination freed the assured elect from fears for their salvation, and gave coherence and confidence to the godly congregation. The new *Book of Common Prayer* provided for dignified worship, shorn of the ceremonies and superstitions which some had found idolatrous and insulting. Above all, the Reformation brought a freely available vernacular Bible, for Christians to read the pure Word of God and intensify individual faith – an opportunity which prompted young William Malden of Chelmsford to learn to read so he could study the New Testament for himself, and not be dependent upon others.[12] For those gripped by Protestantism, it was a

[9] J.-P. Moreau, *Rome ou L'Angleterre? Les Réactions Politiques des Catholiques Anglais au Moment du Schisme (1529–1553)* (Paris, 1984), pp. 134–66.
[10] See above, pp. 120–32. The restoration of altars, images, etc. was speedily accomplished even in Essex: see J. E. Oxley, *The Reformation in Essex* (Manchester, 1965), pp. 188–91.
[11] A. G. Dickens, review of J. J. Scarisbrick, *The Reformation and the English People*, in *J.E.H.*, XXXVI (1985), pp. 125–6. Professor Dickens's *The English Reformation* (London, 1964) remains the best account of what the new religion could mean to those who espoused it.
[12] *Narratives of the Days of the Reformation*, ed. J. G. Nichols (Camden Society, 1859), pp. 349–51. For those who could not read, of course, Protestantism did not bring spiritual independence;

powerful and life-changing faith, which would later lead some to the stake in confidence that God's hand was upon them. But one may recognise the Protestant dynamic and still question the scale of its operation.

The available, admittedly imperfect, indicators do not suggest that Protestantism swept the country, rather that it created small cells of committed adherents.[13] And that, surely, is what one would expect. For the religion of the preached and printed Word would not make much headway when, as in mid-Tudor England, there was little preaching and not much more reading. It is true that some illiterate men and women did turn to the new faith, but it seems clear even from Foxe's examples that they were singular and spiritually disadvantaged individuals.[14] So the seventy per cent of men and the ninety per cent of women who could not read were largely impervious to Protestantism (at least until preaching became more widespread), and it is probable that religious allegiance, like literacy, tended to follow social rank and occupational categories.[15] Though Catholic writers presented Protestantism as the creed of rebels and the rabble, it is likely that the new religion made proportionately more progress among higher and more literate social groups.[16] The State Reformation therefore found its most willing collaborators among those with influence: country gentlemen who might enforce Protestant laws, and might press servants and tenants towards new ways; merchants and masters who might staff civic administrations, and might persuade their journeymen and apprentices to adopt new beliefs; yeomen and artisans who might serve as churchwardens, and ensure that altars came down and Bibles were set up. The Reformation appealed to minorities, certainly – but to minorities in key positions.

Yet even those groups most open to Protestant persuasion were not uniformly converted. In 1564, after thirty years of official Reformation, an investigation by the bishops found that just over half of the justices of the peace were favourable towards the settlement of 1559 – and that was *after* government manipulation of the

they relied upon the literate for Bible readings as they had relied upon priests for sacraments: see below, p. 213 n. 14.
[13] See above, pp. 24–6 and 95–108. P. Clark, *English Provincial Society from the Reformation to the Revolution: Religion, Politics and Society in Kent, 1500–1640* (Hassocks, 1977), pp. 37–49, 58–61, 73–7, suggests a more general swing of opinion, but this is on the basis of a rather uncritical use of will-preambles. Even the formulae show little positive Protestantism, and the fluctuations seem to reflect official attitudes rather than real conversions.
[14] See, for example, the cases of Protestant converts learning to read (J. Foxe, *Actes and Monuments*, ed. G. Townsend (London, 1843–49), VII, p. 325; VIII, p. 463), and, especially, the examples of the dependence of the illiterate on those who could read to them (Foxe, *Actes*, VII, pp. 29, 323, 325; VIII, pp. 102–3, 247–8, 498).
[15] D. Cressy, *Literacy and the Social Order: Reading and Writing in Tudor and Stuart England* (Cambridge, 1980), pp. 104–69.
[16] For some of the problems involved in converting the lower orders, see P. Collinson, *The Religion of Protestants: the Church in English Society, 1559–1625* (Oxford, 1982), pp. 189–241.

commissions and a purge of leading Catholics.[17] There was some resistance to the new religion at all levels of society, and this prevented Protestantism from becoming a class-based movement: if the Marian Protestant exiles were drawn mainly from the upper ranks, the Marian martyrs came primarily from the lower orders.[18] Though Protestantism remained top-heavy, the social division between the Protestants and the rest was a vertical rather than a horizontal one, within classes rather than between them. At all levels, and in all places, the new religion brought disunity. Its adherents came together as self-conscious godly groups, and mocked the icons and rituals which conservatives held dear – while the Catholics retaliated against 'heretics and two-penny book men'.[19] Although the English Reformation lacked much of the drama and fire of religious change on the continent, it was by no means a trouble-free Reformation: it was peaceful, but not uneventful. There were conflicts between Catholics and Protestants at Bristol, Gloucester, Oxford and Rye in the 1530s; at Canterbury and London in the 1540s; at Bodmin, Exeter, Poole and Salisbury under Edward VI; in several Essex parishes in the reign of Mary; and at Hereford and York in the 1560s.[20] The Reformation was a struggle, in the localities as well as in the Court.

By the 1580s, however, the Protestants had effectively won the struggle. The settlement of 1559 had given them command of the Church and the universities, and so the opportunity to mould the next generation of magistrates and ministers. With each age-cohort, Protestants gained a higher proportion of the positions of power, until by the 1580s they controlled the Privy Council, the Court, Parliament, county commissions of the peace, and civic governments, and were well on the way to control of churches and schools.[21] The cautious enforcement of royal Injunctions gradually drove old ceremonies from parish services, and the Catholics began to organise themselves as a seigneurial sect.[22] But Protestantism was still a divisive creed, and trouble followed whenever enthusiasts tried to impose Protestant ways upon the recalcitrant multitude. A campaign to clean up the towns by suppressing maypoles, Whitsun ales and morris dancing, and imposing stricter Sunday observance, provoked widespread resistance in 1588–9: there were street demonstrations in

[17] M. Bateson, ed., 'A Collection of Original Letters from the Bishops to the Privy Council, 1564', *Camden Miscellany*, IX (Camden Society, 1895), p. iii; A. H. Smith, 'The Personnel of the Commission of the Peace, 1554–1564: a Reconsideration', *Huntingdon Library Quarterly*, XXII (1959), pp. 309–10; R. H. Fritze, 'The Role of Family and Religion in the Local Politics of Early Elizabethan England: the Case of Hampshire in the 1560s', *H.J.*, XXV (1982), p. 278.

[18] P. Hughes, *The Reformation in England* (London, 1963 ed.), II, pp. 199, 259–60; see above, p. 101.

[19] J. Vowell, *alias* Hooker, *Description of the Citie of Excester* (Devon and Cornwall Record Society, 1919), p. 75.

[20] See above, p. 32 and refs., and Oxley, *Reformation in Essex*, pp. 180, 205, 212, 231–3.

[21] Collinson, *Religion of Protestants*, pp. 92–188.

[22] Haigh, 'Church of England, the Catholics and the People', pp. 196–203.

Banbury, and a protest morris was danced against the godly mayor of Canterbury.[23]
The Protestants had defeated Catholicism, but they had failed to capture the people:
everywhere, Protestant preaching brought dispute and discord. 'Hath not Minge
[what a name for a preacher!] brought Ashford from being the quietest town of
Kent to be at deadly hatred and bitter division?', asked a critic in 1588,[24] and it
was much the same elsewhere. The Reformation had created not a united Protestant
England but a deeply divided England.

[23] *Ibid.*, p. 215; A. Beesley, *The History of Banbury* (London, 1841), pp. 242–4, 615–16; Clark, *English Provincial Society*, p. 157. There were widespread troubles in Essex, discussed in W. Hunt, *The Puritan Moment: the Coming of Revolution in an English County* (Cambridge, Mass., 1983), pp. 130–55.

[24] *The Seconde Parte of a Register*, ed. A. Peel (Cambridge, 1915), I, p. 238.

INDEX

Common Pleas, court of 65
communion in both kinds 121
communion tables 125, 128, 133
compurgation 43
confession 105, 168, 180, 196, 204, 206
Confirmation 170
confraternities 8
continental Protestantism 21, 25–6, 95, 104
Convocation 54, 96, 141n., 148n.
Cooper, J. P. 63
Coppingford, Huntingdonshire 88
Cornwall 27–8, 32, 98–101, 104
Cornworthy, Devon 136n.
Corpus Christi, feast of 122, 130
Corpus Christi play 25
Corwen, Merioneth 136
Coulton, G. G. 56–7
Council of the North 103, 126
Counter-Reformation 103, 128, 133, 139,
    141, 178, 192, 194, 202, 204, 207
court act books 22, 68, 77
Court politics 21, 30, 31, 59, 61–2, 73, 191
    see also faction
Coventry 4, 95, 100, 104
    parish of Holy Trinity 136n.
Cowfold, Sussex 46
Cranmer, Thomas, Archbishop of
    Canterbury 16, 20, 25, 47, 53, 120, 123,
    160
Cratfield, Suffolk 116n., 117n., 118n.
Craven, Yorkshire 108
Crediton, Devon 124n., 129n., 130n., 134
creed 132, 170–1
Creuddyn, Caernarvonshire 199
Criplyng, Robert 109
Cromwell, Thomas 10, 12, 14, 16, 20, 30, 47,
    48, 60, 63–5, 76, 78, 108–9, 158–9
Crondall, Hampshire 118n., 123n., 130n.
Cross, Claire 21, 105
crucifixes 9, 16, 102, 129, 132–5, 187
Culworth, Northamptonshire 116n.
Cumberland 70, 108, 120, 200
cunning men 25, 73
Curteys, Richard, Bishop of Chichester 51–2,
    109
Cyprian, Saint 170
Cyrus of Persia 144

Darcy, George, Lord Darcy 165
Darcy, Thomas, Lord Darcy 97
Dartington, Devon 130n.
Dartmouth, Devon 116n.
Davie, Alice 51
Davies, C. S. L. 35n., 96
debt 65
Dedham, Essex 167

defamation 48, 65, 67, 72, 169
Delumeau, Jean 177n., 204
Denton, Norfolk 117n.
Derby, Earls of
    see Stanley
Derbyshire 99, 181, 193, 197, 206
Devizes, Wiltshire, parish of St Mary 125
Devon 98–101, 107–8, 119, 125, 136n.
Dickens, A. G. ix, 1, 3–4, 7–8, 29–30, 95, 98,
    104, 108, 112–13, 176, 180, 212
Dobson, Thomas, vicar of Orwell,
    Cambridgeshire 105, 112
Doctors' Commons 38
Doncaster, Yorkshire 121, 186
Dorset 99
Douai, seminary 192–3, 195, 201, 203
Dover 25
    parish of St Mary 124, 130n.
Dovercourt, Essex 161
Downham, William, Bishop of Chester 111,
    189–90
Draper, William 39
Dromyn, John 88
Dry Drayton, Cambridgeshire 24
Dudley, John, Duke of Northumberland and
    Earl of Warwick 11, 125
Dunmow, Great
    see Great Dunmow
Durham
    cathedral 111, 147, 185
    county of 27, 105, 188
    diocese of 78, 92n., 154
Dursley, Gloucestershire 137n.

East Anglia 11, 95, 101–3, 109, 117, 136, 191,
    196, 208
Easter sepulchre 116, 123, 127, 130, 134
Eastwell, Kent 13
Ecclesiastical Commission 27, 52, 54, 110,
    184, 186, 190
Eddenham, Edward 79
Edgeworth, Roger 105
education 3, 122, 125, 140, 170–1, 192–5,
    204, 211, 214
Edward VI 8, 10, 19–20, 26, 107, 119, 123,
    127, 146, 212
Edwardian Reformation 7, 11, 13, 20, 26–7,
    29, 32, 99–100, 107, 111, 112, 119–28,
    132, 135, 137, 145–9, 152, 159, 166–7,
    169, 176–7, 212, 214
Elizabeth I 6–9, 16, 21, 101–2, 115, 133
Elizabethan Church 6, 8–9, 16, 19, 27, 29, 52,
    54, 58, 61, 66, 68, 72–4, 100, 102–3, 105,
    109–13, 115, 132–3, 137–9, 157,
    176–209, 214
Elizabethan settlement (1559) 7, 11, 16, 25,

Elizabethan settlement (*cont.*)
27, 31, 50, 103, 112, 133, 178, 180n.,
188, 192, 200, 213
Elmham, North
see North Elmham
Elmstead, Kent 12
Eltham, Kent 129, 194
Elton, G. R. 20, 29–31, 63, 96–7, 105, 109
Ely, diocese of 23, 35, 111, 127
employment 3
enclosure 70, 99, 108
episcopal registers 22, 39, 71, 77
Erasmus, Desiderius *Paraphrases* 120, 124–5,
133, 137
erastianism 57, 66
Essex 4, 22, 26, 28, 99–102, 104, 128, 135,
161–2, 164–9, 172, 174n., 181, 186–7,
192, 197, 205, 212n., 214
Everitt, Alan 112
Exchequer Court 62
excommunication 49, 50, 53–4, 66, 127–8,
136n., 164, 172, 174–5
Exeter
diocese of 12, 34, 78, 92n., 181, 191
parish of St John Bow 122n., 125n.
priory of St Nicholas 96
parish of St Petrock 111–2, 115n., 116n.,
129n.
Exmouth, Devon 107
exorcism 185, 207
extreme unction 170

faction 2–3, 10, 30–1, 33, 191
fasts 184, 202, 206
Feckenham, John 158, 194
Filgrave, Buckinghamshire 89n.
Fish, Simon 29, 59
Supplication for the Beggars 59
Fishbourne, Sussex 36
Fisher, John, Bishop of Rochester 14–16, 59,
70
FitzAlan, Henry, Earl of Arundel 147
Fitzherbert, Thomas 193
Fitzjames, Richard, Bishop of Chichester and
London 38
Fleshmonger, William 38–40, 50
Flixborough, Lincolnshire 87–8
Florence, merchant of 153–4
font 122, 130
fornication 37
Fortescue, Francis, knight 195
Foster, Isabella 163
Fowler, Robert 49
Fox, Richard, Bishop of Winchester 53
Foxe, John 1, 3–4, 8, 22, 29, 111, 157, 160,
162–5, 167, 174n., 175, 213

Acts and Monuments 1, 157, 167
France 158, 190
Reformation in 7
Francis I, King of France 158
Freake, Edmund, Bishop of Norwich
109
Fredewell, James 13
freewillers 167
Frende, William 39
Friesland 104
Fulham, Middlesex
church 174
Palace 173–4
Furness, Lancashire 25, 200
deanery of 200
Fust, Thomas 163n.
Fylde, Lancashire 207
Fyley, John 87–8

Gardiner, Stephen, Bishop of Winchester
10, 23, 26, 53, 59, 143, 147, 155n., 158,
159
De Vera Obedientia 158
Garlick, Nicholas 193
Garnet, Henry 198
Garrett, Christina 101
Geneva 106
gentry 2, 11, 14, 20–2, 25, 27, 32, 46, 59, 74,
95–8, 101, 105, 107–10, 122, 128, 133,
141, 147, 165–6, 182, 183–5, 187–92,
194, 198–9, 201, 203, 205–7, 210–11
Gerard, John 178, 193, 195, 207
Germany,
Reformation in 7
Gilpin, Bernard 105, 111
Glamorgan 127
Gloucester 32, 105, 214
diocese of 26, 51, 54, 66
parish of St Michael 122
Gloucestershire 22, 25, 26
Gold, Henry 57n., 68
Goodman, Christopher 9
Granada, Luis de 205
Granvelle *see* Perrenot
Great Catsworth, Huntingdonshire 88
Great Dunmow, Essex 116n., 129
Great Hallingbury, Essex 119n., 124n.
Great Hampden, Buckinghamshire 89n.
Great Packington, Warwickshire 115,
136n.
Great Witchingham, Norfolk 115n., 117n.
Greek 193
Greenham, Richard 24, 178n.,
Greenwich, Kent 86
Greves [?] 74
Grey, Jane 11